# The Art of Bicycling

# THE ART OF BICYCLING

## A Treasury of Poems

Edited by Justin Daniel Belmont

BREAKAWAY BOOKS
HALCOTTSVILLE, NEW YORK
2005

The Art of Bicycling: A Treasury of Poems

ISBN: 1-891369-56-3
ISBN-13: 978-1-891369-56-8
Library of Congress Control Number: 2005920866

Published by Breakaway Books
P.O. Box 24
Halcottsville, NY 12438
(800) 548-4348
www.breakawaybooks.com

FIRST EDITION

# CONTENTS

Prologue: On Bards and Bicycles     11

| | | |
|---|---|---|
| From Song of the Open Road | Walt Whitman | 27 |
| On the Road | Ninon Neckar | 30 |
| The Flying Wheel | Ernest de Lancey Pierson | 31 |
| Winter Resolve | Peter Grant | 33 |
| Bowl Over, Wheel | Edmund Vale | 34 |
| North of Amsterdam | Larry Rubin | 35 |
| Lament | Gregory Orr | 36 |
| Bicycle Days | Robin Becker | 38 |
| No Hands | Helena Nelson | 41 |
| Riding Bike with No Hands | Julia Kasdorf | 42 |
| Learning the Bicycle | Wyatt Prunty | 43 |
| Learning to Ride My Bike | George Held | 44 |
| Like Riding a Bicycle | George Bilgere | 45 |
| I Never Dream of My Father | Eva Hung | 47 |
| Almost Communication | Rita Ann Higgins | 48 |
| The Bicycle Ride | Henry Israeli | 49 |
| My Bicycle Bell | Dobashi Jiji | 50 |
| At Jong-Jhou Train Station | G. Timothy Gordon | 52 |
| The Three Ladies | Lawrence Kearney | 53 |
| Phoebe on a Bicycle | D. W. Faulkner | 54 |
| Split | George Held | 55 |
| The Bicycle | James Brown | 56 |
| [Bicycle] | David Malouf | 58 |
| Mobile City | Machine Wilkins | 60 |
| From Out the Heated City | S. Conant Foster | 61 |
| Away from the Office | Willis Boyd Allen | 63 |
| Morning Ride | Anonymous | 65 |
| Town and Country | Arthur Waugh | 67 |
| Angry | Suki Wessling | 73 |
| The Rider | Naomi Shihab Nye | 75 |
| The Companion | Anonymous | 76 |
| Joy | Eben E. Rexford | 77 |
| King Tommy's Rise and Fall | Ella Wheeler Wilcox | 79 |
| Not My Knees | Stazja McFadyen | 81 |
| The Bicycle | Risa Lichtman | 83 |

| | | |
|---|---|---|
| The Bicycle | James Reaney | 85 |
| A Song of the Wheel | Arthur H. Lawrence | 87 |
| The Old Road Map | Arthur Waugh | 89 |
| Eden | Leslie Norris | 92 |
| No Goalies | Phil Ilton | 93 |
| Ballads of the Wheel | Clinton Scollard | 94 |
| The Whirling Wheel | Anonymous | 95 |
| Toasting Song | S. Conant Foster | 97 |
| Wheelmen's Song | Will Carleton | 98 |
| The Men Who Ride for Fun | Walter G. Kendall | 99 |
| [By Bicycle] | Matthea Harvey | 101 |
| On Rainy Days | Anonymous | 102 |
| A Rain of Bicycles | Jonathan Harrington | 104 |
| Bicycles | Andrei Voznesensky | 105 |
| Blue Bicycles | Charles Fishman | 106 |
| Zeno's Progress | Thomas Centolella | 109 |
| Turning Thirty, I Contemplate Students Bicycling Home | Rita Dove | 111 |
| An Old Maid's Reverie | Anonymous | 112 |
| Stationary Bicycle | Linda Pastan | 114 |
| Beating the Drum in Reverse | Miroslav Válek | 116 |
| Buffalo | Eugenio Montale | 118 |
| The Bicycle Race in Beowulf | David Galef | 119 |
| Fearless Rider | Jim Clawson | 120 |
| The Gol-Darned Wheel | Anonymous | 122 |
| Mulga Bill's Bicycle | A. B. "Banjo" Patterson | 125 |
| The Silent Steed | Paul Pastnor | 127 |
| To the Wheel | Charles E. Pratt | 129 |
| To the Bicycle | John Gibbens | 130 |
| Song of the Cycle | Charles S. Crandall | 131 |
| Invention | Robert Clarkson Tongue | 132 |
| The Birth of the Bike | Anonymous | 134 |
| Bicycle Song (For Women) | Robert Buchanan | 137 |
| The Maiden | Anonymous | 139 |
| Dames of Washington | Grace Duffie Boylan | 140 |
| When Gerty Goes A-Wheeling | Manley H. Pike | 141 |
| Daisy Bell (A Bicycle Built for Two) | Henry Dacre | 143 |
| Shovelin' Coal | Tony Pranses | 144 |
| The Smithville Tandem Bike | W. T. Goodge | 146 |
| Cycles | Alison Brackenbury | 148 |
| Sonnet at Three-Speed | J. Lorraine Brown | 149 |
| In Cold February Twilight | Frederic William Kirchner | 150 |

| | | |
|---|---|---|
| Silver Creature | Maxwell Boyle | 152 |
| Wheels Within Wheels | Seamus Heaney | 153 |
| Cut | David Feela | 155 |
| The Lesson | Claudia M. Reder | 156 |
| Oh, Woe Ith Me! | Bruce Lansky | 157 |
| The Boycycle | S. Conant Foster | 158 |
| Me and My Bike | Dylan Thomas | 159 |
| By Proxy | Amos Russel Wells | 163 |
| Bike Ride with Older Boys | Laura Kasischke | 164 |
| The Young Boys | Linda Hogan | 166 |
| Ode to Bicycles | Pablo Neruda | 167 |
| Roll On, Shining Wheel! | C. T. Mitchell | 170 |
| Beard and Bicycle | Guy Boas | 172 |
| Cycles in Flight: The Racing Bike | Allison A. deFreese | 173 |
| Rider | Mark Rudman | 175 |
| Down-Hill on a Bicycle | Louis Untermeyer | 177 |
| Going Down Hill on a Bicycle | Henry Charles Beeching | 180 |
| The Bicyclers | Harriet Monroe | 181 |
| Among Goldfinches | Bill Morgan | 182 |
| A Pastoral | Franklin Verzelius Newton Painter | 183 |
| A Centurion | William Carleton | 185 |
| Riding Their Bikes | Ellen Kirvin Dudis | 187 |
| The Old Bike | Anonymous | 190 |
| A New Cycle | Edward Field | 191 |
| We | Ryn Gargulinski | 192 |
| A New Blue Bike | C. J. Stevens | 194 |
| Moon Landing, 1969 | Mary Jane Nealon | 195 |
| Moon in the Mirror | Brenda Brooks | 196 |
| Instructions for How to Get Ahead of Yourself While the Light Still Shines | Jenny Bornholdt | 197 |
| To My Cycle | Adriel Vere | 198 |
| Swiftly We Fly | James Clarence Harvey | 199 |
| My Magic Wheel | N. P. Tyler | 200 |
| A Bicycle Glee Song | Glory Anna | 202 |
| Her Majesty | Arthur Waugh | 203 |
| The Queen of Girlhood | Margaret E. Sangster | 205 |
| The Romaunt of Cecilia | Arthur Waugh | 206 |
| I Stand at the Window and Wave My Arms About | Angela Cooke | 211 |
| The Enigma | Alan Bold | 212 |
| Reasons to Commute by Bicycle | Frederic William Kirchner | 213 |

| | | |
|---|---|---|
| Bicycle | Livingston Taylor | 215 |
| My Wheel and I | Alberto A. Bennett | 217 |
| The Bicycle and I | Anonymous | 218 |
| To Flight | S. Conant Foster | 220 |
| The Scorcher's Farewell to His Steed | Charles Dryden | 221 |
| The Scorcher | Edward F. Strange | 223 |
| Bicycle Sprint | Pamela Alexander | 224 |
| Constellation: Prose Poem | Bruno Schulz | 225 |
| Galileo and the Bicycle | Anonymous | 226 |
| Cyclolotry | Anonymous | 227 |
| Leonardo's Bicycle | Cal Bedient | 229 |
| Hampton Lock | Dave McClure | 232 |
| God on a Bike | Pat Winslow | 233 |
| Old Man on a Bike | Peter Sizer | 235 |
| Sunday Morning Services | Michael S. Smith | 236 |
| Wheel Ethics | Charles Richards Dodge | 237 |
| A New View of Sunday Cycling | Anonymous | 238 |
| Little Things | Anonymous | 240 |
| Puncture Near Wittedrif | Gus Ferguson | 241 |
| Puncture Wounds: A Baiku | Rowena M. Love | 242 |
| Highroller | Mary F. Nixon | 243 |
| Bicycle Dream | Lauris Edmond | 244 |
| The Way a Child Might Believe | Olga Broumas | 246 |
| Island of Miracles | Catherine Phil MacCarthy | 247 |
| Along the River | Ad Zuiderent | 249 |
| Cycling the Rosental | W. D. Ehrhart | 250 |
| Training on the Peninsula | Brian Turner | 251 |
| The Cyclist | John Morgan | 253 |
| Maybe Alone on My Bike | William Stafford | 256 |
| At Eventide | James Clarence Harvey | 257 |
| A Versicle | James Clarence Harvey | 259 |
| A Bicycler's Song | Anonymous | 260 |
| The Song of the Wheel | George Lynde Richardson | 261 |
| Ode to the Bicycle | C. Buddingh | 263 |
| An Accident | Gjertrud Schnackenberg | 265 |
| Dragonfly | Tania Pryputniewicz | 266 |
| The Ballade of the Devout Husband | Arthur Waugh | 267 |
| Wooing the Bicycle | Grace Duffie Boylan | 269 |
| To a Daughter Leaving Home | Linda Pastan | 270 |
| At the Crossroads | Mary Scott | 271 |
| Visitation Rites | Jack Elliott Myers | 273 |
| A Constable Calls | Seamus Heaney | 274 |

The Yellow Bike                            John Lancaster                276
Two Sonnets                                Anonymous                     277
Buying a Cycle                             Walter Parke                  279
Bicycles, Tricycles!                       John Banister Tabb            280
The World's Greatest Tricycle Rider        C. K. Williams                281
Our Bicycles                               James Laughlin                282
She Waits for Me                           Anonymous                     283
The Bicycle Slow Race                      Claire Bateman                284
Tour de France                             Michael Cantor                286
Logocyclegram                              Audrey Hughes                 287
Place for Four-Letter Words                Peter Sears                   288
A Quiet Revery                             Anonymous                     289
The Rain Race                              Post Wheeler                  290
Bicycling Away from the Library            William Hedrington            291
Entirely You                               Anton Korteweg                292
After Cycling                              Gary Young                    293
Puritan Against the Wind                   Gus Ferguson                  294
The Eight-Mile Bike Ride                   Philip Schultz                295
Girls                                      Lauris Edmond                 297
Autumn                                     Michael Schein                299
The Bicycle                                Stan Rice                     301
The Lesson                                 James Brown                   302
The Trail                                  Myra Stillborn                305
The Noiseless Wheel                        James B. Kenyon               306
On a Bicycle                               Yevgeny Yevtushenko           308
Pedaling Paranoia                          Jane Mayes                    310
The Bhakti Yogi Buys a Bike                Gus Ferguson                  311
For Fausto Coppi (1916-60)                 Jeff Cloves                   312
Mont Ventoux                               Jan Kal                       314
Sometimes We Close Our Eyes                Marco Pantani                 315

Epilogue: Rhythm and Rhyme                 William Saroyan               316
Poet Biographies                                                         318
Credits                                                                  331
Index of First Lines                                                     337

# PROLOGUE
## On Bards and Bicycles

Bicycling has long been appreciated for its poetic qualities. Rarely does a sport lend itself so graciously to movement; to metaphor; to style; to thought. Your mind races on the road. It *dances on the pedals.* Sometimes it's about love, loss, the meaning of life; other times, about whether the brake pads are rubbing. I don't know which is more profound.

On returning home from a ride, you begin to wonder. Where did all those great thoughts *come* from? And, perhaps just as puzzling, where did they *go*? Novelist R. K. Narayan offers the following character portrait in *The Painter of Signs*: "While bicycling, his mind attained a certain passivity, and ideas bubbled up, lingered a while, burst and vanished." So there you are, afterward, back indoors, endorphins gone, left with only a vague muscle memory of the mental exercise that, at the time, seemed so utterly essential and precious and brilliant. Time to remount the saddle.

Of course, unless your first name happens to be Jan or Lance, though you may feel you live to ride, you don't ride for a living. Thoughts about biking are squeezed around work and weekdays.

If only.

If you're reading this (which I suspect you are), chances are your passion lacks an on-and-off shifter. Your school and workdays pass by on visualized cranksets, daydreams of derailleurs and Gu; Monday on last weekend's dirt, Friday on the smooth tarmac ahead. Before long it's time: The sun shining high, the tar sparkling, you and your slick wheels are all pumped up and ready to go. *Free at last. Breaking Away.*

Still, the philosopher nags: Away from *what*? Troubles? Responsibility? Real life? "Where are you *going*?" asks a concerned spouse or Lycra-skeptic friend, bemused by the sight of a full-grown *you* clad in clown tights racing by the Joneses at the speed of an adolescent fantasy, trying, vainly, to beat your own times.

"To John's house and back." "Just down the block?" "Dunno, back by dinner." "Out."

With an enigmatic smirk you exit the scene of domesticity, parting the side door to reveal in ecstasy, astride your singsong steely steed, an untouched jungle paved in possibility, calling you to play. Then, invariably, you ask yourself the same question: "Where *am* I going?" What the hell am I doing out here?

This book won't tell you. It doesn't know you well enough. At best, it will do more. It will speak to you. *The Art of Bicycling* marks the first attempt to compile the world's greatest poetry about bicycles and bike riding. Not just the machine itself, in its bare essential elements, its cranks and sprocket clusters, but the range of joys and pains and memories it inspires in the psychology, the psyche, of the cyclist.

You might be thinking, "Poetry . . . about bicycling?" It's an odd concept to be sure. But not a new one. Bike bards have been around for as long as the bike itself, from the late nineteenth century up through the modern era. Paul Fournel, a contemporary avant-garde French writer, introduces the connection between cycling and the poetic process:

> There are a lot of walker-poets who write their verses to
> the rhythm of their feet. Cyclist-poets are less numerous, it
> seems, but that's due to inattentiveness, since the bike is a
> good place to work for a writer. First, he can sit down; then
> he's surrounded by windy silence, which airs out the brain
> and is favorable to meditation; finally, he produces with his
> legs a fair number of different rhythms, which are so much
> music to verse.

As you can probably tell, this is not a how-to book. It will not instruct you how to get inspired while riding—likely you already do. Nor is it a book of style and technique, though in a way, it contains both. In short, this book will not make you a better rider. With luck, it may help to make you a stronger, leaner learner, a better reader of the world around you in the sights and sounds and senses such as you encounter along the road, hence revitalizing what remains magical but has grown, over time, habitual. But primarily, these pages are meant to entertain. They can be turned and returned to from time to time as inspiration strikes or flags, either before a big ride or when you're stuck on the trainer in the deep throes of winter. Or simply, whenever you feel like being understood.

"Everything is bicycle."
—Stephen Crane

That you enjoy riding is no secret—to anybody. It's part of your life. In a large part it defines your identity. In the words of author William Saroyan, "What is the bicycle? Well, my bike is himself (myself)." That is to say, by riding, you are *being yourself*.

The obvious corollary is this: By riding, *you are not someone else*. However hard you try, however many clubs you join, the truth is you can never know, viscerally, emotionally, intellectually, what anything—cycling—fully means to another person. You can get close. A brief look over your shoulder and you can tell, often, if your roadie buddies are in pain or heaven, or if you can beat them to the town line. But never can you *be* them.

So we bridge the gap. We communicate. We share nonverbal signs like a pat on the back, a gesture, a hand, even a finger. Even the act itself of sharing a ride is an occasion for bonding.

Assuming we possess minimal social skills, we may even use words. There's a lot to talk about on the road. We can express deep feelings ("uh, good ride") or sincere concern ("you dead?"), talk shop ("how expensive was *that*?"), grunt (""), hypothesize ("where are we?"), even philosophize ("so I was reading Spinoza"). Cyclists are smart. They like to conserve energy; they give few-word answers. They're not blowing you off; it's all you need to know. You know the rest. Don't you?

Poetry is communication, condensed. Quick. To the point. Without the small talk. Without the bull. Guys are good at it. They use the fewest words to say the most. The lightest gear. The leanest language. The best words. In the best order.

A claim often leveled against poets and cyclists, the creative and largely solitary bunch they are, is that their activities are a form of cheap escapism, a flight from the demands of real life. But life, you know, is still there; you're just experiencing it on a higher plane. Your everyday speaking life has been translated, essentially, into the language of the road: the whirring and whispers of spokes and traction; the crackling of leaves; of tires treading tar; of the private cognitive sound tracks that go off in your mind on a clear day, when you think clearly and can make sense of things.

Poetry translates it back. It takes those ineffable clusters of free-flowing thought on the road and puts them back into the language of daily life. This is the aim of this book and its poems, to put the language of cycling into words. It fails beautifully. Continues writer Paul Fournel:

> When you get on your first bike you enter a language you'll spend the rest of your life learning, and you transform every move and every event into a mystery for the pedestrian.

Cyclists are indeed a mysterious bunch. From a pragmatic or economic or even a physical standpoint, they don't *need* to ride. Most own cars. And there are other aerobic exercises, like swimming and polka dancing. There is something more that drives them. Something hidden. One can't help but think, in driving by riders, that they're observing some strange ritualistic creed, some sacred, secret society, and they're right. Bikes pass cars without interest. They pass other bikes and they perk up, able to sniff each other out from a mile away. "Bikes talk to each other like dogs," writes author Daniel Behrman; "they wag their wheels and tinkle their bells." With a tacit smirk or an all-knowing nod, secret handshakes are exchanged.

Join the Bike Club. This book is a testament to and for that club. It isn't the club that plans Sunday doughnut rides and charity tours. It's the covenant, or the glorious myth of such a covenant, that is unwritten and largely unspoken for and which binds you to the wider world of riders. The language none of us knows only all too well.

So who came up with the idea for this silly anthology? In a way, you did.

Fresh out of college, as an assistant editor at *Bicycling* magazine, I had the unique privilege of reading reader mail. Letters poured in on all topics, from cranksets to calf toning, leaky water bottles to fluid retention. More than half were love letters. About bikes.

Neither submissions nor formal requests, these mystery manifestos had no apparent reason for being written or sent. They simply appeared, waiting, wanting to be read. Steeped in recurrent images of thrashing wheels and fresh air and aromatic azaleas, the documents recounted both specific rides and riding philosophies, everything from the "wide array" of roadside sights to the "child-like thrill" of going downhill to the feeling of being "free as a bird." They were about the simple joys of cycling. And they read like private diaries. They read . . . sort of like poetry.

Each letter described in more or less the same idiom that which asserted itself as a fully unique and individual quest. Freedom. Speed. Childhood. Happiness. Rhododendrons. I couldn't blame them. I began to think: With only so many words in the language, really how many ways are there to say one enjoys the sensation of manually pedaling a two-wheeled contrivance over a hard surface?

In a famous passage by French novelist Marcel Proust, the narrator sees the sea and is overcome by its sublime beauty. By nature an articulate and highly descriptive poet, he finds himself confined to muttering "gosh, gosh, gosh, gosh!" It doesn't seem a stretch to imagine the same spectator on wheels, cruising up hills and feeling on top of the world as he admires in passing flashes of speckled foliage and sun, reflecting. "Dude," he might say at ride's end, "unreal." Good ride, good ride. Same time tomorrow?

Reduced to idiots, in a way, in more than the minds of motorists, riders have the habit of journeying from inspired philosophers "in the moment" to inarticulate athletes after the game. *Yeah, I guess I pulled through today, just doing my thing. Woohoo!* You know? Sportsmen just aren't sensitive enough. They always look at a loss for words. They can't express what they "feel." Words are for airy intangibles like glory and pain; physical action is raw and real and baby, there's nothing else like it. A rhyme, however persuasive and well reasoned, can't argue the real rhyme and reason of a ride.

Reality check: When you say these things, no longer are you speaking sensibly or literally. You're thinking . . . like a poet. You are feeling what you feel cannot be said, at least in full. Poetry isn't the opposite of an "I can't describe it" moment. Often it's its fullest, loudest, most cultivated expression. It realizes that while some things are hard to say, one must try anyway. In doing so, it acts out a struggle with which all riders can relate.

A good pro's poem doesn't start out on sublime, halcyon peaks, on Alpe d'Huez, looking down on us with our puny, inadequate expressions. More often it begins at an impasse, a gap, a difficulty, and proceeds to work its way up like the best of us, using the same linguistic equipment (okay, theirs is a little better), only with far more grace and greater flair, and talent, and with more intensely fueled desire.

Bob Roll, pro cycling commentator, describes the Zen of mountain biking in this way:

> The more you cease seeing trails as problems to be solved, the more you will transcend the forces of gravity and mechanics. When you finally disconnect, the trail will look different. There will be no obstacles. You'll see it like a canvas or piece of paper on which you can express yourself.

So what does this mean for reading? Do we attack a poem or let it flow by? A poem takes getting used to. Before it can adjust *us*, poetry requires an adjustment, however slight, in the way we regard it. If we look at free verse simply as inadequate or broken prose, or prose on speed, we won't get far. For better or worse, bicycles are neither faster nor more time-efficient than cars. But that was never the question. To appreciate things, we take on their own logic; we challenge the argument itself that equates *speed* with *good*. If cycling is a language, our goal is not to gloss it over, like cars over a road, or to get it over with as if the road were itself a roadblock. We read. We revel in the process, in the challenge.

A poem's composition is interesting: Not just the way a poem is written, but the fact it was written at all. Well beyond their shared interest in bicycling, all the poems here, perhaps anywhere, draw from a common athletic imperative: action over inaction. We wonder where they came from, why the authors ever bothered. What *drives* a bike writer? Where's the fuel? Wherefore grunt and sweat and be made weary over such an obviously antiquated vehicle, an outmoded form of conveyance?

Passion's a strange thing. We suspect we read and write poems and songs because we feel we must, much as one determines to rise early on a brisk Saturday morning, away from plush comforts of home, to ride. Perhaps it's an act of subtle rebellion, a refusal to pass through experience passively, like a body, without reinvigorating it in spirit.

Work isn't a bad thing, if it's self-motivated. As riders, we like making extra work for ourselves. Reading, too, is work and play. Its motivation is not to feel happy but to feel energy. Like a good ride, good writing both challenges and expands us, as German theorist Wolfgang Sachs suggests in *For Love of the Automobile* (1992):

> To attack the pedals may be strenuous over the short run, but is an expression of trust in one's own powers, for with the bicycle everything depends on the self. Those who wish to control their own lives and move beyond existence as mere clients and consumers—those people ride a bike.

Occasionally there is something in the way a poem moves— we're talking about poems, right?—that makes you feel something or moves you, something to their bare-bones economy that rattles and absorbs through you freely, collapsing thoughts with hubs, spokes with feeling, spinning, so that no longer can you tell bars from tendons, balls from ball bearings, so balanced they are. When it burns, it just feels good.

Bike bards are as old as the bike itself. They first surfaced in the 1880s and '90s, a period generally known as the belle époque ("the golden age")—"the cycling craze." As the bi-cycle became a household name, daily periodicals became flooded with verse, songs, and odes in praise of the dazzling new invention, a machine that combined recreation and utility and provided an alternative mode of transport to smelly horses. In the preface to his 1897 bike song anthology, *Lyra Cyclus*, Edmond Redmond explicates the connection:

> A new school of poesy has arisen to celebrate the tribu-
> lations and triumphs of the Bicycling world. The Bards of
> the Bicycle have invaded Helicon in force and have drunk
> deeply from the waters of its sacred rill.

A hundred years later, we return to the rill of this bygone "new school of poesy" and hark! once more, dear friends, ride among those since de-saddled original Bards of the Bicycle. This anthology emerged largely out of a desire to reprint these truly vintage poems, largely forgotten for the last century. Selections from the late 1800s comprise roughly half the collection. It's only fair; it was the bike song revolution. These older poems lay the conceptual roots for what we know to be the *language* of cycling. Youth, love, first rides, letting go, commuting, communing with nature—these light, witty ditties say it all, differently. Whereas their contemporaries use slightly slicker equipment, experimenting more freely with representations of subject and metric style (say, "free verse," or nonrhyming), the early Bards more faithfully recycle traditional, classical forms. The early poems are rhyming paeans to an infant sport; by the 1960s, when bike verse occasioned a strange resurgence, cycling had already become its own discourse, and words struggled to keep up. The very idea of riding had become metaphor. Bikes were figured not as symbolic objects but also as subjects, rhetorical vehicles, for exploring such deep personal issues as memory, psychology, and an irrevocable fear of trucks.

The bicycle, the bicycle surely, should always
be the vehicle of novelists and poets.
—Christopher Morley, *The Romany Stain*

Poetry is an art of balance. Many components must work together, including the human participant. Too many tricks and allusions, the reader falls behind; too much cliché, he grows frustrated, waiting for meaning to show up like a riding buddy dropped at the last turn.

Balance isn't static, however. Good poems are made of successful transitions, in the form of successive words. Analogies. You don't know where they came from. They're strange pairings that generate more energy than the sum of their parts. And they transform the field and revise each other. Take a word like *gutter*. Add *bunny*. No longer are we talking about a drain, or fur, or reproductive euphemisms, but a bike commuter. Neither word in the slang "gutter bunny" makes sense by itself; sense is created only in context.

How do our thoughts come together, poets ask, if not by gulfs and leaps? Strange pairings? Arranged meetings? Chance? From the time bikes were invented, along with "modernism," writers have likened thoughts to streams of consciousness. We change our minds. Our minds change, shift from one lane of thought to another. We wake up, think about breakfast, spoons, forks, then brakes, upward to shifters, last week's hand blisters, cream, the condiments at dinner and the burger bun and everything in between; then we get up and ride. Poetry is a transitive art. It aims to articulate the essence of thought and action, how one thing leads to another.

Accidental bunch that they are, cyclists and poets revel in strange distances. With equally strange recording instruments, they actively explore and record the steps they took (figuratively) to get to where they are now, starting out with a vague direction and ending up someplace else; poetry logs what happens on the way.

Like any muscle, some poems are invariably stronger than others. They may be leaner, more developed, or have a more chiseled look to them, while others may take on too much weight, lose interest too easily, or appear to lack motivation altogether. While distinctions in quality are evident in this collection, as is inevitable whenever Tour and Nobel winners share the podium with novices, I felt each selection had a strong enough voice to hold its own, something adding to the collection. In short, I liked how the poems looked and moved and felt. I admired their lasting power, their endurance, their ability to sustain complex and often contemporaneous lines of thoughts over time with lucidity, fluidity, vitality, and grace. Some moved me more than others, but all of them *move*. William Golding, author of *Lord of the Flies*, once suggested the following analogy:

> Consider a man riding a bicycle. Whoever he is, we can say three things about him. We know he got on the bicycle and started to move. We know that at some point he will stop and get off. Most important of all, we know that if at any point he stops moving and does not get off the bicycle he will fall off of it. That is a metaphor for the journey through life of any living thing.

Good poems are dynamic; so too, potentially, are groupings of poems. Specifically, I have often wondered the effect of taking a film editor's approach to a verse anthology, such that each poem, like a shot or scene, would appear to stream seamlessly into the next. The adjoining texts might share a common theme or subject, or describe a similar feeling, or use comparable words, or structures, or appear so radically different in scope that their collision somehow resounds. Together these parts would comprise a cycle or series of episodes, a kind of "macro poem" in which individual components are assembled to produce a sense of motivated movement.

This collection is constructed in a similar spirit. Rather than organizing the poems by author or title (many are creatively called "Bicycle"), I have sought to arrange, to integrate them, however tenuously, by way of progressive associations. A poem that recalls an old racer might dovetail into one about an abandoned high-wheeler; a poem about a child losing his wheels in winter might be followed by the midsummer musings of a father learning to ride.

If poetry can capture anything of the way we think or the way we ride, it must find a way to articulate life in movement. Every race has a life of its own, a combination of raw energy, speed, history, craft, and series of successive, overlapping narratives. These things make it exciting and give it life. All poems, and perhaps some anthologies, might aim for a similar effect.

To help you select the right words for the right mood, provided on page 338 is an "Index of First Lines." As the plural noun suggests, the first two lines of each selection are rendered, so as almost to reproduce the feel of a writer's notebook, to follow in depth whatever moods or phrases feel most natural at the time.

Above all, the aim of this collection is recreation. Poems are meant to give pleasure. Recreation need not be idle, of course; we are serious about what we love and work hard at it. Some poems take more work than others. When they succeed, you feel it was a worthy investment. They take time and give it back to you.

The art of bicycling is ultimately a personal art. This book cannot begin to tell you what it means to you. At best it can do the next best thing—sharing what riding means to others, speaking on behalf of a passion that moves you beyond words, and helping to run a finger on its fine edges.

This project has been a compilation of multiple talents. First and foremost, acknowledgment is owed to the hundreds of passionate readers, writers, and riders who contributed—leads, submissions, advice, and general enthusiasm. Thanks also to the entire team at *Bicycling* magazine; I couldn't have done this without you. And to Francois, bringer of fine photos, I couldn't ask for a better collaborator.

To all my friends, relatives, and grandparents, I love you. (Echo too.) Above all, I wish to thank my family. All freewheeling requires a solid grounding; Brian, Adam, Mom, and Dad, the true lover of cycling, you inspired this just as you continue to inspire me. Thank you. Let's ride.

—J. D. B.

# From SONG OF THE OPEN ROAD

I take to the open road,
Healthy, free, the world before me,
The long brown path before me, leading wherever I choose.

Henceforth I ask not good-fortune—I myself am good fortune;
Henceforth I whimper no more, postpone no more, need
    nothing,
Strong and content, I travel the open road.

The earth—that is sufficient;
I do not want the constellations any nearer;
I know they are very well where they are;
I know they suffice for those who belong to them.

O highway I travel! O public road! do you say to me,
    *Do not leave me?*
Do you say, *Venture not? If you leave me, you are lost?*
Do you say, *I am already prepared—I am well-beaten and
    undenied—adhere to me?*

O public road! I say back, I am not afraid to leave you—
    yet I love you;
You express me better than I can express myself;
You shall be more to me than my poem.

I think heroic deeds were all conceiv'd in the open air, and
    all great poems also;
I think I could stop here myself, and do miracles;
(My judgments, thoughts, I henceforth try by the open air,
    the road;)

I think whatever I shall meet on the road I shall like, and
    whoever beholds me shall like me;
I think whoever I see must be happy.

From this hour, freedom!
From this hour I ordain myself loos'd of limits and imaginary
    lines,
Going where I list, my own master, total and absolute,
Listening to others, and considering well what they say,
Pausing, searching, receiving, contemplating,
Gently, but with undeniable will, divesting myself of the holds
    that would hold me.

I inhale great draughts of space;
The east and the west are mine, and the north and the south
    are mine.

I am larger, better than I thought;
I did not know I held so much goodness.

All seems beautiful to me.

Allons! whoever you are, come travel with me!
Traveling with me, you find what never tires.

The earth never tires;
The earth is rude, silent, incomprehensible at first—
    Nature is rude and incomprehensible at first;
Be not discouraged—keep on—there are divine things,
    well envelop'd;

I swear to you there are divine things more beautiful than
    words can tell . . .

Allons! with power, liberty, the earth, the elements!
Health, defiance, gayety, self-esteem, curiosity;
Allons! from all formules!

Allons! yet take warning!
He traveling with me needs the best blood, thews, endurance;
None may come to the trial, till he or she bring courage and
    health.

Come not here if you have already spent the best of yourself;
Only those may come, who come in sweet and determin'd
    bodies.

Allons! whoever you are! come forth!
Allons! the road is before us!
Mon enfant! I give you my hand!
Will you give me yourself? will you come travel with me?

*Walt Whitman*

# ON THE ROAD

Away we go on our wheels, boys,
 As free as the roving breeze,
And over our pathway steals, boys,
 The music of wind-swept trees;
And round by the woods and over the hill
 Where the ground so gently swells,
From a thousand throats in echoing notes
 The songster melody wells.

Along we speed o'er the road, boys,—
 The road that we know so well;
Those oaks know the whir of our wheels, boys,
 And they welcome the cycle's bell;
And down in the hollow the streamlet flows
 In rollicking humor along;
While flinging its wavelets' cadence up
 To challenge the cycler's song.

Above us we feel in the air, boys,
 A spirit that's kin with ours,—
A spirit that gives to our life, boys,
 The brightest of earth's best flowers;
For the health and strength that are beauty's own,
 That are stamped with nature's seal,
Are securely bound and circled round
 In the spokes of the flying wheel.

*Ninon Neckar*

# THE FLYING WHEEL

When the hedgerows are sweet with bloom and bud,
   And blossoms are covering apple-trees;
When the air is spicy and daisies stud
   The velvety turf and emerald leas;
When drowsily ramble the honey bees
   In perfumed nooks their sweets to steal,
And birds are rehearsing their August glees—
   Then ho for a spin on the flying wheel!

When the brain is sluggish and slow the blood
   And you're idling in knickerbockered ease,
Deep in meadow-sweet while the bitter cud
   You are ruminating of memories;
When a pipe and a glass can not appease
   The phantoms that follow upon your heel,
And no song for sorrow will bring surcease—
   Then ho for a spin on the flying wheel!

When Winter grim takes the summer's keys
   The devil in blue march can steal,
But when rose birds come, and the snow bird flees,
   Then ho for a spin on the flying wheel!

*Ernest DeLancey Pierson*

# WINTER RESOLVE

A wintry chill is in the atmosphere,
  As from the heaving lake the storm wind blows;
And weak-kneed brethren of the cycle fear
  That brings the riding season to a close.
Jack Frost assails us with his wicked thrusts;
  Our polka-dotted mufflers are on guard;
And many a good wheel in the basement rusts
  Which should be speeding down the boulevard.

And shall we join the patient, suffering throng,
  Which crowds the rumbling street cars to the door?
Which kicks against the service loud and long,
  But keeps on riding as it did before?
Nay! Perish such a thought. On every street
  The hardy wheelman has the right of way;
No ancient female comes to claim his seat;
  No cable breaks, no lumbering teams delay.

Our hearts beat high, our life-blood dancing flows,
  Though ice-flakes sparkle in the biting air;
While street-car heaters, every patron knows,
  Are but a vain delusion and a snare.
The steed that bore us through the woods aglow
  With sunshine, where the morning glories creep,
Will bear us safely through the mud-streaked snow
  Until it lies at least five inches deep.

*Peter Grant*

# BOWL OVER, WHEEL

The crimped clouds swim full low
Over the long chalk breast.
The cold wind bodes of snow
As it blows me along to the West.

Bowl over, bowl over, Bicycle Wheel!
Who feels what I feel?
I'm no sad winter's guest!
On the road I'm my best,
Full of zest!
Love's my lode.

Bad weather's no crime
In the mid-winter time,
Though there's mud under tire
Or it rain or it blow
Or the water's spell-crossed,
Or come whirling snow,
Our young blood's at the prime,
There's no sight like the rime,
There's no hush like the frost.

Bowl over, bowl over, Bicycle Wheel!
There's some life in cold steel
When you're urging amain,
Joints astir,
Frame astrain,
Flowing chain,
Spokes awhirr!

*Edmund Vale*

# NORTH OF AMSTERDAM

### For Hans Wijman

The wind blows hard across the polder;
Pedaling in silhouette, the cyclists lean
Into the wind, racing the sea along
The line of dikes, sweeping past the straggler
Who stands and pumps his rented bicycle
And, like a storm-lost mariner, searches
The chartless sky, praying for an end
To wind.
　　　　There is no end. But presently
One youth grips the handle of his brake
And speaks, and smiles. The tongue is wrong, but not
The voice, and suddenly the wind is down,
The polder quiet, save for the straggling cyclists—
Laughing as they translate in the gale.

*Larry Rubin*

# LAMENT

I thought of you
as I drove past
the girl kneeling
on the verge
by her upside-down
bicycle.

      I know
she was only
fixing the chain
but for one moment
I saw her playing
a round harp
(and I thought of you
as I drove past).

There on the highway's
edge where gusts
from passing cars
whipped the grass
like wind off the sea
and she was kneeling,
her arms moving
among the metal spokes
plucking from them
a music lost
in the louder
impersonal sound
of traffic (and I thought
of you
as I drove past).

The girl kneeling
on the verge,
adjusting the loop
of metal links
that would propel her
into the future,
but also playing
(and I thought of you
as I drove past)
a round harp
on a desolate coast.

*Gregory Orr*

# BICYCLE DAYS

I heard the jerk
of a chain and turned;
in your palm, the derailleur
cracked in two. *Metal fatigue*,
you called to me, miles
from the car, halfway
into the day's ride.
By what magic did you conjure
a teenage boy, strolling down the hill,
Marlboros snug in his T-shirt's folds?
*I can fix it*, he said. *Wait here.*
Call it karma or luck, he returned
with the part, knelt on the ground
and pulled from his pockets the tools.
Another save.
In an hour we were pumping up the hill.

We pedal into our old ways.
A bend in the road draws
us to a fishing village, a country store,
where I admire jars of local jam
and you order sandwiches.
Panniers, old cycling shorts, grease-
stained gloves: I follow
the bumblebee-yellow helmet
I bought you for a birthday before we left
each other. A year later, we're trading
stories—lovers we've taken, towns we explored
with other people, jobs we didn't get.
Bicycle days. Pedaling hard, uphill,
I know your new apartment fills
with things we never had room for. Forgive me.

A couch, beloved paintings, cupboards of dishes
recovered from friends' basements.
Oh, sweet one,
what fatigue finally forced us apart?
On the beach that day
only the hardy
Maine children made it
into the frigid water.
We watched a boy, legs twisted
from birth, stab the sand unsteadily.
His mother carried the walker
he discarded, and you spoke
of her patience, the way she did not rush
the boy but absorbed the gazes of the curious,
the way a lead apron will take the lethal rays.
I return to the memory
as I return to many others—guarded,
with my old fear that events
and the people inside them
will ask more of me
than I'm prepared to give.
You asked more of me: demanded
I ride the forty-five miles
and complete the day's loop, stay
with you and raise a child.

By morning, dark clouds drifted
over the route, but you insisted
we complete what we started.
Twenty miles into the ride, a steady rain
oiled the asphalt, dripped
from your glasses. *I'm hitching back,*
I said, half-serious, half-thinking
I'd convince you to quit.

*We're riding*, you said. *Trust me.* I followed
angry, frightened of skidding, our positions
fixed as the map in your mind.
We cycled through soggy towns,
past white church steeples gone
gray in the Maine afternoon.
*You'll be glad you did it*, you shouted
as I walked my bike on a slippery turn.
Over dinner we toasted
the route, the rain, the ride.
Beloved, what fear held me back? What kept
me from trusting when you only wanted
to keep going, to bring us home,
to usher us into a life
we could hold, tangible as the handlebars
in our four hands?

*Robin Becker*

# NO HANDS

One look at you and I knew
you'd be able to ride a bike with no hands.

I tried it, of course, but could never do it.
It was written all over your face that you
would have practiced, bare legs, bloody knees,
in the Summer evenings, hours at a time
when no-one was watching the mishaps, until
casually, coolly, at infinite ease,
you'd ride, no-handed, surveying the street,
as if you'd been born on a circus bike.

I wish—But then, we are what we are.
I drive with two hands, walk with both feet
firmly planted on sensible ground. And
I've got you. You can ride with no hands.

*Helena Nelson*

# RIDING BIKE WITH NO HANDS

I have always longed to,
the way I longed to match Mother's
perfect alto those Sundays
she sang into my ear,
hoping her pitch would stay there.

Harder than staying in tune,
it's been years since I tried to ride
no hands, but under this pure sky
I sing "Christ the Lord is Risen, Today"
surprised I still know the words.

And my hands drop from the bars
in that quickening
I felt long ago when Daddy let go
and I coasted off in the lawn,

exquisitely balanced, absolved
from all attachment.

*Julia Kasdorf*

# LEARNING THE BICYCLE

### for Heather

The older children pedal past
Stable as little gyros, spinning hard
To supper, bath, and bed, until at last
We also quit, silent and tired
Beside the darkening yard where trees
Now shadow up instead of down.
Their predictable lengths can only tease
Her as, head lowered, she walks her bike alone
Somewhere between her wanting to ride
And her certainty she will always fall.
Tomorrow, though I will run behind,
Arms out to catch her, she'll tilt then balance wide
Of my reach, till distance makes her small,
Smaller, beyond the place I stop and know
That to teach her I had to follow
And when she learned I had to let her go.

*Wyatt Prunty*

# LEARNING TO RIDE MY BIKE

Just for me, my dad sweeps the entire
sidewalk, tricky with its leaves and twigs.
When I climb onto my freedom,

he takes hold of those handlebars
and guides me with his hands clamped to the fender
and his head bent down so close,

the steady traffic of his breath reassures me.
When he starts to run
and the spokes begin to click with spinning,

and the wind lifts the red
tassels the grips are tipped with?
Don't stop, he says,

but I'm not steady. I'm wobbling.
I want to take momentum from him,
but he has let go.

*George Held*

# LIKE RIDING A BICYCLE

I would like to write a poem
About how my father taught me
To ride a bicycle one soft twilight,
A poem in which he was tired
And I was scared, unable to disbelieve
In gravity and believe in him,
As the fireflies were coming out
And only enough light remained
For one more run, his big hand at the small
Of my back, pulling away like the gantry
At a missile launch, and this time, this time
I wobbled into flight, caught a balance
I would never lose, and pulled away
From him as he eased, laughing, to a stop,
A poem in which I said that even today
As I make some perilous adult launch,
Like pulling away from my wife
Into the fragile new balance of our life
Apart, I can still feel that steadying hand,
Still hear that strong voice telling me
To embrace the sweet fall forward
Into the future's blue
Equilibrium. But,

Of course, he was drunk that night,
Still wearing his white shirt
And tie from the office, the air around us
Sick with scotch, and the challenge
Was keeping his own balance
As he coaxed his bulk into a trot

Beside me in the hot night, sweat
Soaking his armpits, the eternal flame
Of his cigarette flaring as he gasped
And I fell, again and again, entangled
In my gleaming Schwinn, until
He swore and stomped off
Into the house to continue
Working with my mother
On their own divorce, their balance
Long gone and the hard ground already
Rising up to smite them
While I stayed outside in the dark,
Still falling, until at last I wobbled
Into the frail, upright delight
Of feeling sorry for myself, riding
Alone down the neighborhood's
Black street like the lonely western hero
I still catch myself in the act
Of performing.

And yet, having said all this,
I must also say that this summer evening
Is very beautiful, and I am older
Than my father ever was
As I coast the Pacific shoreline
On my old bike, the gears clicking
Like years, the wind
Touching me for the first time, it seems,
In a very long time,
With soft urgency all over.

*George Bilgere*

# I NEVER DREAM OF MY FATHER

I never dream of my father
Cycling twenty miles each way to work.
A small market town called Tai Po sent him off at dawn,
The green valleys of Lam Tsuen cheered him on,
Steep mountain paths pulled him up then
Down to the Yuen Long Plains
And a tiny village school.

Heavy rickety bike
Black paint peeling:
The kind used to make deliveries of
Rice and paraffin and other daily necessities.
He probably bought it third hand.

He cycled in the damp spring,
In torrential summer rains,
In the short golden autumn,
In the wintry cold, his hands numb.

He was young then
With a young family on his shoulders,
An old one in his heart,
The sandwiched generation.

I never dream of my father
With or without his bike.

*Eva Hung*

# ALMOST COMMUNICATION

My father just passed me
in his Fiat 127;
I was cycling my bicycle 'Hideous.'

They stopped at O'Meara's
for the Connacht Tribune.
As I passed I shouted
"road hog" in the window.

The occupants laughed.

Before this he owned
a Renault 12;
we called it the
'Ballyhaunis cow killer.'

Later we met outside the sister's,
"Wouldn't you think
he'd buy you a decent bike, the miser."

"If he had your money," I said
and we laughed.

The neighbors with their ears
to the rose bushes
think that we're great friends.

I haven't seen his eyes for years.

*Rita Ann Higgins*

# THE BICYCLE RIDE

In the country of confusion my father
passes by clumsily on a three-speed
    unaware of the state he inhabits.
You might say he's confused, and mistakes
    long silences for the luscious drone
of an angel's wing sweeping overhead.
    You might say he cannot focus on
confusion, that he rides along the sunny
    streets of disorientation as if he were
gliding over them, an insect following
    the ancestral scent to the cave.
I wave and he nods a little, lowering
    his chin. Think of me, I think aloud,
hoping he registers the amplification
    and frequency somewhere along the ride.
Don't worry, I hear him call out,
    I know this country well. How could you,
I ask. How could you.
    He jerks the handlebars right and left
and turns out of sight. All night I invent
    dreams of betrayal and loss,
where at the end of the road the inexplicable
    divides from the unexplained,
and the ringing of my father's little bell
    stops the traffic cold.

*Henry Israeli*

# MY BICYCLE BELL

Ringing the bell of my bicycle,
I ride through the crowds.
Since I ring the bell persistently,
I never bump into anyone.
Since I don't bump into anyone,
I sometimes want to bump gently into a child
and surprise him.

I want to bump elastically
into a young woman's fresh body.
I want to ride forth over the body of a man
who would not feel pain even if he fell.

But keeping the bell ringing
I pass by without incident.
What a peaceful custom!
What an easygoing sound the bell makes!

But soon
I am stopped
by a train of the Yokosuka Line.
Then I get off my bicycle for the first time
and ring the bell vigorously.
With that,
the train shakes its head
and passes by at full speed.

What an effective bell it is!
(I am surprised
by the pleasant sound it makes.
Amid the rumble and roar
my bell rings with resonance.)

I pass again
through the crowds.

I keep ringing the bell incessantly, until
blood oozes from my fingers,
but I won't let go
of my bell.
No matter how wonderful any other bell may be,
I will keep on ringing mine.

*Dobashi Jiji*

*Translated from the Japanese by Koriyama Naoshi and Edward G. Lueders*

# AT JHONG-JHOU TRAIN STATION

Girls still ride bicycles into Jhong-Jhou Train Station,
The big, black, old-fashioned skinny kind, all solid-steel
And wrought-iron unibodies that lie high up in the saddle
With eaglewing-span handlebars and bell-ringers spread so wide
Apart they must sit postured upright in rat-trap stirrups—
Foot brake a long way down from metal toward ground.

Even the fieldhands in *doulis* with flat, serious faces
        from Kuei-jen
For *tofu* and *won-ton* lunch ride bikes queenly, ones
        with wire baskets,
White muslin saddlebags, ones without crotchbar, inlaid
        spinner spokes—
Aren't embarrassed by their rides' simple sex, the way
        Chinese often are
When they confuse, stumble over, proper-parsed
        English pronouns—"his"/"her,"
"she"/"he"—, so close together are they in some other
        tongues they almost touch.

*G. Timothy Gordon*

# THE THREE LADIES

On the cover of the book of 19th-century
etchings, three lady bicyclists,
their black eyes fixed on the front wheels,
race toward an unseen goal.

Billowing behind them, their hair & skirts & scarves
thrust them continually out of themselves—
till there is only wind & the spokes shivering
to a thin chrome light. And though

at any moment their mushrooming skirts
could catch in the treacherous rear wheels
& drag them down,
                              the skirts
do not catch, & the cyclists race on,

locked in the story the wheels tell
each of them—a story of covering ground;
of a woman who went & never came back;
of nothing at all,

the spokes whirring till they vanish,
the feet & the pedals a single blur.

*Lawrence Kearney*

# PHOEBE ON A BICYCLE

Pitching and darting across the roadway,
Plowing the air like a sail, Phoebe rises
And falls, her eyes popping and firing,
A fading of small spots on the night.

Full folds of her dress billowing
Above pedals in a baleful whorl, her hair
A flaming smudge in the headlamps, Phoebe
Hangs for a moment,

Green-snared against lilac;
Then crashing headlong, she falls.

*D. W. Faulkner*

# SPLIT

It makes me grin to recall my innocence
When I set out on my red and white Schwinn.
High clouds grazed on the azure horizon.
The smell of lilacs promised permanence.
Hormones yet to achieve their dominance,
I was one with the world, ever in season,
With no split between the heart and reason,
No need to pray for deliverance.

I was fishing at Sprain Lake when the storm
Hit, too focused on my float to be forewarned.
When I lit out for home, the tires lost their grip
On the slick concrete, and I did a flip.
Though my senses would never be in sync
Again, I still smile at the smell of lilac.

*George Held*

# THE BICYCLE

I have always been lucky.
When I was seven
my parents gave me
a red bicycle.

I rode it every day until
it became a part of me.

It had a basket on the front,
and my father attached a bell
to make doing the deliveries
more noticeable.

Pedaling up hills
pushed me so far inside my head
that only reaching the top
could bring me back out.

Going down, my mouth would open
as the world became flocks
of many-colored birds
soaring into flight.

I loved that bicycle.

Lying in bed listening
to rain sheet against the window
and knowing that tomorrow
it was Monday,

I would get up and go
into the hall and stare at it,
consoled by the standing
of its beautiful silence.

*James Brown*

# [BICYCLE]
## for Derek Peat

Since Thursday last, the bare living-room
of my flat's been occupied
by a stranger from the streets, a light-limbed traveler:

pine-needle spokes, bright rims, the savage downward
curve (like polished horns)
of its handlebars, denote

some forest deity, or deity of highway
and sky, has incognito set up residence—the godhead
invoked in a machine.

To the other inmates of the room, a bookcase,
two chairs, its horizontals speak
of distance, traveling light. Only the mirror

remains unruffled—holding
its storm of light unbroken, calmly accepting
all traffic through its gaze. Appease! Appease! Even

this tall metallic insect,
this horizontal angel
of green. So much for mirrors! . . . As for myself,

I hardly dare look in. What should I offer
a bicycle? Absurd
to lay before its savage iridescence—

grease-drops' miraculous resin,
blue mist of stars,
a saucer of cold sweat . . .

Now time yawns and its messengers appear:
like huge stick-insects, wingless, spoked with stars,
they wheel through the dusk towards us,

the shock-wave of collision still lifting
their locks, who bear our future
sealed at their lips like urgent telegrams.

*David Malouf*

# MOBILE CITY

You can ride your hangover out.
You can ride your problems into numb little stubs of
The problems they were and you can sleep
Later, if you want to
Because you are tired.
You can ride down flag-lined avenues where rays of light
Reflect off the high windows of buildings
Illuminating other worlds that we can see sometimes
If only for seconds
And you can ride through piss-smelling alleys
Whose ground is littered with the broken
Jewels of the past.
Sometimes, since this is a job,
It can feel like you are riding through the teeth
Of a rich man's dream.
The teeth of a rich man who sits in his helicopter
Making calls on his cell phone.
A rich man wearing sad elation's coat to the dinner
Which you delivered.
Yesterday can shake her hair and pace her one room
With a sky of clouds or rain
Wondering forever what is at stake?
This job thought, this ride
Is less about delivering packages than about searching
For the Truth of the Moment.
And there it is, somewhere out there in the metropolis,
Waiting to be polluted and lied to,
Abused and sent home.
And what do you know, the Truth and the Moment
Keep changing, how do you like that?
They've created a mobile city
But we are here to keep its promise.

*Machine Wilkins*

# FROM OUT THE HEATED CITY

From out the heated city Cyclist takes
  His way; and instant pauses at the gates,
An instant listens as the morning wakes
  The din of life he leaves behind; then waits
No more, but with a cry of pleasure flees
  To where his wheeling song may freely rise
On air more pure; where floats the sweetened breeze
  Between the verdant fields and azure skies.

Through woody hollows carpeted with moss,
  Up daisy-covered hills, o'er babbling brooks,
Down steep, uncertain paths, with vines across,
  In sleep-enticing spots and ivied nooks,
Past cooling caves—from each to each he flies;
  Now sinking deep amid some clover bed,
Now drinking crystal dew of summer skies
  From out some lily cup above his head.

Upon a cliff, in mute amazement lost,
  He stands at last and listens to the roar
And rush of waters, by late tempests toss'd,
  That crush in anger on a rocky shore.
Below him, up the beach and to the right,
  Makes in a cove, one of those sheltered spots
That win a sailor's heart, a cozy bight,
  Safe haven for some fifty fishers' cots.

'Tis here, in this secluded fishing town,
  Where hollyhocks and china-asters grow
Before the doorways weather-worn and brown,
  And o'er the shelly paths their petals strow,
That wandering Cyclist, lulled by moaning sea

And sighing wind, by stormy petrel's scream
And flying mist, reposes 'neath the lea
   Of an embedded wreck and dreams his dream.

He sees a narrow street, to him well known,
   Where busy men go rapidly along,
With woeful care upon their faces shown;
   And lo, he, too, is of the anxious throng
Of hurrying ones; a frown of fretting thought
   Sits on his forehead and unrests his eye;
Anon he passes down a sultry court,
   Then gains a heated office wearily.

*S. Conant Foster*

# AWAY FROM THE OFFICE

Away from the office and desk at last,
The business-haunted room,
The roar of a city, hurrying past,
The heat, the worry, the gloom,
To the glorious red of the sunset sky,
The sweet, cold wine of the air,
On the frozen road, my wheel and I,
A dusty, rusty pair!

Push—Push—
Two birds in a bush
Are laughing to see me hop;
On, with a bound
From the frozen ground,
With never a sway nor stop.

Over and over the pedals fly—
"Come on!" to the twittering bird I cry,
As over and over the wheels fly past her,
Over and over, still faster and faster,
On through the ice-cold stream of air,
On where the road is frozen and bare.

Roll—Roll—Roll—Roll—
Silent and swift as a death-freed soul.
Glide—Glide—
On the smooth, black tide
Of the ocean of night flowing in from the West,
Over and over, and on without rest,
Swifter and swifter, till over the crest
Of the hill, and down to the valley below,
Through the murk of the mist and the white of the snow—

Now my steed falters, as, breathless and slow,
Up the steep hillside he labors and grinds,

Grinds—Grinds—Grinds—Grinds—
Across and across he turns and winds,
Sand-clogged and rock hindered, without hope or faith,
No longer a soul, but a sin-burdened wraith—
Till, reaching the summer he spurns the dark hill,
And onward he plunges, for good or for ill,
Over and onward, and onward and over,
He reels and he spins like a jolly old rover.

Roll—Roll—Roll—Roll—
Backward he flies to our one dear goal,
Where the whirling shall cease and the rider shall rest,
And soft trembling lip to my own shall be pressed.

Slow—Slow—Slow,
Slowly—more slowly—we go—
What, darling, so far on the road to-night,
To welcome us both with your eyes' sweet light!
The wheel no longer has need to roam—
Be quiet, old fellow! we're safe, safe at home.

*Willis Boyd Allen*

# MORNING RIDE

Up with the lark in the first flush of morning,
  Ere the world wakes to its work or its play;
Off for a spin to the wide-stretching country,
  Far from the close, stifling city away.

A spring to the saddle, a spurt with the pedal,
  The roadway is flying from under my wheel.
With motions so sprightly, with heart beating lightly,
  How glorious to master this creature of steel!

Now mounting the hill-slope with slow, steady toiling,
  Each turn of the wheel brings us nearer the goal.
And so on life's journey 'tis patient endeavor
  That opens the path to the conquering soul.

The summit surmounted, we're now wildly dashing
  Through woodland and meadow, past farm-house and dell;
Inhaling the breath of the field and the forest,
  Keeping time as we glide to the tinkling cow-bell.

Lo! at length in the cast, 'mid the radiant glory,
  Great Phoebus Apollo looks forth, bright and fair,
Attended by cloudlets all roseate and golden;
  Oh, joy, to be out on a morning so rare!

As we mount the last hill, to the smoke-clouded city,
  Just beginning to boil with its great human tide,
It calls us to toil, and to enter the conflict,—
  So endeth this morning our twenty-mile ride.

*Anonymous*

# TOWN AND COUNTRY
## (A Moden Eclogue.)

### URBANUS—STREPHON—DAMOETAS

### URBANUS.

I sing the town—

### STREPHON.

                And I the country sing—
The perfect paradise of bicycling!
The country where the lanes are always green—

### URBANUS.

And there are no policemen to be seen!
But, Strephon, if young and native pride
Still finds its pleasure in the country side,
Come, tune your oaten pipe, my foster-brother:
We'll sing in antiphones to one another,
Praising the sport wherein our profit lies,
And old Damoetas shall award the prize.
This brand-new Humber shall the guerdon be—
'Twas lately raffled for a charity—
Let him who praiseth best the cycle win,
And you, the elder poet, shall begin!

### STREPHON.

I sing the country, where the shady way
Resounds melodious with the thrush's lay,
Where from the morning to the evening dusk
The lanes are sweet with eglantine and musk,

Where nature follows her instinctive plan,
Without the aid of interfering Man.

### URBANUS.

And mine the town, where all the stern day long
I hear humanity's incessant song,
Where thro' the deep pulsation of the streets
The heart of an achieving manhood beats.
Where stones and briars never find a place,
And even wood accelerates the pace:
The circling wheel runs regular and true,
And work is light, and punctures very few.

### STREPHON.

I know that "town"—its rude and deafening roar—
Hansom behind and omnibus before,—
Where any momentary indecision
May land you in a perilous collision!

### URBANUS.

And I your country; where your twinkling lamp
Tempts from his lair the unrelenting tramp,
To dash his cudgel on your faltering wheel,
To threaten, to intimidate, and steal,
Then vanish in the thicket dim and grey,
And leave you spoiled and bleeding by the way.

### STREPHON.

Vain stories all! Let him believe who will;
And yet the country has my suffrage still,
When the homefaring toiler, glad and bright,

Touches his cap, and wishes you "Good-night!"
Where hearts are simple as the day is long,
And nobody directs the rider wrong.

## URBANUS.

Where every dreary dullard in the land
Talks in a tongue you cannot understand;
Where sleepy will and ignorant respect
Grow vapid in unmeaning dialect!

## STREPHON.

To ears unsympathetic all tongues cloy:
(Recall the Hellenes and their Βάρβαροι)
To me the Cockney lingo seems as bad,
"Full of strange oaths," and bellowed by a cad!
But leave the language, and return again
To the secluded quiet of the lane,
Where you may pedal—

## URBANUS.

                    Thro' a cloud of dust,
A warm of flies that grows with every gust,
Till under Pharaoh's plague your spirit smarts,
Crying for Local Boards and water-carts!

## STREPHON.

Not in *my* country!  For the shady trees
Do overarch an avenue of ease;
The cool rich sward refreshes burning feet,
And all the world of green rebukes the heat.

## URBANUS.

Until the sudden thunder echoes loud,
And livid lightnings answer from the cloud!
Then you will shun the perilous oak-tree—
Conductor of the electricity:—
While I can house my wheel in Hyde Park Mews,
Rest in my club, and read the morning news.

## STREPHON.

Perfidious Cockney! wedded willy-nilly
To artificial charms of Piccadilly;
Not yours the passions of a manlier sort—
The risks, the fears, the escapades of sport;
You were as well, with Jehu for a guide,
To hire a hansom to the riverside,
Plough up the path from Hampton Court to Kew,
And boast of feats you watch another do.
But be mine, when twilight settles down,
To swing into the sleepy country-town,
Seek out the tavern—

## URBANUS.

Where, no doubt, you'll find
Refreshment suited to a sportsman's mind,—
A well-bared bone, drink muddy at the lees,
And nothing fit to eat but bread and cheese!
While I—

## STREPHON.

Oh, yes; I know your fancy well,
The Café Royal, the Savoy Hotel:

The luscious *paté* and the English pine—

URBANUS.

And what of them?  At least a man must dine.

STREPHON.

Yes; but, my friend, your sybaritic creed
Would fain imply a man must overfeed!

URBANUS.

Not so!

STREPHON.

   You lie!

URBANUS.

   Silence, impetuous youth!
Ill-temper is not wont to speak the truth.

STREPHON.

See, I am calm—

URBANUS.

   Rage mantles all your brow—

STREPHON.

Damoetas!

## URBANUS.

Come, Damoetas; judgment, now!

## DAMOETAS.

First peace, then judgment. Let old Arbitration
Free this your argument from indignation.
Well have you praised where inclination lies,
Yet neither poet has deserved the prize.
He argues best who best his temper keeps,
And both your faces are as black as sweeps'!
Your grey Damoetas is not yet so grey
But he can ride throughout a summer day.
Damoetas, too, impartial, nothing loth,
Knows town and country, and enjoys them both.
He wins the guerdon which he merits well!
Behold, how he bestrides a bicycle!
See, how he pedals merrily away:
Ill-tempered bards, he wishes you "Good-day!"

*Arthur Waugh*

# ANGRY

Had to be was angry full of
thoughts with no voice leaving house
loud with children and father busy with his book
mother at work on a new degree
to make her know more and know less
of me the child angry on my red bike

Guys in their hot cars
would come from the flat country
down that new blacktop
stream of mullets and blue jeans
often balancing a beer between
and always a cigarette and sometimes a girl

No exception today
with red car to match my bike
was down so fast don't even remember
the air in my lungs and whether it stayed
with him or cooled the hot blacktop
along with Oh God, I'm Sorry his prayer

No need for an ambulance, I
skinned knees and road-burn arm, a new curve
to the wheel of my bike went
home to mother cooking in the kitchen
and father with his paper so it must have been late
in the afternoon of the day I knew

my parents didn't see me and never noticed
the scabs I fingered under my shirt
proof that they had lives outside of mine
I was alone in this world and if I
wanted anyone to know it I was
going to have to find a voice

*Suki Wessling*

# THE RIDER

A boy told me
if he roller-skated fast enough
his loneliness couldn't catch up to him,
the best reason I ever heard
for trying to be a champion.
What I wonder tonight
pedaling hard down King William Street
is if it translates to bicycles.
A victory! To leave your loneliness
panting behind you on some street corner
while you float free into a cloud of sudden azaleas,
pink petals that have never felt loneliness,
no matter how slowly they fell.

*Naomi Shihab Nye*

# THE COMPANION

Partaker in my happiest mood,
Companion of my solitude,
Refuge when gloomy thoughts intrude,
My bicycle to you I sing!
With you no cares my brain oppress,
I laugh at fortune's fickleness;
No other sports your charm possess,
Nor match for me the joy you bring.

*Anonymous*

# JOY

It's joy to be up in the morning when the dew's on the grass and clover,
And the air is full of a freshness that makes it a draught divine,—
To mount one's wheel and go flying away and away,—a rover
In the wide, bright world of beauty—and all the world seems mine!

There's a breath of balm on the breezes from the cups of the wayside
    posies;
A hint of the incense-odors that blow through the hillside pines,
And ever a shifting landscape that some new, bright charm discloses
As I flash from nooks of shadow to plains where the sun-light shines.

Along by the brambled hedges where the sweet wild roses redden
In the kiss of morning sunshine that woos their leaves apart,
Over cool, damp sward and mosses that the sound of my swift flight
    deaden—
I leave the world behind me and am close to Nature's heart.

I hear the lark in the heavens and his silver song seems sweeter
Than ever before, I fancy, since I have found my wings.
Ah—the long, smooth stretch before me! and my flight grows blither,
    fleeter—
Good bye to the lark above me who soars in the sun and sings!

I see a flash in the bushes, and I hear a squirrel's chatter,
Half frightened, and full of wonder, as I go gliding by.
Perhaps—who knows?—he is saying that something strange is the matter
In the world beyond the woodland, since its creatures learn to fly!
I am up on the windy hilltop; oh, the fair, bright world below me!
I see the flash of the river through the forest at my feet.
What beauty, what strange, new beauty has Nature deigned to show me
In the world of which I wearied ere I felt her warm heart beat!

I sing in my care-free gladness. I am kin to the wind that's blowing!
I am thrilled with the bliss of motion like the bird that skims the down.
I feel the blood of a gypsy in my pulses coming,—going!
Give me my wheel for a comrade, and the king may keep his crown!

*Eben E. Rexford*

# KING TOMMY'S RISE AND FALL

Tommy was ruled by his father and mother,
Tommy was bossed by his older brother.

Tommy was tyrannized over each hour
By a very small maid with the face of a flower.

But one day Tommy was given a wheel,
And he felt like a king on a throne of steel.

Now a sudden rise from a serf to a king
Has always proven a dangerous thing.

The people who come into power too quick
Go up like a rocket and down like a stick.

King Tom, before the first day was done,
Was Emperor, Sultan, and Czar in one.

He owned the pavement, he owned the street,
He ran the officers off their beat.

He frightened the coachmen out of their wits
As he scorched right under their horses' bits.

Pedestrians fled when they saw him approach,
He caused disaster to carriage and coach;

For he never turned out, and his pace never slowed:
His bell was a signal to clear the road;

And I would not repeat, indeed, not I,
What the truckmen said when his bike went by.

King Tom only winked in their eyes with a grin,
Proud of his power to make them sin.

And bolder and bolder each day he grew,
And faster and faster his bicycle flew;

And he was certain he owned the earth,
And all that was on it from girth to girth;

And he always got off without hurt or scratch,
Till all of a sudden he met his match.

Reigning one time in his usual splendor,
He came face to face with a Cable's fender.

He rang his bell for the right of way,
But a biker may ring till his hair turns gray,

And a Cable Car, or its Cousin Trolley,
Will pay no heed to that sort of folly.

All that King Tom recalls of that day
Was riding into the Milky Way,

Where he saw all the stars in the heavens. Well,
There isn't much more of his reign to tell.

He gave his wheel to his brother Bill,
And walks on two crutches, and always will.

And he says as he looks at his wooden leg,
"I went up like a rocket and down like a peg."

*Ella Wheeler Wilcox*

# NOT MY KNEES

I will not expose
my scabby knees,
mercurochromed
like the eight year old
I was the first time I tried to fly.
What did I know of aerodynamics
when Sputnik was only a gleam
in Russian rocket scientists' eyes?

I've seen trick cyclists
loop-the-loop their bikes from ramps,
making Evel Knievel's jumps look like gramps
in slo mo, but I was oh-so-proud
of my three-speed English racer.
The whistling whirr of plastic cards
clothes-pinned to tire spokes
sounded like jet propulsion to me.

And that launch pad rock
planted square in the unpaved road
that passed by Ernie Catucci's house,
that rock said "inclined plane" to me.
If I aligned my handlebars just right
and pedaled a thousand miles an hour,
I knew I could make the leap
with perfect two point landing.

When Schwinn met rock, the bike went down.
In that nanosecond between free flight
and biting the dust, I realized
what might be common knowledge
among the modern bicycle pilots:

pull up on the handlebar at lift off.
Did I mention the fractured arm?
I'll show you my elbow, but not my knees.

*Stazja McFadyen*

# THE BICYCLE

It was before the white wicker basket fell
from the handlebars, before the red
white & blue streamers faded into a collective
dusty pink, sunburned and bathing in rain.

It was after the 4th of July but before
my feet could comfortably reach the ground
from atop the long, white banana-seat,
the one that started far behind my bottom

and protruded forward between my thighs.
I still had tonsils and strep-throat every month,
wore shoes without socks and let my bangs fall
into my eyes, hair sweeping against my ears.

It was before my girlfriends came for sleepovers,
before we burrowed under heavy quilts
naked and silent except for the breath that whispered
from our fingertips. Before I knew

that the quiet space between my legs
could sing, or scream. I rode down that hill
every day, the wind pushing against my cheeks,
my hair waving behind my head like a flag.

I would lean forward into the handlebars, into
the downward slope of the road, eyes squinting
into the sun, focused on where the smooth gravel
leveled into flat ground ahead. I became

a tunnel in the biting morning wind and I
was flying. But the day I felt the gravel slip

from under the tire treads I squeezed so hard the pink
rubber handlebars oozed between my gripping fingers

and before I could throw my airy weight back into
the direction of the road I felt the seat pulled
from under my bottom as the front tire stabbed a tree,
my pelvis thrown ahead then caught by the metal bar

between the two tires, the pain piercing deep
into my undeveloped sex, my legs wrapping around
the tree as that silent space began to shriek,
releasing the muted body nestled safely under my skin.

*Risa Lichtman*

# THE BICYCLE

Halfway between childhood & manhood,
       More than a hoop but never a car,
The bicycle talks gravel and rain pavement
       On the highway where the dead frogs are.

Like sharkfish the cars blur by,
       Filled with the two-backed beast
One dreams of, yet knows not the word for,
       The accumulating sexual yeast.

Past the house where the bees winter,
       I climb on the stairs of my pedals
To school murmuring irregular verbs
       Past the lion with legs like a table's.

Autumn blows the windfalls down
       With a twilight horn of dead leaves.
I pick them up in the fence of November
       And burrs on my sweater sleeves.

Where a secret robin is wintering
       By the lake in the fir grove dark
Through the fresh new snow we stumble
       That Winter has whistled sharp.

The March wind blows me ruts over,
       Puddles past, under red maple buds,
Over culvert of streamling, under
       White clouds and beside bluebirds.

Fireflies tell their blinking player
       Piano hesitant tales

Down at the bridge through the swamp
  Where the ogre clips his rusty nails.

Between the highschool & the farmhouse
  In the country and the town
It was a world of love and of feeling
  Continually floating down.

On a soul whose only knowledge
  Was that everything was something,
This was like that, that was like this—
  In short, everything was
The bicycle of which I sing.

*James Reaney*

# A SONG OF THE WHEEL

When the air is rushing past us, and our
    ride has just begun,
With the hard white road beneath us,
    and above, the blazing sun,
What a happiness is in us, what a joy
    it is we feel,
When it's ride, ride, ride, a-riding on
    the wheel.

There's a heavenly sky above us, and
    Nature laughs aloud!
In our little rustic arbor we forget the
    "madding crowd."
But now we must be stirring, and down
    the street we steal,
And it's ring, ring, ring, of the bell above
    the wheel.

When Old Time has cycled past me, and
    my ride is almost done,
And my life will all be evening, and
    above, the setting sun,
I shall watch the roving cyclist, I shall
    still be full of zeal.
'Twill be glad, glad, glad memories
    of the wheel.

*Arthur H. Lawrence*

# THE OLD ROAD MAP

*Haec Olim Meminisse Juvabit.* *

When the drifting rain on the window-pane
    streams over the pattering ledge,
When the clouds never break, and the road is a
    lake in flood at the pavement's edge,
When it's vain to ride, and the blurred hillside the
    driving mists enwrap,
There's a charm never fails in the stirring tales that
    are writ in the old Road Map.

It stands by itself on the fireside shelf, with the
    cricket books beside:
All tattered and torn, but on many a morn it has
    proved a trusty guide.
Tho' its cover's marred, and its pages scarred by
    the grip of the wallet strap,
There are secrets kind I can seek and find in the
    fold of the old Road Map.

See, it's scrawled about, and in and out, with lines
    and circles strange,
What time we planned the lie of the land, and
    marked the Mendip range.
'Twas overnight, with our tour in sight, we
    broached the foaming tap,
And drank to the chance of the mazy dance we
    had traced on the old Road Map.

That summer is dead, and its friends are fled: but
    I follow their passage still,

Where the pencil-black still wanders back from
    Wells to Cranmore Hill:
It was here that we lay after lunch that day for a
    pipe and a noontide nap,
Till the market-cart woke us all with a start, as we
    dozed o'er the old Road Map.

It was here we were found upon stony ground,
    with a three-mile rise to pace,
And Will hung fire with a punctured tyre, and a
    thundering frown on his face.
Here we stopped for tea at the "Cocoa-Tree," till
    Bob ate every scrap,
And at Rowberrow Hill was as red in the gill as
    the cloth of the old Road Map.

'Twas a sultry way from day to day, when the sun
    on our shoulders streamed:
And we learned that to roam so far from home
    wasn't all our fancy dreamed!
But when, two days late, we sighted the gate with
    no malign mishap,
It was something to show how far we could go on
    the squares of the old Road Map.

So it happens still, with the rain on the hill, and
    the wind in the creaking tree,
That my heart's desire is the sturdy fire, and a
    friend to sit with me;
With a pipe supplied, and the dog by my side, and
    the kitten asleep on my lap,
I can sit and prose (oh! goodness knows) of the
    tales of the old Road Map.

For I count that man but a cubit's span whose
   memory doesn't last,
Or who hasn't the heart to play his part in the
   dreams of another's past.
So,—romance, my friend, till the evening's end!
   your knuckles I'll never rap!
I'm the man for you: I can tell lies, too,—when we
   turn to the old Road Map!

*Arthur Waugh*

* "Some day it will be pleasing to remember these things."
   —(Vergil, *The Aeneid*)

# EDEN

Climbing from Merthyr through the dew of August mornings
When I was a centaur-cyclist, on the skills of wheels
I'd loop past The Storey Arms, past steaming lorries
Stopped for flasks of early tea, and fall into Breconshire
A thin road under black Fan Frynych—which keeps its winter
Shillings long through spring—took me to the Senni valley.

That was my plenty, to rest on the narrow saddle
Looking down on the farms, letting the simple noises
Come singly up. It was there I saw a ring-ousel
Wearing the white gash of his mountains; but every
Sparrow's feather in that valley was rare, golden,
Perfect. It was Eden fourteen miles from home.

*Leslie Norris*

# NO GOALIES

Not a hill to highlight the landscape.
Not a tree to treat the eyes.
Nature nullified on this northern Nullabor.*

Only one thing to aim for,
the next ten-kilometer sign;
goalpost of the outback cyclist.

*Phil Ilton*

* An arid and treeless plain in southern Australia.

# BALLADS OF THE WHEEL

Through the winding lanes where willows lean,
  And the stately elms their shadows throw,
Past the woodland bowers of sunlit green,
  Where the dusky brave, with bended bow,
  In the haloed time of the long ago,
Would soft, like a stealthy panther, steal,
  We fling dark care to the winds that blow,
And spin away on the whirling wheel.

By the highways broad, where, fair, is seen
  The bloom of the alder, white as snow,
Down hillsides steep on the road between
  The vineyards wide with their vines a-row,
  Nigh meads where the murmuring brooklets flow
And rushes tall in the breezes reel,
  We fling dark care to the winds that blow,
And spin away on the whirling wheel.

On days when spring is a verdant queen
  And bright-eyed buttercups gleam and glow,
'Mid hours when the forest's emerald sheen
  Is scorched by suns that the tropics know,
  In autumn-tide, ere the winter's woe,
Whether bells of morn or eve outpeal,
  We fling dark care to the winds that blow,
And spin away on the whirling wheel.

Come, riders all, be ye swift or slow,
  And join in the praise of the steed of steel!—
We fling dark care to the winds that blow,
  And spin away on the whirling wheel.

*Clinton Scollard*

# THE WHIRLING WHEEL

Have you never felt the fever of the
    twirling, whirling wheel,
Of the guiding and resisting of the
    singing cranks of steel;
    Never felt your senses reel
In the glamour and the gladness of the
    misty morning sky,
As the white road rushes toward you,
    as the dew-bathed banks slip by,
    And the larks are soaring high?

Never known the boundless buoyance of
    the billowy, breezy hills,
Of the pine scents all around you, and
    the running, rippling rills,
    Chasing the memory of life's ills;
Dashing, flashing through the sunshine,
    by the windy wold and plain,
The distant blue heights luring, onward,
    upward, to the strain
    Of the whirling wheels' refrain?

Fled from prison, like a prisoner, sped
    the turning, spurning wheel,
Changed the city's stir and struggling,
    jar and vexing, none can heal,
    For the peace and the fields reveal,
And with spirit separate, straining above
    the town's low reach,
Found a tender satisfaction, which the
    steadfast summits teach?
    In their silence—fullest speech.

Never known the wistful, wand'ring
        back, in pleasurable pain?
Met the kine from milking sauntering to
        pastures sweet again,
    Straggling up the wide-marged lane?
You have never felt the gladness, nor
        the glory of the dream
That exalts, as tired eyes linger still on
        sunset, mead and stream?
    Haste then! Taste that bliss supreme.

*Anonymous*

# TOASTING SONG

Away, dull care, away!
Till night doth bud in day,
    Till dawn doth lie
    In the eastern sky
With a promise bright and gay;
    For Joy is King,
    And his subjects sing
To the wheel forever and aye.
        Away!

Uncork the wine so red
The grape of France hath bled:
    Libations pour
    Till sorrows thaw,
And the ice of life is dead;
    Till morning steals
    On our glistening wheels,
And the order "Mount" is said.
        Uncork.

Hurrah, my friends, hurrah!
Fast fades the morning star;
    The sun doth shine
    Like the red, red wine,
And our road runs smooth afar.
    Let's fill one up
    As a treadle cup—
To ourselves and wheels—ha! ha!
        Hurrah!

*S. Conant Foster*

# WHEELMEN'S SONG

Good-morning, fellow-wheelman; here's a warm
      fraternal hand,
As with a rush of victory we sweep across the land!
If some may be dissatisfied to view the way we ride,
We only wish their majesties could travel by our side!
      For we are pure philanthropists,—
      Unqualified philanthropists;
And would not have our happiness to any one denied.
We claim a great utility that daily must increase;
We claim from inactivity a sensible release;
A constant mental, physical, and moral help we feel,
Which makes us turn enthusiasts, and bless the silent wheel!

*Will Carleton*

# THE MEN WHO RIDE FOR FUN

We're the healthy, happy heathens, the Men Who Ride for Fun,
The faithful friends of bicycling, that sport surpassed by none.
We've ridden through long seasons past; we'll ride long seasons more;
And while we've gained both health and strength, we have had fun galore!

We're close to Mother Nature, and she greets us every year
With blossoming flowers, budding trees and sunny atmosphere.
We hear her voice low-calling, just as soon as spring's begun.
She tells her choicest secrets to the Men Who Ride for Fun.

We start the season's wheeling when the frost first leaves the ground.
We know the roads in every town for fifty miles around.
Our minds are clear, our hearts are light, digestion Number One.
We've three big appetites a day, the Men Who Ride for Fun.

There are men who ride for mileage and men who ride for speed,
And in a few short seasons they get all the wheel they need
While we keep on year after year; our wheeling's never done.
We hearty, hungry vagabonds, the Men Who Ride for Fun.

We wear each other's burdens and enjoy each other's jokes;
Respect each other's feelings and the rights of other folks.
Bring out your wheels and join us. You'll be welcome, everyone,
To the Brothers of the Bicycle, the Men Who Ride for Fun.

*Walter G. Kendall*

# [BY BICYCLE]

it's not good or bad it's how you get around these
tiny hedged-in lanes that criss-cross town
maneuverable only by bicycle because the larger
roads are for sheep and cows who have to move
together in a brief season when there are two ruts
in the mud instead of one but rain romancing always
leads to rust and that of course leads to one place only
hope there isn't a waiting list and a reprimand
waiting when you arrive at the repair shop smile
and speak quietly and give your explanation
it is not a place for banter go to the barber
these men were all once like the boy I knew
would end up here when I watched him
run the bicycle chain along his chin to see
how it felt bumpy he said I said you have grease
on your chin fooled around with a shuttlecock and left
it at that he doesn't recognize me turns away
murmuring to enter the back room to enter
the back room is every non-apprentice's dream
no facts but lots of rumors that the vicar has the firstborn
lamb shorn to pad his seat that Mrs. Stavely once slashed
her own tires in a fit of pique which is why she doesn't
have one now she walks with a cane and is a lesson
to us all this is possible but what of the stories about
that room and the bicycles upside down on benches
and those men with the clear eyes and hands in their pockets
singing and the spokes all spinning in response

*Matthea Harvey*

# ON RAINY DAYS

What though the rain weeps down the pane,
  And all the streets are muddy gray,
And cycling hopes are worse than vain
  This wet, unhallowed, dismal day—
Still shall my soul know joy and peace,
  And sweet delight shall thrill my heart,
As, armed with rags and wrench and grease,
  I take my bicycle apart.

One half the pleasure, I opine,
  Which focuses upon a wheel
Is that ecstatic and divine
  Enjoyment I am wont to feel
When I remove the nuts, or screw
  The saddle off, or loose the chain,
Or pull the inner tube to view,
  And try to put it back again.

I love to tinker with the forks—
  To readjust the mud-guard strips—
To cut deft patches out of corks,
  Wherewith to mend the handle-grips;
I take the bearings out, and clean
  Them with a piece of an old sack,
And I am happy and serene
  Until I seek to put them back.

Oh, rainy days do fill my heart
   With rapture which I deem sublime,
For then I take my bike apart,
   Just as I did the other time;
I file and rub and twist and chop,
   And wrench and pull and paint and scrape,
And next day take it to the shop,
   And have it put back into shape.

*Anonymous*

# A RAIN OF BICYCLES

All night the sprockets have fallen from the sky.
The clouds have unzipped
dropping spokes all over the world.

Chains, inner tubes, handlebars and kickstands,
Oh when will this godforsaken rain of bicycles cease?

Twisted frames
are lying all over backyards and baseball diamonds.
There are bicycles hanging
in the trees
like strange fruit.

They are cluttering the sidewalks,
falling into swimming pools;
they smash and clatter
on the roof of my house
crushing the azaleas
in the flower boxes out front.

Oh I'm sick of it—
days and days and days on end
bicycles, bicycles, bicycles.

*Jonathan Harrington*

# BICYCLES

The bicycles lie
In the woods, in the dew.
    Between the birch trees
    The highway gleams.

They fell, fell down
Mudguard to mudguard,
    Handlebar to handlebar
    Pedal to pedal.

And you can't
Wake them up!
    Petrified monsters,
    Their chains entwined.

Huge and surprised
They stare at the sky.
    Above them, green dusk
    Resin, and bumblebees.

In the luxurious
Rustling of chamomile, peppermint
    Leaves they lie. Forgotten,
    Asleep. Asleep.

*Andrei Voznesensky*

*Translated from the Russian by Anselm Hollo*

# BLUE BICYCLES

Under the dogwood the bicycles are blue
and still, but blurred enough
to make them seem to move
                              behind his pane
the child keeps watch   and what he sees
is real

The wheels on the bikes are blue—barely
in focus: blue as ice on a petrel's mouth . . .

The child dreams he is gliding in a park
—his father runs behind, steadying,
steadying, and then moves off    The bicycle
rises under him like a star

The wheels are coldly beautiful . . .
the child sees how right they are
for moving: he could float with them
under the milky sky, under trees blowing
like visible green wind
                              could fly with them
into the earth's elegant houses, into the bronze
eye of a god
                    could move deliberately, paddling
like a turtle with webbed feet, navigating
narrow channels, sailing down the white throat
of time
              with them, he could go back—drifting—

he could retreat: back to his father's arms,
the meaty hands, back to the glimpsed penis,
the black shock of hair

Hazy and blue as a dream, light fills the room
where the child waits for life to come to him:
in his mind all things arrive—a train
with its million miniature cars comes toward him
brimming with oil and grain, comes booming
and clattering, engulfed in whistles and steam

He knows where the train must stop but sees
it will keep on going: he is the only station
on the map

The hair on his father's chest grows
in a perfect cross: he is so vividly poised
on the tall rock it seems he is about to jump

The child is looking up at the sun: he sees his mother
seated on her bicycle—he sees she has come into the glare
of the rock, he sees she is gliding toward him,
naked and impossible to touch

All things arrive and depart: the bicycle
pulls light into him—like a pyramid of quartz, he glows
with mineral change
            The world is burning

like a photograph: it is going nowhere, but up

He begins to see
how the night empties light into time,
how silence opens—a blue flower—in the brain:

reason enough to make his soul climb, wheeling faster
and faster

*Charles Fishman*

# ZENO'S PROGRESS

It is always late at night and always the night in mist
when these paradoxes are felt the most.
How can the boy leave a life force behind
in that dream house of his, and make it back on his bike
along the winding brick side streets,
through alleys no wider than two shoulders,
if at any one point his Peugeot is not moving?

It must be agony, wanting as much as he does
to get away quickly as possible, and getting nowhere.
On our way home across the street
we study him as we would the still
from a movie at the neighborhood theater:
we know that inside, larger than life, he is moving

and move on ourselves. In a fog
that blurs even the streetlamps, the boy
is certainly not lit up. But the idea of being
someday beyond this impasse, of thriving
under a cupola that pinpoints Andromeda,
is a possibility seen in a natural light.

Though he doesn't seem to mind
his young life is caught in this freeze frame,
his hands and nose and feet are getting cold.
And with that reminder he's off again,
until the next light that will stop him and hold him,
he's down the road again, an arm's length from traffic,
hunched over the elegant bones of his bicycle,
his progress blind, surging, prehistoric.
While farther and farther behind him, two floors
above the street, a man gets up in the night

recalling how interminable those still points seemed
that got him here, and step by slow step
makes it to his desk to write all of this down.

*Thomas Centolella*

# TURNING THIRTY, I CONTEMPLATE
# STUDENTS BICYCLING HOME

This is the weather of change
and clear light. This is
weather on its B side,
askew, that propels
the legs of young men
in tight jeans wheeling

through the tired, wise
spring. Crickets too
awake in choirs
out of sight, although
I imagine we see
the same thing
and for a long way.

This, then, weather
to start over.
Evening rustles
her skirts of sulky
organza. Skin
prickles, defining
what is and shall not be . . .

How private
the complaint of these
green hills

*Rita Dove*

# AN OLD MAID'S REVERIE

Shall I tell you what I'm thinking
  As I sit alone to-day,
While the ruddy coals are shrinking
  Into ashes wan and gray?

I am thinking of my cycle,
  Swift as any Arab steed;
Graceful in its revolutions,
  Geared exactly right for speed.

I am old and nearly sixty,
  Staid and settled in my ways,
Yet my heart will throb with pleasure
  Thinking of my cycling days.

Tell me not of balls and dances,
  O ye folk of feeble wits,
Scottish, polka, waltz, or barn-dance,
  Cycling beats them "all to fits."

In the dance how many giddy
  Revolutions must you do;
While in cycling you sit steady.
  And your wheel gyrates—not you.

In the dance the conversation
  Is the silliest you have heard!
But the wheel—your iron partner—
  Ne'er interpolates a word.

In the dance the air is poisoned
  With carbonic acid gas,
On the wheel you meet the freshness
  Of the morning as you pass.

So I think I've made my case clear,
  And you'll all agree with me
That there's naught comes up to cycling
  If you've "goodlie companie."

I say my age was sixty,
  And my riding days were o'er?
Perish such a dreary notion!
  I will cycle more and more,

Till my limbs no more support me,
  And my vision clouded be,
All the present, past and future
  Merge into eternity.

*Anonymous*

# STATIONARY BICYCLE

You pedal furiously
into a future you're trying
hard to prolong
by this exercise,
though the landscape
that rolls by here is time
passing, with its lists
of things undone
or not done properly,
and all this effort,
the fierce monotony
of this ride feels
much like life itself—
going nowhere
strenuously,
redeemed in part
by the imagination, its trance
of rivers and trees,
its shady roads unwinding
just beyond your closed eyes,
or even on the tv screen
you sometimes watch
as you ride, mile
after mile of drama
unfolding while you pump
and pump, proceeding
from here to here
at twenty theoretical
miles per hour, your legs

beginning to throb as if
the body communicates
in a code of pain, saying
never mind the future,
you're here
right now, alive.

*Linda Pastan*

# BEATING THE DRUM IN REVERSE

Shortly before my death I'm buying
a chrome-plated
bicycle.
I ring my bell to let the whole world know you're
beautiful.
Shortly before my death, and yet only
half-way there,
like a man who knows he won't make it to the top of
the hill,
but doesn't give up and won't stop pedaling.
The last man in the race has long since passed from
his sight
and he has no connection,
he doesn't write home, gets no letters,
hasn't fallen in love with the brunette in the window
and hasn't drunk from others' wells.
Feeling himself behind him he makes a break
only to meet himself, having only himself,
his other self
that he senses but vaguely,
as the apple-tree senses a bird.
And, maybe, that is the point of it all,
of that teeth-gritting and obstinate ride. . .

We recognize ourselves in the rider with the tense
face
rounding the corner,
in our legs we can feel the ascent, as abrupt as a
storm,
the jangling of bells in our voice.

This is the journey that each must make
individually
within himself
and all together, each along his own track.
This is that miraculous perpetuum mobile,
the exchange of energy, division of cells,
the infinity
of man,
his blood, his glory.

*Miroslav Válek*

*Translated from the Slovak by David Short*

# BUFFALO

A sweet inferno, gusting, funneled
crowds of every color in the oval
echoing with megaphones. The buses
emptied out in waves into the evening.
The heat evaporated into smoke
above the seething gulf: a shining
are inscribed a current down below
and the crowd was ready at the crossing.
A black man dozed inside a beam of light
that sliced the shadows: in a box
breezy, easy women waited
for a ferry to arrive. I whispered:
Buffalo! —and the name took.
                        I plummeted
into the limbo where the voices of the blood
are deafening and gleaming burns the sight
like mirror flashes.
I heard the dry whip crack and everywhere
saw striped backs, bent and churning
on the track.

*Eugenio Montale*

# THE BICYCLE RACE IN *BEOWULF*

The leader of the pack, long seasoned in the saddle,
Hands clenched as if in prayer, bends over the ram's horn bars,
Spokes flashing like sunrays across the long, level road.
The winding trail of men extends beyond the curve.
With fifty lengths to go, from behindmost comes Big Thighs,
The sprinter in the group, searching for a slot.
He passes middlemen who try to suck his wheel.
He edges around blockers who hook his handlebars.
He steers to free himself, till, just behind the leader,
With a calculated kick, he upshifts into seven-gear
And plunges knifeward to penetrate the windwall.

*David Galef*

# FEARLESS RIDER

Unspoken Creed
Fearless Rider
Ride like Lighting
Crash like Thunder

Battered Frame
Mangled Derailleur
Adrenaline, Fear
Bliss and Anger

Pain is Temporary
Glory . . . Forever
Muddy and Bloody
The More, the Better

Man and Machine
Trails to Conquer
Neither Weather nor Wife
Can Tear Them Asunder

Gnarled Roots, Jagged Rocks
Slippery as a Salamander
Big Gear, Granny Gear
Force, Finesse . . . Whatever

Ride like Lighting
Crash like Thunder
Unspoken Creed
Fearless Rider

*Jim Clawson*

# THE GOL-DARNED WHEEL
## (A Cowboy Song)

I can take the wildest bronco in the tough old woolly West;
I can ride him, I can break him, let him do his level best.

I can handle any cattle ever wore a coat of hair,
And I've had a lively tussle with a tarnal grizzly bear.

I can rope and throw the longhorn of the wildest Texas brand,
And in Indian disagreements I can play a leading hand;

But at last I got my master and he surely made me squeal
When the boys got me astraddle of that gol-darned wheel.

It was at the Eagle Ranch, on the Brazos, when I first
Found that darned contrivance that upset me in the dust.

A tenderfoot had brought it, he was wheeling all the way
From the sunrise end of freedom out to San Francisco Bay.

He tied up at the ranch for to get outside a meal,
Never thinking we would monkey with his gol-darned wheel.

Arizona Jim begun it when he said to Jack McGill
There was fellows forced to limit bragging on their riding skill,

And he'd venture the admission the same fellow that he meant
Was a very handy cutter far as riding broncos went;

But he would find that he was bucking 'gainst a different kind of deal
If he threw his leather leggins 'gainst a gol-darned wheel.

Such a slam against my talent made me hotter than a mink,
And I swore that I would ride him for amusement or for chink.

And it was nothing but a plaything for the kids and such about,
And they'd have their ideas shattered if they'd lead the critter out.

They held it while I mounted and gave the word to go;
The shove they gave to start me warn't unreasonably slow.

But I never spilled a cuss word and I never spilled a squeal—
I was building reputation on that gol-darned wheel.

Holy Moses and the Prophets! how we split the Texas air,
And the wind it made whip-crackers of my same old canthy hair,

And I sorta comprehended as down the hill we went
There was bound to be a smash-up that I couldn't well prevent.

Oh, how them punchers bawled, "Stay with her, Uncle Bill!
Stick your spurs in her, you sucker! Turn her muzzle up the hill!"

But I never made an answer, I just let the cusses squeal,
I was finding reputation on that gol-darned wheel.

The grade was mighty sloping from the ranch down to the creek,
And I went a-galliflutin' like a crazy lightning streak—

Went whizzing and a-darting first this way and then that,
The darned contrivance sort o' wabbling like the flying of a bat.

I pulled upon the handles, but I couldn't check it up;
And I yanked and sawed and hollowed but the darned thing wouldn't stop.

Then a sort of a meachin' in my brain began to steal,
That the devil held a mortgage on that gol-darned wheel.

I've a sort of dim and hazy remembrance of the stop,
With the world a-goin' round and the stars all tangled up;

Then there came an intermission that lasted till I found
I was lying at the ranch with the boys all gathered round,

And the doctor was a-sewing on the skin where it was ripped,
And old Arizona whispered, "Well, old boy, I guess you're whipped,"

And I told him I was busted from sombrero down to heel,
And he grinned and said, "You ought to see that gol-darned wheel."

*Anonymous*

# MULGA BILL'S BICYCLE

'Twas Mulga Bill, from Eaglehawk, that caught the cycling craze;
He turned away the good old horse that served him many days;
He dressed himself in cycling clothes, resplendent to be seen;
He hurried off to town and bought a shining new machine;
And as he wheeled it through the door, with air of lordly pride,
The grinning shop assistant said, "Excuse me, can you ride?"

"See here, young man," said Mulga Bill, "from Walgett to the sea,
From Conroy's Gap to Castlereagh, there's none can ride like me.
I'm good all round at everything as everybody knows,
Although I'm not the one to talk—I hate a man that blows.
But riding is my special gift, my chiefest, sole delight;
Just ask a wild duck can it swim, a wildcat can it fight.
There's nothing clothed in hair or hide, or built of flesh or steel,
There's nothing walks or jumps, or runs, on axle, hoof, or wheel,
But what I'll sit, while hide will hold and girths and straps are tight:
I'll ride this here two-wheeled concern right straight away at sight."

'Twas Mulga Bill, from Eaglehawk, that sought his own abode,
That perched above Dead Man's Creek, beside the mountain road.
He turned the cycle down the hill and mounted for the fray,
But 'ere he'd gone a dozen yards it bolted clean away.
It left the track, and through the trees, just like a silver streak,
It whistled down the awful slope towards the Dead Man's Creek.

It shaved a stump by half an inch, it dodged a big white-box:
The very wallaroos in fright went scrambling up the rocks,
The wombats hiding in their caves dug deeper underground,
As Mulga Bill, as white as chalk, sat tight to every bound.
It struck a stone and gave a spring that cleared a fallen tree,
It raced beside a precipice as close as close could be;

And then as Mulga Bill let out one last despairing shriek
It made a leap of twenty feet into the Dead Man's Creek.

'Twas Mulga Bill, from Eaglehawk, that slowly swam ashore:
He said, "I've had some narrer shaves and lively rides before;
I've rode a wild bull round a yard to win a five-pound bet,
But this was the most awful ride that I've encountered yet.
I'll give that two-wheeled outlaw best; it's shaken all my nerve
To feel it whistle through the air and plunge and buck and swerve.
It's safe at rest in Dead Man's Creek, we'll leave it lying still;
A horse's back is good enough henceforth for Mulga Bill."

*A. B. "Banjo" Patterson*

# THE SILENT STEED

The shadow of my silent steed
  Flies over hill and vale,
As swiftly as the clouds that speed
  On Notus' fav'ring gale.

No whip, no spur, its sleek thigh wounds;
  Nor galls the chafing rein;
But, free as Helios' steed it bounds
  Along the shining plain.

Fly on, fly on, my glorious wheel,
  And round the belted earth
Go flashing with thy spokes of steel,
  Like star on heaven's girth!

Look how the grooves go by the fields,
  The fields go by the groves!
What joy the flying 'cycle yields,
  As swiftly on it moves!

Now cleaving with its noiseless hoof
  The white dust of the plain;
Now sliding down the mountain's roof
  Like a silver drop of rain!

Oh, merry are the wheelman's days;
  His dreams are deep and sweet;
He glides down all life's troubled ways
  With velvet 'neath his feet!

*Paul Pastnor*

# TO THE WHEEL

Come with me out into the road, my wheel,—
  Out into the road, ere the sun goes down!
Thy hoofs of round rubber and ribs of true steel
  Shall bear me away from this tiresome town.

Aloft on thy saddle, set safe from all harm,—
  The saddle ne'er mounted by trouble or care,—
I'll hie me away where the woodlands yet charm,
  Where valleys are smiling and fields are yet fair.

With feet on thy quick-moving pedals impressed,—
  The pedals that speed from the hurrying street,—
I'll seek the calm hills and the landscapes at rest,
  Where green leaves are fresh and breezes are sweet.

Out over the road while the sun is yet high,
  While sunlight and shadows are nimbly at play,—
O Bicycle! free as the swallows that fly,
  We'll hover, we'll hasten, as joyful as they.

*Charles E. Pratt*

# TO THE BICYCLE

Humane chariot, most valuable,
most laughable of machines,
complete companion of the human form
and to the human bottom bosom friend,
we are more intimate than most friends.
Cousin to the umbrella
and elder brother of the sewing machine,
an example to all your family,
you testify of an heavenly engineering
which angels do not need.
Once you went unrecognized,
bore eccentrics asymmetrically about,
stopped to pose for engravings.
What you gained in simplicity and equity
you gained also in beauty and usefulness.
You are our invention's
hymn to balance;
with the horse and the steam-train
you write the perfect poem of distance
overland—its sonnet.
Poised between your wheels,
between your pedals,
I feel I know your future
is secure. You cannot be replaced
any more than I can.

*John Gibbens*

# SONG OF THE CYCLE

This is the toy, beyond Aladdin's dreaming,
　　The magic wheel upon whose hub is wound
　　All roads, although they reach the world around,
O'er western plains or orient deserts gleaming.

This is the skein from which each day unravels
　　Such new delights, such witching flights, such joys
　　Of bounding blood, of glad escape from noise,
Such ventures beggaring old Crusoe's travels.

It is as if some mighty necromancer,
　　At king's command, to please his lady's whim,
　　Instilled such virtue in a rubber rim
And brought it forth as his triumphant answer.

For wheresoe'er its shining spokes are fleeting
　　Fair benefits spring upward from its tread,
　　And eyes grow bright and cheeks all rosy red,
Responsive to the heart's ecstatic beating.

Thus youth and age, alike in healthful feeling,
　　And man and maid who find their paths are one
　　Crown this rare product of our century's "run"
And sing the health, the joy, the grace of wheeling.

*Charles S. Crandall*

# INVENTION

Spun in some mighty wizard's brain,
   The potent spell that gave thee birth!
He questioned nature, not in vain,
   And called thy being from the earth;
To share the task, he summoned fire;
   Æolus at his bidding came;
He fashioned by his vast desire
   The mystic bond of steel and flame.

The subtle genius of the Greek,
   That bade swift Hermes tread the air,
And Icarus, on pinions weak,
   The vast ethereal spaces dare,
And Phaeton forget his fears,
   And speed the cloud-borne chariot free,—
Prophetic looked adown the years,
   And dreamt a deed fulfilled in thee.

What if he wrought not what he sung?
   The vision into being came;
And it were meet the Grecian tongue
   Should lend the magic wheel a name.

For sure, the god-like force that woke
   The pulsings of the Attic heart
Is present here in every spoke,
   And latent dwells in every part.

The Caliph's carpet, magic-spun,
   The Lord of Baghdad bore alone,
None other ever gazed upon
   Or mounted on that airy throne;

The modern necromancer weaves
  A myriad mystic steeds of steel.
Alike, or king or common cleaves
  The gale upon the ready wheel.

Outdone, outdone, O genii, ye
  Who wrought that Orient fabric rare!
A nobler steed is waiting me,
  And I am regent of the air.
With regal foot I spurn the dust,
  All baser barbs are left behind,
I launch me like the lance's thrust,
  And speed triumphant down the wind.

*Robert Clarkson Tongue*

# THE BIRTH OF THE BIKE

In the beginning,
Ere the artificer
Built him the wood thing
Names the *célérifère,*
Baron von Draise—
Four years from Waterloo—
Vengefully pondering,
Impotent Gaul,
As he heard how the thunder
Of Wellington's soldiery,
England's artillery,
Wheeled through the world—
Grinning, he scrawled
In the dust with his walking-stick
A shape for a sign,
Two circles: circumference
Perfectly flawless,
Joined and united them,
One, indissoluble,
(Wondrous intelligent!)
That was the birth of me:
I am the Bike.

High and round, rude and haughty,
Big-wheeled, little saddled,
I froze into steel;
And he knew me and named me,
Bone-shaker, Velocipede,
Father of Bicycles,
Winger of woman,
Banishing petticoats,
Bringing the female

(Long since irrational)
Rational dress.
Ho! then the polish
And pride of my ministry.
Ho! then, the gleam
Of my glittering nickel-plate.
Ho! then, the park,
And the pleasaunce of Battersea.
Ho! then, the hose
Of my deftly shod womankind.
I, the ubiquitous
Angel of exercise,
I am the Bike.

Mount, then, my children,
Follow, oh, follow me,
Forth through the daylight
Into the shadow-land
(Time to light up!)
Rush by the omnibus,
Halting not, tiring not,
Pedaling evenly
Over the stones.
On, till the turbulent
Traffic grows fainter,
All of you, each of you.
Clerk from the counting-house,
Peer from the imperious
Portals of Westminster,
"Devils" from Fleet Street,
Maidens from Lockhart's,
Costers from Whitechapel.
Follow, oh, follow, then,
Follow the Bike.

I am the coin maker.
Hark, through the deathly
Depression of Stock Exchange,
Hark, how the companies
Limitless, limited
Under the Act,
Spring into life
At the touch of my wheel,
See them capitalize
Million on million,
Gear Case and Handle-Bar,
Wallet and Tire:
Everything patented,
Everything profiting.
Mark the advertisements—
Vast, multitudinous—
All the world conquered,
All things subservient,
I am alone triumphing,
I, the Victorious,
I am the Bike.

*Anonymous*

# BICYCLE SONG (FOR WOMEN)

Changed in a trice you find me,
Man, my master of yore!
Vainly you seek to bind me,
For I'm your Slave no more.
Fast as you fly behind me,
I now fly on before!

Out from my prison breaking,
Wherein so long I lay,
Into my lungs I'm taking
Draughts of the glad new Day—
Out! where the world is waking!
Presto! up and away!

Praise to the Luck which sent me
This magical Wheel I ride,
For now I know God meant me
To match Man, side by side!
Wings the good Lord hath lent me,
And oh, the world is wide!

Scornful of all disaster,
On to the goal I flee!
My wheel grows faster and faster,
My soul more strong and free!
Pedal your best, good Master,
If you'd keep pace with me!

Bees may hum in the clover,
Sheep in the fold may cry,
My long siesta is over,—
Onward at last I fly—

He who would be my lover
Must now be swift as I!

All that I missed he misses
Who lags behind distressed,—
Sweet were the old-time blisses
But Freedom and Life are best—
Still, there's a time for kisses,
When now and then we rest!

And now I heed not a feather
The chains I used to feel—
Soon in the golden weather,
Edenward back we'll steal!
Adam and Eve together!
Throned on the Double Wheel!

*Robert Buchanan*

# THE MAIDEN

The maiden with her wheel of old
Sat by the fire to spin,
While lightly through her careful hold
The flax slid out and in.
Today her distaff, rock and reel
Far out of sight are hurled
And now the maiden with her wheel
Goes spinning round the world.

*Anonymous*

# DAMES OF WASHINGTON

The Capital ladies are gloomy this year,
And the pavements of Washington lonely appear
Because the good President thinks it his right
To put his foot down with 300 pound might
On bicycle riding for women of place
Lest some of their thoughts take the bicycle pace
And then the wheel costume, though modest it be,
He thinks unbecoming to dames of degree
And says with a frown quite forbidding and grim,
That Cabinet ladies must listen to him;
Their husbands he hires for wars and such like
To give him more leisure to cope with the "bike"
And while they are puzzling o'er Cuban affairs
And over wise statecraft are splitting fine hairs,
The President keeps weather eyes over the town
(Like Officer Rowan of local renown)
And when ever on a wheel a fine lady he sees
He sends her right home just as cool as you please.
The beautiful streets of the Capital gay
Are made by a prophet, the wheelwomen say
Each one is as smooth as a ribbon of white
With all its magnificent distance in sight,
And if one's abroad in the fresh morning hours,
The country breeze brings her the essence of flowers
The ladies of Washington bow to their fate
And find at a ball or dinner of state
The sole recreation propriety yields
Though they sigh at the freedom of pony-set fields,
And say as they murmur their wishes so strong
"Well Mr. G. Cleveland, you can't boss us long."

*Grace Duffie Boylan*

# WHEN GERTY GOES A-WHEELING

When Gerty goes a-wheeling half the people in the place
Come out to gaze, admire and praise, as she skims by apace;
They never tire of lauding her activity and grace,
And of the while there's not a soul but loves her bonny face.
   So fast she flies,
  She has fluttered past and gone
   Before their eyes
  Have been fairly cast upon
The rippling skirt, which half forgets its duty of concealing
Those little feet that pedal fleet when Gerty goes a-wheeling.

When Gerty goes a-wheeling it has been observed that few,
However quick and hard they kick, can keep her wheel in view.
According to appearances, they've crawled while Gerty flew,
Though they have trained and toiled and strained and done the
  best they knew.
   The lissome lass
  Always leads them on the course;
   They cannot pass,
  And must be resigned perforce
To smother in their jerseyed breasts the deep chagrin they're feeling,
And take her dust, because they must,
When Gerty goes a-wheeling!

When Gerty goes a-wheeling, it's a pleasant sight to see,
For light and lithe and brave and blithe and beautiful is she;
Her brown hair blowing backward, and her cheeks aglow with glee.
The cream she seems of what one dreams a wheel girl ought to be—
   Like sylph on wing,
  In a sky forever fair,
   A happy thing
  Of the sunshine and the air.

You fancy you are touched by some celestial breath, revealing
In very truth, the joy of youth, when Gerty goes a-wheeling!

*Manley H. Pike*

# DAISY BELL (A BICYCLE BUILT FOR TWO)

There is a flower within my heart,
Daisy, Daisy!
Planted one day by a glancing dart,
Planted by Daisy Bell!
Whether she loves me or loves me not,
Sometimes it's hard to tell;
Yet I am longing to share the lot—
Of beautiful Daisy Bell!

> (Refrain) Daisy, Daisy, Give me your answer do!
> I'm half crazy all for the love of you!
> It won't be a stylish marriage,
> I can't afford a carriage,
> But you'll look sweet upon the seat
> Of a bicycle built for two!

We will go 'tandem' as man and wife,
Daisy, Daisy!
Ped'ling a-way down the road of life,
I and my Daisy Bell!
When the road's dark we can both despise
P'licemen and 'lamps' as well;
There are 'bright lights' in the dazzling eyes
Of beautiful Daisy Bell!

I will stand by you in 'wheel' or woe,
Daisy, Daisy!
You'll be the bell(e) which I'll ring, you know!
Sweet little Daisy Bell!
You'll take the 'lead' in each 'trip' we take,
Then if I don't do well,
I will permit you to use the brake,
My beautiful Daisy Bell!

*Harry Dacre*

# SHOVELIN' COAL

There are those who think the tandem is the instrument sublime
For the serious cycle-tourist, and the man concerned with time.
It has drive and rolls much faster as it gobbles up the track,
But it's quite another matter to the guy who sits in back . . .
    shovelin' coal.

But just look at the advantages with twice the power at hand,
And half the wind resistance as it travels o'er the land.
The weight is less than double. This alone gives peace of mind.
But it's still another matter to the guy who sits behind . . .
    shovelin' coal.

Yes, the man up front is master. It is he who shifts the gears.
He decides when brakes are needed, and on top of this he steers.
He can go the wrong direction and wind up in Timbuktu;
But refuses any protest from the guy who's number two . . .
    shovelin' coal.

It's just like a locomotive, with the front man engineer,
He sits back and shouts instructions to the fireman in the rear.
It's the way to run a railroad. With a bike it's not so sweet
To the sweating, swearing fellow on the secondary seat . . .
    shovelin' coal.

True, the pilots work the throttles while their partners work the flaps.
They are barely more than slaves—a society of saps.
Co-pilots do the labor. They are not supposed to feel.
It's likewise with the suckers above the rearward wheel . . .
    shovelin' coal.

His view ahead is blank and to peek would be a sin;
So he can't see where he's going—only places where he's been.
He would love to lean to starboard when to port they make a turn,
But such pleasure is verboten to the fellow in the stern . . .
    shovelin' coal.

Yet there will be retribution on some future day in hell,
When all tandem frames have melted, and the tandem leaders yell.
In agony they writhe, and some mercy they request;
But the back men just keep doing the thing they've done the best
    . . . shovelin' coal.

*Tony Pranses*

# THE SMITHVILLE TANDEM BIKE

Now Henry Jones and William Brown
   Were built as nature planned 'em,
Although the swells in Smithville town
   Perpetually banned 'em.
They'd long been chums in fights and frays,
Together "on the burst" for days,
And when they got the cycling craze,
   Of course they bought a tandem!

But tandem bikes, though right enough
   For those who understand 'em,
Are very apt to cut up rough
   On folks who ride at random;
When Brown desired to take the right,
Jones screwed to left with all his might,
And then they'd start to swear and fight
   While riding on the tandem!

And Jones would swear that Brown was bound
   Upon the road to land 'em,
And all the people standing round
   A pair of fools would brand 'em.
Some twenty miles they went in rain
When Brown got off and took the train,
And Jones was left and tried in vain
   Himself to ride the tandem!

He tried the front and hinder seat,
   But Jones could not command 'em,
With observations choice and sweet
   He swore he could n't stand 'em.

Next day the folks who saw the start
  Saw Mr. Henry Jones the smart
Returning in a horse and cart—
  A-bringing back the tandem!

*W. T. Goodge*

# CYCLES

Would I go back? The childhood bike
Was secondhand, painted thick blue.
Yet scratch the hedge, dull black showed through.
I rattled blank lanes where I liked.
I had a college bike, caught hard
In its top gear, when I met you.
Uphill, I fought for every yard.
When I first worked, roads gave more space.
I steered cheap bikes through tall streets, full
Of selfish hopes, the first air cool.
Some came, some went. Sun scorched my face.
I whirred electric windows down.
Caught in the traffic's throb and pull
I drove my daughter into town.
This bike is new. It shines and purrs.
I shake, but can still pedal, swoop
From our workshop's door in crazy loops
Behind old roofs. My fine gears whirr,
I set off home. Lit trees storm past,
Late rain holds off, stiff knees hold out.
Oh never have I gone so fast.

*Alison Brackenbury*

# SONNET AT THREE-SPEED

She eased the bike onto the park's curved path
and stepped into the shade beneath a tree
that dipped its branches like a sultan's fan
and filtered morning light and mottled ground.
Around her she could hear the gentle swish,
the steady hum, the tick of wheels in flight.
The path flowed twisting toward a distant hill,
the center line a winding yellow beam.
She looped her leg around the bar and lurched
the bike along the path until she gained
a lovely, languid rhythm of her own,
and then she stood and strained each pedal till
she pressed against the wind and seized the top
to quickly gather speed and disappear.

*J. Lorraine Brown*

# IN COLD FEBRUARY TWILIGHT

Loping silhouettes ahead of me
on the bike path. At first I thought dogs,
hounds of the moor, canine wraiths.
As I neared, white tails revealed deer.

The path here is narrow.
One edge fenced; the other, scree climbing
to freeway overpass. No place to flee.
We—the three of us—headed down
the blacktop, hooves clicking
on surface made for tires.

I wore synthetic, hydrophobic bike gear,
crash helmet, reflective safety vest.
They traveled light:
fur, bones, muscle, organs, blood.

I felt the power of the chase.
They ran from me instinctually.
For a moment
I deluded myself, thought
we had chosen to travel together.

As the path opened onto a field,
they left blacktop, accelerated,
bound a frozen stream, slipped bloodlessly
through dense bramble. I used the bridge,
kept wheels straight, watched for black ice.

They vanished into a barren region
of stunted trees surrounded
by grid-locked city street,

7-foot chain link, and an alien interstate
lit with the vapor of mercury,

thrumming with the numberless
pulses of steel, glass, and rubber
that flash by, each dark cockpit revealing
one head staring fixedly
toward the end of the highway.

*Frederic William Kirchner*

# SILVER CREATURE

I left it, precious, balanced
against the rotting wood post
of the gate. My new bicycle;
bright and special in the rain,
a strange silver creature,
handlebars like antlers.

Mother had called and I was
running to the house for dinner
when the front wheel turned
and, like a stag at a rifle shot,
it jerked and crashed to the ground.

I saw it on its side
one wheel angled, spinning slowly.

I righted it and wiped it clean.

*Maxwell Boyle*

# WHEELS WITHIN WHEELS

## I

The first real grip I ever got on things
Was when I learned the art of pedaling
(By hand) a bike turned upside down, and drove
Its back wheel preternaturally fast.
I loved the disappearance of the spokes,
The way the space between the hub and rim
Hummed with transparency. If you threw
A potato into it, the hooped air
Spun mush and drizzle back into your face;
If you touched it with a straw, the straw frittered.
Something about the way those pedal treads
Worked very palpably at first against you
And then began to sweep your hand ahead
Into a new momentum—that all entered me
Like an access of free power, as if belief
Caught up and spun the objects of belief
In an orbit coterminous with longing.

## II

But enough was not enough. Who ever saw
The limit in the given anyhow?
In fields beyond our house there was a well
('The well' we called it. It was more a hole
With water in it, with small hawthorn trees
On one side, and a muddy, dungy ooze
On the other, all tramped through by cattle).
I loved that too. I loved the turbid smell,
The sump-life of the place like old chain oil.
And there, next thing, I brought my bicycle.

I stood its saddle and its handlebars
Into the soft bottom, I touched the tyres
To the water's surface, then turned the pedals
Until like a mill-wheel pouring at the treadles
(But here reversed and lashing a mare's tail)
The world-refreshing and immersed back wheel
Spun lace and dirt-suds there before my eyes
And showered me in my own regenerate clays.
For weeks I made a nimbus of old glit.
Then the hub jammed, rims rusted, the chain snapped.

III

Nothing rose to the occasion after that
Until, in a circus ring, drumrolled and spotlit,
Cowgirls wheeled in, each one immaculate
At the still centre of a lariat.
Pepetuum mobile. Sheer pirouette.
Tumblers. Jongleurs. Ring-a-rosies. Stet!

*Seamus Heaney*

# CUT

Filming a motion picture
about a small town life
must be difficult: things happen
so slowly that when the director says
"Action" the crew must be content
to watch a short farm boy pick up
his bicycle from a dusty road
and imagining it to be a close friend,
walk beside it toward the creek,
kicking pebbles like dreams
into a ditch. They told him
he was being filmed but
he wouldn't believe them because
nothing interesting ever happens
here. After he reaches the creek
the bicycle falls from his hands
and the boy picks up a few
flat stones to skip across
the water. In his mind he pretends
each skip betters his chances
of any dream coming true.
He throws another
only to watch it sink.
Discouraged, he turns toward home
but finds a camera crew
surrounding his fallen bicycle,
filming that one wheel
still spinning in the motionless air.

*David Feela*

# THE LESSON

Stand next to your bike, like that,
says my father, holding the new Minox camera
that fits in his shirt pocket. I am a chubby ten,
in profile, the worst, my too tight shirt
over tight stretch pants, holding the handle bars.
How many lessons will it take?

        In Atlantic City
my mother rents a bike. I practice
on the boardwalk, children whizzing past,
age five or six. To compensate,
my mother stuffs a giant bear in my arms.

The bear is blue, the bike is blue, the sky is blue,
and I cannot ride, I cannot ride, my fingers
grip bars that are supposed to hold me
and do not. My feet turn pedals
that are supposed to take me somewhere
and they do not.

At twenty four, in graduate school,
I practice on a rusty blue bike
my boyfriend found in a park after rain.
He holds the back and lets go.
I think, I can do this,
but each time I feel the surge of power,
I waver and shout,
I'm going to crash into that tree, and I do.

*Claudia M. Reder*

# OH, WOE ITH ME!

Ath I wath biking
down the thtweet,
I hit a bump
and lotht my theat.

I cwathed my bike
into a twee,
I thcwathed my fathe,
oh, woe ith me.

My bike ith wecked,
I've no excuthe.
And wortht of all,
my tooth ith looth.

*Bruce Lansky*

# THE BOYCYCLE

An' fare 'ave yer bin to? An' phat is it, Terrence?
  A boycycle is it! An' phat is it for?
To roide on ashtraddle! go lang wid yer, Terrence,
  Yer'd break ivery bone in yer back on thur floor.

Now don't yer be thryin' yer tricks wid yer mother;
  An' phy wan't ye home to yer supper before?
An' me wid thur babby, an' only yer brother
  To draw all thur wather an' wait on thur sthore.

An' phat is that thing hanging there in thur middle?
  A lantern! faix, hang it up over thur door!
'Twill loight up thur notice as foine as a fiddle:
  "Here's Mrs. O'Flaherty's Grocery Sthore."

Yer hans are that filthy, an' black beyont menshun;
  An' how did it come as your breeches wuz tore?
The boycycle did it! thur divil's invention!
  I'll not have yer roidin' thur thing anny more.

Get down from there, Terrence! come back yer young villin!
  Och, mother av Moses! an' ain't there no law
To punish a poor widdy's son, as ain't willin'
  To sthop wid his mother, an' wait on thur sthore?

*S. Conant Foster*

# ME AND MY BIKE
## *An excerpt from an unpublished operetta*

*. . . And the two lovers burst into a kind of song, half operatic, and recitative.*

GEORGINA.
How stern you appear
With your penny-farthen,
Augustus my dear,
So imposing astride it
And not scared a bit
Oh, I'd have a fit
If I even tried it!

AUGUSTUS.
For you I would ride it,
Georgina my dear,
From here to Carmarthen.

GEORGINA.
Oh how brave you are then
On your penny-farthen!

AUGUSTUS.
Though it is, I admit,
Very sharp where you sit.

GEORGINA.
How impressively you pedal!

AUGUSTUS.
How excessively it shakes!

GEORGINA.
Your monster made of metal

AUGUSTUS.
And every whisker aches.

GEORGINA.
How aggressively you pedal!

AUGUSTUS.
Though it hasn't any brakes.

*Georginia turns from Augustus and addresses the audience—*

GEORGINA.
How handsome my love
Upon his boneshaker!
How high up above!
How the winds reel behind!
But the day I get on it
I'll eat my best bonnet
And the small wheel behind.

AUGUSTUS.
Oh for a steel behind!
Then I would take her
From here to Jamaica.

GEORGINA.
Oh he'd never take her
Upon his boneshaker.

AUGUSTUS.
Bicycles rot 'em, yes!
Hell is not bottomless!

GEORGINA.
How swivelly
You are then

AUGUSTUS.
Oh my liverly
And lights

GEORGINA.
On your nasty penny-farthen

AUGUSTUS.
Where the saddle sits and bites

GEORGINA.
How busily

AUGUSTUS.
How dizzily

GEORGINA.
How knobbily

AUGUSTUS.
How hobbily

GEORGINA.
You wobble and you sway!

AUGUSTUS.
O speedily

GEORGINA.
Indeedily

BOTH.
Take the brute away!

*The butler, outside the servants' quarters, passes at arm's length, and with a look of well-bred loathing, the penny-farthing to a footman.*

Take this hobject away.
It's a heysore to horsemen.

*Now the footman, with repugnance, is passing it to an under-footman.*

Take this error away.
To 'orsemen it's 'ell.

*Now the under-footman is passing it, with a scandalized expression, to a parlormaid.*

Take this 'otch potch away.
It's a insult to 'orseflesh.

*Now the parlormaid is passing it, with upturned nose and a refined accent, to an under-parlormaid.*

Take this engine away.
All bicycles smell.


*Dylan Thomas*

# BY PROXY

Young Timothy Timid is cautious and wealthy;
He has heard that bicycle owners are healthy;
And being himself but a weak-chested youth,
He bought him a wheel,—and a beauty, in truth.
"A pity," he said, as he viewed it with pride,
"To scar it and batter it learning to ride;
And worse (what is likely) to batter myself.
I cannot do better than hire with my pelf
Some cycler to ride in my stead, and be rid
Of all danger and worry and work." So he did.

*Amos Russel Wells*

# BIKE RIDE WITH OLDER BOYS

The one I didn't go on.

I was thirteen,
and they were older.
I'd met them at the public pool. I must

have given them my number. I'm sure

I'd given them my number,
knowing the girl I was . . .

It was summer. My afternoons
were made of time and vinyl.
My mother worked,
but I had a bike. They wanted

to go for a ride.
Just me and them. I said
okay fine, I'd
meet them at the Stop-n-Go
at four o'clock.
And then I didn't show.

I have been given a little gift—
something sweet
and inexpensive, something
I never worked or asked or said
thank you for, most
days not aware
of what I have been given, or what I missed—

because it's that, too, isn't it?
I never saw those boys again.

I'm not as dumb
as they think I am

but neither am I wise. Perhaps

it is the best
afternoon of my life. Two
cute and older boys
pedaling beside me—respectful, awed. When we

turn down my street, the other girls see me . . .

Everything as I imagined it would be.

Or, I am in a vacant field. When I
stand up again, there are bits of glass and gravel
ground into my knees.
I will never love myself again.
Who knew then
that someday I would be

thirty-seven, wiping
crumbs off the kitchen table with a sponge, remembering
them, thinking
of this—

those boys still waiting
outside the Stop-n-Go, smoking
cigarettes, growing older.

*Laura Kasischke*

# THE YOUNG BOYS

It's springtime and young boys
ride by, the moving spokes
of their bicycles like nothing.

They turn
as water in a wheel
or earth
with invisible speed,
the gods of Mount Olympus
bent over handlebars.

Come watch the race.
Stand at the corner
and give the drivers water with lime.
Don't tell them their wheels
are ready to collapse
at the end of the track.
Don't say how the black market is a bobbin
unwinding veins from living bodies
to fill itself.

Don't tell the beautiful gods on their bikes
about our other lives
in swamps, with trembling earth
and islands of peat floating up
growing cypress overnight
and the mosses
and birds with boomerang wings,
the goddesses of inner earth
bent over the cauldron.

*Linda Hogan*

# ODE TO BICYCLES

I was walking
down
a sizzling road:
the sun popped like
a field of blazing maize,
the
earth
was hot,
an infinite circle
with an empty
blue sky overhead.

A few bicycles
passed
me by,
the only
insects
in
that dry
moment of summer,
silent,
swift,
translucent;
they
barely stirred
the air.

Workers and girls
were riding to their
factories,
giving
their eyes

to summer,
their heads to the sky,
sitting on the
hard
beetle backs
of the whirling
bicycles
that whirred
as they rode by
bridges, rosebushes, brambles
and midday.

I thought about evening when
the boys
wash up,
sing, eat, raise
a cup
of wine
in honor
of love
and life,
and waiting
at the door,
the bicycle,
stilled,
because
only moving
does it have a soul,
and fallen there
it isn't
a translucent insect
humming
through summer
but

a cold
skeleton
that will return to
life
only
when it's needed,
when it's light,
that is,
with
the
resurrection
of each day.

*Pablo Neruda*

*Translated from the Spanish by Margaret Sayers Peden*

# ROLL ON, SHINING WHEEL!

As I rise from my couch at the first dawn of day,
  E'er the sun earth's beauties reveal;
The fresh morning air drives away all my care,
  As I fondly caress my new wheel.

Roll on, shining wheel, bear your master on the road,
  With a rapture he cannot conceal;
And never, never once need the jockey's cruel goad,
  Urge along, my swiftly gliding wheel.

On the wings of the wind we speed over the plain,
  And glide through the forest so still;
The swift-running brook babbles on while I look
  At the meadows, the fields, and the hill.

Now we come to the grade up whose steep we must climb,
  And bend to the work with good cheer;
And as we reach the top, we do not even stop,
  For the slope we can coast without fear.

As the sun mounts the sky with his beautiful gleam,
  And the lark from on high trills his lay;
I check my nickelled steed, and return with all speed,
  Well prepared for the work of the day.

Oh, happy the man, though his years have declined,
  Who the vigor of youth still doth feel;
For many, many days may he gladly sing the praise
  Of the hours he hath spent on his wheel.

*C. T. Mitchell*

# BEARD AND BICYCLE

Alas, how many years have flown
    Since first your silvery note I sounded
And on a cycle of my own
    First o'er the bumps in boyhood bounded,
And felt, like Icarus, the delight
Of suddenly acquiring flight.

The roads were peaceful then; no noise
    More strident than your ring intruded,
And bells of other little boys
    Who also cycled (as a few did),
And those of elder people who
Sedately pedaled two-by-two.

But the inventive brain of man,
    As restless as the winds that fan it,
Is always making some new plan
    To work commotion on our planet;
Especially if it thinks we need
Devices for increasing speed . . .

When in the future I retire
    (So runs my fanciful reflection)
And find some land of heart's desire
    Where everything will be perfection,
Motors shall vanish like a dream
And cycles be once more supreme.

*Guy Boas*

# CYCLES IN FLIGHT: THE RACING BIKE

I have slipped
off my car,

undressed
from it
fresh

as a snake
easing clean
of its slough,

hatched
timeless
and light,

then perched
myself
high:

slender frame,
I have
straddled
a damsel-
fly. I am

motion
rotation
and spoke,
flighty creature
half-evolved

melding
of metal
and flesh,

full of fight
and alive
I alone

will take on
this road
inhale

any hill
in a heartbeat

*Allison A. deFreese*

# RIDER

There was only one problem—the steepness of the hill
so that the moment I got any momentum
it would become too hard to keep my balance *and*

press one pedal forward enough to get my weight
onto the other one. I fell more times
than I could have counted but was more

than a little aware that there were
witnesses: rubbernecking
hordes dragging home from Sears, Caterpillar and John

Deere, made somehow more than punily human while in
the fabulous, unimpeachable yellow
of their company vehicles, loaned to them

"at no charge for the duration"
by the invisible gods who ran these
beneficent institutions . . .

It was clear from the moment when I was airlifted
to "the Heights," that every other able bodied kid
at the advanced age of six could handle a two-wheeler;

there was no question that for the other
children it would have required massive regression,
a dip into the archaic, bicameral mind—

recapitulating the history
of the species' struggle out of the ooze
to mastery—to begin to dredge up

an image of themselves grappling so clumsily
with simple tools, handlebars and pedals,
like "lead-footed" Parnelli Jones

after another brave victory at the Indy 500
being asked—while his tires were still scorched—
who invented the wheel.

I was fine while I could ride in circles,
circumnavigating the flat patch
that, guarded by sawhorses, fronted

the prefabricated yet eternally
unfinished ranch house where idle bull-
dozers and cranes were petrifying fast.

I never rode in circles, I would not
ride without slight lurches
to the left and right,

the zigzag pattern I felt compelled
to retrace without knowing what I was
doing; and who knows but that from an aerial height

or view from the highest mound
my awkwardness might have been mistaken
for acrobatic grace!

The sight and smell of my own blood did
make me queasy; but you know
how pain is: it goes beyond itself.

I don't know what stopped the crowd
from splitting its sides, what turned
their faces ashen—a cloud blocking out

the sun's last rays, or some animal sense
of the blood—bright on my extremities;
or . . . the ruin of a good pair of jeans. . . .

Of course I would have preferred
to carry out this rite in private—
say on a rich man's sequestered driveway,

under the silent tunnel of his elms,
but what did it matter, in the end, how
I learned to get where I wanted to go.

*Mark Rudman*

# DOWN-HILL ON A BICYCLE

The rolling earth stops
As I climb to the summit,
Then like a plummet
It suddenly drops . . .

Down, down I go—
Past rippling acres;
Hillsides like breakers
Over me flow.

Wildly alive
I hail the green shimmer,
Fresh as a swimmer
After the dive.

Like banners unfurled
The skies dip and flourish—
The keen breezes nourish,
While the bright world

Is a ribbon unrolled
With a border of grasses;
And tansies are masses
And splotches of gold.

Still I whirl on—
Startled, a sparrow
Darts from the yarrow,
Flash—and is gone . . .

Faster the gleams
Die as they dazzle—

And roadsides of basil
Turn to pink streams.

Sharp as a knife
Is each perfume and color . . .
To feel nothing duller—
God, that were Life!

*Louis Untermeyer*

# GOING DOWN HILL ON A BICYCLE
## A BOY'S SONG

With lifted feet, hands still,
I am poised, and down the hill
Dart, with heedful mind;
The air goes by in a wind.
Swifter and yet more swift,
Till the heart, with a mighty lift,
Makes the lungs laugh, the throat cry:—
"O bird, see; see, bird, I fly.
Is this, is this your joy,
O bird, then I, though a boy,
For a golden moment share
Your feathery life in air!"

Say, heart, is there aught like this
In a world that is full of bliss?
'Tis more than skating, bound
Steel-shod to the level ground.
Speed slackens now, I float
Awhile in my airy boat;
Till when the wheels scarce crawl,
My feet to the treadles fall.
Alas, that the longest hill
Must end in a vale; but still,
Who climbs with toil, wheresoe'er,
Shall find wings waiting there.

*Henry Charles Beeching*

# THE BICYCLERS

Like gray moths tasting the scented world
　　When the young flowers wake in June,
They take the first breath of the summer, whirled
　　To the swift wind's daring tune.

Their thin wings glide through the docile air
　　And gleam at the gaudy day;
They skim the rich earth of her odors rare,
　　And silently flit away.

And when blue night sighs through her spheric dome
　　For the worlds that shine afar,
Like will-o'-the-wisps they come trooping home,
　　And each one bears a star.

*Harriet Monroe*

# AMONG GOLDFINCHES

I am floating in a thin cloud
of them—simultaneous with
their soft whistles and rhythmic,
undulating flight—their tiny bodies
suspended just next to my ears
and shoulders, as we inhabit
each other's space and speed
and direction for a dozen wingbeats
and easy pedal strokes,
coasting on the morning wind.
Then they bank off, settle,
and sit like bright blossoms
in scrubby trail-side locusts, watching
my ordinary bicycle plunge ahead
into a canyon of Queen Anne's lace.
Later, as I struggle home against
the wind, their ghosts are glazing
my arms like dew and wrapping
the street full of traffic and starlings
in a yellow nimbus, dropping
an airy twitter and flutter of wings
onto the rolling earth, then drifting off
with a shy glance—feathered spirits
teasing like a voice that whispers:
Some riders here still believe in angels.

*Bill Morgan*

# A PASTORAL

The sun looks o'er the mountain fair,
Its smiles the landscape greet;
The songs of birds are in the air,
As I spring upon the seat:
A quick press on the pedal strong
And, like a bird, I skim along.

Farewell to cares that may annoy,
To toil that tires the brain;
New vigor sends a thrill of joy
Through every tingling vein,
As on I swiftly speed my way
'Mid beauteous scenes of rising day.

My soul responds to each appeal
Of nature's varied grace;
The charm of stream and wood I feel,
Each lovely prospect trace,
As swift and silent on I fly
'Mid rural scenes and azure sky.

At length I stop beneath a tree
Where wells a cooling spring,
And drink, inclined on bended knee,
Its waters murmuring;
A moment on the grass I rest,
My brow by grateful breeze caressed.

Then homeward I as quickly fare,
With heart and brain elate,
To take again, with lightened care,
The duties that await,

Exulting that my wheel each hour
Can bring me such a joy and power.

*Franklin Verzelius Newton Painter*

# A CENTURION

He tumbled from his weary wheel,
 And set it by the door;
Then stood as though he joyed to feel
 His feet on earth once more;
And as he mopped his rumpled head
 His face was wreathed in smiles;
"A very pretty run," he said,
 "I did a hundred miles!"

"A hundred miles!" I cried. "Ah, think!
 What beauties you have seen!
The reedy streams where cattle drink,
 The meadows rich and green.
Where did you wend your rapid way—
 Through lofty woodland aisles?"
He shook his head. "I cannot say—
 I did a hundred miles!"

"What hamlets saw your swift tires spin?
 Ah, how I envy you!
To lose the city's dust and din
 Beneath the heaven's blue;
To get a breath of country air,
 To lean o'er rustic sites!"
He only said: "The roads were fair—
 I did a hundred miles!"

*William Carleton*

# RIDING THEIR BIKES

1
I love it when he rides standing.
The mastery in his muscles shows.
The drive shows. His height and commanding
swell with a shy boy's acceptance. He feels
limitless now and he goes

like wind, rivers, winged horses.
I know, for it was I who appealed
to such power and forced such forces
to take hold as he wobbled down the lane,
I who steadied the seat, steeled

his nerve, let go. Horses, rivers,
wind surged to the cliff's edge! And the reins—
those traces embroidered with favors
by the Old Woman who sits on her heels
in the great cave which contains

seeds of everything—I threw them
after. Now the road, the whole world peel
open. His knees' assertive rhythm
marshals his straight thin shoulders. Still, the charm
to carry him through ordeals

and combat can't be this prowess
alone. There's an obedient *form*,
and even as he yells "how's this?"
back to the cave, the earth-conquering real-
ization shows, the brainstorm

that set everything rolling!
      The Old Woman loops rivers like eels,
she is crocheting a doily.
The wind comes full circle and, above that,
horses like fetuses kneel

into themselves. This memento
she will wear over her heart, to cover
its battling sentiments. *Go man go!*
What if my father likes to blame the wheel
for all man's ills? I love it

when my son rides standing. I laugh
that I should be so proud and my thrill
so unselfish. Think of the times I catch
a glimpse of him elsewhere, times I feel
the wind die, my heart stand still.


2
When she fell she threw the bike in the dirt,
    the stupid bike. She kicked its grounded tires
        and stormed back to the garage, nothing hurt

but the image. Beauty the world admires
    is shallow, meaningless, if not skillful.
        *Once more?* I beg. But urging from me only fires

her disappointment. Left to herself, she'll
    do it. *Get back here then and pick it up!*
        She won't look at me. Oh, she is willful.

Five minutes later she's riding—her grip,
    her profile, the perfect description. Voila!
        I note the Old Woman, stern and tight-lipped

before, smiles. Together we laugh out loud.
　　Willful? How well she knows! Sparks fly. Tell me,
　　　　Old Mother, how much fury may we allow

daughters like this? The question is silly.
　　Her answering fingers blaze with design,
　　　　beating the silver. No lace, no frills. Lee-

way doesn't exist for arrows, only line,
　　Up and down the lane, two wheels, red fenders,
　　　　a kid's squat-looking knees hardly define

man's progress. The point, with her windblown hair
　　and high chin, is continuing presence;
　　　　an ideal portrait in which bystanders

can't hope to see themselves. Yet she's her own
　　worst critic! And I know how deeply she loves,
　　　　don't I? . . . Violets and pink moccasins

flutter, her favorites. The Old Woman weaves
　　a garland. There isn't one little girl
　　　　she's forgotten. Mine, using both hands, shoves

the kickstand down. Free, her quick legs twirl
　　two perfect cartwheels. See how versatile
　　　　art can be?, this—or composed as a pearl

at an Amtrak station, sitting so still
　　on a bench with my mother that I leave
　　　　running, crying real tears against my will.

*Ellen Kirvin Dudis*

# THE OLD BIKE

I love it, I love it, and who shall dare
To chide me for loving that old bike there?
I've treasured it long as a sainted prize,
And its battered old frame brings the tears to my eyes;
'Tis bound with a thousand bands to my heart,
Though the sprocket's bent and the links are apart.
Would you know the spell? My grandma sat there,
Upon that old saddle, and zipped through the air.
In childhood's hour I lingered near
That old machine, with listening ear,
For grandma's shrieks through the house would ring
If I even happened to touch the thing.
She told me to wait until she dies,
Then I could take it and learn to ride.
And once I caused her to tear her hair,
When I cut the tire of that old wheel there.
'Tis old, 'tis wrecked, but I gaze on it now
With quivering breath and with throbbing brow.
'Twas there she sat—ah, how she could ride,
With grandpa humping along at her side!
Say it is folly, call it a joke,
But the scrap-man can't have even a spoke,
For I love it, I love it, and can not bear
To part with my grandma's old bike there!

*Anonymous*

# A NEW CYCLE

My father buying me the bicycle that time
Was an unusual thing for him to do.
He believed that a parent's duty meant the necessities:
Food, clothing, shelter, and music lessons.

I had hardly dared to ask him for it
And I didn't believe he really meant to buy me one
Until I saw him take out the money and hand it over—
Eight dollars secondhand, but newly painted, and good rubber.

And I couldn't thank him, a hug was out of the question with us,
So I just got up on it and rode a ways shakily
And then I made him ride it—
He didn't even know he was supposed to say it was a good bike.

I rode off on it into a new life, paper route, pocket money,
Dances in other towns where girls found me attractive,
And sexual adventures that would have made my father's hair
Stand up in horror had he known.

Daddy I can thank you now for the bike you gave me
Which meant more to me than you knew, or could have stood
    to know.
I rode away to everywhere it could take me, until finally
It took me to this nowhere, this noplace I am now.

I just passed my thirty-fifth birthday,
The end of a seven-year cycle and the beginning of a new one,
And sure enough I woke up the first day quite empty,
Everything over, with nothing to do and no ideas for the
    future.

Daddy whom I now can hug and kiss
Who gives me money when I ask,
What shall I do with this life you gave me
That cannot be junked like a bicycle when it wears out?

Is it utterly ridiculous for a man thirty-five years old and graying
To sit in his father's lap and ask for a bike? Even if he needs one?
Whom shall he ask if not his father?
Daddy, darling Daddy, please buy me a bicycle.

*Edward Field*

# WE

Me and my new bike.

We go everywhere together
except the laundromat
the supermart
the gambling hall
the john

We do everything together
except visit graves
run errands
make love
graduate

We scale new heights
except when it's windy

We reach new lows
except when it rains

We tour new worlds
except when there's traffic

Me and my new bike.

*Ryn Gargulinski*

# A NEW BLUE BIKE

I remember the smell of cut grass
sweetening my tattered pant cuffs
and the magic of daylight clinging
to a new blue bike. Back then
I would skim the 'Lewiston Sun'
over the graveled sidewalks and watch
the papers flop like wounded pigeons
as the news of Dunkirk and the Third Reich
targeted the doorsteps. Then I
would drop my hands from the handlebars,
whistle, and pump out of sight. Only
a magician's cape of daylight is now
thrown carelessly over the cut grass,
and the 'Lewiston Sun' arrives by van.
Hitler is history, and many blitzkriegs have come.
But when I least expect to be trapped
by nostalgia, when I am unwilling
to daydream or to become sentimental,
a piece of sky seen in the eye
of a puddle or a bluebird plunging
from a telephone line reminds me
that once there was a time
when a new blue bike was mine.

*C. J. Stevens*

# MOON LANDING, 1969

It starts to rain, and my blue
Schwinn is tilting
in the mud. *You have time,*
my father says, *the rain will ruin your bike.*

My family is a circle of silhouettes
before the gray TV light. I'm alone in the rain
with my bike. There's salt

water in the air. I taste it.
I watch the moon from the yard.
Shouts from the houses.

Fireworks like gunshots
release their sparks
over Shark River. I stay in the yard,

poised between the mundane
and the extraordinary. I am 13 years old,
in a navy blue bathing suit,

leaning on a kickstand, thinking
that soon I'll be missed
and will have to huddle with all the excited

neighbors and strangers, but for a moment
I am watching the moon, and the smoky
sky around it,

feeling something large taken from me,
like a wing, or a lung.

*Mary Jane Nealon*

# MOON IN THE MIRROR

New light on an old bike,
new legs since I ran away.

Getting back my cadence coming up the hill;
these nights my only anticipation

is going down the other side with a full scarf,
that prolonged rush only the wind can promise

and make good. And I am not my age
when the moon rises full of rushes too

so I don't slow until it fills my broken
mirror from behind and sends me news

through the curving hang of telephone line,
the ravenous drape of cedar branch,

news, I swear, of everyone I've ever known
caught in my scarf like a rush—prolonged,

endless, caught in myself, filling me
to breaking. No hands on the hill,

moon in the mirror and me in flight
down the mountain and into the night.

I am not my age.

*Brenda Brooks*

# INSTRUCTIONS FOR HOW TO GET AHEAD OF YOURSELF WHILE THE LIGHT STILL SHINES

If you have a bike, get on it at night
and go to the top of the Brooklyn Hill.

When you reach the top
start smiling—this is Happy Valley Road.

Pedal at first, then let the road take you down
into the dark as black as underground
broken by circles of yellow lowered by the street
lights.

As you come to each light
you will notice a figure
racing up behind.
Don't be scared.
This is you creeping up on yourself.
As you pass under the light
you will sail past yourself into the night.

*Jenny Bornholdt*

# TO MY CYCLE

Dear other self, so silent, swift and sure,
My dumb companion of delightful days,
Mighty fairy fingers from thy orbit rays
   Of steel strike music, as the gods of yore
   From reed or shell, what melodies would pour
On my glad ears; what songs of woodland ways,
Of summer's wealth of corn, or the sweet lays
   Of April's budding green; while ever more
We twain, one living thing, flash like the light
Down the long tracks that stretch from sky to sky.
   Thou hast thy music, too, what time the noon
Beasts sultry on broad roads; when, gathering night,
We drink the keen-edged air; or, darkling, fly
   'Twixt hedgerows blackened by a mystic moon.

*Adriel Vere*

# SWIFTLY WE FLY

Gliding, gleaming, speeding along,
Waking the echoes with shout and song,
      Swiftly we fly,
      Cycle and I,
Making the woodlands ring, hurrah!
With the gladsome joy that we bring, hurrah!
Even the birds pause in their flight,
Watching us speed, so swift, from sight.

Away from the struggle and strife and sin,—
Out of the city's roar and din,
      Cycle and I
      Swiftly fly,
Leaving behind all care, hurrah!
Buoyant and free as the air, hurrah!
Racing with squirrels, at break of day,
Like a sunbeam out on a runway.

Swift as a bird, on pinions fleet,
Under the trees where the branches meet,
      Swiftly we fly,
      Cycle and I,
Happy at noon or night, hurrah!
With a reckless, mad delight, hurrah!
Born of the shining steed of steel,
The pride and joy of the knights of the wheel.

*James Clarence Harvey*

# MY MAGIC WHEEL

O magic wheel
Of burnished steel
How part of myself thou art!
   As we roll along
   'Mid the hurrying throng
That peoples the busy mart.

   Let's haste away
   From the heat of the day
To the woods' refreshing shade,
   Where the babbling brook,
   In some sheltered nook,
Is gurgling a down the glade.

   Where the oriole swells
   His throat as he tells
Of his flight through ethereal space,
   And his music flows
   While the earth's repose
Is deeper because of his grace.

   I can talk as we roll,
   And I know that a soul,
Must lurk in thy wonderful frame;
   A spiritual essence,
   Some far hidden presence,
Some genius of magical fame.

   I know well thy power
   In each trying hour,
Thou servant so faithful and true;
   When the swift rushing wind

Is left muttering behind,
As thou sippest the sweet morning dew.

Or when Sol dips his crest
'Neath the glorious west,
And the sunlight congeals into dark;
We will skim by the sea,
We will shoot o'er the lea,
We will follow the meteor's mark.

Thou life-giving wheel,
Whose sinews are steel,
My veins imbibe life from thine own;
And I sink, to my rest
With a true loyal zest,
While my dreams are my cycle's alone.

Rest, then, on the moss
Where the soft zephyrs toss,
Thou circlet of beauty and pride;
While, th' invisible wings
Attached to thy strings
Are folded in peace at thy side.

*N. P. Tyler*

# A BICYCLE GLEE SONG

*(To the tune of "Battle Hymn of the Republic")*

I have seen the dazzling beauty of the swiftly flying wheel,
I have seen its air-filled tires and its bars of flying steel;
And I know just how its rider, as he flies along, does feel—
  As he goes riding on.

Chorus: —
Glory, Glory, Hallelujah; so they go riding on.

I know that they are happy, happy, happy all the day,
I know they feel like singing "Yankee Doodle" all the way;
I know they are rejoicing that they did not stay away
  As they go riding on.

Chorus.

So come, my brothers, sisters, all, and let us have some fun;
Come far out in the country bright for just a little "run,"
We surely shall reach home before the setting of the sun;
  As we go riding on.

Chorus.

*Glory Anna*

# HER MAJESTY
### (A song of the morning.)

O the mountaineer to the summit clear,
   The sailor-soul to the sea:
And the driver to his team, and the dreamer to his dream,
   But the white high-road for me!
For the sun is awake, and in wood and brake
   The birds make glad appeal:
"Come out, come out: there is sport about!"
   Then come, my trusty wheel.
Then come with a hum, with a stir, with a whirr:
   Thro' the air with a rush run free:
Let the world be abed; I have heard, I have sped,
   And the white high-road's for me.

O the hum of the wheel, my steed of steel,
   And the rush of the welcoming wind:
I'm a cavalier of old, and my spirit waxeth bold,
   For my lady fair is kind.
While her sire's asleep from her pane she'll peep,
   She will flutter down to my side;
Come forth, come forth: for the wind blows north—
   To the saddle, my own, my bride.
Then, off! we can scoff at the rest: we are blest:
   For the wheel runs free, runs true!
What matter the odds? We are kings: we are gods:
   And the road's for me and you.

See, the hamlets wake, and the windows shake,
   As the good dame smiles to the sun:
And the herd is at the gate, and the milk-pans clash and grate,
   And the life of the farm's begun.
O the hill climbs white, but the crest's in sight:

Push on to the lonely tree!
Then the river's streak, and the morning reek,
   And the valley for you and me.
Then, oh, for below in the light, left and right,
   The fields of our country shine:
Let prophets bray, it is ours for to-day—
   This England of yours and mine.

Dear England, bright in the morning light:
   Strong Mother of brave men yet;
You have borne us, you have bred us: you have taught us: you
      have led us!
   Not ours to forego, to forget!
And our morning song, as we speed along,
   Is swept to the listening sea:
We can keep her still from fear and from ill.
   And hold her for ages to be!
Whirl, wheel, soul of steel! Iron heart, bear a part:
   As the winds of the world we are free.
We have heard the cry: be it live, be it die,—
   *Her* road is for you and me!

*Arthur Waugh*

# THE QUEEN OF GIRLHOOD

It's ho! for a ride in the open,
　With the cool winds blowing free,
And nothing but joy in dale and hill
　For my trusty wheel and me.
It's ho! for the dew of the morning
　That sparkles on leaf and spray,
And ho! for the charm of the sunset light
　When the glad day fades away.

With muscles that answer quickly
　To call of the resolute will,
With cheeks that glow and eyes that shine
　And pulses that bound and thrill,
I fly through the beautiful kingdom
　That beckons my wheel and me,
Queen of the world of girlhood,
　And sovereign of all I see.

*Margaret E. Sangster*

# THE ROMAUNT OF CECILIA

The shining afternoon was his at last;
And at the altar of his passion's flame
He waited till his own Cecilia came.
For full four years, in spring and winter weather,
These two had shared their afternoons together.
For full four years had Robert Bliss been loathed
By local youth, for why? they were betrothed.
Yet since the cost of setting-up is dear,
And little thrives on ninety pounds a year,
They still continued in the old, sweet way,
And no one talked about the wedding-day.
The same,—yet not the same! for fashion's finger
Sweeps e'en the lines where old conventions linger,
And slowly thro' that little country-town
The manners of the Mall came filtering down;
So, while on foot they used to keep their tryst,
Each now aspired to be a bicyclist.

Young fancies bud or e'er their leaves be green;
And soon Cecilia chartered a machine.
Lissome she was, and just their sort who may
Ride without aid upon the second day,
So ere a week had passed beyond recall
She'd been three miles, and "wasn't tired at all!"
Alas! for Robert. Let the truth be told,
He was not cast in an athletic mould:
His long, laborious hours at school and college
He gave to books, and sacrificed to knowledge;
So now his shoulders stooped as tho' with care
The like no boy of twenty-five should bear:
His bony limbs, his knees together knocking,
Made but a piteous show in tell-tale stocking,

And tho' for twice six weeks before the dawn
He'd skipped and slipped across the doctor's lawn,
The line that marked his progress o'er the green
Twisted in shapes unwholesome to be seen!
Let us not say that Miss Cecilia Brown
Greeted his evolutions with a frown.
Let us not whisper that it made her tired
To mark the way he faltered and perspired,
Inflicting wounds that cried for lint and ointment;
Yet we confess: it *was* a disappointment.

Ah! maidens, weep for Robert; for be sure
He eyed his wheel and prayed to feel secure:
And you, ye men, to whom kind Fate affords
The time and talent to be known at Lords,
Regard, I charge you, with a glance forgiving
The man who had perforce to earn his living,
Who felt so keenly all he'd had to lose,—
For there are heroes who were never Blues!

Next, thanks to human energy, which came
To rescue Robert Bliss from half his shame;
And thanks to him—bluff Sergeant-Major Cupp,
Who gave him lessons ere the sun was up.
So that, towards the ending of July,
The bank and office saw him moving by,—
Not yet so safe, perhaps, nor yet so straight,
Nor yet at any actionable rate,—
But at a moderately even pace,
Towards the dear, familiar trysting-place.

Ay! sure there was a flutter 'neath the gown
Of our expectant Miss Cecilia Brown,
What time she witnessed, that imperial day,
Her Robert sailing slowly under way:
What time, with wholly pardonable pride,
He slipped off sideways, and was by her side.
And then, the lips of love! The wings of Hope!
(In vulgar phrase) they gave their fancy rope.
Their wedding-day, they whispered, should be soon;
They'd bicycle one life-long honeymoon.
She praised his prowess (ah, that praise was sweet!),
She thought his whole equipment "very neat;"
Then whispered, "Darling,—nay, it must, must be,
We'll cycle into Andover to tea."

    *O Hope, estranging Hope! what tales you tell!*
    *O Love, that cheatest whom thou lovest well!*

They started: but Cecilia never knew,
While Robert learned, she'd been progressing too.
Down the first hill she led by twenty yards,
(Speed, Robert, speed! What Fate thy wheel retards?)
Along the level flashed her silver bright,
Another moment—she was out of sight;
A hill before her! Warming to the fray,
She pedaled (double action) all the way.
O ecstasy! O grand exhilaration!
She dreamt of nothing but the wheel's rotation.
The sun was bright, the open sky was blue;
"Whirr" went the wheel: it hummed: it sang: it flew.
Swift as a bird toward Andover she fled,
And, for a moment, Robert left her head,
Then memory: contrition: and a stop!
She paused upon a difficult hill-top:

Down in the valley white the roadway wound,
Two miles—but not a sight, but not a sound.
She paused: she fidgeted: she stamped her heel:
She choked the rage she could not all conceal;
Then swung her wheel round with an evil grace,
And took that hill at a terrific pace.

*Ah, God of Love, what pains thy victims cull!*
*As thou are strong, thou should'st be pitiful.*

Four miles away, back in the paling West,
She found her Robert, pedaling his best.
His face was set—dead weary, past denying—
She thought he looked as tho' he had been crying,
Yet with determination brave to see
He panted, "Dear, we'll still be there to tea."
She bade him turn; she led him up the lane;
Slowly she rode till they were home again.
She passed the trysting-tree, nor stayed to tell
The parting secrets that they loved so well.
Into the market square, without one kiss,
She rode, and there took leave of Robert Bliss!
I think he knew his fate. I think that, when
A note was brought to him next day at ten,
With no surprise the words assailed his sight:
*"I fear I cannot ride with you to-night."*
I only know that from that fateful day
He locked his hard-bought bicycle away,
That Dr. Wilson, who's inclined to shirk,
Finds his assistant glad of double work;
And every evening, when the surgery's done,
Poor Robert strolls beneath the setting sun,
Down by the little huddled cottage-streets,
And sometimes takes the village-children sweets,

Yet always keeps the biggest and the best
For Jim, the poor lame son of Widow West.

I also know that Miss Cecilia Brown
Was seen last week careering up and down
With Mr. Watkins, muscular and lank,
Who's bought a Swift, and manages the bank.

*O God of Love, and regent of our days,*
*How unintelligible are thy ways!*
*O God of Love, be merciful in this:*
*Make whole, console the heart of Robert Bliss.*

*Arthur Waugh*

# I STAND AT THE WINDOW
# AND WAVE MY ARMS ABOUT

Each time I passed his place I looked
Sideways and smiled. Friends sniggered.
They said it was not for a woman of taste
To hanker after this rather rigid man
Who wore a working shirt and owned only
A cheap, white bike. Shyly I brought
Him home—stuck his bike on the steep
Shed roof so all the neighbors would see
And he would get the benefit of bracing
Winds. Now when the weather is right
He cycles most of the day, his knees
Taking all of the strain—bending,
Trembling with an intense joy. I stand
At the window and wave my arms about.
I shout encouraging words—marvel at his
Obedience to the breeze—his dedication
To the propeller's needs.

Sometimes he sighs—he knows he is going
Nowhere but his tiny plastic legs have
Pushed him beyond despair. His flat
Black cap has become a martyr's crown.

*Angela Cooke*

# THE ENIGMA

Every morning I see him pedaling past
And wonder what the hell he's doing.
He seems to be getting nowhere fast;
He's always there, fro-ing and to-ing.

It's not so much an art as a skill;
This method of using the old wheel.
The cyclist negotiates a grim hill
Sitting on a tubular triangle of steel.

What's the point? Where's he going?
Just somewhere away from here.
So he goes through the motions, slowing
Briefly as he changes gear.

There's pain in his face as he accelerates,
Relief as he slowly slows down,
Impatience as he stops and waits
While the traffic lights conduct the town.

Still, he's out and about out there:
That's his religious function.
Bless him with a blue gust of warm air,
Not mincing piety, not extreme unction.

*Alan Bold*

# REASONS TO COMMUTE BY BICYCLE

I must look funny
to those of you in cars:
pedaling furiously,
going slow,
reflecting your headlights,
filling up an entire lane.

I know I've been noticed.
The other day a large, bearded man
in a red pickup waited for me
in the post office parking lot.
Lots of people heard him reminding me
to read the motor vehicle laws, goddammit!

There are some reasons why I do this:

*one*
Autumn river at sundown:
washy, neon-pink fluff
of sun-charged clouds mirrored
upon dark, rippled water.

*two*
Once, I caught the full moon
sneaking over the horizon
like a kid playing hide and seek,
his bald, luminous noggin
peering over row homes, checking for it.

*three*
When I crossed the Olentangy
on the new walk bridge,

three construction workers
cheered. I was first
and passed a pedestrian halfway.

*four*
Racing my moon shadow through the park.
Bald trees lining the path
clasped bony branches over me
like prayerful Druid crones,
worshipping night. I looked up.

The moon—before, a fat, playful child—
now mature, austere,
listened silently
to the spin of my tires,
and the smooth clicking
of this simple machine I pedal home.

*Frederic William Kirchner*

# BICYCLE
## Song Lyrics

I ride my bicycle to work each day
It's not so far
It's better for me than my car.
I wear a helmet that is made of
Rigid Styrofoam
Inspected by a French guy named Guillaume.
I downshift my Shimano gears
I pedal hard and I'm out of here
Glad I am that the coast is clear
Glad I am to be
My bicycle and me.

Some Saturdays at six a.m. I get up
With Bill and Flo
In the parking lot of Ho Jo's west of town
We ride light bikes that cost big bucks
We curse at smelly trucks
Mile after mile 'til the sun is almost down.
What a ride, what a life
Maybe I'm crazy, don't ask my wife
I've been in love with these spinning wheels
Since I was maybe three
My bicycle and me.

Pedal that bike, pedal that bike
Don't open that door 'til I go by.

Pedal that bike, pedal that bike
That little old lady in the Dodge Diplomat
I don't think she sees me
I hope she don't teach me how to fly.

I wear Lycra, it fits really closely to my skin
White to purple is the place where it begins
I pad my butt and I'm careful
To stay out of ruts
Wrap around sunglasses, I'm an alien
Feel my heart go pit-a-pat
Hello big hill good-bye fat
Life goes by just like that
A fortysomething spree is
My bicycle and me.

*Livingston Taylor*

# MY WHEEL AND I

There's a road we know,
  My wheel and I.
Where we love to go,
  My wheel and I.
There the briers thick by the roadside grow,
And the fragrant birch bends it branches low,
And the cool shade tempts us to ride more slow,
  My wheel and I.

But through shade and sheen,
  My wheel and I,
By the hillsides green,
  My wheel and I,
We roll along till there's plainly seen
The bridge that crosses the deep ravine,
With its echoing rocks and the brook-laugh between,
  My wheel and I.

Then's a hill we hate,
  My wheel and I;
But we toil up straight,
  My wheel and I,
For beyond the hill is an ivy-crowned gate,
And a pair of eyes that to welcome us wait;
If we do not haste we will surely be late,
  My wheel and I.

*Alberto A. Bennett*

# THE BICYCLE AND I

Thou and I, my noble wheel,
  O'er the highway rolling,
Friends are we for woe or weal,
  Oft together strolling.

Thou and I, my fifty-four!
  Willing steed and master!
How we skin the roadway o'er!
  Never bird went faster!

What care we for weary miles,
  Thou and I together,
When the cloudless heaven smiles,
  Or in stormy weather?

Thou and I leave care behind,
  Bicycle, my beauty!
Fleeter steed I'll never find,
  Ready aye for duty!

May the beauty ne'er grow dim,
  May the strength ne'er fail thee!
Staunch and true each slender limb;
  Noble wheel, I hail thee!

Thou and I, my fifty-four!
  Willing steed and master!
How we skim the roadway o'er!
  Never bird went faster!

*Anonymous*

# TO FLIGHT

Far swifter than e'er Atalanta flew,
  And silent as the working of the mind
  Thou glidest, leaving city walls behind
To fly to where—in many a brilliant hue
Beneath the moon's pale light—the sparkling dew
  In trembling, scintillating drops is found;
  Where odors sweet and fragrant fields abound
And nature breathes to man of life anew.
Amazed, I guide thee, noiseless thing of steel!
  Scarce using force to urge thee thro' the night,
Wondering if thou, like me, dost bondage feel,
  And find relief in this green-pastured flight;
If thro' thy frame the traveled pleasures reel
  Responsive, haply, to mine own delight.

*S. Conant Foster*

# THE SCORCHER'S FAREWELL TO HIS STEED

My beautiful, my beautiful! thou standest meekly by,
With proudly arched and glossy frame, and sprocket geared so high.
Fret not to roam within the Park with all thy winged speed;
I may not scorch on thee again—thou'rt pinched, my silent steed!

Fret not with that impatient tire, sound not the warning gong;
They'll check you in a basement damp because I scorched along.
The bike cop hath thy handle bar—my tears will not avail;
Fleet-wheeled and beautiful, farewell! for thou'rt held for bail!

Farewell! those fat pneumatic wheels full many a mile have spun,
To bask beside the Cliff House bar or do a century run;
Some other hand less skilled than mine must pump thee up with air;
The patent lamp that won't stay lit must be another's care.

Only in sleep shall I behold myself with bended back—
Only in sleep shall thee and I avoid the trolley track;
And when I churn the pedals down to check or cheer thy speed,
Then must I, starting, wake to learn thou'rt pinched, my silent steed.

Ah, rudely, then, unseen by me, some clumsy chump bestride
May wabble into rough brick walls and dish a wheel beside;
And compressed wind that's in thee 'scape in shrill, indignant pain
'Till cruel man that on thee rides will fill thee up again!

With slow, dejected foot I roam, not knowing where or when
I'll meet a good Samaritan who'll kindly loan me ten.
And sometimes to the Park I go, drawn in my hopeless quest;
'Twas here I struck a record clip—the copper did the rest.

Who said that I had given thee up? Who said that thou wert lost?
'Tis false, 'tis false, my silent steed! I fling them fine and cost!
Thus—thus I leap upon thy back and hit the asphalt trail.
Away! my bright and beautiful; I pawned my watch for bail.

*Charles Dryden*

# THE SCORCHER

He scorcheth down the Ripley Road,
  His teeth are set, his eyes a-glare;
In curious curves his back is bowed,
  And weird the raiment he doth wear.
He looketh not on maiden fair,
  Nor anything of beauty sees,
For him, alack, no charm is there,
  Who rides with nose between his knees.

He carrieth but little load,
  And yet thereat shall curse and swear,
For still his demon doth him goad
  To ride more quickly—anywhere.
With bullet head and close cropped hair,
  And labor hard, which may him please,
What convict can with one compare
  Who rides with nose between his knees?

Each Sunday morn from his abode,
  To slaughter dire forth doth he fare;
He saith that by-laws may "be blowed,"
  Nor yet for mounted police doth care.
He catcheth lovers unaware,
  Who saunter underneath the trees;
He hath no conscience whatsoe'er,
  Who rides with nose between his knees.

A crash, a groan, a rigid stare,
  A coal cart plodding at its ease;
Stern Justice waits him who shall dare
  To ride with nose between his knees.

*Edward F. Strange*

# BICYCLE SPRINT

I crouch over the bare
bones of speed, jacket
snapping like silks, face
against the wind's neck.
My steps don't touch ground,
and spokes sprinkle light
like flint-strikes. Pavement blurs
under me-and-machine. I'm
its muscle! and the centaur
I imagined myself as a child.
We gallop the straight roads
of Ohio. Chainring, chain,
freewheel, derailleur—all
fit, click, ratchet right,
catch and quiet into flight.
Down the long flat road at
the bottom of the atmosphere
we're flung. A wheel before me,
one behind, I tuck, hands low.
Frame trembles. Road
leaps. Knees lift and fall.
I sit the saddle, velocity's
clairvoyant, while what's below
spins—cranks and hubs and
planet. For a moment we ride
the earth the bike was mined from
and I will lie in, which turns
as calmly as a story being told.

*Pamela Alexander*

# CONSTELLATION: PROSE POEM

Oh, skies of those days, skies of luminous signals and meteors, covered by the calculations of astronomers, copied a thousand times, numbered, marked with the watermarks of algebra! With faces blue from the glory of those nights, we wandered through space pulsating from the explosions of distant suns, in a sidereal brightness—human ants, spreading in a broad heap on the sandbanks of the milky way spilled over the whole sky—a human river overshadowed by the cyclists on their spidery machines. Oh, stellar arena of night, scarred by the evolutions, spirals and leaps of those nimble riders; oh, cycloids and epi-cycloids executed in inspiration along the diagonals of the sky, amid lost wire spokes, hoops shed with indifference, to reach the bright goal denuded, with nothing but the pure idea of cycling! From these days dates a new constellation, the thirteenth group of stars, included forever in the zodiac and resplendent since then in the firmament of our nights: THE CYCLIST.

*Bruno Schulz*

*Translated from the Polish by Celina Wieniewska*

# GALILEO AND THE BICYCLE

Galileo from his retreat
Of silence came on noiseless feet
One day to earth and turned his eyes,
With keenest glances of surprise,
To countless thousands of mankind
Speeding along as speeds the wind;
To maids and matrons, sires and sons,
And immaturest little ones,
All whirling on revolving things
That bore them swift as swiftest wings;
Through every busy thoroughfare,
In rural highways, coursing where
The prairies reached o'er endless space,
Where rivers ran, where'er the face
Of earth revealed an open way,
A wheeling, whirling fleet array
Of human forms in ceaseless flight
Was shown unto his wondering sight;
And standing there as one aghast,
His hands before his eyes he passed,
Then, proudly lifting up his head,
In self-applauding tone he said:
"I knew, by Jupiter! it moved,
As my researches grandly proved;
But, by my great-grandfather's hat!
I never thought 'twould move like that."

*Anonymous*

# CYCLOLOTRY

I often drift, on fancy's wondrous stream,
Far out into the vagaries of a dream,
And wonder what the ancients had been like
    Had they the bike.

Think of big Hector tied up by the heel
Tight to the step of strong Achilles' wheel;
And Dad Aeneas scorching out of Troy
    Behind his boy.

See Aristotle with a humped-up back
"Peripateting" on a four-lap track;
And Socrates a-pedaling for his life
    From his sharp wife.

If Alexander had a wheel, would he
Have cut so wide a swath in history?
Or spent his youth like modern royal sons
    In century runs?

Just fancy Julius Caesar (if you will)
A coasting down the Capitolean hill;
Or Cleopatra touring by the Nile
    In royal style.

Can your imagination dwell on Cain
Cycling the world in spite of wind and rain?
Or on our mother Eve (I do not jest)
    In bloomers dressed?

It seems to me that if the chosen race
Had some speedy man to make the pace,

'Twould not have taken forty years to reach
   The promised peach.

The world went different then; but what's the odds?
They didn't have the bike; they had the gods.
No gods rule us (the change I rather like);
   We've got the bike.

*Anonymous*

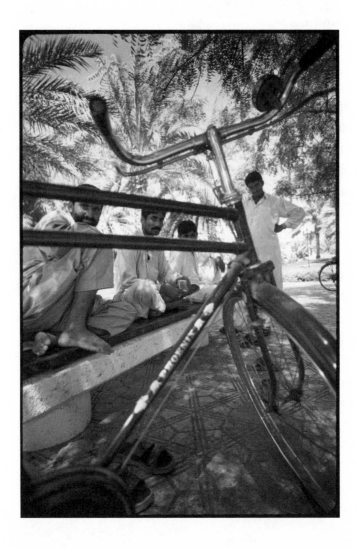

# LEONARDO'S BICYCLE

Like Ceres trying to free her daughter
Before Jove clipped her, a queen card, to the spokes
Of light and dark, where she still flaps, stiff and sore,
You're married to one condition.

You could leave the island whose shore
You circle distractedly, your feet
Bleeding from its cut-tin-can-lid sharpness,
If you swam out beyond your three-chord

Grammar, as Scarlatti flew like a prince,
On a weave-it-as-you-ride-it carpet, "into
Remotest tonal regions," being a
Specialist in investigative harmony.

Leonardo drew a *bicicletta*
Of wood and metal, sleeker than his deck-
Umbrella flying machine. Why should he *build* it?
It was born intact, outlandish, as idea.

(Besides, the wheels could turn neither right
Nor left, they went straight as a dream, with that
Kind of determination and perfection.)
Do you see? You could practice a certain

Stationary vibration, like a bicycle
Just leaned against a wall, and still make
A revolution, cliff-browed like Beethoven's,
Whose forms stand as solid as Haydn's

But whose heart was clouded with the genius
Of taking drama to be normal—as it was

For Proserpine, who, given a whirl,
Uttered now phlox, now roots,

Quite as if an impatient hand
Should draw and erase, draw and erase
An imperfectly penciled bicycle wheel.
Which freed Ceres to hear Arethusa's tale

Of terrified pursuit: how, after she hung
Her clothes on a yielding willow bough
And dived into the stream, she felt the god's
Lung-deep breath sweep through her hair

And screamed. Whereupon the goddess Ortygia
Doused the whole scene in fog, leaving
The god to thrash about blind in white night
While he felt for her salmon calves, her otter back.

But then she became a cataract; she lived
A dramatic life. As you would if you turned
So deaf a child's shriek from the street
Could make you smile over your meal,

Which as usual you eat alone, dipping a heel
Of bread into your soup, before you hear again,
*Vivace e con brio*, the silver wheels
Of a rondo no tricky instruments are riding,

Like water plunging down a cliff
On an imaginary island,
As tears fall in the realms of drama,
Where nymphs take off their clothes and die.

*Cal Bedient*

# HAMPTON LOCK

We cycled on the water. No one thought
to ask us how we managed such a feat,
nor could we tell. It seemed so natural
to choose the smooth canal. The water lapped
around the tires, a softly splashing sound
rose to our ears and made us sing aloud.

At Hampton Lock, freewheeling to the bank,
we joined the tow-path once again. We thought
to use the lock would take an age. Besides,
somehow we knew that if we were to stop
within the basin (as we surely would)
we'd sink like gold on setting down our feet.

*Dave McClure*

# GOD ON A BIKE

God on a bike going twenty miles an hour
over speed ramps, ignoring the pinch-space
cars that would topple him, helmetless
and roaring at road-ragers, mobile phone users,
the guess-where-I'm-going school of motorist.
His long white beard parts in the wind.

God speed, God. He stops at red lights
if he has to, but prefers to sail through.
Lycra shorts in all weathers, hairy legs
pistoning past churches and bingo halls.
God on a bike is good news. He knows
when to apply severe body torque.

God's a rock hopper, a weekend mud churner,
a star on wheels. He can fix a puncture
in five minutes flat, slalom through gravel,
go twenty-four hours without sleeping.
He's the captain of the Cat and Fiddle,
Box Hill, C2C. He's a mashed gear man.

God cycles forty days and forty nights
alone in the wilderness. He stokes up
on Mars Bars, forks more transport café
breakfasts, smokes more fags than I could.
He's a seven-day wonder. The whole world
in a week. That's God the father.

Son Jesus does his own repairs, prefers
Reynolds tubing. He's had the same frame
for thirty odd years. He wears toe clips
that bruise his feet—that's

what comes of wearing sandals.
A chain guard keeps his robes clean.

There's a silver bell he rings each time
he rounds a bend in case of donkeys
or a man carrying a bed. Jesus on a bike
does the shopping. Bread and fish fingers,
a little wine. Abstemious Jesus with hair
in a ponytail under a kitemarked helmet.

There's an orange flag on a stick to warn
drivers to steer clear. Jesus isn't fearful
just careful. He carries batteries and cables,
a cape for bad weather. He's chairman of a club.
Twelve good mates. Though one's a bit suspect.
Drives a car that cost thirty thou. Flash git, Judas.

*Pat Winslow*

# OLD MAN ON A BIKE

I'm pedaling in to work
thinking about God's works.
He's pedaling in to work.
Old man and old grid.
Not far to go now
to the end of the ride.
Look at him, weaving
slower and slower, in and out
of the hating, snarled-up traffic.
He's old and slow
but skilful;
he's doing no harm
but patient
under unjust rebuke . . .

Come, friend, let's go.
The lights are green.
Let's away
to the green places.
And Gabriel will not hoot us
on a hectoring horn.
I hear his bell,
blinkling, brinkling.
And thy rood
and thy verge
shall lead us
safely
under the ring roads.

*Peter Sizer*

# SUNDAY MORNING SERVICES

The noise goes nowhere down the corridor
Of rigid corn, bubbling tar popping off,
Debris of gravel leaping like faith for
A better venue, as I bike the soft

Pavement over church hours to have it all
To myself. Concrete lots of cars weigh down
The earth, while steeples rise untaxed and tall
As watch towers, and the dark front doors frown

And hoard the words inside. Bright flowers nod
And bow, and I smile at their graceful charm,
And the cows turn with my progress, their god-
Like eyes wide. I speak my peace. The moist warm

Air swaddles me, and the life-giving sun
Answers the prayers of everything green.

*Michael S. Smith*

# WHEEL ETHICS

"Tell me, O Wheelman, ere you ride away,"
I asked, "where have you been this Sabbath day?"

Then the cyclist replied from his lofty perch,
With gracious mien, "I have been to church;
I have been to church, though strange to tell,
I have heard neither parson nor tolling bell.

" 'T was a volunteer choir, and the rapturous notes
That fell on my car, as the tiny throats
Seemed bursting with praise of the Maker's name,
Thrilled with such joy I was glad that I came.

"And the air was so pure, so fresh and sweet,
Though I sat on a softly-cushioned seat,—
That I never once thought of going to sleep;
Nor was the sermon too dull or deep.

"I remember the text, too, 'God is love,'—
'T was everywhere written, around me, above,
On the stately columns that rose at my side,
To the vaulted arch so blue and wide.

"Upreaching to the very throne of Grace,—
'T was a grandly solemn, sacred place,
And I almost forgot how cold and drear
Is the earth, sometimes, heaven seemed so near."

Thus I hold that pure worship has no part
In the *time* or the *place*, but springs from the *heart*.

*Charles Richards Dodge*

# A NEW VIEW OF SUNDAY CYCLING

They're complaining from the pulpit, with an energy undue,
That the craze for Sunday cycling now is emptying the pew;
But we think these hasty parsons are mistaken when they throw
On the wheel so much in fashion all the burden of their woe.

As it seems to us, the cycle, on which many perch,
Does not lure away each Sunday those who ride it from the church;
It is from the club it takes them, from the pot-house, from the street,
As it bears them off rejoicing to the country fresh and sweet.

White-faced office-boys it carries to the woods, where thrushes sing,
To the fields, where whirring coveys from the wavering wheat-stalks
    spring;
Care-worn city clerks it hurries off to nature's fairest scenes—
Flower-decked meads and trellised hopgrounds; babbling brooks
    and village greens.

Round-backed artisans it bears, too, from the small and stuffy room,
To the lanes where trailing roses all the summer air perfumes;
And it makes them grow forgetful of the stifling, man-made town,
As they climb the breezy roadway o'er the swelling, God-made down.

Can a change like this be vicious? Can the exercise do harm,
That thus adds to lives so weary, once a week a healthful charm?
No, it seems by far more likely that the cyclists thus may learn
From the fairest sights of nature to that nature's God to turn.

Moved to thought and to reflection by the wonders that they see,
They may long in grateful homage once again to bend the knee;
And the parsons may discover that their pews are filled anew,
Not because their flocks don't cycle, but, forsooth, because they do!

*Anonymous*

# LITTLE THINGS

The preacher spoke of little things,
    Their influence and power,
And how the little pitted speck
    Made all the apple sour.

He told how great big, sturdy oaks
    From little acorns grew,
And how the tiny little stone
    The burly giant slew.

But the cyclist sat there unimpressed
    By all the speaker's fire,
Until he went outside and found
    A pin had pierced his tire.

*Anonymous*

# PUNCTURE NEAR WITTEDRIF

What bliss to be alive this morn,
With land and lake awake to raucous dawn

And every instant serendipitous
I praise, head bowed, the moment I was born

And each unconscious step that led to this
Epiphany of pantheistic bliss

But revelation's brief: a single thorn
Deflates it with a disillusioned hiss!

*Gus Ferguson*

# PUNCTURE WOUNDS: A BAIKU

Hawthorn bares its fangs;
the tire retaliates with
a sibilant hiss.

*Rowena M. Love*

# HIGHROLLER

High rolling cycler! pilgrim of the land,
   Thou dost despise the earth where cares abound,
And lov'st thy wheel, whose well-filled rubber band
   With sudden puncture, casts thee to the ground,
That cold, hard ground, where safeties drop at will
The fool who tries to coast on them downhill.

To thy pneumatic saddle, not beyond,
   Mount, daring rider! Thy most ardent strain
In praise of safeties, a ne'er failing bond,
   Is still 'twixt thee and that long lost of slain,
Who, though they sprinkle all the earth with gore,
The praises of the wheel sing evermore.

Leave to the nightingale the shady woods,
   A blaze of glorious open road is thine.
And if thou hast a score of bruises, floods
   Of misery and curses not divine,
Thou art a type of those most wise, who roam
Far from the kindred points of heaven and home!

*Mary F. Nixon*

# BICYCLE DREAM

I have a dream of bicycles
of the sun on us when we spin quickly
and how easily after a short wobble
we capsize, and sprawl ignominiously.
Some I know believe in decoration,
winding rufflettes of crêpe paper
into their spokes and waving gloriously
as their pierrot suits billow by;

I see too how we keep changing speed
(but only by remembering the principles
of balance) and there is a head wind
to consider, or the one behind driving hard
on our backs—is it luck, that,
or care in choosing the route?

Today you've drawn up beside me
and put your foot to the ground—
I've stopped too, we have everything
to say; it's thrilling, even though
we are constantly interrupted
by the noise of the larger traffic. Still,
this is a love poem—though
at another time it could be a lament
and if we stayed long enough
on this corner for the whole world
to loiter beside us and pass the time of day
that would compose an epic.

As it is, it's just a moment
before we leave the door
of the old second-hand shop, run
to get going, then take off into the wind
pedaling like mad; and alone.

*Lauris Edmond*

# THE WAY A CHILD MIGHT BELIEVE

I think now how we biked toward the sand
all day and up the hill at Devil's Elbow
in time to see a green ray, magma of the sun,
darken the dazzled rim of the Pacific.

We liked to feel the earth under our feet
turning as though our pedals made a difference,
as though it turned from Florence to Eugene
to kiss our wheels as we rode west to meet it,

sweaty and blissed. A borrowed bike at twenty-one
was like a Guggenheim. It rained. We laughed.
The sixty miles of woods have left a sound,
an imprint I return to in your image,

the way a childhood talismanic word
repeated will repeat the walls it echoed.
There are no walls. The day is green.
Green is the night, midfield on our returning,

cowed by the rain, asleep in our tube of tarp.
There is no who I was before that happened,
placeless and innocent, filled only
by a desire to have seen, have had

the carpet of stars infixed. As with your face.

*Olga Broumas*

# ISLAND OF MIRACLES

Forty degrees. Not a soul on the beach.
I began to dream of rain
as we lay in our shuttered room,
blood growing thin,

of standing out in a field
drenched to the skin, tongue out
drinking as it poured down
of falling to my knees before the heavens.

We sped north and east,
the hot wind from Africa burning our heels,
rose with the road, with our fear,
the breath of an angry god

through mountains above a ravine
round Kera pass,
you could no longer steer
and our bike was a trembling reed.

I turned my face from the precipice
as you steadied the wheel
in that land of the mother goddess,
and drove at full throttle.

I could feel our lives in our hands,
then mercy of the elements
as we flew to the plain
of a thousand springs

where the gale ceased
by the Cave of baby Zeus,
and we glimpsed the shadow
of an eagle floating downstream.

*Catherine Phil MacCarthy*

# ALONG THE RIVER

We biked along the Amstel heading south.
Not long ago I was happy here.
What would I do if I should be again? Think back?


There was no music though to order recollections
—this south was anything but warm—no heavy-duty bike now
called 'The Poetic Ecstasy,' and me upright upon it overlooking
the world.


Happily, bent over my ten speeds,
I thought about my health, my boy's dream of a sedentary life
and exorcizing everything, the chubby church at Nes, enameled
signboards.


Tires slithered silently over the road. Beneath the fumes of
Uithoorn I knew that this
would be my future, a training for a longer life filled full with
remembering,
no inspiration any more for more.


*Ad Zuiderent*


*Translated from the Dutch by James S. Holmes*

# CYCLING THE ROSENTAL

### For Adi Wimmer

The River Drau flows swiftly here,
and cold, and such a pale green
it whispers in a waking dream
we pedal through beneath the near

and jagged Slovene Alps, "Let go
of all that troubles you—believe
in all the world can be—I'll weave
a little spell to let you know

the song I sing is meant for you."
So it is, and so the flowers
also sing through all the hours
we ride together, sky so blue

we finally have to stop and strip,
jumping into the River Drau
like a couple of kids. And how
the icy pale water grips

us till our hearts cry out in pain
or joy, my friend, I don't know which,
nor does it matter: even if
we never pass this way again,

we'll know the river's always here,
these mountains, and the sky above
the Valley of Roses, and the love
that makes a day like this so dear.

*W. D. Ehrhart*

# TRAINING ON THE PENINSULA

The blue and yellow light
on the rolling land
and the sea
begins, the longer I look,
to feel as if it radiates
in me, and the day before
this lights up the day
before that, and so on
endlessly until the blue and white
sky stretches as far and as high
as the mind's eye
imagines and is completely
unrestrained.
    I push the gear lever
down a little and the chain
drops on to a small sprocket
and the wheels begin to spin
faster, and the air's
like a quick tongue
in my hair as I descend
swinging in wide curves
around the hill.

How easy to do something
different, how hard to do
it better, is the message I get
as I hear the tires purr
over the smooth seal, and sense
the kind of peace that one can
rarely bear for long
because it fetters
wholeheartedness.

On the flat
I take the long road back
in and out of the bays, spinning
steadily, enjoying a tail wind
home for the first time
in I don't know how many days.

*Brian Turner*

# THE CYCLIST

*Alaska in those days seemed open-ended.*
　　　　　　*—John Haines*

A chill summer day, the sky
a varied gray with squalls to the north
and west, as I pedal shifting gears,
watching for glass. A swallow-tail
flirts for a second with the eye,
a runner passes, bare-chested
in green shorts. And in the bushes

beside the road as my bicycle coasts,
the smell of rotting flesh. Objects
and our ideas about the world
grow and decay. One
month from forty; to my right the river
slides its scaly back. "The world
is flat"—such facts for text,
grasped trembling like that aspen
leaf, twisting on a point I can't
connect: as I move among
gusty ghosts, however fast,
I am this single place,
a man on a bike—he goes
and the world stays.

The woman on the back of the bike
is old and brown. Bones
bruise her skin, breasts flap.
The men putting pipe in the ground

watch us go by and make remarks.
We swerve past their yellow hats.
Her skin a drainage map, behind

which a candle burns, she's like
the withering world. "Sun," she says,
"You are lucky to see us; though
each word you speak is light,
we enhance your self-esteem!"
A sore on her lip looks cancerous,
green liquid oozes from one eye;
yet we celebrate the day's
long season of space and tilt. She
whispers a tune to my ear.—*Einstein
was right, touching disturbs.*
We make a formidable team in this
bicycle riding dream: one of
us is wise and one can steer.

Trees fall to the river, the bank
is swept away. A portion of
ego flees the self, lodging in leaf
or fern, in broken glass,
or the flat black ring of a tire
from which a yellow sign ascends,
a warning. Now between me

and the river (I sit at my desk)
orange trucks pass hauling dirt.
A bicycle coasts by, dust rising
scatters. Like an outlaw, the gray

goose guards her nest. The sky
and sea, blue-gray, lie cold and far.

By the late sheen of an arctic sky
alive with branches shimmying with
light he comes to me: the cyclist,
active, floating, magical, observant,
and the poem comes from him—
whatever he can make it: the hope
that what he turns to will take hold.

*John Morgan*

# MAYBE ALONE ON MY BIKE

I listen, and the mountain lakes
hear snowflakes come on those winter wings
only the owls are awake to see,
their radar gaze and furred ears
alert. In that stillness a meaning shakes;
And I have thought (maybe alone
on my bike, quaintly on a cold
evening pedaling home), Think!—
the splendor of our life, its current unknown
as those mountains, the scene no one sees.
O citizens of our great amnesty:
we might have died. We live. Marvels
coast by, great veers and swoops of air
so bright the lamps waver in tears,
and I hear in the chain a chuckle I like to hear.

*William Stafford*

# AT EVENTIDE

When golden sunbeams gleam athwart the sky,
    Like Daylight's armies hastening to the sun,
On pinions, swift as light, I seem to fly,
    Among the shadows, till the day is done.

My steed of steel, beneath me, seems to know
    The joy intense which thrills in every nerve,
And, like a maiden proud her grace to show,
    From each obstruction doth unbidden swerve.

The god of day, at the horizon's rim,
    Seems lingering there, to watch my silent flight,
And o'er the hills, as though in fear of him,
    Peeps the pale moon, the silvery queen of night.

Between those two, the almost silent sound
    Of yielding tire, among the drifting leaves,
Sings lullaby, as gliding o'er the ground
    I seem to dream,—so well delight deceives.

The shadows lengthen, and the far-off west
    Is glowing, with the last long kiss of day.
The song birds, twittering secrets in the nest,
    Forget to listen, as I wind my way.

And now a truant squirrel hears my call,
    And scampers off, beneath his bushy tail,
Or runs a race along the rough stone wall,
    And hides, at last, within a hollow rail.

Oh! Nature finds within the wheelman's heart
    An echoing chord for every living thing.

At her command the warm blood seems to start
    Through every vein. He cannot help but sing.

And through the stillness, on his homeward way,
    The rich notes of his ringing, manly voice
Burst forth, for very joy, into a lay,
    Whoever hearing must with him rejoice.

*James Clarence Harvey*

# A VERSICLE

I will write you a rollicking, nonsense rhyme,
   Of a man on a wheel of steel,
Who was always singing, in tuneful time,
   In praise of his shining wheel.
He sang at the break of the dawning day,
   He sang when the night grew chill,
In a sort of a reckless, roistering way,
   With a right good royal will.

And sorrow slid off from his careless life,
   Like drops of rain from a spire,
And he hadn't a fretful thought of strife,
   Nor a hopeless vain desire;
So wherever he went, and whenever he sang,
   His manner, so free from guile,
Made every one glad, and the welkins rang
   At the sight of his sunny smile.

And the women and children, and grown-up men,
   Would beg of him, all the while,
To tell them the secret, there and then,
   Of his everlasting smile.
"I ride a good deal, on a wheel of steel,"
   Said the man; "and a conscience clear
Will make you feel that a real steel wheel
   Is a source of endless cheer."

*James Clarence Harvey*

# A BICYCLER'S SONG

## I

Oh, beautiful bicycle, noiselessly gliding,
    How happy the wheelman when trav'ling with thee!
When high on thy saddle he's fearlessly riding,
    How grand and inspiring thy motion so free
While horsemen may gather and jockeys may scorn us,
    Yet dearer the bicycle daily shall be;
And ev'ry true wheelman shall join in the chorus—
    "Oh, bicycle, ever we'll rally to thee!"

## II

When far from the city, where wild flow'rs are growing,
    And through the green lanes where the violets hide
While breathing the health-giving gales that are blowing,
    How happy the wheelmen as gaily they ride!
And sharply the shining bell's musical warning
    Rings out on the air as they rapidly move.
Oh, never Arabian courser's adorning
    Can win our true hearts from the steed that we love!

## III

Then come, brothers, come! with our bicycles hasting,
    No longer at books or at work let us stay!
No longer in cities the sunny hours wasting,
    Let us skim with the birds to the woodlands away!
The sunlight and breezes our strength shall restore us,
    And health to the spirit our freedom shall be;
And ev'ry true wheelman shall join in the chorus—
    "Oh, bicycle, ever we'll rally to thee!"

*Anonymous*

# THE SONG OF THE WHEEL

Whirl and click of sprocket and chain,
    Shimmer and flash of steel,
Throb of pedal and saddle-creak,
    This is the Song of the Wheel.

Think you, you of the shoulder-shrug, you of the scornful glance,
That I am only the season's fad slipped into vogue by chance;
Toy of the moment's childish whim, 'til next year's fancy? Nay,
I am the balanced, whirling, swift, still Spirit of To-day.

Tyrant I of the woodland road; Mercury of the street,
Slipping soundless athwart the rush, fragile, elusive, fleet;
Whispering over the asphalt, ghost-like I glide through the Park,
Flickering my firefly light along the driveways in the dark.

Where'er the sun my cobweb strands (spun wire of spoke)
    hath kissed
The annals praised of feudal days hath faded like a mist.
Flight of machine where once was seen knight errant brave and gay?
Ah, yes, I am the whirling, swift, still Spirit of To-day.

Pleasure hath drunk the draught of haste, and learned to laugh
    to scorn
All the sauntering ease and free of a leisured age outworn.
Tense she speeds! Imperative her clanging summons ring!
I am the sprit of To-day—and I am Pleasure's King.

Whirl and click of sprocket and chain,
    Shimmer and flash of steel,
Throb of pedal and saddle-creak,
    This is the Song of the Wheel.

*George Lynde Richardson*

# ODE TO THE BICYCLE

### For Wim de Vries

You too, you realize, began your days as a conveyance
  for the rich: stylishly moustachioed
    gentlemen in stylish, pricey tweed
      with their downy ladies free-wheeling along
        narrow rustic roads, where not even a farmer
        would dare sully the pristine scene.

And now: so proletarian that you're in danger
  of once more becoming a status symbol for overweight
    managers now overexposed
      in the Jag or MG: no problem: should their
        thigh muscles give them some evening twinges
        you'll probably go to their chauffeur.

No, you are and will stay what you've been for about
  half a century: the extension of poor people's legs:
    just look in the morning, around seven
      o'clock, when the first factory hooters sound:
        in their tens of thousands they come swarming
        past still shut garage doors.

That's why it is fine to live in a town or a village
  with plenty of cyclists: and what's more, there's
    no smell and no sound—well alright, you squeak
      and you creak just a bit, but the gears
        that send your wheels spinning for next to nothing
        are that much more eroded by rust.

Today or tomorrow, you'll hear the smack: already
  here and there Lancias, Studebakers and Bentleys

are swarming like lemmings along the roads.
    Although a Mercedes can go at a lick,
        on a bike we can catch it, for we are that quick
        and then we will laugh in its face!

*C. Buddingh*

*Translated from the Dutch by John Irons*

# AN ACCIDENT

Crossing a bridge in our VW bus
In Stratford-on-Avon, you swerved but grazed
A skinny man riding a bicycle.
God! Was he mad! You pulled off to the side
Beyond the bridge, and he came after us
Shouting, Police! and pedaling furiously
In his black suit. You stood by the bus
As he pulled up and flailed at his kickstand
And rained vituperation on your head.
You quietly cut through his narrative,
"Are you all right?" your face kindly and wry.

Through the bus window I saw the moment when
He first saw you, first looked you in the eye.
He straightened up. His hands moved fast
To straighten his bow tie. Well, yes, he supposed
That he was fine. You asked more questions, asked
So quietly I couldn't hear, but I could see
His more emphatically respectful answers
As he began to nod in affirmation
Of all you said. Then he smiled, sort of,
Offering his hand, and when he pedaled off
He waved and shouted, Thank you very much!

That's what you were like—you could sideswipe
A bow-tied Englishman wobbling across
A narrow bridge on his collapsible bike,
And inspire him, somehow, to thank you for it.

*Gjertrud Schnackenberg*

# DRAGONFLY

In lieu of the ring, a carbon fiber frame.
You had it custom done, turned it for me
in the sun outside our one-room flat,
this way: violet green, that: honey red.
First ride: a pair of shag-lumped llamas,
a kestrel on the wire, a sheep and two lambs
you never saw. Twenty-three miles of hairpin curves
above Cazadero: staring down the cleft of muscle
in your calves, clinging to the promise of the descent
down Meyer's Grade, blocking out the downshifting
gear directives streaming from your mouth. Summit's
view: redwoods to pastures to ocean cliffs
where you stopped long enough for water,
long enough to hear me wonder aloud:
what did I do to you on life back?
We laughed, agreed: *I* was the rider.
This time around, I'll try my hand
at raising the children, and you,
slow enough to see the kestrel,
color of the sky, me.

*Tania Pryputniewicz*

# THE BALLADE OF THE DEVOUT HUSBAND

When the gas-lamps are lighted, when twilight grows grey,
And our road is as bare as the lonely sea-shore,
I slip like a felon who's off with his prey
From the sheltering shade of our little back door.
There's a rattle of steel on the scullery floor,
Then a rustle of petticoats sweeps by my side:
In the dead of the dark we set out to explore,
For my Lady Godiva is learning to ride.

She chooses the darkness: she shrinks from the day:
She is shy of the milkman she dare not ignore;
She declares Mrs. Bangs, who lives over the way,
Will watch from her window from mid-day till four.
So every night, when I'm weary and sore,
She leans on my shoulder with womanly pride,
And I trot by the wheel of the wife I adore;
For my Lady Godiva is learning to ride.
She is pedaling hard; let him hold her who may:
She plunges about in great circles galore;
From the left to the right her magnificent sway
Cuts sixes and sevens and threes by the score.
Then—crash! It's the railing that yesterday tore
The sleeve of my coat with a slithering slide:
She has struck it again as she struck it before!—
O, my Lady Godiva *is* learning to ride!

O still moonlit lovers, light-laughing and gay,
(We have missed you, thank Heaven!—an inch and no more!)
Has she whispered a "Yes"? Has she faltered a "Nay"?
With a dozen soft accents from Venus's store,—
Come, follow our progress; regard, and deplore,
For to this you must come with the turn of the tide;

And the true test of love is as stern as of yore,
When your Lady Godiva is learning to ride!

Queen of Love! Queen of Troth! from afar I implore!
At your palace the faithful were never denied.
Shall I rank as a King for the hardships I bore
When my Lady Godiva was learning to ride?

*Arthur Waugh*

# WOOING THE BICYCLE

To mount the wheel with perfect grace
First see the pedals are in place;
The right, the center half around,
The left, the nearest to the ground
Draw back the wheel a little thus,
To give it proper impetus.
Your hands upon the handlebar
Should be as saintly touches are,
Then press the right foot, till you see
The inside pedal rising free.
Don't be in haste, the pedal right
Describes the circle, sinks from sight;
But ere it meets your foot, once more
You've mounted and the lesson's o'er.

*Grace Duffie Boylan*

# TO A DAUGHTER LEAVING HOME

When I taught you
at eight to ride
a bicycle, loping along
beside you
as you wobbled away
on two round wheels,
my own mouth rounding
in surprise when you pulled
ahead down the curved
path of the park,
I kept waiting
for the thud
of your crash as I
sprinted to catch up,
while you grew
smaller, more breakable
with distance,
pumping, pumping
for your life, screaming
with laughter,
the hair flapping
behind you like a
handkerchief waving
goodbye.

*Linda Pastan*

# AT THE CROSSROADS

Tonight I buy my son a mountain bike.
Independent of his father
we pick a bicycle from a rack of wheels.
It's already assembled and has eighteen speeds,
more than an eleven-year-old needs.

George walks the bike out to the car but refuses
to let me carry it home in the trunk. He says
the frame will get nicked where the latch hits it.
I don't argue much, remembering how my ex-husband
gouged the cabinet on my new sewing machine
removing it from the van and how the scratch ruined
my pleasure every time I sewed.

It's dark now but my son begs to ride home,
three miles from the shopping center.
I can't let him venture out alone like that,
not yet. We compromise. I accompany him,
monitor his progress along the route.
He takes off and I follow, track him like a radar.
No parking allowed on the main street, so I forge ahead,
stop at parking lots and side streets to wait.

He takes longer than I think he should.
I know his father wouldn't approve,
would have hoisted the bike into the trunk and hauled it home,
made him wait another day to try his wheels.
I'd be home now instead of standing on an isolated corner
peering down a dark corridor of trees for my son to emerge.
It's always been this way, me just ahead watching
my child clambering after, searching for me like a landmark.

At each junction he appears, weary and relieved.
Every day he pedals farther away from me
and I sense the time approaching
when he won't need me to navigate the night with him
like two bats squeaky as hinges at twilight
but tonight he still looks for me at every intersection.
Just as much, I need to measure how much distance
I must put between us in order to stay this close.

*Mary Scott*

# VISITATION RITES

My gentle son is performing tricks for me on his bicycle.
He's fourteen and has just cracked open the storm door
to manhood with his gently lowered voice shredding
into shadows until he's surrounded by the calls of
tan young girls whose smooth brown skin calls out, "We're alone."

It will not be long before he masters standing still
on one wheel, elegant jumps over obstacles, riding
upside down and backwards until he will have made
of danger a pretty colored bird to delight him,
sending it away, calling it home, calling it home
as it sails and grows longer, darkens and adds weight.

I watch how well he has done without me all these years,
me with my iron sled of guilt, my cooked-out piles of
worry smoldering. I have been his only model, he says,
and shares with me what a typical day of winning is like.
I sit on a little hill watching my son show off his
light dominion over gravity, knowing in the next few minutes

I will leave again for another year, and again our lives
will pull apart and heal over like bubbles separating in two.
This is how he says goodbye—without speech or reasons or
the long looking after that I have honed through time—
just in a flash in the sun he's suddenly perfected, and I'm gone.

*Jack Elliott Myers*

# A CONSTABLE CALLS

His bicycle stood at the window-sill,
The rubber cowl of a mud-splasher
Skirting the front mudguard,
Its fat black handlegrips

Heating in sunlight, the 'spud'
Of the dynamo gleaming and cocked back,
The pedal treads hanging relieved
Of the boot of the law.

His cap was upside down
On the floor, next his chair.
The line of its pressure ran like a bevel
In his slightly sweating hair.

He had unstrapped
The heavy ledger, and my father
Was making tillage returns
In acres, roods, and perches.

Arithmetic and fear.
I sat staring at the polished holster
With its buttoned flap, the braid cord
Looped into the revolver butt.

'Any other root crops?
Mangolds? Marrowstems? Anything like that?'
'No.' But was there not a line
Of turnips where the seed ran out

In the potato field? I assumed
Small guilts and sat
Imagining the black hole in the barracks.
He stood up, shifted the baton-case

Farther round on his belt,
Closed the domesday book,
Fitted his cap back with two hands,
And looked at me as he said goodbye.

A shadow bobbed in the window.
He was snapping the carrier spring
Over the ledger. His boot pushed off
And the bicycle ticked, ticked, ticked.

*Seamus Heaney*

# THE YELLOW BIKE

Arguing over its cost died to silence,
the birthday cake to a plate of crumbs
as through the open door we watched
the big 5 pinned to his jersey touring
the yard, the circuit growing wider,
steadier as each finish framed him then
took him away into another year,
his singing fading then coming back
always stronger, happier, closer.

*John Lancaster*

# TWO SONNETS

## AFTER THE PORTUGUESE AND ITALIAN

### I. *In a Riding Rink.*

Stay not, with lingering foot, O learner, here,
  Seek the expansion of the country ride;
Firm be thy step, thy heart will banish fear
  In brighter scenes this *posy* path denied,
Far from the shade of tall and brick abodes,
  Where stand the suburb mansions of delight.
Stay not, but on the superior turn*bike* roads
  Find the best basis of bicycling height.
And there to cheer thy firstly toilsome way,
  See many a coaster glitter down the hill!
Pure gales refreshing softly round thee play,
  Warm sunshine smiles; beware of headers still.
Once skilful there, free of beginner's strife;
Health is a certainty, and ride is life.

### II. *A Senior's Intent.*

Bicycle, ride! more lively than serene,
  Whether in urban streets or rural ways,
Where health led me with so mercurial mien,
  Winging my feet these five years' fleeting days;
I must forebear your heights! and though my heart
  Declines the chances of your harms before,
'Tis but ambition for a greater part—
  Still strengthening limbs will manage one wheel more!

Let Tricycle through many a future day
To distant towns this mortal form convey,
  Journeying inland or skirting ocean's wave;
Yet my song musical, to memory true,
On thought's light pedals oft shall fly with you,
  And still, Bicycle, in your praises rave.

*Anonymous*

# BUYING A CYCLE

One Autumn eve, when, sharp and chill,
The wind blew like an icicle,
I met, fast speeding o'er the hill,
A youth upon a bicycle.

'How glorious thus to skim!' I cried,
'By Jove! I too will try-cycle;
And when like him I've learnt to ride,
Why, then, I'll also buy-cycle.'

That very day I made a start,
First practicing the tricycle,
Then soaring to that nobler art,
The riding of the bicycle.

So well I liked my hired machine,
That, having ask'd the price-ical,
I bought it, and it since has been
My own peculiar bicycle.

And now, at morn, and noon, and night,
My life is paradisical;
I emulate the eagle's flight,
When mounted on my bicycle.

Oh, all ye gay and festive youth,
Remember my advic-ical,
And haste to prove this precious truth—
There's nothing like the bicycle!

*Walter Parke*

# BICYCLES, TRICYCLES!

Bicycles! Tricycles! Nay, to shun laughter,
Try cycles first, and buy cycles after;
For surely the buyer deserves but the worst
Who would buy cycles, failing to try cycles first.

*John Banister Tabb*

# THE WORLD'S GREATEST TRICYCLE RIDER

The world's greatest tricycle-rider
is in my heart, riding like a wildman,
no hands, almost upside down, along
the walls and over the high curbs
and stoops, his bell rapid-firing,
the sun spinning in his spokes like a flame.

But he is growing older. His feet
overshoot the pedals. His teeth set
too hard against the jolts, and I am afraid
that what I've kept from him is what
tightens his fingers on the rubber grips
and drives him again and again on the same block.

*C. K. Williams*

# OUR BICYCLES

"At Versailles only the Queen may have pompons on her coach-covers; fastened with nails, and of any color that she pleases. Dutchesses have blue covers. Wives of eldest sons of dukes have red covers. Widows have black velvet."
—The Duc de Saint-Simon, *Historical Memoirs*

My brother being the eldest had
for his bike the most elaborate

accouterments    a pair of squirrel
tails (one grey one brown) which

flew from his handlebars    Cousin
Ham had an extra gear for attack-

ing the hills of Shadyside where
we lived    Cousin Georgie (the shy

one) had two bells with different
tones but when he took his hands

off the bars trying to sound both
of them at once his front wheel

swerved and he ended up at the
hospital for 4 stitches    As for

me (the youngest) I was still on
a tricycle and had nothing but

tears when the others sped on a-
head of me (wait for me wait for

me I would cry) leaving me far be-
hind wailing and eating their dust.

*James Laughlin*

# SHE WAITS FOR ME

When worn and tired with toil and care,
  I homeward wheel my way,
A thought dispels my dark despair
  And lights the homeward way;
A vision fair far up the street
  With straining eyes I see—
I hurry then my love to meet—
  I know she waits for me.

She waits for me, my love, my own,
  She greets me with a smile,
I hear again her tender tone,
  It shortens every mile.
She waits for me, because, you see,
  Like lightning she can go—
At every turn she waits for me—
  I ride so awful slow!

*Anonymous*

# THE BICYCLE SLOW RACE

Often I've seen friends brake when I drive the car,
the cables of their minds tightening
as they jam the spectral pedal
all the way down to the carpeted floor.
I guess, though, that as they watch me now,
their muscles must burn with vicarious speed.
But this is my race, my impossibility.
I want to break the world record
for slowness, to be by a long shot
the last one there, to wish this bicycle
a quarter inch off the ground so that together
we become a single stationary beast
under which the earth turns leisurely,
bringing the finish line beneath me as I hang
motionless, suspended through nebulae of gnats
and subtle barometric changes,
as close as I can come
to that passion where there is no difference
between the willed absence of motion
and the still absolute of speed.
I want to force myself to admit for once
that this is the only way my life arrives,
wave after wave, breaking on my head, entering
through the five portals of the senses to become
the self, as that man discovered
who slit the retina from a rabbit's eye,
developing the frail tissue to find
the image of his study window,
every arch and space and bar—

the rabbit's last sight transformed
into rabbit itself, into particular rabbit,
imprinted by the weight of light.
See, the crowd approaches me in a torrent!
Oh, that there is anything in this world,
and that it should pass through me in such a way!

*Claire Bateman*

# TOUR DE FRANCE

I think of what it's like to team with Lance
for three weeks through the peaks and flats of France
and have no chance; to ride with worker ants,
a mere *plongeur*, a windbreak to advance
another's goal; to pedal with your pants
piss-drenched each day, and then—just when the trance
of pain plateaus—to catch a sideward glance,
of praying mantis eyes and limbs that dance

past in an instant: I know I'd want to prance
in yellow once; dream that, perhaps today,
I bolt the *peleton*, slash through the pack
and pull away—a savage, swift attack
that stirs the crowd's, "allez"—and shrug, and say:
*"C'est pour la France—et pour la liberté!"*

*Michael Cantor*

# LOGOCYCLEGRAM

*A French speaker's English exercise*

Two wheels to roll along the w A
A cyclist's what I want to  B
So far to go so much to   C
On every cycling holi  D
Good company and scener  E

One might be blind or dumb or d  F
Yet cycling stops you growing stod  G
You may feel tired or suffer  H
In headwinds or on mountains h  I
Yet speed like hawk or swift or  J
Pollution free , retard de  K
In fitness and in health ex  L
While pedalling your "Campagnolo" syst  M
Companionship is freely give  N

At night with lamps or dynam  O
Much healthier than your old jalo  P
Avoid the Jam and traffic  Q
And find, come down, you've travelled f  R
To legendary Lyon  S

Then turn and pedal home for  T
Your bicycle will see you thr  U
To ham and eggs and tasty gra  V
Such food of course may tend to  W
Then off to bed and rest, rel  X
No need for me to tell you  Y
The day's ambitions reali  Z

*Audrey Hughes*

# PLACE FOR FOUR-LETTER WORDS

I had it all wrong from the start
about four-letter words. I thought
they were big words with four letters.

Sure, I thought about being wrong.
I kept it quiet, cobweb quiet,
like our house, even our garage.

All but the shed where I kept
my bike. I looked for a place
to hear these words, all of them

Before someone tried to tell me
where this one belonged and that
one didn't. Leaning streamlined

Over the handlebars, I heard them
in the tire's lick and spin. Faster,
tearing all out down a hill, hunched

Under the wind, blinking at the rain,
I yelled every four-letter word I knew,
yelled them until they were as real

As the hill, yelled them until I
broke them in my throat and they were
just words spinning in the spokes.

*Peter Sears*

# A QUIET REVERY

All day without he hears the roar of trade,
  Within the hum and noise of laboring clerks;
Below accounts lie waiting to be made;
  And though the day is done, yet still he works;
Though temples throb, yet still within this den
  He lingers on, companion of dull pain,
Till his hand can guide no more the stubborn pen,
  And on his desk he rests a weary brain.

In sleeping Cyclist's breast a sigh now burns;
  He wakes; looks long upon the land and sea;
Arises; then to beauteous nature turns
  And cries aloud, in joyous ecstasy,
"God bless my wheel! it knows nor care nor strife,
  For one day out the ever-coming seven
I run with it far from the hells of life,
  To find in nature's handiwork a heaven."

Now all is silent as the falling dew;
  The sun has set; the moon, ascended high,
Doth light the slumbering earth with silvery hue;
  A night-hawk gives his solitary cry,
Safe in the confines of the heavenly blue.
  Again doth Cyclist leave his day of weal;
And, when the city's gates he passes through,
  Once more with joy exclaims, "God bless my wheel!"

*Anonymous*

# THE RAIN RACE

Sing me a song of the whirling wheel that paced the coming rain,
Of the riding on the pounded path by gate and hedge and lane.
A lilt to be sung when the spokes are strung to the tune of the
    paling stars,
When the blood of the wire, like a vibrant fire, creeps up thro' the
    handle bars.

Lane and marl and sand-white road and pattering drops at last.
Never a turn till the fingers burn and the breath comes stabbing fast.
On and down to the sleepy town on the staggering wagon trace,
Till the blood can feel the soul of the steel flame up to the rider's face.

Fast, fast, more fast, until at last, while dawn and tempest blend,
In, in, thro' flash and thunder crash, with tumbling rain at end.
Ne'er saw such ride the Oxus side, nor knew it the tribes of Dan,
But such is a race that findeth place in the love of the heart of a man.

*Post Wheeler*

# BICYCLING AWAY FROM THE LIBRARY

Rosewater and dust the dawn;
whir and grit of tires,
grumble of gear and chain
and the fine rain
nerve-white along the skin
as the round webs turn
their long miles down the day . . .
push and push, right and left,
the pedals down and down
riverrun your revolution
downstream drift of wheel and dream
by book and magazine past paper drain
our unloosed lives in your dark run
that we may join our urgent night
allow the turning waterwheel
lost to the buzz of black and white,
that clash of opinions
a Tower of Babel and confusion of tongues.

*William Hedrington*

# ENTIRELY YOU

As motionless as possible in movement;
it's best with mist in the meadow
it's light, but there's nothing that
must already be something, no cow
nor gate nor city in the distance;
what there is, is just a bike
with circling legs each side.

Even if, however far from home
and however dark the night, you pedal
your own kindly light with ease.
And even if your front light is broken,
the dynamo still sings its song,
which itself brings peace to the mind.

But above all, on arrival, it is
entirely you that arrives—
empty, cheery, dead tired.

And so, later, it should be you
that comes to a halt and no other.

*Anton Korteweg*

*Translated from the Dutch by the author*

# AFTER CYCLING

The air's cruel whip which deafened me
down the long descent still sings. My ears
chime and tears well up as if I were still
sailing, wind-borne and weightless down the mountain.
I splash pond water over my face and watch
without my usual envy the gaudy carp,
oranda and koi, as they rise, stop,
and dart away from my hands above them.
I swam in dreams that way as a boy,
breathing the thick water in like air
and moving at will through a brilliant, thrashing sea.
I never had a flying dream,
never leapt from the demons
of sleep and floated safely away.
But I did fall, some nights endlessly,
and woke to see myself settle
into my small and startled body.
I feared sleep, feared dying there
and somehow missing heaven
where everyone spent eternity
soaring like splendid, white birds.
Today, descending the ridge to the whine
of my wheels and the wind, I flew.
And when I stopped, breathless and drenched
with sweat, I felt I had returned from paradise,
or the shadow cast down from paradise
we pass through when we rise above the earth.

*Gary Young*

# PURITAN AGAINST THE WIND

When every pedal stroke's a bore
When bum and back and neck are sore

When flesh is mortified for sure,
Then, I believe, my soul will soar.

*Gus Ferguson*

# THE EIGHT-MILE BIKE RIDE
## IN MEMORY OF JOHN CHEEVER

Sundays we cranked old bikes up hills
until our legs burned and our faces glowed
and our breath twisted down winter inroads
and wind froze our hands as trees measured
the glide of seasons. Splendid was his word
for that rich winding Hudson Valley country,
the hills' swaggering color, gravel sparkling,
rain on our smiling faces, the bridge slick
with first snow, each hill a challenge of chains
*whish whish* the sibilance of macadam—Geronimo!
he'd yell, as we'd go headlong, hands like sails.
Once he somersaulted over handlebars and gashed
his head leaving a looping red trail eight miles long
we spotted months later. But nothing mattered,
not pain which was familiar, a kind of knowing,
like skies opening deeper into light, only trees
and weather and hills mattered, as we drifted reckless
in surrender. No one told a better story. Even
the trees listened, bending to that pure Yankee
hone of language flowing like the spicy stink
of river. The air cracked as we rode around
seasons, as in his story of the swimmer,
the light beginning in summer, fierce and dark
in windows, all those lives hurrying toward
an end which is always surprising, even
when expected. Once we stopped to watch
the night rinse through the heavens, the stars
so silent he said they looked lonely. I think
he meant to tell me that all good stories

are sad, finally, and we make such good stories,
but the window lights grow brighter, burning
with all the others as they do now in memory,
where we are splendid still, every Sunday.

*Philip Schultz*

# GIRLS

This top is the pitch of the world
and they've got there, two girls golden
as stamens of wheat, their bicycles burning
—all still now and tingling
receiving their fierce anointing of sun.

Past the high towns they came
Te Pohue Tarawera
tossed on the horn of the hill
past the rivers Rahunga Rangitikei Mohaka
past the sheep seen creeping like maggots
up tracks to the osier's body of shade—

now they stand shining
proclaiming Look! I'm alive!
I've got red hair that tilts
at the tips, I've got freckles
a melon-slice grin
—or I'm taller, more sallow
with boy's hips and a frizz . . .

we've arrived, we're located
we've found an address at the center
of four horizons
a hawk hung in one corner
and a cattle truck dripping with dung
rolling by . . .

They are bright dust, two sparks
in a traveling galaxy
spun to this moment
for taking a sip of eternity

pause on the road to the hillsides of thunder
Turangakuma Titiokura—yes, yes
they know they're at last for the dark.
But look how they blaze in the light.

*Lauris Edmond*

# AUTUMN

On the first day of Autumn,
a chrysalis day of slanted light,
I am drawn back to my bike,
the sleek steel Bianchi
I rode one-hundredth of the way
to the moon this year,
then abandoned in August to the spiders.

Oh, what joy,
to be pedaling again
into the headlong rush
of the September breeze,
into bird songs
and swirling sepia leaves,
past sculls cutting the canal,
my purring crank and derailleur
a clockwork of wheels within wheels
shifting light and dark
like this gloaming Equinox.

A bicycle is balance and momentum,
the music of the spheres
distilled in steel or aluminum.
It requires no balance
to ride in an automobile:
one devours terrain
oblivious to its texture,
to pleasure or pain,
lusting only for the next destination.

Perched on my saddle,
I am soft and observant
as the day I was born,
calm as in my mother's arms.

"It's as easy as riding a bicycle" we say,
and it is easy, this gentle machine,
the most efficient way to transmit
our small strength into motion.
With ninety-nine more such autumns
and the solar wind pressing me forward,
I believe I could pedal to the moon,
and never miss a single hummingbird.

*Michael Schein*

# THE BICYCLE

That which is, for example,
the bicycle
stands out
among things, its wheels, fierce,
its substance. For example
the spokes are. Spinning
they are even more surely, by which
we recognize the life-light around the hub
and under the brain's thin skin work
a thought for the rightness with which
its fenders join with the frame,
the handlebars, the accuracy, the pureness.
In the same radiance most things
stand, ugly, harmonic, stand
for us to mount
and ride out, clicking, handbrakes cool steel
handbrakes, alive more than ever
to what is, our vision fashioned to please
the legs, the way things
devicelessly wreck us with their perfect chains
on two oily wheels and wreck our
bodies, that we might somehow
rise out of this twofold spinning or leaning,
happy at last, at rest, furiously at rest,
a thing so rightly joined
the chain and frame
will never pull, for example, apart
from where we are going.

*Stan Rice*

# THE LESSON

## 1. Body and Bike

Cleaned, lubed and wiped
      to within a sheen of conception,
          or tossed like a bad hand,
     an untenanted bicycle
        equals
    a tenanted motor vehicle
—strength without muscle,
     bravery without courage
         beauty without heart.
The drivetrain (an essential element)
    can be refined
         beyond the visible
by the body's bellowing heart
        and resonant angles,
   till it pings like love
      in the open air.
    But not always.
What would life be
    with the injustice of always?
Is a body always heavenly?
     Are today's legs any good?
Will today's fluids gain or reduce traction?
   Is today's mind such that
      today doesn't matter?

## 2. The Downhill

What I like about rain
   is its gravity.
What goes up, must come down,

may not be
 rocket science,
but the perfecting of it
 is.
Descent is the straight line
 between
crescendo and nightmare.
 Welcome to the fast . . . the flow,
 like water over impediment,
 narrowing the air's gasps.
It's about being slightly
 out of control,
each thimble shift in weight
 refining the line
 dividing
cadence and catastrophe; every
 nip and tuck
through each declining
 contour
 popping
 the inner ear
with a new definition
 of justice.
Or, because velocity is not free, the other
 ever-present scenario: the hard
 slap
and full stop of
 move
 ment.


## 3. Pear-shaped

Where did last year's lessons go?
 Be honest, sometimes you are

               pushing the envelope
when it folds in on you;
          trying to ride
                    through custard
                              as it turns to it;
          out on a limb
                    when it

But other times
          it falls like fish
                    from clear blue sky.
Too much speed, not enough . . .
          Would hindsight really be
                    a wonderful thing,
                              or plain boring?
After all, there is no foretelling
          the ground effect.
Too much speed, not enough . . .
          You curl into a ball,
you bounce or burst or break
                    your fall,
your mind's returned,
          marooned
                    or called.
Step into the light
          poor Lazurus.

*James Brown*

# THE TRAIL

The path
    down the slope
        is a zipper,
           sand-colored
               in a cloth of green.

I on my bike
am the tab,
gleaming in sunlight of May.
Poised at the top
I wait
    and then
        in a smooth descent
           I glide through the soft, spring air
               unzipping the coat of green

*Myra Stillborn*

# THE NOISELESS WHEEL

How fair they lie!—the circling hills,
Down whose green slopes the summer spills
Her lavish wealth of sun and rain,
Of light and dew. Along the plain,
The errant spice-winds, breathing balm
And scent of southern pine and palm,
Whisper amid the rustling corn
That shakes its plumes beneath the morn.

Through grassy closes, clear and bright
The brooks dance in the misty light,
And one blithe bird, loud caroling,
Dips in the flood a glancing wing.
The flowers that bloom beside the way,
The glistening hedge, the thorny spray,
And myriad beaded blades of grass
Sparkle with diamonds as we pass.
Hark! from the field the farmer's song,
And answering echoes, sweet and long,
Redouble round the emerald vale,
Till o'er the wold they faint and fail.

Still as we pass on noiseless wheels,
The changing landscape glows and reels;
The flaming sun, high and more high,
Mounts up the cloudless summer sky:
We catch the shouts of lads at play
Amid the fragrant new-mown hay,
And sounds of shrill-voiced grigs that sing,
And whetted scythes that cheerly ring.
Through many a shifting scene we flash:
We hear the busy mill-wheel dash;

We hear the shaft that creaks and groans,
The ceaseless whirring of the stones;
Then on we fare; the clattering mill
Is left behind, and all is still.
Ay, all is still; high noon o'erhead
A poppied influence hath shed;
The very insects cease to hum,
And all the breathless world is dumb.

Still on with noiseless wheels we go,
Till in the west the sun dips low—
Till whip-poor-wills begin to call,
And o'er the fields slim shadows fall.
Along our way the midges spin;
Hushed is the day's melodious din,
While piping voices, far and near,
With sweet lamenting vex the ear.
The forest aisles are still and dark,
Save where the fire-fly lights his spark;
And o'er the marish by the way
A mist is rising, ghostly gray.
Now softly glows the evening star
Above us; we have ridden far,
And night is come; a sound of bells,
Like sudden music sinks and swells
In yonder vale, and through the night
A lamp shines like a beacon-light.
Ah, happy inn! ah, happy guest!
How sweet is night! how sweet is rest!

*James B. Kenyon*

# ON A BICYCLE

Under the dawn I wake my two-wheel friend.
Shouting in bed my mother says to me,
"Mind you don't clatter it going downstairs!"
I walk him down he springing step to step:
those tires he has, if you pat him flat-handed
he'll bounce your hand. I mount with an air
and as light a pair of legs as you'll encounter,
slow into Sunday ride out of the gates,
roll along asphalt, press down on the pedals,
speeding,        fearless,
            ring,
                ring,
                    ring

Flinging along my happiness my fever,
incapable of breaking out of it,
overtaking the lorries on the road
taking each of them in a single swoop
flying behind them through cut open space
hanging on them uphill. Yes I know.
It's dangerous. I enjoy it. They hoot
and lean out and yell out,
"We'll give you a hand on the hills;
give you some speed; after that
you tear along on your own."
Careering full tilt, pelting along

in a flurry of jokes. Turn a blind eye
to my crazy career; it's the fashion.
You can't tell me how terribly I ride.
One day I'll learn how to ride.

*Yevgeny Yevtushenko*

*Translated from the Russian by Robin Milner-Gulland and Peter Levi, S.J.*

# PEDALING PARANOIA
## (Thoughts while cycling alone on M-53)

I might survive
if hit by an old VW,
but a semi? . . . I'd be
no-turning-back dead.

Would I die happier
from beer-truck deliverance
rather than, say, a lumbering,
waste disposal vehicle?
And would the transition
be made easier
if it were a *lite* beer truck?

It would be out of character
for the trash truck
to *make* a mess,
but it would be handy
for cleanup . . .
and it's accustomed
to re-cycling.

*Jane Mayes*

# THE BHAKTI YOGI BUYS A BIKE

Astride my dual prayerwheel
I meditate at speed
Devotion to my dharma is
The only call I heed.

I never lust for victory
Nor crave frenetic motion
But gentle like the Ganges
Flow calmly to the ocean.

To cycle through the Cosmos is
A karmic task and thrill,
I just adjust my cadence to
The rhythm of each hill.

I have a little mantra that
I murmur on my way
And if you pay attention
You are sure to hear me say:

"Though heavy is the Samsara
And hard to pedal solo;
I do believe Eternity
Is fully *Campagnolo*."

*Gus Ferguson*

# FOR FAUSTO COPPI (1916–60)

## Et tous les copains de la bicyclette

When you were king of the mountains
Fausto
the kilometers hissed by
like busy moments
beneath your tires
and the pavé was no more than grit
on your tongue
young Italian girls
threw wayside flowers
as you ticked past
spokes flashing in the sun
and in the Tour de France
peasants in the Alps
leaned from windows and shouted
*Allez Coppi!*
and forgot their own man

I remember how
you never seemed to lose
and how
you pushed your goggles
on to the brow
of your thin face
and smiled
as you crossed the line
and how
the photographers hounded
your lady in white
as she waited
for her lean brown prince to race
to her embrace

And when that dreadful disease
did for you
as for any mortal
I thought again
of the pain
that might have been
behind those goggles and the tight grin
behind the private smile
for the waiting lady
the quiet lady in white
who waited at the line to give
the greatest prize
of all

But it's long gone now
Fausto
the flash pop picture press
the gossip column glare
has switched to another scene
you can relax
it's time to sit up in the saddle
ride on the tops
freewheel a little
you're out in front
and they'll never catch you
now

*Jeff Cloves*

# MONT VENTOUX

Writing verse is cycling up Mont Ventoux,
where Tommy Simpson met his tragic end,
before he ever made the final bend
the once world champion collapsed from view.

Here riders all try shaking off the pack,
a category one col, now taboo.
It has a pinewood scent, Sunsilk Shampoo,
which you could need to use when you get back.

It's so exhausting you run out of fuel;
cycling up Mont Ventoux's a bitter pill,
so 'look before you leap' applies, you'll find.

Despite all this, although the heat is cruel,
I reach the summit of this windswept hill:
vanity and the hot pursuit of wind.

*Jan Kal*

*Translated from the Dutch by John Irons*

# SOMETIMES WE CLOSE OUR EYES

Sometimes we close our eyes,
Because reality doesn't please us . . .

. . . if we however should stop to communicate,
we could no longer succeed in tasting life
and writing our history.

My language is my bike . . .
and I want to continue writing
the last chapter of my book
that I much too long
have left unfinished . . .

*Marco Pantani*

# EPILOGUE

## RHYTHM AND RHYME

*An excerpt from* The Bicycle Rider in Beverly Hills

Before I was sixteen I had many bicycles. I have no idea what became of them. I remember, though, that I rode them so hard they were always breaking down. The spokes of the wheels were always getting loose so that the wheels became crooked. I bore down on the handlebars with so much force in sprinting, in speeding, making quick getaways, that the handlebars were always getting loose and I was always tightening them. But the thing about my bicycles that I want to remember is the way I rode them, what I thought while I rode them, and the music that came to me.

First of all, my bikes were always rebuilt second-hand bikes. They were lean, hard, tough, swift, and designed for usage. I rode them with speed and style. I found out a great deal about style from riding them. Style in writing, I mean. Style in every-thing. . . . The style I learned was this: I learned to go and make it fast. I learned to know at one and the same time how my bike was going, how it was holding up, where I was, where I would soon be, and where in all probability I would finally be.

A man learns style from everything, but I learned mine from things on which I moved, and as writing is a thing which moves, I think I was lucky to learn as I did.

A bike can be an important appurtenance of an important ritual. Moving the legs evenly and steadily soon brings home to the bike rider a valuable knowledge of pace and rhythm, and a sensible respect for timing and the meeting of a schedule.

Out of rhythm comes many things, perhaps all things. The physical action compels action of another order—action of mind, memory, imagination, dream, hope, order, and so on. The physical action also establishes a deep respect for grace, seemliness, effectiveness, power with ease, naturalness, and so on. The action of the imagination brings home to the bicycle rider the limitlessness of the potential in all things. He finds out that there are many ways to ride a bike effectively, and the acquaintanceship with the ways and the comparing of them gives him an awareness of a parallel potential in all other actions. Out of the action of the imagination also comes music and memory.

In the early days of the search I heard many great symphonies which no composer ever put to paper and no orchestra ever performed.

On the way I found out all the things without which I could never be the writer I am. I was not yet sixteen when I understood a great deal, from having ridden bicycles for so long, about style, speed, grace, purpose, value, form, integrity, health, humor, music, breathing, and finally and perhaps best, of the relationship between the beginning and the end.

*William Saroyan*

# POET BIOGRAPHIES

**Pamela Alexander** won the Yale Younger Poets Award for *Navigable Waterways* (1985). She has received numerous fellowships and formerly taught at the Iowa Writers' Workshop. Co-editor of *Field Magazine* (Oberlin College Press), Alexander is associate professor and co-director of the creative writing program at Oberlin University.

**Willis Boyd Allen** (1855–1938) was a lawyer, author, and editor. Born at Kittery Point, Maine, Allen graduated from Harvard and Boston University Law School. He edited various small publications including *The Cottage Hearth* and *Our Sunday Afternoon*, and published poems in larger publications like *Scribner's* and *Harper's*. His poetry collection, *In the Morning*, was published in 1890.

**Claire Bateman** graduated from Kenyon College and received her MFA from Vermont College. She has authored four books of poetry: *The Bicycle Slow Race* (1991), *Friction* (1998), *At the Funeral of the Ether* (1998), and *Clumsy* (2003). She has received an NEA Fellowship and Pushcart Prize. Bateman teaches at the Fine Arts Center in Greenville, South Carolina.

**Robin Becker**, born in Philadelphia, earned degrees from Boston University and taught for seventeen years at MIT. Her poems and book reviews have appeared in such venues as *American Poetry Review*, the *Boston Globe*, and *Ploughshares*. She is a professor of English and Women's Studies at Pennsylvania State University, where she also serves as poetry editor for *The Women's Review of Books*.

**Cal Bedient** is a literary critic and author of two books of poems, *Candy Necklace* (1997) and *The Violence of the Morning* (2002). His critical study *Eight Contemporary Poets* was nominated for the National Book Award. Co-editor of the *New California Poetry Series* and of the poetry magazine *VOLT*, Bedient is currently professor of English at UCLA.

**Henry Charles Beeching** (1859–1919) was an English clergyman, author and poet. Educated at the City of London School and at Balliol College, Oxford, he took holy orders in 1882, and thereafter worked in a Liverpool parish. Beeching was later named Dean of Norwich. He delivered the distinguished Clark Lecture in 1900 on *The History of Lyrical Poetry in England*.

**George Bilgere**, Ph.D., has published three books of poetry, including *The Going* and *Big Bang*. His poems have appeared in *Poetry*, *Ploughshares*, and *The Iowa Review*. A recipient of NEA and Fulbright Fellowships, Bilgere earned a doctorate in British and American Poetry from the University of Denver. He is professor of English at John Carroll University in Cleveland, Ohio.

**Alan Bold** (1943-98) was a writer, visual artist, and anthologist. Born in Edinburgh, Scotland, where he went to college and was trained as a journalist, he published many books of poetry including *To Find the New*, *The State of the Nation*, and *In This Corner: Selected Poems from 1963–83*. His many anthologies include *The Poetry of Motion: An Anthology of Sporting Verse*.

**Jenny Bornholdt** was born in Wellington, New Zealand. A poet and anthologist, she was awarded the Meridian Energy Katherine Mansfield Fellowship, and edited *An Anthology of New Zealand Poetry in English* (1998). Her most recent poem collection is *Summer* (2004).

**Alison Brackenbury** was born in Lincolnshire, England, and studied English at St. Hugh's College, Oxford. Since 1990, she has worked in the family metal finishing business. Her most recent collection of poems is *Bricks and Ballads* (2004). She lives in Gloucestershire with her husband and daughter.

**Brenda Brooks** was born in Rivers, Manitoba. She attended York University in Toronto, and worked for many years at the Canadian Press. She has published two poetry collections. Brooks resides on Salt Spring Island, British Columbia, where she is working on a new collection of poems and a novel.

**Olga Broumas** was born in Syros, Greece. She has published one Greek and seven English books of poetry, one of which, *Beginning with O*, was a Yale Younger Poets selection. She has received Guggenheim and NEA Fellowships. Broumas is director of the Creative Writing program at Brandeis University, where she is the Poet-in-Residence.

**James Brown** lives in Wellington, New Zealand, and is the author of *Lemon* (1999) and of *Go Round Power Please* (1995), which won a Best First Book Award. Former editor of the literary journal *Sport*, Brown serves as the 2004 Victoria University/Creative New Zealand Writer in Residence. His most recent collection is *Favourite Monsters* (2003).

**Robert Williams Buchanan** (1841–1901) was a British poet, novelist and dramatist, known best for his narrative poems. His poetry collections include *Undertones* (1863) and *Idyls and Legends of Iverburn* (1865). He also authored a study of mysticism, *The Book of Orm: A Prelude to the Epic* (1870). Buchanan's best-known novel is *The Shadow of the Sword* (1876).

**Michael Cantor** was born in New York City. A retired business *plongeur*, he writes and pedals on Plum Island on the Massachusetts coast. His poems have appeared in *The Formalist*, *The Atlanta Review*, and *The Cumberland Review*. Cantor was a 2003 finalist for the Robert Penn Warren Award, and won the NAA poetry competition in 2004.

**Will Carleton** (1845–1912) wrote sentimental poems of rural life, the most famous being "Over the Hill to the Poorhouse." Born near Hudson, Michigan, where he learned farming and gained a scholarship to the local college, Carleton published such works as *Farm Ballads* (1873), *Farm Legends* (1875), and *City Ballads* (1885). He worked as editor of the *Detroit Weekly Tribune*.

**Thomas Centolella**'s several books of poetry include *Terra Firma*, selected for the 1990 National Poetry Series, and *Lights & Mysteries* (1997). He was a Stegner Fellow at Stanford University and has taught at UC-Berkeley and in the California Poets in the Schools Program. A former recipient of the American Book Award and a Lannan Foundation Fellowship, Centolella lives in San Francisco.

**Jim Clawson** is married with three kids, and lives in a log cabin on a lake in the highlands of New Jersey. He rides his Turner 5-Spot on a nearby technical singletrack, where he has built bridges, trails, and friendships. He has received lacerations, bruises, a broken front tooth, and temporary dysfunction. Clawson credits mountain biking with cleansing his mind, nourishing his body, and rejuvenating his soul.

**Jeff Cloves** lives in England. He is a longtime poet, self-publisher, self-proclaimed freelance hack, and cyclist.

**Angela Cooke** is a poet, playwright, and sculptor. Her first collection, *Behind*

*Glass*, was published by Tarantula in 1996.

**Charles S. Crandall** (1840–?) was a newspaper editor and hardware store owner. Born in Erie County, Ohio, he lived for many years in Owatonna, Minnesota, where he served in the state House of Representatives and Senate.

**Harry Dacre (Frank Dean)** (1860–1922) was an English popular music composer. On his first visit to New York, he brought a bicycle, to which fellow songwriter William Jerome remarked, "It's lucky you didn't bring a bicycle built for two; otherwise you'd have to pay double duty [tax]." Dacre applied the phrase to the song "Daisy Bell," which was rejected by American music publishers until an English singer, Katie Lawrence, brought it to London; it became an international hit.

**Allison A. deFreese** lives in Portland, Oregon, and has published verse in *The Indiana Review*, *Midwest Poetry Review*, and *Many Mountains Moving*. A former James A. Michener fellow at The University of Texas at Austin, she recently returned to the States after a year of writing and teaching in Shizuoka-ken, Japan.

**Rita Dove** served as Poet Laureate of the United States from 1993 to 1995 and is currently Poet Laureate of the Commonwealth of Virginia. Her numerous awards and honors include the 1987 Pulitzer Prize in Poetry and the 1996 National Humanities Medal. Born in Akron, Ohio, Dove received an MFA from the Iowa Writers' Workshop, and went on to publish numerous books. Her most recent poetry collection is *American Smooth* (2004).

**Charles Dryden** (1860–1931) was a humorist and newspaper sportswriter in San Francisco, Chicago, Philadelphia, and New York. A charter member of the Baseball Writers' Association of America, Dryden was regarded as the master baseball writer of his time, and is known to this day for his sports witticisms. He suffered a stroke in 1921 that left him paralyzed.

**Ellen Kirvin Dudis** has published verse in *Poetry*, *The Nation*, *Christian Science Monitor*, *Cream City Review*, and *The National Poetry Review*. She lives on a farm on the Eastern Shore of Maryland.

**Lauris Edmond** (1924–2000) was born in Dannevirke, New Zealand, and published her first book at age fifty-one. Since that time she published sixteen volumes of poetry and a three-volume autobiography. A former speech therapist and English teacher, Edmond received the 1975 PEN Best First Book Award for *In Middle Air*, along with a Katherine Mansfield Fellowship and a Commonwealth Poetry Prize.

**W. D. Ehrhart** lives in Philadelphia with his wife, Anne, and daughter, Leela, and teaches English and history at the Haverford School. His most recent poetry collection is *Beautiful Wreckage: New & Selected Poems* (1999).

**Gus Ferguson** is a poet, cartoonist, and publisher. Born in Scotland, Ferguson currently lives in Cape Town, South Africa. He has published roughly a hundred poetry collections under the imprint of Snailpress and Firfield Press, including six of his own. His most recent collection is *Arse Poetica: Musings on Muse Abuse: Prose, Poems, Drawings, Intertextualities* (2003).

**Edward Field** was born in Brooklyn. Before pursuing poetry, he studied acting at the Moscow Art Theatre. His collections include *Magic Words: Poems* (1997); *Counting Myself Lucky: Selected Poems 1963–1992*; and *Stand Up, Friend, with Me* (1963), which was a Lamont Poetry Selection. He also wrote the narration for the documentary film *To Be Alive*, which won an Academy Award in 1965.

**Charles Fishman** is director of the Distinguished Speakers Program at Farmingdale State University, associate editor of *The Drunken Boat*, and poetry editor of *New Works Review*. His poetry collection *The Death Mazurka* was nominated for the 1990 Pulitzer Prize. In 2004, Fishman published two poetry collections, *Country of Memory* and *5,000 Bells*.

**David Galef** has published over seventy poems in magazines including *Shenandoah*, *Witness*, *The Laurel Review* and *The Formalist*. A former bike racer, Galef is currently professor of English and administrator of the MFA Creative Writing Program at the University of Mississippi. He was a Cat 3 bike racer for many years. "The Bicycle Race in Beowulf" mimics the feel and typography of a poetry translation from Middle English.

**Ryn Gargulinski** is a Brooklyn-based poet, journalist, and stand-up comic. She completed her master's degree with a thesis on the folklore of New York City subway workers. She hosts numerous poetry-reading series across Brooklyn and Manhattan.

**John Gibbens** lives in London, where he has worked as a typesetter, receptionist, playwright, actor, jazz doorman, printmaker, dogwalker and journalist. His poems have appeared in anthologies devoted to Elvis, the Beatles, and nuclear war. Recent publishing credits include *Collected Poems* (2000) and *The Nightingale's Code: A Poetic Study of Bob Dylan* (2001), both by Touched Press. In 2004 he began to publish Inkjet Books.

**W. T. (William Thomas) Goodge** (1862–1909) was born in London and died in Sydney, Australia. He was a prolific writer of light and satirical verse, along with newspaper columns and skits on sports and politics.

**G. Timothy Gordon**, Ph.D., lives in Taos. He teaches and writes on topics of poetics, modernism/postmodernism, and creative writing at The National Cheng Kung University in Taiwan. His poetry collections include *Everything Speaking Chinese* and *Ground of This Blue Earth*.

**Jonathan Harrington** is a graduate of the Iowa Writers' Workshop. He has published one poetry chapbook, *Handcuffed to the Jukebox*, along with a collection of essays, *Son: Essays on the Nature of Florida*. Harrington has published five novels. He currently lives in Mexico.

**Matthea Harvey** is poetry editor of *American Letters & Commentary*. Her most recent poetry collection is *Sad Little Breathing Machine: Poems* (2004). She lives in Brooklyn.

**Seamus Heaney** is considered to be among the greatest living poets. Born in 1939 in County Derry, Northern Ireland, Heaney is best known for such collections as *Opened Ground* (1999); *The Spirit Level* (1996); and *Sweeney Astray* (1984). His recent translation, *Beowulf* (2000), won a Whitbread Award. In 1995 he received the Nobel Prize in Literature.

**William Hedrington** (1948–1971) was the recipient of a Stegner Fellowship in Creative Writing in Poetry at Stanford University. He died at age twenty-three in an automobile accident in Syracuse, New York, where he had just taken up a writing fellowship; his collection, *On the Downhill Side,* was published posthumously.

**George Held**'s poems have been published in *Antigonish Review*, *Concho River Review*, and *Brooklyn Review*. He received a 2005 NEA Fellowship and has been nominated for a Pushcart Prize.

**Rita Ann Higgins** was born and lives in Galway. One of thirteen children, she left school at age fourteen; since then she has published seven books of poetry, including *Sunny Side Plucked: New & Selected Poems* (1996). She regularly reads her poems in public, including spots on various radio shows.

**Linda Hogan** has published six volumes of poetry, including *Savings* (1991) and *The Book of Medicines* (1993), along with two volumes of short stories and two novels, *Mean Spirit* (1990) and *Solar Storms* (1995). A member of the Chickasaw tribe, Hogan was born in Denver, Colorado, and currently serves as associate professor of American Indian Studies at the University of Minnesota.

**Eva Hung**, Ph.D., was born and educated in Hong Kong. After receiving her doctorate from London University in 1986, she joined the Chinese University of Hong Kong, where she currently edits *Renditions*, a journal specializing in the translation of Chinese literature into English. She also writes short fiction and essays in Chinese.

**Phil Ilton** is an Australian poet, writer, and cyclist, whose featured poem was inspired by a seventy-two-hundred-kilometer solo ride through the outback. Ilton's work has appeared in numerous literary journals, and he has conducted various writing workshops and writers' groups.

**John Irons** is a professional translator. He studied modern languages at Cambridge, and since 1968 has resided in Scandinavia. For the last ten years he has specialized in the translation of poetry—mainly Dutch and Flemish, but also Danish, Swedish, Norwegian, and German.

**Henry Israeli** is a poet and playwright. A graduate of the University of Iowa's Writers' Workshop and Theater Arts Department, his books include a collection of poetry, *New Messiahs* (2002), and *Fresco: The Selected Poetry of Luljeta Lleshanaku* (2002), which he edited and co-translated. The recipient of numerous fellowships, including an NEA grant, Israeli is the founder of Saturnalia Books, a small press dedicated to poetry and art books.

**Julia Kasdorf** was born in Lewistown, Pennsylvania. Her books of poetry include *Eve's Striptease* (1998) and *Sleeping Preacher* (1992), with work featured in *The New Yorker*, *Paris Review*, and *Poetry*, as well as numerous anthologies—most recently, the 2003 Pushcart collection. Kasdorf teaches creative writing at Pennsylvania State University.

**Laura Kasischke** is a writer of poetry and prose. In addition to receiving the Pushcart Prize, she has received fellowships awarded by the NEA, the Ragdale Foundation, and the MacDowell Colony. Kasischke holds an MFA from the University of Michigan and teaches creative writing at Washtenaw Community College in Ann Arbor.

**Lawrence Kearney** was born in Oxford, England and grew up in Buffalo, New York. His first collection of poems was *Kingdom Come* (1980). He has published verse in the *Chicago Review*, *Massachusetts Review*, *Paris Review*, and *Atlantic Monthly*.

**Dr. Walter G. Kendall** (dates unknown) was captain of the Boston Bicycle Club, the first cycling club in America, for fifty-two years. He was a horticulturist who developed new strains of plant life and produced many prize flowers and fruits. The land feature Kendall Kettle Hole, located on his former estate in North Quincy, Massachusetts, remains a mecca of sorts for geologists and glaciologists.

**James B. Kenyon** (dates unknown) was a writer, publisher, and sonneteer.

Onetime protégé of Henry Wadsworth Longfellow, Kenyon was editor of *The Standard Dictionary* and remains best known for his poetry collections *Out of the Shadows* (1886) and *In Realms of Gold* (1887). His daughter, Doris Kenyon, was a famous American actress.

**Frederic William Kirchner** is publications director and events manager for Pudding House Publications, a literary press in Columbus, Ohio. He taught elementary school for ten years and has published poems in various venues. He can yo-yo while he rides. Known by the Internet handle "Pedalin' Poet," Kirchner wears Lycra to poetry open-mike events.

**Naoshi Koriyama** is a Japanese poet and teacher. He formerly worked as a translator for U.S. military occupation forces in Okinawa. He completed his undergraduate studies at the New York State College for Teachers, and is author of *Selected Poems, 1954–1985*. His work has been widely reprinted in the English-speaking world.

**Anton Korteweg** lives in the Netherlands. He published his first poetry collection in 1971, following it with a further six collections. He is the director of Holland's Literary Museum.

**John Lancaster** is an English poet living in Scotland. His poetry collections include *Here in Scotland* (2000), *The Barman* (1993), and *Split Shift* (1990).

**Bruce Lansky** has written and edited numerous children's poetry books. Collections of his own verse include *My Dog Ate My Homework, If Pigs Could Fly*, and *Funny Little Poems for Funny Little People*; his editorial credits include *Kids Pick the Funniest Poems, Miles of Smiles*, and *Rolling in the Aisles*. Many of his poems rhyme.

**James Laughlin** (1914–97) was a publisher, editor, and poet. As founder of New Directions, one of the most important and influential publishing companies in the United States, he is best known for having published the works of such revolutionary writers as Vladimir Nabokov, Tennessee Williams, Ezra Pound, and F. Scott Fitzgerald.

**Risa Lichtman** is a master's student in Creative Writing at Bar-Ilan University in Israel, where she serves as editorial assistant for the academic journal *Common Knowledge*. While studying at Vanderbilt University for her bachelor's in Creative Writing, she was the recipient of the Merrill Moore Award for Poetry.

**Rowena M. Love** is a freelance Scottish writer based in the west of Scotland. Her poetry has appeared in such publications as *Poetry Scotland, Reach Poetry Magazine, Psychopoetica, Quantum Leap*, and *The Fireside Book*. In 2004 she published her first collection of poetry, *The Chameleon of Happiness*.

**Edward G. Lueders** (1923–2002) was a poet, teacher, author, and editor. He served as chairman of the English department and director of the creative writing program at the University of Utah. He published works of fiction and nonfiction and edited several books of poetry.

**Catherine Phil MacCarthy** has published poems in Ireland and the United States. Her collections include *This Hour of the Tide* (1994), *The Blue Globe* (1998), and *One Room an Everywhere* (2003). She was awarded Arts Council Bursaries for poetry in 1994 and 1998. "Island of Miracles" recalls a storm-plagued bike trip across Crete.

**David Malouf** is the author of ten novels and six volumes of poetry. Born in Brisbane, Queensland, Australia, he formerly taught English in Britain and at the University of Sydney. His novel *The Great World* was awarded the Commonwealth

Prize, and *Remembering Babylon* was shortlisted for the Booker Prize. His most recent novel is *The Conversations at Curlow Creek*. Malouf lives in Sydney.

**Stazja McFadyen** has published two collections of poems, *If You Can't Eat 'em, Join 'em*, and *Dream Songs*. She hosts weekly poetry readings in her native Austin, Texas, where she lives with husband Cody, son Mikey, and dog Chelsea. She is poetry editor of *Austin Downtown Arts*.

**Harriet Monroe** (1860–1936) was an editor, critic, and poet. Born in Chicago, in 1912 she founded *Poetry: A Magazine of Verse,* which is currently the most widely read poetry journal in the United States. She helped introduce to readers such luminaries as Carl Sandburg, Rupert Brooke, and Robert Frost. Her own works include several volumes of poetry; a book of essays, *Poets and Their Art* (1933); and *A Poet's Life* (1938), an autobiography.

**Eugenio Montale** (1896–1981) is considered perhaps the greatest Italian poet of the twentieth century. His works include *Ossi di seppia* (*Cuttlefish Bones*, 1925), *Le occasioni* (*The Occasions*, 1939) and *La bufera e altro* (*The Storm and Other Things*, 1956), a trio that earned him the Nobel Prize for Literature in 1975. His featured poem, "Buffalo," describes a long-distance velodrome race (a *nocturne*) in the Parisian suburb of Montrouge.

**Bill Morgan** taught English for thirty-one years at Illinois State University; he took early retirement in June 2000. His poems have appeared in *Pikestaff Review, The Susquehanna Quarterly,* and *Spoon River Poetry Review*. Morgan co-produces *Poetry Radio,* a poetry-in-performance radio show on WGLT, a local NPR affiliate in Normal, Illinois. He also manages a website on the poetry of Thomas Hardy. Morgan rides 15-30 miles daily on the roads and trails of Normal.

**John Morgan** has published three books of poetry, and his work has appeared in *The New Yorker, The New Republic, Poetry,* and *The Paris Review*. A former Discovery Award winner, Morgan held a scholarship at Bread Loaf and was a writing fellow at the Fine Arts Work Center in Provincetown. "The Cyclist" is excerpted from a longer poem of the same name, published as a chapbook by Dooryard Press, and in *Walking Past Midnight*. Morgan lives in Alaska.

**Jack Elliott Myers** is the author of seven collections of poetry, including *As Long As You're Happy*, winner of the 1985 National Poetry Series open competition. He is director of Creative Writing at Southern Methodist University and a faculty member of Vermont College's low-residency MFA program. He lives in Dallas, Texas.

**Mary Jane Nealon** was raised in Jersey City, New Jersey and lives in Missoula, Montana. Since receiving an MFA from Warren Wilson College, she has received two fellowships from The Fine Arts Work Center in Provincetown, along with awards from the Mid-Atlantic Arts Foundation and the Poetry Society of America. Her most recent collection is *Immaculate Fuel* (2004).

**Helena Nelson** lives in Fife, Scotland, where she teaches creative writing at a community college. Her first collection, *Starlight on Water*, was a joint prize-winner of the Jerwood Best First Collection Award at the 2003 Aldeburgh Festival. She is a regular contributor to the webzine *Snakeskin*.

**Pablo Neruda** (1904–1973) was arguably the greatest Spanish poet of the twentieth century. Born in Parral, Chile, he published his first book, *Crepusculario* (*Twilight*), in 1923, and became a celebrity the following year with *Veinte poemas de amor y una canción desesperada* (*Twenty Love Poems and a Song of Despair*). He shared the World Peace Prize with Paul Robeson and Pablo Picasso in 1950, and received the Nobel Prize for Literature in 1971.

**Leslie Norris** was born in Wales and is Humanities Professor of Creative Writing at Brigham Young University. His *Collected Stories* and *Collected Poems* were both published in 1996, followed by the poetry volume *Holy Places* (1998). An honorary D. Litt. of the University of Glamorgan, in Wales, Norris is a fellow of The Royal Society of Literature and of The Welsh Academy, and lives in Utah with his wife, their two dogs, Gwenno and Porter, and their cat, Sophie.

**Naomi Shihab Nye** was born in St. Louis, Missouri, and received her bachelor's from Trinity University in San Antonio, Texas, where she still resides with her family. Her poetry collections include *19 Varieties of Gazelle: Poems of the Middle East* (2002), *Fuel* (1998), and *Red Suitcase* (1994). She has twice traveled to the Middle East and Asia for the United States Information Agency promoting international goodwill through the arts.

**Gregory Orr** has written eight collections of poetry, including *The Caged Owl: New & Selected Poems*. He has written three critical books on poetry and co-edited *Poets Teaching Poets: Self and the World*. The recipient of NEA and Guggenheim Fellowships, Orr currently serves as professor of English at the University of Virginia and as poetry editor of the *Virginia Quarterly Review*.

**F. V. N. (Franklin Verzelius Newton) Painter** (1852–1931) was a writer, editor, and professor of modern languages at Roanoke College in Virginia. His publications include *Introduction to Bible Study: The Old Testament*, *Introduction to American Literature*, and *Poets of the South*.

**Marco Pantani** (1970–2004) was an Italian cyclist, widely regarded as one of the best climbers of his generation. Known as Il Pirata (the Pirate), Pantani won both the Tour de France and the Giro d'Italia in 1998. He also suffered from clinical depression and drug addiction, which resulted in a premature death. He enjoyed painting and writing poetry.

**Linda Pastan** was born in New York City, graduated from Radcliffe College, and received her master's from Brandeis. From 1991 to 1994, she served as Poet Laureate of Maryland. Her collection of selected poems, *Carnival Evening*, was a finalist for the National Book Award, and was followed by *The Last Uncle* (2002). A former recipient of the Pushcart Prize and the Dylan Thomas Award, Pastan resides in Potomac, Maryland.

**A. B. "Banjo" Patterson** (1864–1941) was a humorous ballad writer perhaps best known for "Waltzing Matilda." Born in New South Wales, Patterson moved to Sydney, Australia, at age ten to attend school. He worked variously as a solicitor, a journalist, a soldier, and an ambulance driver, and published under the pseudonym "The Banjo," taken from the name of his horse. His first book, *The Man from Snowy River* (1895), has sold more copies than any other book of Australian poetry.

**Margaret Sayers Peden** is an award-winning translator and has worked closely with numerous eminent Latin American writers, including Carlos Fuentes, Isabel Allende, and Octavio Paz.

**Walter Polk Phillips** (1846–1920) was a newspaper editor and a famous telegrapher, who once served as understudy to Samuel Morse. A Massachusetts native, he was one of the fastest Morse code transmitters of his time. He remains best known for inventing the Phillips Code, a code of abbreviations for telegraph operators, many elements of which remain in use today.

**François Portmann**, a Swiss photographer based in New York City, is the poetic eye behind the book's striking black-and-white images. A specialist in action-adventure and travel photography, Portman spends much of his time on the road, shooting assignments in the mountains, deserts, and urban jungles. As a freelancer, he has contributed to such magazines as *Bicycling, Mountain Bike, Ski, Skiing,* and *S.I. Kids,* with a roster of clients that includes Red Bull and Swiss Airlines. His portfolio is available on fotoportmann.com.

**Charles E. Pratt** (1845–1898) was a pioneer bike advocate. An early spokesman for the public acceptance of the bicycle, Pratt served as the first president of the League of American Wheelmen (now the League of American Cyclists), and wrote the handbook *The American Bicycler* (1879), which contained the first-ever set of road signals for use in the United States.

**Wyatt Prunty**, Ph.D., was born in Tennessee and raised in Athens, Georgia. He has written six volumes of poetry, including *Unarmed and Dangerous: New and Selected Poems* (2000). Prunty is Carlton Professor of English at Sewanee: The University of the South (Tennessee), where he founded and directs the Sewanee Writers' Conference and edits the Sewanee Writers' Series, which is published in conjunction with Overlook Press.

**Tania Pryputniewicz** is a graduate of the Iowa Writers' Workshop. She writes, rides, and resides in Sonoma County, California, with her two children and ten-time Hawaii Ironman finisher husband.

**James Reaney** was born in Ontario and has taught English at the University of Western Ontario and the University of Manitoba. In 1966, he established a workshop for theatrical experiments in London, Ontario, and from 1969 to 1979 he edited and printed *Alphabet: The Iconography of the Imagination.* In addition to experimental collages for radio, he has coauthored three operas.

**Claudia M. Reder**, Ph.D., is a graduate of the Iowa Writers' Workshop and of NYU, where she received a doctorate in Educational Theater. Her first book of poems, *My Father and Miro and Other Poems,* won the Bright Hill Contest in 2001. A former resident at the Millay Colony and recipient of two fellowships from the Pennsylvania Arts Council, Reder teaches at California State University at Channel Islands. In 2003, she helped found the Ojai Valley Poetry Festival.

**Eben E. Rexford** (1848–1916) was born in Johnsburgh, New York. He composed hymns, short sketches, and over a thousand poems for the *Saturday Journal* and the *Banner Weekly.* His best-known secular work was *Silver Threads Among the Gold,* which was made into a popular song by Hart Danks. Rexford died of typhoid fever.

**Stan Rice** (1942–2002) authored eight collections of poetry, including *Red to the Rind, Radiance of Pigs,* and *False Prophet* (published posthumously). He was a long-time professor at San Francisco State University, where he also served as chairman of the creative writing program. In 1977, he received the Edgar Allen Poe Award for *Whiteboy.* Rice, who was also a painter, lived in New Orleans with his wife, the novelist Anne Rice, and their son, Christopher.

**Larry Rubin** has published hundreds of poems and four collections. He retired in 1999 from a long career as English professor at the Georgia Institute of Technology. "North of Amsterdam" was inspired by Rubin's 1959 trip to Holland: "I cycled out on the polder north of the city and met a young Dutch fellow (Hans Wijman), also cycling. He spoke very little English and I knew no Dutch, but we got along. To this day he and his wife invite me to dinner when I visit Amsterdam every other summer."

**Mark Rudman** is a poet, essayist, and translator. His recent books include a long poem, *Rider*, which received the 1994 National Book Critics Circle Award in Poetry; a book of essays, *Realm of Unknowing: Meditations on Art, Suicide, and Other Transformations* (1995); and *The Millennium Hotel* (1996)—all three with Wesleyan University Press. He is the author of seven books of poetry and three books of prose.

**Margaret E. Sangster** (1838–1912) was an author and editor, most noted for her work as editor of *Harper's Bazaar*. Born in New Rochelle, New York, Sangster was also a prominent member of the Dutch Reformed Church, editing two periodicals, *Christian at Work* and *Christian Intelligencer*. In 1897 she published *The Art of Being Agreeable*.

**William Saroyan** (1908–1981) was born in Fresno, California, the son of Armenian immigrants. His story "The Daring Young Man on the Flying Trapeze" (1934) launched a successful writing career, which resulted five years later in a Pulitzer Prize for *The Time of Your Life*. He refused to accept the award, believing that business had no place in the arts. His novel *The Human Comedy* (1942) was made into a movie, for which he won an Academy Award in 1943. Saroyan published over sixty books.

**Michael Schein** was born in Vermont and attended Reed College. He has been published in the online zine *Slowtrains* and is currently writing his first novel. Schein is married with two daughters and three cats, and loves Bianchi, the Beatles, and baseball. He first learned to love language at the hand of his high school writing teacher, Gladys LaFlamme Colburn.

**Philip Schultz**'s latest poetry book is *Living in the Past* (2004), which followed *The Holy Worm of Praise* (2002). His work has won the Levinson Prize from *Poetry*, the Lamont Prize, and a National Book Award nomination. He lives in East Hampton, New York, and directs The Writers Studio in New York City.

**Bruno Schulz** (1892–1942) was a Polish writer and painter of Jewish lineage, widely considered to be one of the greatest Polish prose stylists of the twentieth century. His first short story collection, *The Street of Crocodiles* (1933), was followed by *The Sanatorium Under the Sign of the Hourglass* (1937); elaborately poetic, his style has often been likened to that of Kafka and Proust. Schulz was murdered on the street by a Gestapo officer. In 2001 fragments of one of his murals were discovered and restored to Yad Vashem, Jerusalem.

**Clinton Scollard** (1860–1932) was a poet, editor, and writer. Born in Clinton, New York, he graduated from Hamilton College and studied at Harvard before traveling to Europe, Greece, Egypt, and Palestine. He published two volumes of poems, *Pictures in Song* (1884) and *With Reed and Lyre* (1886).

**Peter Sears** was born in New York and graduated from Yale and the Iowa Writers' Workshop. He won the 1999 Peregrine Smith Poetry Competition for his book of poems, *The Brink*. In addition to co-founding The Friends of William Stafford, Sears founded and currently manages the Oregon Literary Coalition. He works at the Community of Writers in Portland.

**David Short** has taught Czech and Slovak at the School of Slavonic and East European Studies, University College London, since 1973. His publications include *Czechoslovakia* (1986), *Teach Yourself Czech* (1993), *Customs and Etiquette in the Czech*

*Republic* (1996), and a 2004 collection of symposium papers on writer Bohumil Hrabal.

**Michael S. Smith** has published over four hundred poems in literary journals and anthologies, along with over twenty short stories. In 2004 he retired as Director of Safety and Insurance Services at GROWMARK, an international agricultural cooperative. He lives in Illinois.

**William Stafford**, Ph.D. (1914–1993), was born in Hutchinson, Kansas. After the Second World War, to which he was a conscientious objector, he earned a doctorate at the newly created Iowa Writers' Workshop, and taught English at Lewis and Clark College until his retirement in 1980. His first major collection of poems, *Traveling Through the Dark*, won the National Book Award in 1963. Stafford went on to publish more than sixty-five volumes of poetry and prose, and in 1970 was named the Consultant in Poetry to the Library of Congress (a position currently known as the Poet Laureate).

**C. J. Stevens** was born in Smithfield, Maine, in 1927. He has written sixteen books, three of which are about treasure hunting in Maine, along with over five hundred stories, poems, textbook articles, and Dutch and Flemish translations. He lives in Maine with his wife, Stella.

**John Banister Tabb** (1845–1909) was born near Richmond, Virginia. Despite bad eyesight, he served on the *Robert E. Lee* steamer for the South in the Civil War and was imprisoned by the North. After the war, he taught at various schools and became a priest in 1884. From then until his death, Father Tabb was chair of English at St. Charles College. His amusing lyrics appeared in eight collections, including *Bone Rules, or Skeleton of English Grammar* (1897). He died a Confederate.

**Livingston Taylor** was born in Boston and has been performing music professionally for over thirty years. He tours extensively, working over one hundred performances per year, and is a professor at Berklee School of Music, where he teaches Stage Performance Techniques. "Bicycle" is the title track of his 1996 album by the same name.

**Dylan Thomas** (1914–1953) was born in Wales, and published his first book, *Eighteen Poems*, at age twenty, to great acclaim. In 1948, during his screenwriting days, Thomas wrote the first part of what he planned to be a much longer film operetta, later abandoned, titled *Me and My Bike*. The premise, wrote Thomas, concerned a man who rode "penny-farthings, tandems, tricycles, racing bikes—and when he dies at the end, he rides on his bike up a sunbeam straight to heaven, where he's greeted by a heavenly chorus of bicycle bells."

**Robert Clarkson Tongue** (1869–1904), born in Nebraska, was a poet as well as an ordained reverend. His wife was Minnie Wyatt Tongue.

**Brian Turner** lives in central Otago, New Zealand, and is the Te Mata Estate New Zealand Poet Laureate for 2003–5. He won the Commonwealth Poetry Prize for his first collection, *Ladders of Rain* (1978), and the New Zealand Book Award for Poetry for *Beyond* (1992). Turner has previously worked as a customs officer, rabbiter, sawmiller, editor for Oxford University Press, national-class hockey player, senior cricketer, and road race cyclist; he continues to race at age sixty. The peninsula in the poem is the Otago Peninsula (South Island of New Zealand).

**Louis Untermeyer** (1885–1977) was a renowned poet and anthologist. In 1923, he resigned as vice president of his father's company to concentrate on writing. Over the next fifty years he wrote, edited, or translated over one hundred books. He is best known for editing anthologies including *Modern American Poetry* (1919) and *Modern British Poetry* (1920). In 1956, he was awarded a Gold Medal by the Poetry Society of America.

**Miroslav Válek** (1927–1991) was a Slovak poet, translator, children's book author, and journalist. Influential in the 1960s, when he edited two major literary journals (*Mladá tvorba* and *Romboid*), he was president of the Union of Slovak Writers from 1967 to 1968 and from 1969 to 1989 he served as Minister of Culture for the Slovak Socialist Republic.

**Arthur Waugh** (1866–1943) was an English publisher, editor and critic. Born in Somerset, England, he was a book review editor for the *Daily Telegraph*, and served as managing director and chairman of Chapman & Hall, Publishers. He was the father of distinguished author Evelyn Waugh.

**Amos Russel Wells** (1862–1933) was a journalist. Born in Glens Falls, New York, he published the periodicals *The Golden Rule* and *Christian Endeavor*, along with religious poetry collections such as *Social Evenings*, *The Caxton Club*, and *A Treasure of Hymns*. Wells died in Massachusetts.

**Suki Wessling**'s prose and poetry have appeared in various journals, including *The Literary Journal*, *The Carolina Quarterly*, and *Pacific Review*. She received an MFA in Creative Writing from the University of Michigan, and currently serves as publisher of Chatoyant, a small poetry press. Wessling lives in Santa Cruz County, California.

**(George) Post Wheeler** (1869–1956) was a poet, politician, and Freemason. Born in Owego, New York, he served as U.S. minister to Paraguay and to Albania.

**Walt Whitman** (1819–1892) is widely considered to be the father of American poetry. Born on Long Island, Whitman ended his formal schooling at age eleven to become a printer's apprentice; he spent the next two decades as a printer, freelance writer, and editor in New York. His self-published *Leaves of Grass*, unconventional in content and technique, remains arguably the most influential volume of poems in American literature.

**Ella Wheeler Wilcox** (1850–1919) was a poet, novelist, and spiritualist, known primarily for her poems in support of temperance and conventional family values. Born in Johnstown Center, Wisconsin, Wilcox published nearly forty volumes of verse, including *Drops of Water* and *Poems of Passion*, the latter of which was denounced as immoral when it first appeared. Shortly after publishing her autobiography, *The World and I*, she died of a nervous breakdown.

**Machine Wilkins**, also known as Steve Gibson, lives in Washington, DC, where he was formerly a bike messenger. He co-founded and currently edits *Mobile City*, which began as a messenger zine passed out by hand in Dupont Circle and is now a thriving urban arts and literary magazine. His most recent poetry collection is *City of Midnight Skies* (2001).

**C. K. Williams** was born in Newark, New Jersey. He is the author of numerous books of poetry, including *The Singing* (2003); *Repair* (1999), which won the 2000 Pulitzer Prize; and *Flesh and Blood* (1987), which won the National Book Critics Circle Award. Williams has also published five works of translation. He has won numerous other awards. Williams teaches creative writing at Princeton University and lives part of the year in Paris.

**Yevgeny Yevtushenko** was born in Siberia near Lake Baikal in 1933. He remains the best-known of the post-Stalinist generation of Russian poets. A social revolution-ary, Yevtushenko gained international fame and controversy in 1961 with *Babi Yar*, in which he denounced Nazi and Russian anti-Semitism; he was considered a leader of Soviet youth during the 1950s and '60s. Since 1990 he has served as Vice President of Russian PEN.

**Gary Young** is the editor of Greenhouse Review Press. He is the author of five books of poems, the most recent of which, *No Other Life*, won the William Carlos Williams Award. His other honors include the Phelan Award, a Pushcart Prize, and both NEA and NEH Fellowships. A husband and father of two, Young is a master letterpress printer, teacher, and visual artist, and lives and works in California's Santa Cruz mountains.

**Ad Zuiderent** was born in 1944 near Rotterdam, Netherlands, and has spent much of his life in Amsterdam. A lecturer in modern Dutch literature at Amsterdam's Free University, he is also a poetry critic for the Dutch weekly *De Tijd* (*Time*) and edi-tor of an ongoing critical collection of contemporary Dutch-language writers. The river Amstel, referenced in the poem, is the one that gave Amsterdam its name; the town of Uithoorn is a thriving industrial center.

# CREDITS

Every effort has been made to identify, locate, and secure permission from those parties who hold rights to the poems in this anthology. Any omitted acknowledgements brought to the editor's attention will be added to future editions.

**Pamela Alexander:** "Bicycle Sprint." Published in *American Scholar* (October-December 1999). Reprinted by permission of the author. ❖ **Claire Bateman:** "The Bicycle Slow Race" from *The Bicycle Slow Race* © 1991 by Claire Bateman and reprinted by permission of the author and Wesleyan University Press. ❖ "Bicycle Days" is from *All-American Girl,* by **Robin Becker,** © 1996. Reprinted by permission of the University of Pittsburgh Press. ❖ **Cal Bedient:** "Leonardo's Bicycle." Published in *Harvard Review* 24 (spring 2003). Reprinted by permission of the author. ❖ **George Bilgere:** "Like Riding a Bicycle," from *The Good Kiss,* The University of Akron Press, copyright 2002 by George Bilgere. Reprinted by permission of The University of Akron Press. ❖ **Alan Bold:** "The Enigma," originally published as "The Cyclist" in *The Poetry of Motion: An Anthology of Sporting Verse,* ed. Alan Bold. Edinburgh: Mainstream Publishing Company, 1984. ❖ **Jenny Bornholdt:** "Instructions for How to Get Ahead of Yourself While the Light Still Shines." From *An Anthology of New Zealand Poetry in English* (Oxford University Press, 1998). Reprinted by the permission of Victoria University Press. ❖ **Maxwell Boyle:** "Silver Creature," originally published as "Bike" in *The North* 8 (1990). Reprinted by permission of The Poetry Business (UK). ❖ **Alison Brackenbury:** "Cycles." Published in *Critical Quarterly.* Reprinted by permission of the author. ❖ **Brenda Brooks:** "Moon in the Mirror." From *Blue Light in the Dash* (Polestar, 2000). Reprinted by permission of the author and Raincoast Books. ❖ **Olga Broumas:** "The Way a Child Might Believe," from *Rave: Poems 1975–1999.* Copyright © 1999 by Olga Broumas. Reprinted with the permission of Copper Canyon Press, P.O. Box 271, Port Townsend, WA 98368-0271. ❖ **J. Lorraine Brown:** "Sonnet at Three-Speed." Reprinted by permission of the author. ❖ **James Brown:** "The Bicycle" and "The Lesson." The latter is excerpted. Reprinted by permission of the author. ❖ **C. Buddingh,** trans. John Irons: "Ode to the Bicycle." Originally titled *"Ode aan de fiets."* From *It Stops Raining Softly* (*Het houdt op met zachtjes regenen*). Amsterdam: De Bezige Bij, 1976. Reprinted in *TLC: The Low Countries. Volume 12. Arts and Society in Flanders and the Netherlands.* Flanders, Belgium: Flemish-Netherlands Foundation, 2004. ❖ **Michael Cantor:** "Tour de France." Reprinted from the e-zine *Eratosphere.* Reprinted by permission of the author. ❖ **Thomas Centolella:** "Zeno's Progress." From *Terra Firma* (Copper Canyon Press, 1990). Reprinted by permission of the author. ❖ **Jim Clawson:** "Fearless Rider." Reprinted by permission of the author. ❖ **Jeff Cloves:** "For Fausto Coppi (1916–60) et Tous les Copains de la Bicyclette." (1971) From *The Poetry of Motion: An Anthology of Sporting Verse,* ed. Alan Bold. Edinburgh: Mainstream Publishing Company, 1984. Reprinted by permission of author. ❖ **Angela Cooke:** "I Stand at the Window and Wave My Arms About." Published in *The North* (No. 8, 1990). Reprinted by permission of the author. ❖ **Allison A. deFreese:** "Cycles in Flight: The Racing Bike." Variation published in *The Southern Poetry Review.* Final stanzas first appeared under the title "Cycling" in *Poetry Kanto* (Yokohama, Japan). Reprinted by permission of the author. ❖ "Turning Thirty, I Contemplate Students Bicycling Home," from *Grace Notes* by **Rita Dove.** Copyright © 1989 by Rita Dove. Used by permission of the author and W. W. Norton & Company, Inc. ❖ **Ellen Kirvin Dudis:** "Riding Their Bikes."

Reprinted by permission of the author. ❖ **Lauris Edmond:** "Bicycle Dream" and "Girls." From *New & Selected Poems*. Newcastle upon Tyne: Bloodaxe Books Ltd., 1992. ❖ **W. D. Ehrhart:** "Cycling the Rosental." From *Beautiful Wreckage: New & Selected Poems*. Easthampton, MA: Adastra Press, 1999. Reprinted by permission of the author. ❖ **D. W. Faulkner:** "Phoebe on a Bicycle." Published in *Conjunctions* 2 (spring-summer 1982). ❖ **David Feela:** "Cut." Reprinted by permission of the author. ❖ **Gus Ferguson:** "The Bhakti Yogi Buys a Bike," "Puncture Near Wittedrif," and "Puritan Against the Wind." From *Past Applegarth in Radiance: A Cycling Miscellany* (Cape Town: The Unpublished Manuscript Press, 1999). Reprinted by permission of the author. ❖ **Edward Field:** "A New Cycle." From *Counting Myself Lucky: Selected Poems, 1963–1992* (Black Sparrow Press, 1992). ❖ **Charles Fishman:** "Blue Bicycles." From *Country of Memory* (Uccelli Press, 2004). Reprinted by permission of the author. ❖ **David Galef:** "The Bicycle Race in Beowulf." Reprinted by permission of the author. ❖ **Ryn Gargulinski:** "We." Reprinted by permission of the author. ❖ **John Gibbens:** "To the Bicycle." From *Collected Poems* (Touched Press, 2000). Reprinted by permission of the author. ❖ **G. Timothy Gordon:** "At Jhong-Jhou Train Station." Reprinted by permission of the author. ❖ **Jonathan Harrington:** "A Rain of Bicycles." From a chapbook, *Handcuffed to the Jukebox*. Reprinted by permission of the author. ❖ **Matthea Harvey:** [By bicycle]. From *Pity the Bathtub and its Forced Embrace of Human Form: Poems*. Reprinted in *Boston Review* 23, Nos. 3–4 (Summer 1998). Reprinted by permission of the author. ❖ **Seamus Heaney:** "Wheels Within Wheels," from *Seeing Things* (Noonday Press, 1993); "A Constable Calls," excerpted from "Singing School," from *New Selected Poems 1966–1987* (Faber and Faber, 1990). ❖ **William Hedrington:** "Bicycling Away from the Library." From *On the Downhill Side: The Collected Poems of William Hedrington* (Shambling Gate Press, 2002). Reprinted by permission of the publisher. ❖ **George Held:** "Learning to Ride My Bike" and "Split." Reprinted by permission of the author. ❖ **Rita Ann Higgins:** "Almost Communication." From *Goddess & Witch* (1988). Reprinted by permission of the author. ❖ **Linda Hogan:** "The Young Boys." From *Savings* (Coffee House Press, 1988). Reprinted by permission of the author. ❖ **Audrey Hughes:** "Logocyclegram." Reprinted by permission of the author. ❖ **Eva Hung:** "I Never Dream of My Father." From the e-zine *Archipelago*, 1999. Reprinted by permission of the author. ❖ **Phil Ilton:** "No Goalies." Reprinted by permission of the author. ❖ **Henry Israeli:** "The Bicycle Ride." From *New Messiahs* (Four Way Books, 2002). Reprinted in *Black Warrior Review*, 24, No. 2 (spring–summer 1998). Reprinted by permission of the author. ❖ **Dobashi Jiji**, "My Bicycle Bell" from *Like Underground Water: The Poetry of Mid-Twentieth Century Japan*, translated by Naoshi Koriyama and Edward Lueders. Copyright © 1995 by Naoshi Koriyama and Edward Lueders. Reprinted with the permission of Copper Canyon Press, P.O. Box 271, Port Townsend, WA 98368-0271. ❖ **Jan Kal**, trans. John Irons: "Mont Ventoux." From *Cycling on the Mont Ventoux* (*Fietsen op de Mont Ventoux*). Amsterdam: De Arbeiderspers, 1974. Reprinted in *TLC: The Low Countries. Volume 12. Arts and Society in Flanders and the Netherlands*. Flanders, Belgium: Flemish-Netherlands Foundation, 2004. ❖ "Riding Bike with No Hands" is from *Sleeping Preacher*, by **Julia Kasdorf**, © 1992. Reprinted by permission of the University of Pittsburgh Press. ❖ **Laura Kasischke:** "Bike Ride with Older Boys." Reprinted by permission of University of Massachusetts Press from *Dance and Disappear*, 2002. Copyright 2002 by Laura Kasischke. ❖ **Lawrence Kearney:** "The Three Ladies," originally published as "The Cyclists" in *The Paris Review*. Reprinted in *Anthology of Magazine Verse*, ed. Alan F. Pater. Beverly Hills: Monitor Book Company, 1980. ❖ **Frederic William Kirchner**: "Reasons to Commute by Bicycle" and "In Cold February Twilight." The former was published in *Talking Leaves: A Journal of Our Evolving Ecological Culture*. Reprinted by permission of the author. ❖ **Anton Korteweg**, trans. by author: "Entirely You," originally titled "Ode to the Bicycle" ("Ode aan de fiets"). From *While Whistling* (*Al fluitend*, 2001). Reprinted in *TLC: The Low Countries. Volume 12. Arts and Society in Flanders and the Netherlands*. Flanders, Belgium: Flemish-Netherlands Foundation, 2004. Reprinted by permission of the author. ❖ **John Lancaster**: "The Yellow Bike." From *Split Shift* (Smith/Doorstop Books, 1990), and *The North* 7 (1989). Reprinted by permission of The Poetry Business (UK). ❖ **Bruce Lansky**: "Oh, Woe Ith Me!" Copyright © 1996 Bruce Lansky. Reprinted from *My Dog Ate My Homework* by permission of its publisher, Meadowbrook Press, Minnetonka, MN. ❖ "Our Bicycles." By **James Laughlin**, from *Poems New and Selected*, copyright © 1997 by the Estate of James Laughlin, copyright © 1989 by James Laughlin. Reprinted by permission of New Directions Publishing Corp. ❖ **Risa Lichtman**: "The Bicycle." Reprinted by permission of the author. ❖ **Rowena M. Love**: "Puncture Wounds: A Baiku." Reprinted by permission of the author. ❖ **Catherine Phil MacCarthy**: "Island of Miracles." From *The Missouri Review*. Reprinted by permission of the *Review* and the author. ❖ **David Malouf**: "[bicycle.]" From *Bicycle and Other Poems* (St. Lucia, Queensland: University of Queensland Press, 1970). Copyright © David Malouf, 1970. ❖ **Jane Mayes**: "Pedaling Paranoia." Reprinted by permission of the author. ❖ **Dave McClure**: "Hampton Lock." ❖ **Stazja McFadyen**: "Not My Knees." From *Love Poems to My Road Atlas* (2000), and from *Garland* (2002). Author retains all copyright. Reprinted by permission of the author. ❖ **Eugenio Montale**, trans. William Arrowsmith: "Buffalo." From *The Occasions, Part I*. © 1987 by William Arrowsmith. Rights held by Estate of William Arrowsmith. ❖ **Bill Morgan**: "Among Goldfinches." Reprinted in *The Spoon River Poetry Review*, XXIII, No. 2 (summer-fall 1998). Reprinted by permission of the author. ❖ **John Morgan**: "The Cyclist." From *The Cyclist* (Dooryard Press, 1986). Copyright © 1986 by John Morgan. Reprinted by permission of the author. ❖ **Jack Elliott Myers**: "Visitation Rites." Reprinted by permission of the author. ❖ "Moon Landing, 1969" from *Immaculate Fuel* by **Mary Jane Nealon**. Four Way Books 2004. By permission of Four Way Books, all rights reserved. ❖ **Helena Nelson**: "No Hands." From *Starlight on Water* (Rialto Press, 2003). Reprinted by permission of the author. ❖ **Pablo Neruda**, trans. Margaret Sayers Peden: "Ode to Bicycles." From Pablo Neruda, *Selected Odes of Pablo Neruda*, ed. M.S. Peden. Copyright © 1990 Regents of the University of California, © Fundacion Pablo Neruda. Reprinted by permission of University of California Press. ❖ **Leslie Norris**: "Eden." Excerpted from the poem "A Small War," published 1974. Reprinted by permission of the author. ❖ **Naomi Shihab Nye**: "The Rider" from *Fuel*. Copyright © 1998 by Naomi Shihab Nye. Reprinted with the permission of BOA Editions, Ltd., www.BOAEditions.org. ❖ **Gregory Orr**: "Lament." From *The Caged Owl: New and Selected Poems* (Copper Canyon Press, 2002). Reprinted by permission of the author. ❖ **Marco Pantani**: "Sometimes We Close Our Eyes." ❖ **Linda Pastan**: "To a Daughter Leaving Home" and "Stationary Bicycle." From *Carnival Evening: New and Selected Poems, 1968–1998*. New York: W. W. Norton, 1998. Reprinted by permission of the author. ❖ **Tony Pranses**: "Shovelin' Coal." Reprinted from the Greater Boston Council, AYH, *Spokesman*. ❖ **Wyatt Prunty**: "Learning the Bicycle." From *Balance as Belief* (Johns Hopkins University Press, 1989). Reprinted by permission of the author and the Press. ❖ **Tania**

Pryputniewicz: "Dragonfly." Reprinted by permission of the author. ❖ **James Reaney:** "The Bicycle." From *Twelve Letters to a Small Town* (Toronto: The Ryerson Press, 1962). ❖ **Claudia M. Reder:** "The Lesson." Published in the journal *Phoebe* (1999). Reprinted by permission of the author. ❖ **Stan Rice:** "The Bicycle." From *Whiteboy* (Mudra, 1976). Reprinted by permission of Lew Thomas and the Stan Rice Gallery. ❖ **Larry Rubin:** "North of Amsterdam." From *Commonweal* (1961) and *The World's Old Way* (University of Nebraska Press, 1963). Copyright © Larry Rubin. Reprinted by permission of the author. ❖ **Mark Rudman:** "Rider." Excerpt from pages 101–104, *Rider* © 1994 by Mark Rudman and reprinted by permission of Wesleyan University Press. ❖ **Michael Schein:** "Autumn." Reprinted by permission of the author. ❖ **Gjertrud Schnackenberg:** "An Accident." From *Supernatural Love: Poems 1976–1992* (New York: Farrar, Straus and Giroux, 2000). ❖ **Philip Schultz:** "The Eight-Mile Bike Ride." From *The Holy Worm of Praise: Poems* (Harcourt, 2002). ❖ **Bruno Schulz:** "[Constellation: Prose Poem]." Excerpted from *The Street of Crocodiles* (New York: Penguin Books, 1977). ❖ **Mary Scott:** "At the Crossroads." From *We'd Wanted Quiet, We Would Have Raised Goldfish* (Meadowbrook Press, 1994) and *Essential Love* (Poetworks/Grayson Books, 2000). Reprinted by permission of the author. ❖ **Peter Sears:** "Place for Four-Letter Words." Reprinted by permission of the author. ❖ **Peter Sizer:** "Old Man on a Bike." From *Old Man on a Bicycle*, 1977. ❖ **Michael S. Smith:** "Sunday Morning Services." Reprinted by permission of the author. ❖ **William Stafford:** "Maybe Alone on My Bike" © 1975 William Stafford from *North by Northwest* (Spring Rain Press). Reprinted by permission of The Estate of William Stafford. ❖ **C. J. Stevens:** "A New Blue Bike." Reprinted by permission of the author. ❖ **Myra Stillborn:** "The Trail." From *On Common Ground 1*, copyright © Myra Stillborn. Reprinted by permission of the author. ❖ **Livingston Taylor:** "Bicycle." From the musical album *Bicycle* (Coconut Bay, 1996). Reprinted by permission of the songwriter. ❖ **Dylan Thomas:** Excerpted from *Me and My Bike* (McGraw-Hill Book Co., 1965). ❖ **Brian Turner:** "Training on the Peninsula." From *All That Blue Can Be* (John McIndoe, 1989). Reprinted by permission of the author. ❖ **Miroslav Válek**, trans. from the Slovak by David Short: "Beating the Drum in Reverse." Originally titled *"Bubnovanie na opaènú stranu."* Comprises excerpts from the first and last section of a longer poem. Reprinted by the permission of the translator. ❖ **Andrei Voznesensky**, trans. Anselm Hollo: From *Selected Poems of Andrei Voznesensky*, trans. Anselm Hollo (1964), © 1964 by Grove Press. Reprinted by permission of Grove/Atlantic, Inc. ❖ **Suki Wessling:** "Angry" originally published as "Red Bicycle" in *The Literary Review*, 45, No. 3, (spring 2002). Reprinted by permission of the author. ❖ **Machine Wilkins:** "Mobile City." First published in *Mobile City* (Bike Messenger zine, 4). Reprinted by permission of Stephen Gibson. ❖ **C. K. Williams:** "The World's Greatest Tricycle Rider." Published in *The New Yorker*. Farrar, Straus and Giroux. ❖ **Pat Winslow:** "God on a Bike." Reprinted by permission of the author. ❖ **Yevgeny Yevtushenko**, trans. Robin Milner-Gulland and Peter Levi, S.J.: "On a Bicycle." Reprinted by permission of Yevgeny Yevtushenko. ❖ **Gary Young:** "After Cycling." From *The Dream of a Moral Life* (Copper Beech Press, 1990). Reprinted by permission of the author. ❖ **Ad Zuiderent**, trans. James S. Holmes: "Along the River," originally published as "Trip Along the River" (*"Tocht Langs de Rivier"*). From *Cycling; Recycling: Poems by Ad Zuiderent in Translation*, ed. and trans. by James S. Holmes. Amsterdam: Uitgeverij De Arbeiderspers, 1984.

The following poems are in the public domain; many are listed under their respective anthologies. Authorial credit is given where originally supplied.

S. Conant Foster, editor. *Wheel Songs: Poems of Bicycling*. New York: White, Stokes, & Allen, 1884. ❖ S. C. Foster: "Toasting Song." ❖ Foster: "From Out the Heated City." ❖ Foster: "The Boycycle."

Walter P. Phillips, editor. *Songs of the Wheel*. New York: George Munro's Sons, 1897. ❖ Ella Wheeler Wilcox: "King Tommy's Rise and Fall." ❖ Anonymous: "The Birth of the Bike." From *St. James's Gazette*. ❖ Anonymous: "Little Things." From *Wilkes-Barre News-Dealer*. ❖ Mary F. Nixon: "Highroller." From *New York Sun*. ❖ Anonymous: "The Old Bike." From *Cleveland Leader*. ❖ Anonymous: "The Song of the Wheel." From *Chicago Daily Tribune*.

Edmond Redmond, editor. *Lyra Cyclus: The Bards and the Bicycle*. New York: M. F. Mansfield, 1897. ❖ Anonymous: "The Whirling Wheel." From *London Sketch*. ❖ Peter Grant: "Winter Resolve." From *Chicago Record*. ❖ Arthur H. Lawrence: "A Song of the Wheel." From *Cycling World*. ❖ Margaret E. Sangster: "The Queen of Girlhood." ❖ George Lynde Richardson: "The Song of the Wheel." From *Outing*. ❖ Charles S. Crandall: "Song of the Cycle." From *Youth's Companion*. ❖ Manley H. Pike: "When Gerty Goes A-Wheeling." From *Buffalo Express*. ❖ Glory Anna: "A Bicycle Glee Song." From *L.A.W. Bulletin*. ❖ Charles Dryden: "The Scorcher's Farewell to His Steed." From *San Francisco Examiner*. ❖ Edward F. Strange: "The Scorcher." From *Cycling World*. ❖ Anonymous: "Cyclolotry." From *Bearings*. ❖ Anonymous: "An Old Maid's Reverie." From *C.T.C. Gazette*. ❖ Anonymous: "She Waits for Me." From *Cleveland Plain Dealer*. ❖ William Carleton: "A Centurion." From *L.A.W. Bulletin*. ❖ Adriel Vere: "To My Cycle." From *The Spectator*. ❖ Post Wheeler: "The Rain Race." From *New York Press*.

Volney Streamer, editor. *The World Awheel*. London and New York: Frederick A. Stokes Company, 1896. ❖ Ernest De Lancey Pierson: "The Flying Wheel." ❖ Eben E. Rexford: "Joy." ❖ Robert Clarkson Tongue: "Invention." ❖ Alberto A. Bennett: "My Wheel and I." ❖ Harriet Monroe: "The Bicyclers."

Arthur Waugh, editor. *Legends of the Wheel*. Bristol, UK: J.W. Arrowsmith, 1898. ❖ A. Waugh: "The Old Road Map." ❖ Waugh: "The Wheel and the Wind." ❖ Waugh: "The Ballade of the Devout Husband." ❖ Waugh: "Town and Country (A Modern Eclogue)." ❖ Waugh: "The Romaunt of Cecilia." ❖ Waugh: "To My Bicycle."

Willis Boyd Allen: "Away from the Office." ❖ Anonymous: "[Beyond the city's . . . ]." First published in *The Wheelman*, 1883. ❖ Anonymous: "[Partaker in my happiest mood . . . ]" First published in *The Cycling Magazine*, 1896. ❖ Anonymous: "The Maiden." Reprinted in the *OAH Magazine of History* (summer 1992). ❖ Anonymous: "A Bicycler's Song." ❖ Anonymous: "Morning Ride." First published in *The Wheelman*, 1883. ❖ Anonymous: "A New View of Sunday Cycling." First published in *The American Wheelman*. ❖ Anonymous: "Bicycle and I." ❖

Anonymous: "On Rainy Days." First published in *Answers*. ❖ Anonymous: "The Gol-Darned Wheel." Reprinted in *Cowboy Songs: And Other Frontier Ballads,* ed. John A. Lomax and Alan Lomax. New York: Macmillan Company, 1943. ❖ Anonymous: "Two Sonnets." First published in *The Wheelman*, 1883. ❖ Henry Charles Beeching: "Going Down Hill on a Bicycle: A Boy's Song" (1895). ❖ Guy Boas: "Beard and Bicycle" and "To a Bicycle Bell" (1933). ❖ Grace Duffie Boylan: "Wooing the Bicycle" (1896) and "Dames of Washington." The latter was published in *Wheel Talk,* 1896. ❖ Robert Buchanan: "Bicycle Song (For Women)" From *The Complete Poetical Works* (1901). ❖ Will Carleton: "Wheelmen's Song." First published in *Outing,* 1884. ❖ Harry Dacre: "Daisy Bell (A Bicycle Built for Two)" (1892). ❖ Charles Richards Dodge: "Wheel Ethics." First published in *The Cycle*. W. T. Goodge: "The Smithville Tandem Bike." ❖ James Clarence Harvey: "Swiftly We Fly," "At Eventide," and "A Versicle." ❖ Dr. Walter G. Kendall: "The Men Who Ride for Fun." ❖ C. T. Mitchell: "Roll On, Shining Wheel!" ❖ Ninon Neckar: "On the Road." ❖ F. V. N. Painter: "My Bicycle." ❖ Walter Parke: "Buying a Cycle." From *Songs of Singularity* (1874). ❖ Paul Pastnor: "The Silent Steed." ❖ A. B. "Banjo" Patterson: "Mulga Bill's Bicycle." First published in *The Sydney Mail,* 1896. ❖ Charles E. Pratt: "To the Wheel." ❖ Clinton Scollard: "Ballads of the Wheel." ❖ John Banister Tabb: "Bicycles, Tricycles!" (1899). N. P. Tyler: "My Magic Wheel." ❖ Edmund Vale: "Bowl Over, Wheel." From *Cycling Song* (1924). ❖ Amos Russel Wells: "By Proxy." ❖ Walt Whitman: "Song of the Open Road" (excerpts). From *Leaves of Grass* (1855).

# PROLOGUE: QUOTATIONS

**R. K. Narayan**. From *The Painter of Signs* (New York: The Viking Press, 1976), pp 13–14. ❖ **Paul Fournel**. From *Need for the Bike*, translated with an intro by Allan Stoekl. Lincoln: University of Nebraska Press, 2003. (*Besoin de vélo* © Editions du Seuil, 2001.) Translation and Translator's Introduction © 2003 by the Board of Regents of the University of Nebraska. pp 29, 127. ❖ **Stephen Crane**. From "Transformed Boulevard," essay. ❖ **William Saroyan**. From *The Bicycle Rider in Beverly Hills* (New York: Scribner's, 1952). ❖ **Daniel Behrman**. From *The Man Who Loved Bicycles: The Memoirs of an Autophobe* (New York: Harper's Magazine Press, 1973). ❖ **Marcel Proust**. From *In Search of Lost Time: Volume One*, trans. D. J. Enright, from original translation by Terence Kilmartin and C. K. Scott Moncrieff (New York: The Modern Library, 1992), p. 218. ❖ **Bob Roll**. Reprinted in *The Quotable Cyclist*, ed. Bill Strickland. Halcottsville, NY: Breakaway Books, 1997. ❖ **Wolfgang Sachs**. From *For Love of the Automobile: Looking Back into the History of Our Desires* (Berkeley: University of California Press, 1992). ❖ **William Golding**. From the essay "Utopias and Antiutopias," address 13 Feb. 1977 to Les Anglicistes, Lille, France. As reprinted in Golding's *A Moving Target* (New York: Faber and Faber, 1982). ❖ **Edmond Redmond**, editor. *Lyra Cyclus: The Bards and the Bicycle* (New York: M. F. Mansfield, 1897). ❖ **Christopher Morley**. From *The Romany Stain* (Garden City, NY: Doubleday, Page & Company, 1926). ❖ **William Wordsworth**. From *Lyrical Ballads* (1798), ed. W. Wordsworth and S. T. Coleridge.

# INDEX OF FIRST LINES

A boy told me
if he roller-skated fast enough      75

A chill summer day, the sky
a varied gray with squalls to the north      253

A sweet inferno, gusting, funneled
crowds of every color in the oval      118

A wintry chill is in the atmosphere,
As from the heaving lake the storm wind blows;      33

Alas, how many years have flown
Since first your silvery note I sounded      172

All day without he hears the roar of trade,
Within the hum and noise of laboring clerks;      289

All night the sprockets have fallen from the sky.
The clouds have unzipped      104

An' fare 'ave yer bin to? An' phat is it, Terrence?
A boycycle is it! An' phat is it for?      158

Arguing over its cost died to silence,
the birthday cake to a plate of crumbs      276

As I rise from my couch at the first dawn of day,
E'er the sun earth's beauties reveal;      170

As motionless as possible in movement;
it's best with mist in the meadow      292

Astride my dual prayerwheel
I meditate at speed      311

Ath I wath biking
down the thtweet,      157

Away, dull care, away!
Till night doth bud in day,      97

Away from the office and desk at last,
The business-haunted room,      63

Away we go on our wheels, boys,
As free as the roving breeze,                                          30

Bicycles! Tricycles! Nay, to shun laughter,
Try cycles first, and buy cycles after;                              280

Changed in a trice you find me,
Man, my master of yore!                                             137

Cleaned, lubed and wiped
to within a sheen of conception,                                    302

Climbing from Merthyr through the dew of August mornings
When I was a centaur-cyclist, on the skills of wheels                 92

Come with me out into the road, my wheel,—
Out into the road, ere the sun goes down!                           129

Crossing a bridge in our VW bus
In Stratford-on-Avon, you swerved but grazed                        265

Dear other self, so silent, swift and sure,
My dumb companion of delightful days,                               198

Each time I passed his place I looked
Sideways and smiled. Friends sniggered.                             211

Every morning I see him pedaling past
And wonder what the hell he's doing.                                212

Far swifter than e'er Atalanta flew,
And silent as the working of the mind                               220

Filming a motion picture
about a small town life                                             157

Forty degrees. Not a soul on the beach.
I began to dream of rain                                            247

From out the heated city Cyclist takes
His way; and instant pauses at the gates,                            61

Galileo from his retreat
Of silence came on noiseless feet                                   226

Girls still ride bicycles into Jhong-Jhou Train Station,
The big, black, old-fashioned skinny kind, all solid-steel           52

Give me a pair of sturdy legs,
And fair outfit of feet, 186

Gliding, gleaming, speeding along,
Waking the echoes with shout and song, 199

God on a bike going twenty miles an hour
over speed ramps, ignoring the pinch-space 233

Good-morning, fellow-wheelman; here's a warm fraternal hand,
As with a rush of victory we sweep across the land! 98

Had to be was angry full of
thoughts with no voice leaving house 73

Halfway between childhood & manhood,
More than a hoop but never a car, 85

Have you never felt the fever of the
twirling, whirling wheel 95

Hawthorn bares its fangs;
the tire retaliates with 242

He scorcheth down the Ripley Road,
His teeth are set, his eyes a-glare; 223

He tumbled from his weary wheel,
And set it by the door; 185

High rolling cycler! pilgrim of the land,
Thou dost despise the earth where cares abound 243

His bicycle stood at the window-sill
The rubber cowl of a mud-splasher 274

How fair they lie!—the circling hills,
Down whose green slopes the summer spills 306

How stern you appear
With your penny-farthen, 159

Humane chariot, most valuable,
most laughable of machines, 130

I am floating in a thin cloud
of them—simultaneous with 182

I can take the wildest bronco in the tough old woolly West;
I can ride him, I can break him, let him do his level best.                     122

I crouch over the bare
bones of speed, jacket                                                          224

I had it all wrong from the start
about four-letter words.  I thought                                            288

I have a dream of bicycles
of the sun on us when we spin quickly                                          244

I have always been lucky.
When I was seven                                                                56

I have always longed to,
the way I longed to match Mother's                                              42

I have seen the dazzling beauty of the
swiftly flying wheel,                                                           202

I have slipped
off my car,                                                                    173

I heard the jerk
of a chain and turned;                                                          38

I left it, precious, balanced
against the rotting wood post                                                  152

I listen, and the mountain lakes
hear snowflakes come on those winter wings                                     256

I love it, I love it, and who shall dare
To chide me for loving that old bike there?                                    190

I love it when he rides standing.
The mastery in his muscles shows.                                              187

I might survive
if hit by an old VW,                                                           310

I must look funny
to those of you in cars:                                                       213

I never dream of my father
Cycling twenty miles each way to work.                                          47

I often drift, on fancy's wondrous stream,
Far out into the vagaries of a dream,                    227

I remember the smell of cut grass
sweetening my tattered pant cuffs                         194

I ride my bicycle to work each day
It's not so far                                          215

I sing the town—
And I the country sing—                                   67

I take to the open road,
Healthy, free, the world before me,                       27

I think now how we biked toward the sand
all day and up the hill at Devil's Elbow                 246

I think of what it's like to team with Lance
for three weeks through the peaks and flats of France    286

I thought of you
as I drove past                                           36

I was walking
down                                                     167

I will not expose
my scabby knees,                                          81

I will write you a rollicking, nonsense rhyme,
Of a man on a wheel of steel,                            259

I would like to write a poem
About how my father taught me                             45

I'm pedaling in to work
thinking about God's works.                              235

If you have a bike, get on it at night
and go to the top of the Brooklyn Hill.                  197

In lieu of the ring, a carbon fiber frame.
You had it custom done, turned it for me                 266

In the beginning,
Ere the artificer                                        134

In the country of confusion my father
passes by clumsily on a three-speed                          49

It is always late at night and always the night in mist
when these paradoxes are felt the most.                    109

It makes me grin to recall my innocence
When I set out on my red and white Schwinn.                55

It starts to rain, and my blue
Schwinn is tilting                                         195

It's ho! for a ride in the open,
With the cool winds blowing free,                          205

It's joy to be up in the morning when the dew's on the grass and clover,
And the air is full of a freshness that makes it a draught divine,—    77

it's not good or bad it's how you get around these
tiny hedged-in lanes that criss-cross town                 101

It's springtime and young boys
ride by, the moving spokes                                 166

It was before the white wicker basket fell
from the handlebars, before the red                        83

Just for me, my dad sweeps the entire
sidewalk, tricky with its leaves and twigs.                44

Likes Ceres trying to free her daughter
Before Jove clipped her, a queen card, to the spokes,      229

Like gray moths tasting the scented world
When the young flowers wake in June,                       181

Loping silhouettes ahead of me
on the bike path. At first I thought dogs                  150

Me and my new bike.
We go everywhere together                                  193

My beautiful, my beautiful!  thou standest meekly by,
With proudly arched and glossy frame,                      221

My brother being the eldest had
for his bike the most elaborate                            282

My father buying me the bicycle that time
Was an unusual thing for him to do.                                    191

My father just passed me
in his Fiat 127,                                                        48

My gentle son is performing tricks for me on his bicycle.
He's fourteen and has just cracked open the storm door                 273

New light on an old bike,
new legs since I ran away.                                              196

Not a hill to highlight the landscape.
Not a tree to treat the eyes.                                          93

Now Henry Jones and William Brown
Were built as nature planned 'em,                                      146

O magic wheel
Of burnished steel                                                     200

O the mountaineer to the summit clear,
The sailor-soul to the sea:                                            203

Often I've seen friends brake when I drive the car,
the cables of their minds tightening                                   284

Oh, beautiful bicycle, noiselessly gliding,
How happy the wheelman when trav'ling with thee!                       260

Oh, skies of those days, skies of luminous signals and metors,         225

On the cover of the book of 19th-century
etchings, three lady bicyclists,                                       53

On the first day of Autumn,
a chrysalis day of slanted light,                                      299

One Autumn eve, when, sharp and chill,
The wind blew like an icicle,                                          279

One look at you and I knew
you'd be able to ride a bike with no hands.                           41

Partaker in my happiest mood,
Companion of my solitude                                               76

Pitching and darting across the roadway,
Plowing the air like a sail, Phoebe rises                             54

Ringing the bell of my bicycle,
I ride through the crowds.                                        50

Rosewater and dust the dawn;
whir and grit of tires,                                          291

Shall I tell you what I'm thinking
As I sit alone to-day,                                           112

She eased the bike onto the park's curved path
and stepped into the shade beneath a tree                       149

Shortly before my death I'm buying
a chrome-plated                                                 116

Since Thursday last, the bare living-room
of my flat's been occupied                                       58

Sing me a song of the whirling wheel
that paced the coming rain,                                      290

Sometimes we close our eyes,
Because reality doesn't please us . . .                          315

Spun in some mighty wizard's brain,
The potent spell that gave thee birth!                           132

Stand next to your bike, like that,
says my father, holding the new Minox camera                    156

Stay not, with lingering foot, O learner, here,
Seek the expansion of the country ride;                         277

Sundays we cranked old bikes up hills
until our legs burned and our faces glowed                      295

"Tell me, O Wheelman, ere you ride away,"
I asked, "where have you been this Sabbath day?"                237

That which is, for example,
the bicycle                                                     301

The air's cruel whip which deafened me
down the long descent still sings. My ears                      293

The bicycles lie
In the woods, in the dew.                                       105

The blue and yellow light
on the rolling land                                        251

The Capital ladies are gloomy this year,
And the pavements of Washington lonely appear             140

The crimped clouds swim full low
Over the long chalk breast.                                34

The first real grip I ever got on things
Was when I learned the art of pedaling                   153

The leader of the pack,
long seasoned in the saddle,                             119

The maiden with her wheel of old
Sat by the fire to spin,                                 139

The noise goes nowhere down the corridor
Of rigid corn, bubbling tar popping off,                 236

The older children pedal past
Stable as little gyros, spinning hard                     43

The one I didn't go on.
I was thirteen,                                          164

The path
down the slope                                          305

The preacher spoke of little things,
Their influence and power,                              240

The River Drau flows swiftly here,
and cold, and such a pale green                         250

The rolling earth stops
As I climb to the summit,                               178

The shadow of my silent steed
Flies over hill and vale,                               127

The shining afternoon was his at last;
And at the altar of his passion's flame                 206

The sun looks o'er the mountain fair,
Its smiles the landscape greet;                         183

The wind blows hard across the polder;
Pedaling in silhouette, the cyclists lean                    35

The world's greatest tricycle-rider
is in my heart, riding like a wildman,                       281

There are those who think the tandem is the instrument sublime
For the serious cycle-tourist, and the man concerned with time.    144

There is a flower within my heart,
Daisy, Daisy!                                                143

There's a road we know,
My wheel and I.                                              217

There was only one problem—the steepness of the hill
so that the moment I got any momentum                        175

They're complaining from the pulpit,
with an energy undue,                                        238

This is the toy, beyond Aladdin's dreaming,
The magic wheel upon whose hub is wound                      131

This is the weather of change
and clear light. This is                                     111

This top is the pitch of the world
and they've got there, two girls golden                      297

Thou and I, my noble wheel,
O'er the highway rolling,                                     218

Through the winding lanes where willows lean,
And the stately elms their shadows throw,                     94

To mount the wheel with perfect grace
First see the pedals are in place,                           269

Tommy was ruled by his father and mother,
Tommy was bossed by his older brother.                        79

Tonight I buy my son a mountain bike.
Independent of his father                                    271

'Twas Mulga Bill, from Eaglehawk, that caught the cycling craze;
He turned away the good old horse that served him many days;    125

Two wheels to roll along the w A
A cyclist's what I want to  B                                    287

Under the dawn I wake my two-wheel friend.
Shouting in bed my mother says to me,                            308

Under the dogwood the bicycles are blue
and still, but blurred enough                                    106

Unspoken Creed
Fearless Rider                                                   120

Up with the lark in the first flush of morning,
Ere the world wakes to its work or its play;                     65

We biked along the Amstel heading south
Not long ago I was happy here.                                   249

We cycled on the water. No one thought
to ask us how we managed such a feat,                            232

We're the healthy, happy heathen, the Men Who Ride for Fun,
The faithful friends of bicycling, that sport surpassed by none. 99

What bliss to be alive this morn,
With land and lake awake to raucous dawn                         241

What though the rain weeps down the pane,
And all the streets are muddy gray,                              102

When every pedal stroke's a bore
When bum and back and neck are sore                              294

When Gerty goes a-wheeling half the
people in the place                                              141

When golden sunbeams gleam athwart the sky,
Like Daylight's armies hastening to the sun,                     257

When I taught you
at eight to ride                                                 270

When the air is rushing past us, and our
ride has just begun,                                             87

When the drifting rain on the window-pane streams
over the pattering ledge,                                        89

When the gas-lamps are lighted, when twilight grows grey,
And our road is as bare as the lonely sea-shore,                    267

When the hedgerows are sweet with bloom and bud,
And blossoms are covering apple-trees,                              31

When worn and tired with toil and care,
I homeward wheel my way,                                           283

When you were king of the mountains
Fausto                                                             312

Whirl and click of sprocket and chain,
Shimmer and flash of steel,                                        261

With lifted feet, hands still,
I am poised, and down the hill                                     180

Would I go back? The childhood bike
Was secondhand, painted thick blue.                                148

Writing verse is cycling up Mont Ventoux,
where Tommy Simpson met his tragic end,                            314

You can ride your hangover out.
You can ride your problems into numb little stubs of               60

You pedal furiously
into a future you're trying                                        114

You too, you realize, began your days as a conveyance
for the rich: stylishly moustachioed                               263

Young Timothy Timid is cautious and wealthy;
He has heard that bicycle owners are healthy;                      163

"Anybody with an interest in screenwriting should read Chris Keane — to learn just how it's done. He demystifies the process so that any screenwriter, aspiring or accomplished, can understand the craft and be eager to give it a go."

— Joseph Wambaugh, *New York Times* bestselling author of *The Choirboys* and *The New Centurions*

"Any successful screenwriter knows that it's all about attracting A-List talent to your story. Christopher Keane teaches you everything you need to know to get the attention you want by writing a script no actor, producer or director could resist. This is a priceless guide to creating a saleable script with magnetic appeal and should be on the bookshelf of any writer serious about breaking into the business."

— Marie D. Jones, book reviewer, *AbsoluteWrite.com*, *BookIdeas.com*

"Mr. Keane takes an excellent approach to the subject matter of screenwriting, breaking it down in new and different ways and giving the reader a whole new level of understanding of how to write a quality script. Even in a world where it seems that there are too many books on screenwriting, you can't pass up Mr. Keane's fresh look. It will help you immensely."

— Matthew Terry, *www.hollywoodlitsales.com*

"Chris Keane hits the nail on the head — most often it takes star actors to get a screenplay sold, but it's his insightful instruction that helps to get you there."

— Steve Duncan, Associate Professor and Chair, Screenwriting Department, Loyola Marymount University School of Film & Television

"Chris Keane's emphasis on developing a central character as the way to get A-list actors to come on board is quite simply brilliant."

— Margaret Lazarus and Renner Wunderlich, Oscar winners for *Saving Our Lives* and members of the Motion Picture Academy of Arts and Sciences.

"Here's the difference between *Romancing the A-List* and every other screenwriting book clogging the shelf: Chris Keane has not only been through the movie and TV wars, he's still engaged in them. His insights aren't dated or theoretical — they're as real as the studio notes he got last week. Even more impressive, he doesn't just linger on his successes. He's confident enough to analyze his failures and those hard-earned lessons are some of the most instructive in the book."

— David Himmelstein, screenwriter (*Power*)

"Chris Keane's *Romancing the A-List* stands head and shoulders above a very crowded field of 'how to' books. Successful both as a writer and teacher, Keane explains the tactics necessary for building a story and getting it into the marketplace. Essential reading for anyone interested in a career in screen writing."

— Michael Miner, director, *The Book of Stars*, co-writer,
*Robocop* and *Anacondas: Hunt for the Blood Orchid*

ROMANCING

# THE A-LIST

HOW TO WRITE THE SCRIPT THE BIG STARS WANT TO MAKE

## CHRISTOPHER KEANE

MICHAEL WIESE PRODUCTIONS

Published by Michael Wiese Productions
3940 Laurel Canyon Blvd. – Suite 1111
Studio City, CA 91604
(818) 379-8799, (818) 986-3408 (FAX).
mw@mwp.com
www.mwp.com

Cover design by MWP
Interior design by William Morosi
Copyedited by Paul Norlen
Printed by McNaughton & Gunn

Manufactured in the United States of America
Copyright 2008 Christopher Keane

Printed on Recycled Stock

Library of Congress Cataloging-in-Publication Data

Keane, Christopher.
    Romancing the A-list : how to write the script the big stars want to make / Christopher Keane.
        p. cm.
    Includes bibliographical references and index.
    ISBN-13: 978-1-932907-40-7 (alk. paper)
    ISBN-10: 1-932907-30-0 (alk. paper)
    1. Motion picture authorship. I. Title.
    PN1996.K35 2008
    808.2'3--dc22
                                            2007036688

# TABLE OF CONTENTS

vii   **PREFACE**   THE TARGET

xiv   **ACKNOWLEDGMENTS**

xv   **INTRODUCTION**   WHY SCREENWRITING?

1   **WORKSHOP ONE**   THE NATURE OF CHARACTER

17   **WORKSHOP TWO**   YOU LIKED WHAT!?
Who *Are* You?
Who Are You Up Against?

37   **WORKSHOP THREE**   THE MOVIE THAT INFLUENCED YOU THE MOST

59   **WORKSHOP FOUR**   THE THREE HORSEMEN: SITUATION, CONCEPT, STORY

79   **WORKSHOP FIVE**   WHERE ARE THOSE STORIES?

103   **WORKSHOP SIX**   YOU'RE WRITING IN *WHAT* GENRE?!

117   **WORKSHOP SEVEN**   THE FOURTH HORSEMAN: PLOT

137   **WORKSHOP EIGHT**   THE FIFTH HORSEMAN: STRUCTURE

151   **WORKSHOP NINE**   THE DREADED MINI-TREATMENT & THE TEDIOUS SCENE BREAKDOWN

189   **WORKSHOP TEN**   HOW TO BREAK INTO HOLLYWOOD

205   **WORKSHOP ELEVEN**   ADAPTING ANY IDEA INTO A SCREENPLAY

225   **ABOUT THE AUTHOR**

For the person who feels, life is a tragedy.
For the person who thinks, life is a comedy.
— Federico Garcia Lorca

# PREFACE

## THE TARGET

Not long ago, a producer hired me to write a screenplay based on the extraordinary life of Mary Pinchot Meyer, who among other things spent many days and nights with John F. Kennedy in the White House during the last year of his life. Her influence on him was so significant that she inadvertently contributed to his assassination, and to her own.

During the two years I worked on this script based on Mary Meyer's life, I relied on two nonfiction books and a vast amount of new research. It became clear that the actor best suited to play this star role would be Charlize Theron.

I had paved the road to Charlize through my attorney and her manager. Charlize is an extraordinary actor with great range. For this and many other reasons (mainly her vast talent) I wrote the script with her in mind. She's the right age, she plays elegant and tough, and she can travel in presidential company.

Charlize can open a picture and carry one. The role dominates the spotlight. Mary Meyer rides past Kennedy, no mean accomplishment. In the film, entitled *Lost Light*, they are star-crossed lovers, Romeo and Juliet, in Camelot. But it's Mary we follow from the beginning to her tragic death in the end. She is the horse that will carry and drive the story forward.

It's not Kennedy's story. It's not CIA counterintelligence chief James Jesus Angleton's story. It's her story. She drives it. It was difficult at times when Jack Kennedy's indomitable power took over a room. I tried extra hard to create a balance between them.

Mary walked into his life with an agenda, and she fell in love. She had clout. She came from great wealth and power; she was the daughter of Amos Pinchot, a founder of the American Civil Liberties Union. Both her father and sister committed suicide. Mary went to Vassar; later she wrote for *Harper's* magazine.

She and her husband, Cord Meyer, were the golden couple of the post-World War II peace movement. Her husband betrayed her ideals by going over to the CIA, and she divorced him. Her young son Michael, run over by a car, died in her arms.

Her sister Tony married Ben Bradlee, executive editor of the *Washington Post* and Kennedy's best friend.

When Mary and Kennedy fell in love, his marriage to Jackie had been over for years. Mary was the only woman Jackie ever feared.

During the two years it took me to write the script, I fell in love with Mary Meyer, with her fierce intelligence and dedication to her ideals, her wit and beauty, the way she carried herself, her athleticism.

Kennedy asked her if she would be willing to wait until he left office to marry him. She said she would.

And then forces within his own administration assassinated him. One year later, after the Warren Commission came out, Mary could be silent no more. She told this to James Jesus Angleton, the CIA's counterintelligence chief and godfather to her children, who begged her to keep quiet.

Next day, as Mary took her daily walk along the tow path near her Georgetown, Washington, D.C. home, a jogger approached and put two bullets in her because she knew too much.

I have never cried as much as I did in writing this story.

I wrote for Charlize, knowing the requirements of what an A-list star needs — to be in the film at least 85% of the time; a strong, well-written role; to drive the story from beginning to end; and to drive individual scenes rather than play a passive observer.

This book is about how to write a screenplay with a strong, complex main character, played by a superlative actor you have in mind that will break you out of the pack.

In *Lost Light*, I had a story that had never been told, about an extraordinary woman who played a significant role in the forming of world politics that reverberate today.

In February 2007, the producers decided the script was ready and sent it out. Instead of Charlize they got it to Cate Blanchett and Kate Winslet. It was read by Bill Condon's (director of *Dreamgirls*) manager, who thought it would be perfect for his client. George Clooney's production company was reading. I hope that by the time this book comes out we'll be in production.

## THE CURRENT SCENE

In 2006, when two independent movies that had been passed over for years — one about road rage in L.A. (*Crash*) and another about two gay cowboys (*Brokeback Mountain*) — win all the prizes that same town has to offer, you know that mainstream movies are not what they used to be.

When the big tent pole pictures like Paramount's *War of the Worlds* are iffy, or when the same studio lets go of a major action star like Tom Cruise, focus has shifted. For instance, instead of an action hero who beats back giant creatures from other worlds, we want a quirky tale about a guy who hears a narrator in his head, narrating his own life story (*Stranger than Fiction*), or a picture about an odd romance between a woman of thirty and a man who, at fifty, begins aging backwards (*The Curious Case of Benjamin Button*).

The best way to break into the movie business is to write a well-crafted, low-budget screenplay from your heart and mind, from passion and craft, with a main character who is so well written and complex that the screenplay will attract agents, producers, bankable actors and money. The key is to write a screenplay that will not cost a bundle but will act as a showcase for you, with the possibility of being picked up by the marketplace.

You can't compete against the big studios or Wall Street investment firms that want blockbusters and give their writing assignments to seasoned pros. Write small with big implications. Read *Brokeback Mountain; Maria, Full of Grace; Sideways; Stranger than Fiction;* and the scripts plucked by distributors from Sundance and Slamdance. That's your market.

Sony, Universal, Paramount, Fox; they will always be here. The independent market (the indies) ebbs and flows, always looking for funding and distribution and always the place for new writers to find their niche.

A small movie with big implications catches on and star power shows up because stars bank on roles that will enhance their careers. Showtime and HBO films, Focus Features, and Fox Searchlight have opened doors for new writers and new audiences and will continue to attract A-list talent who want original, well-written roles.

Who doesn't? For a lot of A-list actors, it's not that much fun to compete against special effects for top billing. Sharp, character-driven roles can stretch bankable actors' talent reserves. Look at *King Kong* and what the talented cast had to go up against — Kong himself, the entire animal kingdom from special effects shops, odd-looking natives, fog-shrouded harbors.

Then think about *Brokeback*, with two characters trying to understand their yearnings and the life-threatening risks they take by acting on them. There was more emotional tension in one minute of *Brokeback* than in all of *King Kong*. You can bet that those fine actors in *Kong* would have given anything to trade with Heath Ledger and Jake Gyllenhaal in *Brokeback*.

The old way of thinking — believing you'll break in at a top level — doesn't matter today the way it did a few years ago. Write small and personal, lower budget, and brilliantly. If you want to work in the industry as a screenwriter, forget about retread thinking, the fear-driven need to write derivative junk. My advice is the focus of this book: to write for character, one main character, the horse that will carry the script over the hump and into a bankable actor's hands.

As writers, you can't afford to follow old directions or read screenwriting books that *exclusively* use examples of movies made ten or twenty years ago or which focus on big studio pictures. *Little Miss Sunshine* never would have been made back then, and certainly wouldn't have succeeded at the box office as it did.

I aimed this book toward original thinkers with something fresh to say. There are rules. You need to know them before you can break them. You can't break into Hollywood with old thinking, no matter how many books or teachers insist that the old rules are the ones to follow.

My students convinced me to write this book because, as they said, there is no substitute for getting the scoop from somebody who writes screenplays for a living — for the industry, in the industry, every day, by someone who is deep into the process.

When my students suggested I write this book I thought they should be in it, too. They'd been through my classes, some of them a half dozen times, and many now work in Hollywood. I've included some of their stories here: What they had to go through to climb the Hollywood ladder; what they learned to avoid; and what they knew to chase after. There's no substitute for first-hand experience.

They also suggested that I organize the book in the way I run a classroom, as a workshop, starting at class one — from the tiny sliver of an idea to the finished product, the screenplay itself. And to show what happens to the screenplay when it leaves your hands and finds its way into the Hollywood machine and beyond.

## THE TWENTY-MINUTE METHOD

I teach two graduate courses a semester at Boston's Emerson College. I lecture on film at Harvard, the Smithsonian, and NYU Film School. Every summer at the International Film Workshops, in Rockport, Maine, I teach a one-month, first-draft screenplay class. It turns out that Emerson, along with UCLA and USC, pumps more students into the Hollywood screenwriting system than any other schools.

So what does it take to be a successful screenwriter? You can read every screenwriting book out there and memorize all the guidelines, but there's no substitute for the daily grind and for reading produced screenplays. I work on a screenplay every day, either a spec or one under contract. Every day, I put in my time; otherwise, I feel something is missing. I work under the dual umbrellas of love and guilt.

Call it fear-driven. I fear what my life will become if I work in a traditional job, for other people with their own agendas. I fear giving my entire creative life to other people. I don't want to work on their time. I have to make a living, so when I decided to write I knew I had to learn some rules, create a schedule, discipline myself to write every day.

I read tons of screenplays. I love movies, and try to see them all. I yearn to see movies that are coming out next week, next month, next year. I can't wait to read reviews on *Metacritic* (*www.metacritic. com*). Every day I log onto *Variety* (*www.variety.com*), *The Hollywood Reporter* (*www.hollywoodreporter.com*), and *Done Deal* (*www.scriptsales. com*) to see what the industry is buying and making.

I teach to get out of the house and to have some sort of steady income in an unsteady business of big paychecks or no paychecks for long periods of time. I've written in hotel lobbies, coffee shops, on park benches, in cars, trains, planes and busses. I crave maple walnut scones at Starbucks. There is no way I'll ever own another desktop computer. I live on the road. Give me my computer with battery juice and software from Final Draft and I'm golden.

I have been turned down at least five times by every Hollywood studio. But I keep plugging because steady work gets the job done, good work gets better, better works gets attention, attention gets jobs, and jobs get produced.

Even the most seasoned pros struggle in this capricious business. These are the chances you have to be willing to take for a writing life worth living. The biggest lesson of all is in the work itself — the time alone with your thoughts, plugging the thoughts into a file, spreading them out on a page, putting them on cards on the wall, structuring the story, laying out the story beats.

For those with regular jobs, I recommend twenty minutes a day, minimum. It's like having kids. If you don't feed them every day, malnutrition sets in. If you don't want your screenplay to suffer that fate, feed your story and your characters on a daily basis. As you get more interested, you will find more time. After the twenty minutes, shut down, get up and go. The work isn't going anywhere; it will be waiting for you tomorrow.

Meanwhile, all day long, the thoughts will be rolling around in your subconscious. There's no magic to it. At least twenty minutes a day. And the script will take care of itself.

To get you started, I recommend these movies to see (and read) because they are small breakout movies with signs of personal choices and visions throughout, the writers' and directors' personal choices as seen through the characters:

*The Curious Case of Benjamin Button*
*Stranger than Fiction*
*Maria Full of Grace*
*Story Telling*
*Y Tu Mama Tambien*
*Amores Perros*
*The Fast Runner*
*Hot Fuzz*
*Knocked up*
*The Queen*

So, have fun. I am, writing this book. It's part of my writing life. I hope some of it spills over into yours.

*Chris Keane*

# Acknowledgments

Many thanks to the following for their invaluable contributions: Erin Liedel, Bonnie Christoffersen, Susan Crawford, Michael Wiese, Ken Lee, Paul Norlen.

# INTRODUCTION

## WHY CHARACTER?

I used to think that structure was the most important part of a script. It's not. Then I thought the story carried the water. It doesn't. There's only one element that stands above all others: character.

There's nothing more important in writing a script than developing a character that will get you up to the machine in the morning and then, when it reaches the hands of a bankable actor, she won't be able to say no. Then the picture gets made.

The plot's not going to get you up out of bed in the morning. Neither is the story, nor the structure. Bankable stars don't read for those elements as much as they read for a character that will enhance their careers.

The character drives the story and the movie. Almost all movies are about one man or woman with one big problem that has to be resolved. As the writer you want a love affair with your main character — the highs and lows, the treachery, the star-crossed love affairs, and the battles, on the field and off, but always in the heart.

And by the way, what is character? Character is the progression of choices the character makes during the course of the story. It's how in the beginning the character will make choices that will have changed significantly by the end. Those decisions by the main character, one by one, throughout the movie, become the character arc.

It's so simple. In Act I, let's say the main character is a lawyer. One morning he's racing to work to close a massive deal on which his entire career hinges.

In the road ahead he sees an accident and two couples in a burning car. Our man is torn. He could stop and help them or keep going on to his massive, career-building meeting.

He rationalizes. He thinks to himself that the EMTs will arrive soon enough, he'd only get in the way. In fact, he thinks he hears a siren in the distance. Guilt-ridden, he heads to work.

By the end of the story, the main character might learn a big lesson about getting his priorities straight. This progress, or character arc, will define his character.

## THE EMERSON MAFIA

They're called The Emerson Mafia. Hundreds of grad students and interns from Emerson College's Boston campus streaming to, living and working in — Hollywood.

For one semester Emerson Mafia interns take non-paying jobs at studios, production companies, and talent agencies as part of their program requirement in the Emerson College writing program. Most all of them end up staying, sucked into the phantasmagoria that is known as the movie business.

They move into small apartments, with palm trees sprouting out of grassy back yards, and roommates piled on top of roommates. They have been hooked on industry juice, they are talented, they have ambition.

It doesn't hurt that the Emerson Mafia is a well-respected and trained cadre of young, smart, high-energy drivers with sharp focus.

I've taught screenwriting to most of them. They tell me the American Poetry Society has a hit out on me. Many of these students enter the Emerson Boston program to write poems and after taking my classes end up, a year later, working at Paramount or CAA, writing and analyzing movie scripts. If *I* were the American Poetry Society I'd put a hit out on me.

I didn't mean to do it. It's not my fault. It's this form of writing — the evil screenplay — that caused all these poets to turn their backs on John Donne, Walt Whitman, Elizabeth Barrett Browning, Ezra Pound. But actually they didn't turn their back on them, they incorporated them into their work, turning out better screenplays than ever.

This new manna from heaven, screenwriting, is a bastard art. After months, sometimes years, of toil, drilling images to the page, in a empty room, all alone, living on Tender Vittles with mayonnaise, the Hollywood powers yank your art away and pass it on to fifty strangers — producers, directors, other writers, grips — who mess with it, rip the originality out of it, and slap it up on a screen.

It's an industry with no room for egos. If you go into the business, expect to be stepped on, pushed around, screwed over and knocked down. That's part of "the collaborative spirit" of Hollywood.

As somebody once said to me when I told them I wanted to write screenplays: "Go to a dark corner and wait for the feeling to pass."

I didn't wait for it to pass, nor did my students. We were already addicted. Making movies is the most highly collaborative art in the world. The screenwriter is the architect. Others build the building off our original dream and conception.

If you're afraid of losing control over your work, stop reading. You *will* lose control over your work. But if your vision is strong to begin with, if that 107-page screenplay you've busted your butt writing has the guts and the gumption and the heart and soul of a great story, with wildly compelling characters and dead-on structure, your chances of seeing that work make it up on the screen, in its original conception, is pretty damn good. That keeps me going.

*Romancing the A-List* is about that process of getting your work to a bankable actor and then up on the screen. It is also about what it takes to get your work out there in this highly competitive world, in the best shape possible. This book is also about getting your screenplay read, from a working writer who's been through it.

I have interviewed dozens of former students who now work in the business, at all levels. They have stories to tell, stories filled with hopes, realized and dashed. Some have left L.A., their cautionary tales filled with frustration and grief.

Some of those with tales of frustration turn back East. Others stay in Los Angeles, take jobs with studios or production companies, or teach or become script doctors. They all share one thing in common: they know character and they know story. They know what a strong character is and what it takes to write one, which is a lot more than many people working in the business know. They also know what a bad script is. This information gives them a giant leg up.

They all know how *not* to write a screenplay. They've all done it. They have been in the trenches of despair, and learned from the experience.

They know character. They know concept. They can take you from the beginning of a story to the end, by showing you character and relationship arcs and motivation, and they know how to write a script that that bankable actor will respond to. They can make the reader sit up and take notice.

They know what's been done and what hasn't, and how to take a single character at the most critical moment of her life and make her so appealing in her turmoil that the bankable actor will fight for the part.

The New Hollywood seems to reinvent itself seasonally, the fundamentals of storytelling shift occasionally. A big secret beyond Hollywood, it seems, is the *talent draft*, a draft that is designed to be read quickly by an actor, without much description, focusing mainly on how the main character drives the action through the story.

Topics, once unsavory, are now sought out: pedophilia, incest, graphic everything. The independent market craves odd-ball stories — well-written stories with strong characters. Stories that will lure A-list talent, or at least bankable talent, in order to get the movie financed.

The language and subject matter knows few boundaries, from *Dirt*, the Mötley Crüe biopic, to *Saw III*, to Eric Roth's *The Curious Case of Benjamin Button*, from F. Scott Fitzgerald's short story.

Talent wants to work. Actors need to exercise their skills. Today, solid mid-level actors who used to demand big dollars are paid scale, or they don't work. They look for work out of the mainstream. Consider *One Hour Photo* (Robin Williams) or *The Dancer Upstairs* (directed by John Malkovich and starring Oscar winner Javier Bardem).

And why not? Why should actors take a tiny part (or any part at all) in a studio picture, for low pay, when they could get the lead or second lead in an independent feature that might break out and put their names back where they used to be? That's not to suggest that leads in independent films are taken by former greats. Quite the contrary. The better parts are usually in independent films; they're meatier, more dynamic, and encourage the actor to dive down into the deep layering of character.

The old studio days are fading. The big movies are in-house creations, financed largely by Wall Street, that live for the most part in development hell. *Development Hell is that world to which scripts with "character" are sent to grow up. It's like summer camp for the brighter kids, the ones with promise, where they are developed into potential money-making works-in-progress. Lots of money is spent nurturing these kids. They're given the best educations by the top teachers and artists. They're gussied up to look pretty for investors and stars. They're here to grow their chops. They most often never graduate to the screen for one reason or another – overnurturing, underestimation — and so they end up languishing in development hell, forgotten, or remembered for all the wasted money spent on them and the accompanying frustration. They're like some people who come to Hollywood. There's a sudden flash on the horizon, hoards rush to see what light through yonder window broke. At first they're treated like royalty, these scripts are, until they end up fame's orphans, sparking and jerking in the gutters along the boulevard of broken dreams.*

The Hollywood movie industry admits that the best stories come from the Provinces (anywhere other than Hollywood), stories so original and dramatically shocking they take your breath away, written by new talent who know the fundamentals of screenwriting — character, story, structure. These are often used as writing samples that get writers jobs on other projects.

There are two types of Hollywood writers: the writers of original screenplays and the work-for-hire scribes. Once the original writer gets one or two scripts under his belt, he becomes a studio writer. He can't afford to write spec scripts anymore because his monthly nut — mortgages, families — is so high he can't afford to work for very little, or nothing, on his passion projects.

There are some writers who do both, rare exceptions. On occasion, if time allows, a writer will fiddle with a spec script of his own.

When *The Huntress*, a nonfiction book I wrote about a mother-daughter bounty hunting team, metamorphosed into the USA Network series, I got a dose of reality. I was under the impression that I was hot and Hollywood would want anything I wrote. My next script — an $80 million dollar thriller — hit a wall. You're not as good as your last picture. You're as good as your current screenplay. Your last project will get you seen, but you had better top that last project.

Rejection? Getting turned down is the nature of the beast. It's a staple of the industry. Actors get about one of every thirty jobs they audition for. At those odds you need a powerful anti-rejection shield. Call it tough self-love.

But you soldier on. That old saw — if it doesn't kill you, it will make you stronger — has always been in the Top Ten of Hollywood's survival kit. Who cares if they all don't love you! After rejection, give yourself permission to sit on the pity pot for twenty-four hours and then get on to the next thing. It hasn't killed you and you will get stronger.

Or — you've heard the tales — you can wither away like some sad flower and get blown out of town. You might get angry at those bastards who didn't snap to your brilliance. Or you become disillusioned. Or you can put the "fun" back in fundamentals.

This book is about writing scripts with strong central characters and a workshop about the process. I will take you through a series of classes, and together we'll build a screenplay, from a simple notion to the complete manuscript. Then I'll tell you how to get it into agents' and producers' hands.

My students have finished first drafts in a month, in six months, a year. There is no time limit as long as the work is steady. Devote those twenty minutes each day to keeping the characters fed and clothed, and their story will live. Otherwise they will wither away, relegated to that drawer or cabinet where all partially finished screenplays go to die.

One of my students who has a full-time job as a graphics artist in Cambridge, Massachusetts, with a wife and two children, devotes an hour every evening after work, five days a week, to his scripts. After the hour, no matter where he is in the script, he leaves his computer and goes on with the rest of his life.

For the rest of each day the story spins through his subconscious. His characters confront one another. The plot moves forward. The story unfolds.

He's been doing this for five years. He has taken on a good agent, who likes his work. He's had two scripts optioned, sold one. He's been hired to write four scripts to date by production companies. One hour a day. Every day. Steady work.

I can't teach you the art of writing, but I can show you the craft. The art is yours. It's what makes you tick and see the world as you do and satisfies your need to express your feelings through story and character. It differentiates you from the others and hopefully gives you a strong unique driving voice.

I can show you tricks, ways to do things, methods to build story and character. How to lay the story out on the screenwriting page. How to tweak characters to get the most out of them so that A-List actors will want to play them. How to stay connected to your story and not go rambling off somewhere and, with your characters, and get hopelessly lost, usually in the Act II desert.

I can also, once you're done, show you how to get the script read, how to sidestep the inevitable pitfalls of the business, directly, without flinching.

I can offer you these things, just as you can offer your characters the things you know from the well of your experience. I can't write it for you, wouldn't presume to, just as you should never try to do it all for your characters. Instead, let *them* run the show, as they should. They are the masters of the story. You are their servant. Just as I am your servant. You give the characters guidance, I give you guidance.

You may still fail, for awhile. Hard work and paying attention will get you through the jungle. Think of this book as a machete, hacking through the debris of fear. It's the most frustrating and satisfying journey you'll ever make. If you stick with it. If you learn the lessons and apply them.

# WORKSHOP 1

# THE NATURE OF CHARACTER

A story that made a big impression on me was "Little Red Riding Hood." I was ten and my mother said to me, "Who's the main character in the story?"

I thought for a moment, and said, "Red Riding Hood."

"How so?"

"The story is called that," I said. "Little Red Riding Hood."

"You think so, do you?" my mother said. "I think it's misleading. She's not in the story very much. What about the Wolf? Why don't you take a look at the story from the Wolf's point of view? Ask yourself how the Wolf feels about all this?"

"Okay, but why should we care about the Wolf? All he wants to do is have Red for dinner."

Not true, I would learn once I got thinking about it.

Here is what my mother explained to me about the story, and what I added to it in the years to come.

We have a Wolf, a sad guy who lives in the woods, alone and hungry. One night, through the trees, he sees a light.

He discovers a farmhouse inhabited by a Grandma. The Wolf sneaks a closer look. It's homey in there, with a fire. The Grandma seems very nice. The Wolf needs companionship, a meal; he's desolate.

The next day he picks flowers and puts them on the back porch. The Grandma finds them and that night she puts out a dish of something.

The Wolf wolfs it down and leaves more flowers, or something he's carved out of wood. And so on. One night as the Wolf is eating the food the Grandma has left for him, she appears and invites the Wolf in to eat his meal at a proper table.

Thus begins the best relationship the Wolf has ever had, and probably the best relationship Grandma has had. She likes this Wolf, and she's also in need of companionship.

A bargain is struck. In return for being fed and housed, the Wolf agrees to do handy work around the house.

This goes on for a few weeks. The Wolf has never been happier. Finally, after all his roaming around, he's found a home, and a sweet lovely person with whom to while away the evening hours.

One day the Old Lady asks the Wolf to stay in the woods, just for a short time. Her granddaughter is visiting and the girl wouldn't understand the nature of their friendship.

The Wolf says sure. That day, the Wolf, now hiding in the forest, positions himself to see the visitor.

Ohmygoodness! When he gets a look at Red Riding Hood his heart stops. He can barely control his sudden and overwhelming love for this girl. He hyperventilates, he sweats, his heart pounds.

Red leaves. The Wolf returns and asks Grandma questions about her, but not too many because the Wolf is no fool. If Grandma ever realized how smitten he was with her granddaughter, she would kick him out.

So now the Wolf has another thing to be grateful for — anticipating Red's next visit.

But gratitude is not what he's feeling. It's more like obsession. When she visits again, he hides and watches. Later, when he returns to the house, Grandma asks him what the matter is. He says he must have come down with something; maybe he caught cold in the woods.

Time goes on and Red visits every few weeks. Grandma starts to notice the Wolf's erratic behavior before and after her visits.

Grandma is worried.

On the most recent visit, she catches the Wolf peeking through the window at Red.

Now Grandma has to do something. The Wolf's behavior is unacceptable. As much as Grandma likes the Wolf, she is now afraid for her granddaughter's safety.

She tells the Wolf he has to go.

Now the Wolf's obsession for Red enters the hot zone. He cannot stand the idea of not seeing her, or the idea that he will be thrown out of his happy home. Obsession turns to something else.

It turns to murder.

The poor Wolf who had everything — a friend, a place to live happily, food on the table, some joy — has been destroyed by his obsession for a girl.

So what do we have here? "Little Red Riding Hood" from the point of view of this disturbed Wolf gives me a greater understanding of the story and its complexities, along with the role of the villain, whose job it is to drive the story toward catastrophe.

My mother planted an idea in my head about the Wolf. I have watched her lesson grow and take shape in my work.

## CHOOSING THE RIGHT MAIN CHARACTER

Over the years, using this story as an example, I started to look at other stories from *all* the characters' points of view. One thing that occurred to me was that I had better pay attention to *the character through whom the story should be told*. Which characters drive the story and which are driven by it?

When I started to write my own stories, I'd stepped back to see the stories from the points of view of all the major characters. Often I realized that the main character I had originally chosen was not the right one after all, but another character, through whose eyes the story became much more interesting.

I sometimes changed genders to see what that would do. As a result I realized that making the main character a female instead of a male created all sorts of story opportunities.

I began to ask myself which character made the greatest change in the story. This character, it turned out, usually had more at stake, more to win and/or lose.

Often the story belongs to another of your characters. Unless you take a good hard look around the cast to see which one is the most compelling, you may never choose the right lead. At the beginning of your story you may have chosen the character you identified with most, rather than the character through whose eyes the more dramatic version of the story should be told. *Give the story to the character that changes the most, who is most affected by the story*.

What if Robert Towne, writer of *Chinatown*, had decided to make this a movie about the incestuous relationship between John Huston and Faye Dunaway, instead of focusing on Jack Nicholson? Believe me, he might have. The Huston/Dunaway subplot is incestuous, dark and daring. In this scenario the Nicholson character might have been just a footnote.

Writers have committed this error in judgment and later wondered why they had to put the brakes on the story because it wasn't going anywhere. Those scripts end up in a drawer somewhere, all because the writer failed to look around the cast to see if a more dynamic character has been hiding.

In the Coen brothers' *The Man Who Wasn't There*, what if the story were taken away from the expressionless Billy Bob Thornton character and given to the actor who walked away with the picture, the high-powered lawyer, played by Tony Shalhoub, who might have fallen into this weird world and changed radically, but didn't? The Coen brothers had their main character, the quiet man with a deeply troubled inner life that crept out at crucial times during the story to shock and surprise.

## DRILL

• Take your story or script and climb behind the eyes of the two or three main characters. See the story as they do. Write it down in one page for each character. Ask these questions:

• Who changes the most?

• How do these changes significantly alter the story from one character to another?

• Once you determine who the main character is, build him into a force of nature that, let's say, Russell Crowe is destined to play. Start thinking like that. Start thinking that Russell Crowe will play this part.

The very idea that you're aiming that high will force you to do nothing les than your A-list work. Russell Crowe would settle for nothing less than A-list work. Picture him, put his image up above your machine. Become obsessed with fashion-ing this character for him. And believe that he is waiting for this masterpiece. You will soon come to believe that this work you're doing is your very best ever, and it is. Suspend your disbelief and the work you produce will outdistance anything you've done before.

> If the main character has a strong goal, then why not his creator, you, the writer? Call it unwavering focus, call it fantasy, call it whatever you wish. Just do it.

## WHAT HAPPENED TO MAIN CHARACTERS OVER THE PAST FIFTY YEARS?

In the past, characters lost their dignity, honor, self-esteem, their homes, and jobs — now they lose their minds.

Consider a handful of movies: a paranoid schizophrenic scientist slipping among a variety of lives (*A Beautiful Mind*); a rather likeable pedophile (*L.I.E.*); in *Deja Vu*, an ATF agent (Denzel Washington) travels back in time to save a woman from being murdered and falls in love with her during the process; in a suburban town full of perfect parents devoted to rearing their children for Harvard futures, a stay-at-home mom has an affair with an ex-jock, stay-at-home dad who rebels against his wife's wishes that he become a big-bucks lawyer (*Little Children*).

There are no *It's a Wonderful Life* Jimmy Stewarts anymore, folks, or angry young men. Gone, all of them. As much as we might have loved being brought up on some of these heroes, they reflected an age that has passed into memory.

Today's heroes are far cries from the muscle bound guys like Stallone or the cyber men like Arnold. Today's heroes are more closely aligned with that golden age of moviemaking, the '70s, in which the anti-heroes played by Dustin Hoffman and Jack Nicholson made their bones. But even they were not nearly as mentally and psychologically challenged as the ones today.

Today's heroes are complex amalgams of tortured, idiosyncratic, demon-pursued, vulnerable, often neurotic, even psychotic, characters — men and women whose inner lives crawl out on the surface for all to see.

As psychology keeps coming up with new exotic disorders (in this age of specialization), this generation of characters with inky pasts, incomprehensible presents, and unimaginable futures emerged. More mysterious, more angst-ridden, they face their psychotic ghosts, debilitating mental disorders and paralyzing fears.

A movie that few saw but which I watched five times was *The Man from Elysian Fields,* in which an unsuccessful writer (John Cusack) needing cash takes a job at an escort service (run by Mick Jagger), without telling his wife (Julianne Margolis). One of his first clients (tricks, in the best sense of the word) is the beautiful young wife (Olivia Williams) of an older, world-class novelist (James Coburn).

This struggling writer steps into a world about which he is clueless, where they play games at which he is like the rankest of amateurs. But this writer is willing to do anything to support his family and what's left of his writing career. And look at what he must do to chase the illusive muse, not to mention the almighty buck. He grovels, he becomes an errand boy, he wonders if he should compromise his marriage for the money he's promised by the wife of this famous writer.

The question behind almost all characters is this: What is the character willing, or forced, to do to get what he or she wants? The answer should be: Anything. The field is open. What is *your* character willing to do? Not you. Your *character*.

As the writer, you have to place your character at that proverbial critical moment, and squeeze. For your character, the farther into the story he travels, the more he realizes there is no retreating. You, the writer, have slammed those old doors shut.

The character of course wants to go back, but in that direction is nothing, less than nothing. Ahead is the way to resolve the problem. Back there is death or, worse, *ennui*. There isn't anything worse than a character saddled with ennui for turning a picture into a dishrag.

Look what happened to *Good Will Hunting*. First the writers, Matt Damon and Ben Affleck, had in mind exactly who they wanted in the roles — themselves. In the beginning, Will is a prisoner of his own fears, hiding in Southie, among his pals, working at a non-descript job, janitor at MIT. He's a mess. He can't go much lower. He's also a genius tormented by his own insecurities. He is his own worst enemy, the evil villain in his own ife.

The writers have choices. The one they choose is to bring Will, yowling and pounding, out of the darkness of his prison into the light of the world. How to do it is the next task.

Gradually, slowly, piece by piece, they set up a series of incidents designed to tug and yank and pull Will out of his cave.

They first assail his genius by tempting his ego. They encouraged him to solve a complex math problem on the MIT blackboard. They didn't turn their character into a janitor at MIT, the top math genius school in the world, for nothing. Will was not a janitor at McDonald's. He didn't want to be *of* the action, but *near* the action.

So now Will is exposed for the genius he is. He tries to retreat. Too late, Will, you've been found out.

But the writers can't let it go at only his genius; they need their character to experience a full frontal attack on all his fears and insecurities.

To get at his heart they created the Minnie Driver character, a lovely, smart, exotic Harvard student, to whom he begins to open up. Will resists her, too, but not for long. He tries to retreat from her but, alas, he is captivated. His heart says, "Give it a shot, stupid."

In fear center number three, the Vesuvius of man's fear centers, his darkest fears reside. In Will's psyche. His emotional past, the agony with which he cloaks himself, this shrouded self.

Enter Robin Williams, shrink, who probes the depths of Will's self-protection mechanism. This mechanism has been in place forever and nobody get past that sentry. Will resists mightily and, as a result, now tries harder than ever to retreat.

In all scripts, it's essential to study how the writers work with their main characters — truly the most important relationship in writing a script. Writers and characters. Creators and creations. If this connection is not solidly established, all else fails.

You might say, "What about Robert Altman? What about *Gosford Park*? What about *Nashville*? What about all those ensemble casts that worked so magnificently?"

My question to the naysayers: Who among you is Robert Altman? At this point in your careers, who among you possesses the genius for making that kind of movie?

For the time being, early on in your career, concentrate on bringing one central character to life. It's difficult enough to create one strong central character per script, much less five. Then cast it with a bankable actor, and write it so well that he or she cannot resist.

Will Hunting's heart, genius, and psyche are being simultaneously assailed by secondary characters who represent the paths by which Will can escape from his prison, if he wishes to.

But like all of us, Will falters. He doesn't want to make the effort, a mighty one to be sure. He wants to go back to Southie and the confines of his little shanty on the sea.

But there, in the personages of his pals, his last refuge, is an answer he doesn't want to hear. Even in the end, the character Ben Affleck plays tells him that he is no longer welcomed there, for his own good. You, his best friend tells him, can offer the world a great deal more than you can give from down here in Southie. Out of love, he tells Will to go.

Go forth, Will, into the world. The paths have been laid, your organs transplanted. By the end of the story, Will Hunting has had the doors to the past sealed by a squadron of people who help him enter the present, providing help for the future. By an act of will, he makes the final decision to move forward. At story's end, when his genius and his psyche have been laid out before him, and his past is not the dark secret that it was in the beginning, he will chase his heart and love will prevail. He will find his girlfriend and begin a life.

Here's where a little character legwork will do wonders.

In her excellent book on character archetypes from mythology, *45 Master Characters*, Mia Schmidt breaks the archetypes into simple categories: male heroes and villains, and female heroes and villains. As Linda Seger, in *Creating Great Characters* did before her, Schmidt provides the tools for thinking about character needs.

## WHAT YOU NEED TO THINK ABOUT WHEN YOU'RE COMING UP WITH YOUR OWN CHARACTERS

In creating any story, there's no easy plan. Nobody's going to hand you the total meal. You've got to cook it up yourself.

Reading produced scripts in your genre is the greatest gift. They'll steer you in the right direction. No matter how many treatments or scripts I read, I always find myself asking the question: What does the character want? To get out of a jam? To save the day? To get the guy, to get rid of the girl? To kill the bastard who murdered her son and ruined their lives?

I read a script yesterday afternoon, about a guy who wins the lottery. It was fuzzy, soft in the middle, discombobulated. Like a drunk on the street, the story kept veering off, stumbling around, loosing its footing, careening towards who knows where.

Why? The main character didn't know what he wanted; neither did he have tools for discovering it. He kept looking for something to do. Meanwhile, all this *stuff* was going on around him. The other characters seemed to know what they wanted, but the main character didn't have a clue.

By this time your story is already deeply into Act II, and moving toward Act III. Your main character doesn't need to have all the answers but at least she has to be going after something that will ease the pain.

She will most likely fail the first few times — part of the process. She'll fail and try another avenue in. At least there's movement.

Your main character, at the most critical moment of his life, needs a way to resolve a problem. She's tried this, she's tried that. She's hit a wall, she's veered off and tries yet another route.

Go back to the Bomb, or Inciting Incident, in the first twelve pages. What's the big event that starts the story rolling? That establishes the problem she will have to confront and resolve by the end?

Take a good hard look at her crisis when the bomb explodes. That moment establishes the problem. This is your starting point, the place that establishes the *spine* of the story. The thing about a spine is that you should never let the story or characters wander very far from it.

## THE BAD GUYS

A few years ago I started a novel based on a guy that terrified me. In truth, I terrified myself out of fear for this guy. He was in charge of the English Department where I taught. When he took over the department the halls cleared out.

While the former chairman ran a smooth ship on which everyone worked as a team, the new guy had his own way of steering the ship — through intimidation. Whereas the former guy said, "Let's all sail together and, as a team, we'll do great things," the new guy divided everyone so that he could conquer.

The new guy, who had a lot of insecurity issues of his own, played Iago. He whispered in the ears of this one and that one, denigrating one faculty member to another. Bitterness and fear roamed the halls. The department became a ghost town.

It was ugly. I loathed him, and feared him. I was afraid of losing my job; in fact, he threatened me with the possibility.

In my novel, he was the same egomaniac with an inferiority complex that he was in real life. He was well educated but frustrated by his inability to get published in any significant way. His insecurity stemmed from a life of unrealized expectations.

The heroine of the book was a woman teacher who came into the department and discovered the chairman's last desperate attempt by plagiarizing a student's work. If he couldn't get his own work published, he would steal a sharp grad student's work and make it his own. The heroine, who has her own issues with male authority figures, discovers this. The chairman is willing to do anything to protect himself; the heroine is determined to uncover the crime. The wrinkle here is that the two of them have begun an affair before all this comes out.

In the real story, after a faculty uprising, the dean removed the chairman and he went back to intimidating his students in the classroom. In my version I made the hell more personal.

The chairman is a manipulative, insecure but powerful villain who would eventually, by story's end, fall prey to his own vulnerability and a strong woman's determination.

I love villains. I love to hate them. The hate feeds into my own insecurities and desire for revenge, all of which I try to hand over to my main character, without making the main character the almighty me. Tricky. I take the essence of my fear and dump it on my character, who has to live a life of his own.

Without a strong villain, the hero or heroine has little to fight against. Conflict wanes and the story goes limp. Without his great villains, James Bond would have been just another fey British government worker who liked his martinis stirred, not shaken. Without Hannibal Lecter, we have no story. Without Glenn Close in *Fatal Attraction,* are we willing to watch Michael Douglas's family life?

## WHAT A VILLAIN DOES

**1.** *Drives the story towards catastrophe.* By the time the hero comes on the scene, the villain usually has something already in place. By the time James Bond got the news from his superior, for months, sometimes years, all those great villains had been planning to take over the world. I used to get irked that all Bond had to do was sashay in, spend a couple of days ruining all that work, sleep with two+ women, and then sashay out. Job well done.

The villain has the plan that the hero is going to screw up.

**2.** *Has all the real fun.* The villain sets the agenda, defines the story, ruins lives, usually acts without strong moral or ethical restraint, has a big plan to do big things, believes that he is destined, in his own way, for greatness — and is loaded with complexity (let's hope). Hannibal Lecter. Freddie Krueger. Jack Torrance (*The Shining*). Bruce the shark (*Jaws*). Darth Vader. Norman Bates (*Psycho*). Tony Montane (*Scarface*).

**3.** *Acts.* This character is driven by God only knows what: obsession, revenge, rage, a sense of his own importance, or the absolute belief that what he or she is doing is noble or right, or to which he is entitled.

One of the things a writer should always do is to establish the villain's motivation for what he or she does. The reader should be able to see clearly that the villain has a plan and a way to carry it out, what in fact may be, on certain levels, a good plan. If the writer makes it clear from the beginning that the villain is pure evil, wrong headed, and stupid the story does not do what it's supposed to — give the main characters complexity and intelligence and logic and not forecast the end.

The more fun (by which I mean creative fun) you have with the villain the better the movie will be. The villain is not reactive, he's proactive.

The hero is reactive until he refuses to be the punching board anymore and becomes proactive.

The villain always acts. He kills, manipulates, drives himself and others crazy, protects what he has worked hard for, and obsessively wants and needs whatever that thing is out there he's chasing after, whether it's world domination, to screw with Clarise Starling's head (*Hannibal*), or to seduce young boys (*L.I.E.*).

In the new Hollywood, more than ever before in the history of film, the villain wrestles with his own character, i.e. the villain and hero are often indistinguishable (think *Fight Club* or *The Usual Suspects*). "I am my own worst enemy" is the message.

If you look at the best of the independent and studio films, you'll see this Janus-faced complexity. In a very good British film, *Croupier*, the main character (powerfully played by Clive Owen) recognizes the "two" of him — Jack, the real day-to-day person, and Jake, the wilder character in the novel he's writing.

In *A Beautiful Mind*, Russell Crowe battles his schizophrenia. He is his own worst enemy; or rather his disease is.

In another powerful import, *Lantana*, the Anthony LaPaglia character is an Australian police detective who is beset by his own crumbling marriage, self-doubt, a murder mystery, and an affair he's having. In these movies, and dozens of others, we are fascinated by the complexity of the main character, who battles against self.

**4.** *Is a slave to the appetite.* Somewhere way back in the quagmire of his dark childhood soul, the Kevin Spacey character in *Se7en* got all tangled up in the deadly sins. He has been preparing forever to carry out his mission: to display to the world the most grotesque examples of what these seven deadly sins are all about. In his twisted mind, he seems to believe that he is doing the world a favor by showing how truly awful a human mind can be.

In his mind, he is on a mission of mercy. His appetite is, as the modern God, for providing absolution through death. He *is* the new God. And so it is his mission, in *Se7en*, to reenact, with a modern spin, those gory details of old.

The Kevin Spacey character believes he is a hero of some rank and, if you think of it from his perspective, he is. He will, by vivid example, show to mankind what one of its own is capable of, with a warning: tread not in my footsteps. In this villain you've got a real sicko with an inky past, a mission with Judeo-Christian roots, and a mind that is thorough, determined, and prepared. Look at what he does to Morgan Freeman and especially to poor Brad Pitt.

The Kevin Spacey character drives this movie. He is the fun one to write, unencumbered as he is by the patina of civilized behavior that governs others.

**5.** *Is smart and vulnerable.* Watch out for the tendency to write your villain as a pure bad guy. Make her smart and vulnerable and give her something to do other than going around slaughtering people.

Here's a tip that might solve a bunch of your problems. Ask yourself the question: what is my villain afraid of? Or: If this guy is so smart, maybe he's too smart for his own good. What's he hiding behind his surface brilliance? Or: what is he most afraid of having revealed? What is he hiding? What is his greatest vulnerability, and how can the hero find it, attack it, and bring the villain down?

We all try to hide our insecurities and vulnerabilities from the public, right? We slide those smarmy things behind our strengths so that others won't know we're, in critical ways, just a sack of quivering flesh.

Your villain became a villain for good reasons. What are they? Why does this character act like such an *awful human being*?

And of course the villain, once he discovers what the hero is trying to do, will try to stop him at all costs — providing more conflict and drama. Once the hero discovers the villains vulnerability is when the building comes crashing down.

Take a movie you like. Read it or watch it. In one page, write down the central conflict between hero and villain and how it plays out. For instance, place the adversaries in Act I and define the nature of their conflict. In Act II watch how it escalates, and in Act III discover how the conflict becomes a fight to the emotional (and sometimes physical) death.

You will be astonished by how much this exercise will help you in the creation of your own story.

This axis or spine, which begins at the Bomb and culminates at the Climax, drives the story. It holds the entire story together. Everything that happens in the story revolves around this spine and defines the chief adversaries. The villain and the hero battle on the spine.

Remember that the villain drives the story toward some awful end. For the villain, the hero is at first a pest, then a deterrent and then a force to be reckoned with. Their conflict becomes a battle of wills, with the end result leaving one of them standing.

If you pay attention to the idea that this is the most critical moment in *both* the hero and villain's lives, your story will bubble with conflict and tension. Ready made for the A-list.

## DRILL

Ask yourself: What are my villain's motives? Why does she do these things? Out of what emotional, psychological, or sociopathic/psychopathic well does this character drink? Usually the villain thinks he's the hero; does yours? At some point this character believes, through self-justification or self-delusion, that he's on the right course. Does yours?

# WORKSHOP

## YOU LIKED WHAT?!

At the beginning of every semester, I ask my class, "Seen any bad movies lately?" Hands shoot up. "*The Wicker Man.*" Neil LaBute as hilariously bad? "*Pirates of the Caribbean: Dead Man's Chest*" Another brainless Disney sequel. *RV! My Super Ex-Girlfriend. Bobby. Man of the Year. All the King's Men.*

Other reasons for loathing these dogs: Predictability. Stupidity. Pandering to the audience's lowest common denominator. Ridiculous dialogue. No story. Unbelievable. Logic holes entire conveys of trucks could roll through. Insipid. Confusing. *What* plot? Derivative. Self-conscious. Precious. Too slow. Too long. Too loud. No depth. Dumb!

On and on they go about all the things wrong with movies. When you plunk down twenty bucks for two tickets, another twenty for popcorn, drinks, etc., for that much you expect your money's worth. *Something.*

Whose fault is it? The studios that pump up their trailers by gathering all the wicked glances and car chases and hot music to tease you and seduce you into spending that forty bucks, only to have you discover that the trailer *is* the movie?

Or is it the producers and studio execs who, by trying to keep their jobs, aim for that lowest common denominator: mediocre, supposedly inoffensive crap over which focus groups have the final say.

Or what about the director who is under the studio's financial gun? After fighting for months over "creative differences" with actors and producers, he has given up and let them have their way. The director wants to work again and does not want that kiss-of-death "too difficult" rep shadowing him or her around town.

Take *War of the Worlds* and *Daredevil,* mediocre action movies at best: they were dull, illogical, predictable but one starred Cruise and the other had a relatively popular action hero. Why did Warner Brothers choose workman-like director Chris Columbus (*Home Alone, Mrs. Doubtfire*) to direct the first Harry Potter when they could have had a visionary like Tim Burton or Spike Jonze? They had a guaranteed $250 million domestic box office, giant foreign sales and a forever video life. A squirrel could have directed it and the fans would have come.

Blame has been put on J. K. Rowling, the author, who, they say, had control over director and cast. Or did Warner Bros., who has all seven Potter movies in the works, not want to depart from the book, disappointing the fans and killing the franchise?

Chris Columbus's *Harry Potter* is like the fancy bistro that spends all its money on decor and none on the chef, serving a flat, insubstantial meal. Those restaurants go under. Fast. Franchise or no franchise. It was by no means a bad movie but a safe movie. It had a conventional feel that, in other hands, might have soared as Harry does.

Why *are* bad movies made? Some are made to satisfy the fiscal budget. On the studio docket are four or five films with similar budgets, any one of which can be made so that the studio will not have next year's budget cut back by its parent company.

Sometimes producers, directors, and studio people get so caught up in that insulated world of movie and money making that they can't see (or don't want to see) the piece of junk unspooling before them.

Take *Vanilla Sky*, for instance. It's an ill-conceived piece of highfalutin' extract that made little sense. But Tom Cruise starred and, after many false starts, Cameron Crowe came aboard. This is an element picture (the elements, like Cruise and Cruz, were attached) originally shot as a Spanish picture, a story about an egomaniacal, narcissistic rich guy who has acrophobia and a rich daddy who left him control of a publishing empire. By the end of the picture the Cruise character's ego is intact. He'd been living a nightmare contrived by a cryogenic company. He throws himself off a building to cure his fear of heights. And his message is — don't dream when you can live life without worrying about not looking handsome. Huh? In the theater where I saw it, half the audience left during the first thirty minutes.

As somebody put it, did Tom Cruise need to make a $60 million movie to tell the world that he's losing his looks?

Somebody at the studio level championed it and developed it — to the tune of millions. The studio was in so deep that it needed to make the movie. They had guaranteed deals with talent. They couldn't afford *not* to make it.

When all is said and done, this, and many other marginal films like it, should never have been made. Writers hit a concept, agents get on the bandwagon. Stars, directors, and producers get lathered up. Even with a fundamentally weak concept, everybody can buffalo the studio into ponying up millions on a dumb idea.

Business as usual. The concept got the ball rolling so fast that the deal outpaced it and became the only thing that mattered. As George Lucas once put it, "In Hollywood, they don't make movies, they make deals."

Now everybody has to pay, starting with the writer, without whose idea this could never have happened. But the writer got paid, and got paid more, at this stage, than anyone else. The writer always gets paid, whether the movie is made or not. The big pay-off is if the movie goes before the cameras, but the writer always gets something up front.

In this, the most collaborative of businesses, everyone stands on the sidelines as a project moves toward fruition. If the movie is made, or is in production, and looks as if it will tank, people all over town disassociate themselves, disavowing this or that, pointing fingers. If, on the other hand, that smell of success wafts in, you can't beat the people back who are jumping in to take responsibility.

Business as usual.

It's like the caddy and the golf pro. When the pro hits a lousy shot, the caddy said, "You blew it." When the pro hits one close to the stick, the caddy, head perked up, says, "We nailed that one, didn't we?"

So, have you see any bad movies lately?

In movies, everybody is a critic. All the good reasons you use to criticize a movie should also be applied to your own work. I like Oscar Wilde's take on a critic: "A critic is the one who after the battle is over goes around shooting the wounded."

I always point out to my students that the movies they criticize are movies they have chosen to watch in the first place. For whatever reason, they have gone to the theater and plunked down ten bucks. Was there something about the concept of the picture, or love of the star, that compelled them to spend two hours of their time?

Pay attention to the reasons why you see certain movies and avoid others. In that choice lies the subject matter or genre of the kind of movies you should, or should not, be writing.

## DRILL

Make a list of the last ten movies you have gone to see. Think about them. You will notice patterns forming. Types of pictures emerge — thrillers, romantic comedies, outright comedies, and oddball independents.

From these insights you will discover other things about

the nature of your likes and dislikes. If you had a choice for tonight, would you rather see *Fight Club* or *The 40 Year Old Virgin*? Why?

By answering this question candidly, you're drawing closer to the genre. You have an affinity for this type of movie. You instinctively know what the mechanics are.

You know you can do better than this, you say, and you're probably right. You know this genre, you know this type of movie because you've seen a million of them. When you hear about this type of movie opening something in you goes "ka-wang!", telling you that you will see this as soon as it comes out.

What *is* that "ka-wang!"? It's a tip-off to the kind of movie you love, a genre you should be exploring in your writing, the type of movie you want to master.

## DRILL

Make a list of movies that gave you your own "ka-wang!". Those movies you tracked for months waiting for them to come out. What was behind the "ka-wang!"? What was that itch to see it all about? If you can make a short list of those movies of the past and the ones you're now looking forward to seeing, you'll be a long way toward discovering what kind of movie you should be writing.

## GOING AROUND THE ROOM

There's nothing quite so revealing as first-day students in the room talking among themselves, opening themselves up to total strangers. Call it lower-level group therapy.

It's the first step in the writing process: letting things out of the bag, by speaking your mind and revealing what you feel.

It's not easy. Not many of us like to open up to strangers. But that's what writing is. Just because a page and a piece of celluloid and many miles separate the writer from the eventual moviegoer, it's what the writer puts on the page that reveals the source.

If you back off, or hedge, or try to cover up true feelings, people will not want to read your work. They will pull away after a few insubstantial pages.

I used to worry what people would think of me if they read my stuff, and so I would only deliver emotional half-truths. I paid the price by eliciting their vast disinterest in reading on.

If you're guarded in the first place, as we all often are, the process will take time. One way to do this in writing is to climb out of yourself and give the story over to your characters.

In week one, I ask the students four questions:

**1. Where are you from?**

**2. Why are you interested in writing in this strange form, screen-writing, when most of you have never even read a screenplay?**

**3. What is the movie that influenced you the most?**

**4. Tell us about your Darkest Childhood Memory.**

Questions 3 and 4 I'll cover at length in Workshop Three.

I answer these questions first — sometimes right up front to let everybody know that in this class very little is taboo.

These questions all have to do with *back story*. With influences. The reasons behind what brought the students here in the first place. The questions can be intimidating. They're meant to be.

They all address character. Your characters will have a life before we meet them on the page. They have pasts and influences and dark childhood memories, just as we all do.

The answers to these questions will fuel you through the writing process. They compel you to recreate your past, to discover the movies that formed you, reveal the type of movie you now want to write (the source of your creative urges), and reveal the dark childhood moments that struck at or formed your fears.

Character. If you can ask hard questions about yourself, you will get closer to the crux of your characters. That's not to say that just because you're writing a screenplay about others that you have lay your own feeling all over that character, no. It means that if you dig a tunnel into your own psyche, you'll have an easier time burrowing into other characters.

By continuing to ask yourself these questions you will find paths to the fears, needs, and motivations of your character. You will be able to tap inner resources leading to problem solving of character and story. The answer will reveal to you the writer and creator within, the reasons behind your decisions and the mistakes that may have plagued you in the past.

# DRILL

Get on the computer and type in the first two questions.

**1. Where are you from?**

**2. Why are you interested in writing in this strange form, screenwriting, when most of you have never even read a screenplay?**

Think about them. The students in class don't have your advantage, if you can call it that. They have to blurt out their answers in front of strangers.

When you answer the questions, be utterly honest. Forget about wonderful style or complete sentences. Just do it, from the heart or the soul or the gut. Let it spill or pour out of you. This pouring or spilling is the best way to get unstuck in writing.

## 1. Where are you from?

This goes to the core of how you define yourself and implies so much more than the question suggests. Your answer *is* the essence of you and determines all the choices you make. This *is* autobiography; be honest about it. *Where are you from?* addresses the heart of character, yours and that of the character you're writing.

In class I ask everyone to close his or her eyes and verbally ask the question, and visually see the answer. That won't work here on the page. I'll ask you to do this another way.

Sit in front of your computer and type in the answers or if you hunt and peck after each question close your eyes and *see, then write.* Then go on to the next more specific question.

Where were you born? See the house, the apartment. Rural or suburban or urban? Parents? See them. Both there? What did they do during the day?

With whom did you get along better? Worse? How did this affect your relationship with men? Women? Which parent did you trust more? Did they get along? Did they not? Why? Did you have only one parent? Did they divorce? Ugly? Loving? Was it filled with silent anger? Recreate a moment from their relationship that defines how they treated one another. Go ahead. Visualize it. Write it down.

How does their relationship affect your relationships today? Are you argumentative? Are you easy going? Do you appear placid but underneath are you filled with resentment or rage?

You're going to have to know these things about your main character, this creature that the bankable actor will make his or her own. You may as well use yourself as the template.

Did your family struggle financially? How emotional were the economics? Tight-fisted? Free spending? What are you now? How do you see money now? Do you see yourself as frugal, or not? Do you always worry about money? How do others see you?

Are you an only child? Oldest? Youngest? Were great expectations foisted upon you? Have you met them? Were you ignored?

*At five, my best friend, my grandfather, died. Vanished, disappeared, abandoned me. I blocked out the next eight years, until I was thirteen. Through therapy and self-exploration, I am still trying to sort out.*

Who was the most influential person of your (substitute the "your" for the character's) childhood, negatively *and* positively? Who did you love and trust? Who did you fear? See that person. Paint a mental picture. Or if you can draw, draw it. Or tear out of a magazine a photo of an actor or any person that you think looks like this character.

Write down the description of this person who influenced you the most, positively and negatively. Both of them. Fear drives us. How has that relationship affected your life up until now and the life of your character?

*There was this guy in my family. He terrified me. He drank and he fought and he was a giant. I loved him and feared him. I never knew where he was coming from. I blocked out almost all of him but I remember the feeling. He had a name. Dad.*

This is autobiography. It's a prelude to creating vivid characters. If you are able to be utterly honest about your own past your chances of driving to the center of your characters are that much better.

In school were you a leader or follower? Did you have friends, or were you mainly a loner? How so? How has this affected your later life? Close your eyes. Remember. Are you alone now? Are you comfortable alone?

*I have a friend who, before he goes to bed at night, offers to pay people to stay in the house so that he can go to sleep. He can't stand to be alone, especially with himself.*

As a kid, were you a good student? Were you loved for it? Who was your best friend? Close your eyes. See her or him. What did you admire or like about this person? What did you not like about him or her?

As a child, what was the worst thing you did? The worst! The thing you are most ashamed of. Be honest. Write it down.

Now you're around twelve. You're leaving grade school and moving up into another world. Middle school. Puberty enters. What about those hormones and sexual urges? Close your eyes. How did you handle that? Were you afraid of those urges, or excited by them? How are you now? What is sex to you? Glorious? Fearsome? Are you gay? Straight? Bi?

*I ate a lot. I gained lots of weight. I was a very fat kid, ashamed of my fat. I wore big cardigan sweaters to hide my fat. I was a fat, depressed kid who spent most of his time alone. I wanted desperately to belong. I didn't even have my first kiss until I was sixteen, and I kissed the girl-friend of the football team's star fullback — which ushered me into a world of hell.*

When was your first sexual experience? How was it? With whom? How did you feel about it? What did you think about sex? What do you think about it now? Close your eyes. Think. See. Are you awkward? Experimental. Do you make love in the dark, in the same position?

*As a Catholic, I was brought up on a healthy does of shame. Catholics have shame. Jew have guilt. What do you have? I have lost religion, and lost my virginity to a prostitute in a Columbia, S.C., hotel room, at eighteen. I was drunk and though I don't remember many of the details, I know I had a fairly decent time.*

Close your eyes. When did it happen for you? How did you feel? You should know this experience with your main character. In order to know your characters on the page, in your present story, you have to know what drives them, where the urges began. You cannot know them now without knowing them then. If you don't know what happened to your main characters before we meet them on the first page of the script, you won't know them, and the script will show that.

You're in high school. Close your eyes. Where is that place? Paint a picture. Were you popular? Shunned? Ridiculed? Who were your friends? Close your eyes. See them. Why did you hang around with them?

*There was Belinda, a beautiful girl who lived across the street. The first love of my life. Long, dark hair, dark eyes, she was the daughter of the woman I think my father loved. I was always jealous of the handsome twins Linda said she adored. Back and forth she went between them. She told me I was always steady, at number three.*

*There was Jenna, my true pal, who I told everything to, no secrets. Total trust. Jenna was, as have other women like her throughout my life, my best friend. Having been brought up by women, I trust women more than I do men, get along with women better, and think, on the scale, women are far more wide ranging than men are.*

Do you read? Are you a video freak? What do you do when you're alone? What are your secrets? Name two. See them. See yourself doing them. Close your eyes. Write them down.

Your characters will close their eyes and think of you. Think of them. They have secrets that will invariably be revealed during the course of the story. See these things and write them down. Not what *you* did for the first twenty-five years of your life, what *they* did. Know thyself, know thy characters.

A fatal error writers commit during the course of writing a screenplay is in asking what they, the writers, would do under this or that given set of circumstances. Never ask what you would do, but what your characters would do. By asking yourself what *you* would do gives you the license to write a flat screenplay where every character thinks and speaks the same. Huge mistake.

Considering the nature of the story you want to tell, and the role your main character will play in it, you can begin to create a life for the character. This life before we meet him or her on the page. Of course this is a long-term process, extending through the first and subsequent drafts.

The key is to write that first draft and all subsequent drafts with the idea in mind that your main character is your horse. It's his or her story and must grab focus from the beginning and never let go. The story life is dependent upon your main character's rising and falling dramatic action.

If you get that character right, the rest will fall into place. You will automatically, let's hope, want to bring the other characters up to the standard you have set for your horse.

At every scene, stop and ask the question: what would my main character do under this given set of circumstances? Ask the question and answer it before you go on. At the next situation your characters finds herself in, ask the question and answer it before you move on. *What would she do under this set of circumstances?*

Readers don't care what you the writer would do. We all care, however, what your characters would do, and why. Characters are the masters of the story. You are their servant.

If you can run through the script and answer that question for your main character and other principal characters, whether it's the final answer or not, by the end of the first draft you will be well into crafting a first-rate script. You will know your characters.

**Understand what the writer did here and you'll be a lot closer to understand the concept of building a character from within your own memory arsenal.**

*Where are you from?* means a lot more than place.

One of my students, Ted C., whose father was a dentist, wrote about a crazy dentist who did too much of his own nitrous oxide and lured young patients into his office for sex, thereby destroying his family and ruining his relationship with his son, who had looked up to his father. His world shattered. He lost trust in the man he trusted most. Gradually his trust in others waned. He grew suspicious. His life became a series of endless, unsatisfying encounters, trying to believe if what the man or woman sitting across the table, the bed, or the boardroom could be trusted, ever.

Ted's script is odd, quirky, very funny, with a strong family dynamic — a dark comedy pulled from the annals of Ted's life. It turned out that Ted wrote the script for other reasons. His father *was* remote and stayed to himself most of the time, in his office, which was in the house. Ted carried a big resentment against his dad, who cared little for his family and eventually ran away with one of his patients.

Ted the writer not only has an attention-grabbing world from which to draw, he also has an emotional attitude toward it, which compels him to keep writing. He wrote a lot of the script, he told me, out of anger against and resentment of his father. He took his own experience and ran it through his own emotional filter before taking what he need and creating a fictional character.

Ted's emotions were real. His character is fictional. Yet he gave to the fictional character whatever he needed of himself to become real enough *and* he borrowed from may other sources to fill in the blanks.

On paper it seems simple. In the execution I think its critical to keep telling yourself that the character you're creating is fictional. You divorce him from yourself and you let him live his own world, to do what he will.

He was attached to the story, invested in it. He knew the world well, and he was pissed at Pop. All of these contributed to the writing of an emotionally riveting script.

Ted had had the inclination to write this story in some form, but didn't know how. In class he discovered structure, dramatic build, character development, etc. In six months he had a workable first draft.

Ted went back into his childhood to rediscover feelings for his father and mother, the memories of solitude and loneliness, and the startling conclusions he came to about his father. He spent a number of weeks before he felt equipped to write, before he felt comfortable enough to sort out the painful moments and fashion them into a story worthy of a screenplay.

He got honest with himself, wrote down what he had imagined and told friends and compared these to what he remembered as having really happened, the shame and the resentments he could not bear to tell anyone.

With a screenplay he had found a vehicle he could use to reveal the truth. He created a character — the young man — with whom he could identify even though the young man was more or less himself. Plus he had a purpose — to write and perhaps find a profession. This made the experience more palatable, more purposeful.

In the end, he acknowledged that writing a screenplay was like therapy. He realized things about his father and himself that he might not have discovered otherwise.

Ted was also able to write the villain by taking the story and looking at it through the family members' eyes. By writing down in a couple of pages each character's point of view toward the story of the father's betrayal of trust, Ted was able to get a balanced look. The daughter saw the father as having been seized by an obsession, victimized by it. The mother resented him for his vile behavior and blamed herself for not having been canny enough to have caught it. The son — Ted — initially went into shock over the betrayal. No anger, at first, no blame, just shock. He felt numb. His world had come undone, never to return to the innocent days of youthful trust. He wondered briefly if he should turn his father in. Eventually someone brought charges, but, by that time, Ted's father had run off with the patient.

Merilee L., twenty-five, is tall, thin, and from Oregon. Her black hair has the texture of velvet seaweed rolling in off the Pacific. Merri is mellow on the outside and fiercely emotional on the inside.

When her grandmother died, she nearly lost her mind. She was the only person who meant anything to her. The grandmother's wish was to have her ashes tossed into a lake in Missouri, where she was born.

And so Merilee, who was also born near that lake, got in her car, in Oregon, and headed back to Missouri with a canister filled with her grandmother's ashes. This journey, which started in sorrow, proved to be the most extraordinary one Merilee had ever taken — one worthy of a screenplay.

## THE WORDS GET IN THE WAY

Merilee's journey is based on truth. For the screenplay, she took the events of the journey, shaved away what she didn't need (the exact biographical details), kept the stuff she did (the emotion and psychology). As any biographer would do, she strung the events together, the dramatic highs and lows, sometimes fiddling with chronology, and turned them into a picaresque story of a young woman and a promise she made to herself and to her grandmother, battling fear and mustering courage along the way.

She discovered her character's fear center, and, at critical moments, threw obstacles or hurdles in her path. In other words, she began to adapt her own journey into that of a fictional main character — which allowed her to depart from the truth and find what she needed in order to tell the story well.

She did this in order for her character to *earn* what she got in the end. Merilee selected obstacles emblematic of her characters' fears. For instance, she created a male love interest that her character had often sought out and was always disappointed by, one of those habitual lovers about whom the only thing that ever changes is his name. But this lover Merilee created was a monster in a business suit, older, sophisticated, an authority figure, which associated directly to Merilee's father whom she had always tried, and failed, to please.

For her character to successfully complete this journey, Merilee felt that this pattern had to be broken. The only way she felt she could address this was to make the character so powerful that it would take an extraordinary act of courage on her character's part to break the pattern and free herself.

But something like that can't be broken unless the emblem (the man) pierces her armor so profoundly that the character has to face this fear in order to break it. What better than a sly, sociopathic love interest who leads her down a path at whose end is her destruction.

In order for her to succeed story-wise, Merilee had to select only those details necessary to give her character the challenge of her life.

The process of selecting what's worthy and unworthy is crucial. The shaving away of the superfluous details and retention of the substantive details is critical to story building. On Merilee's journey, she encountered people, places and things that got in the way of her mission, big time. These made her stronger. They scared her. She wanted to turn and run, but in the end, these hurdles gave her courage and changed her life. She started out to deliver on a promise and discovered instead something she had never expected — herself.

Merilee came from Oregon, but mainly she came from emotion, drive, and need. She had a story to tell that changed her, but only after going through trials by fire, physically and emotionally. As a writer she did not rivet herself to the details of the story, but remained true to the *essence* of them. She paid attention to that old adage — don't let the facts get in the way of a good story.

Her story, in reality, is an adaptation. She adapted to the screen a moment in her life, weeding out the dull and inserting the dramatic and the conflicted. She didn't have to go to unfamiliar territory, to write about characters she knew nothing about. She told the story of a time in her life that mattered so critically that without it the story would not have been worth telling.

In the process of going back and then writing their screenplays, both Ted and Merilee understood what character is and how character becomes motivated, and how fear is the driver in life and in screenplays.

The questions they put to themselves they also put to their main characters — protagonists and antagonists alike.

When you track back through your own life — as you have done, and will do, using the question, *Where are you from?*, you should be able to discover volumes of fresh storytelling material. All you have to do is stay tuned.

You don't have to cast yourself as the main character. If you do you could run into a popular problem — you will tend not to be as honest as you would be with a character *not* based on yourself.

Ted and Merilee got stuck. To unstick themselves, they found photos of people they imagined their characters resembled. This enabled them to wean themselves away from their characters, and to create something fresh.

You've met people who have gone through critical moments in their own lives that far out-dramatize anything you've seen on the screen. It's a matter of seeing life's turning points, recognizing their story potential.

As you go back, keep a lookout for stories you've heard, people you've met, relatives that have gone through hell, that make good drama, and that have stayed with you.

Writers work out of their own experiences. It's a matter of seeing. The person who carries a camera with her will see photo ops she would never see if she left the camera home. Take your sense of story with you. Above all, look for big emotional bombs and their big dramatic results.

*Where are you from?* means to a writer: How do I build a past for my main characters?

**2. What made you decide to try this strange form, screenwriting, when you've probably never read a screenplay?**

This question nets a wide variety of answers. "*I needed one more class to graduate and thought I'd take a look at screenwriting, but I've got two backups in case I don't like it.*" I love the honesty.

*"I'm crazy about movies. That's what I do when I'm not doing anything else. And I'm hardly ever doing anything else."* I've had students who have seen just about every movie ever made. With this group of people, who must have spent 40% of their lives watching movies, they are living, breathing human resources in class. They know plots, characters, and truckloads of arcane information.

One thing about teaching screenwriting that you never get with the novel or short story is total context, a complete frame of reference. You mention a movie title in class and everybody has seen it or knows something about it. Everybody can give you plot details or dish dirt on cast members. The frame of reference is immediate and massive.

For people to attempt a novel is like facing a mountain they do not want to climb. Short stories are satisfying but can you make a living writing short stories? Or poetry? Everybody should read poetry, wherein lives the soul of our language.

Screenwriting is the new manna from heaven. One hundred and seven pages. Do-able. If you write three pages a day for forty days you have a first draft. This is attractive to people that have wanted to tell a story but couldn't find the medium with which to tell it. Screenwriting is all about character and action. Character *is* action. In movies, what one does is what one is. In writing movies you can't see thought but you can see the manifestation of thought through action.

For instance, in *A Beautiful Mind*, instead of trying to gauge John Nash's imaginary world through voice over and having others explain his problem, we understand, in one shocking scene, that an entire part of his life that we think is real (as he did) is not.

In this way, screenplays differ from the novel, short story, and poetry: If you can't see it, it doesn't belong on the page. Action replaces thought, dialogue replaces thought. Screenwriting takes place first and foremost in a visible and visual world.

Watching a movie is a passive experience. Reading, on the other hand, is active. The reader controls the environment, can pick up and put down the book at will. In a theater, there is not this option. What does this say about the different audiences? Books take time to read. Watching a movie takes one hundred minutes.

For me, books are lifeblood. They belong to you. In a book, *you* set the pace. Why would you want to write for the movies? After you finish your masterpiece and hand it in, all they want to do is change it.

Let's say your script garners interest from agents and managers and producers, stars and directors, and looks as if it's got a shot at the big screen. The first thing they do is fire you and hand your baby to fifty foster parents, all of whom are convinced they have striking ideas on how to improve it.

Then, let's say it's produced. It comes out in a totally different medium. You write it on paper and it appears on celluloid or it's digitized. The story has changed shape, and look what they did to your characters! And what about that great dark ending you put on it, which is now light and airy and everybody gets what they want? You want to kill yourself. Is this the writing life you want?

They say that in the New York publishing world the writer is king. In Hollywood, he's jester.

And then, the final insult: It might not even have your name on it because the first thing they did when they fired you was to hire another writer, then another, then four others, none of whom you've ever met. The actors and producers and directors added their changes to it, without consulting you. The Writers Guild's arbitration board gathered all drafts and awarded credit to another writer, someone you have never met nor perhaps even heard of.

But, hey, you have a picture on, sort of, and people are willing to meet you, to hear your new ideas, and pitches. All so that you can go through that awful process again. Come *on*! What are you, a masochist?

Why would you want to work in a medium whose writers Louis B. Mayer once called "Schmucks with Underwoods" (a derogatory smear against ancient typewriters), a perception that has changed little in the last fifty years?

Ah, because you want to write. You need to write. And you love movies. And this is *your* manna from heaven. You're determined, huh? You have a story burning in you, fifty stories burning in you, and you need to let them out of their cages. Writing movies is the only way you can do it. This is the only way you think you'll be *able* to do it.

Okay, if that's what you want, give it a shot. You already connect with movies in ways you have never connected with books or short stories or poetry. Digitized or celluloid veins snake through your body. Your blood runs in frames per second. Your eyes are projectors.

It's your manna, your heaven.

A reminder: the writer always gets paid. If your picture is made you get to visit offices of agents and production companies that might have been denied to you. You get to work and hobnob with talented, gainfully employed movie people. You get to pitch treatments, scripts and ideas that prior to this nobody wanted to listen to.

## DRILL

There is something you love about movies and something else that makes you want to write them. If you're going to write, what is it about movies (as opposed to books or short stories, etc.) that give you this urge to scribble in this form? It may seem obvious to you, but a reality check is always a good idea. Write down five to ten reasons why this form is the most attractive to you. What can you say or do in the script that you can't get across in any other form?

# WORKSHOP 3

# THE MOVIE THAT INFLUENCED YOU THE MOST

**W**hat's the movie that influenced you the most? Not the one you liked the best, or loved the least. But the one that *affected* you like no other.

*Citizen Kane? The Godfather? Miller's Crossing? Lawrence of Arabia? Goonies?* You never know how a particular movie is going to grab you.

Here's Scott Sand, a student from Pittsburgh, who is writing a character-driven movie about male bonding, revenge, and betrayal: "*Miller's Crossing* moved me with its loneliness, with the overwhelming sense of being alone in the world, enacted through heartbreaking betrayals and reversals. Eddie Reagan (Gabriel Byrne) doesn't fit in. He is loyal to his boss but is secretly dating his girlfriend. In the end Eddie betrays his boss to save his friend, Bernie, who later betrays Eddie.

"I have always put loyalty above obligation, and sometimes it's hard, so I responded to this. It's not a caper movie but a character story; the complexity is in the hard decisions the characters are forced to make.

"For my computer desktop I've chosen the image of Bernie pleading to Eddie for his life, trying to convince him that they are different from the people they work for. But they're trapped, too, by the things they do.

"It's sad, dark and lonely. For me the image of that hat blowing through the woods sums up the picture. And the line: 'There's nothing sadder than a man chasing after his hat.'"

Here's Allison Elliot, a student who writes about herself in the third person: "Allison Elliot was born prematurely in Rochester, New York, April 10, 1978. The jaundiced infant was placed in an incubator and stored in a room away from the other babies for being yellow and strange looking. This pattern would repeat itself in various guises for the rest of her life."

Here's what Allison says about the movie that most affected her: "When I was ten or eleven, I saw *Amadeus*. My intense reaction focused on the character of Salieri, the court musician, and his complicated feelings for Mozart.

"He befriends Mozart and proceeds over time to destroy him. In so doing, the calculating and vicious Salieri engineers his own demise. As much as I marveled at how low he could sink, I could not get rid of strong feelings of sympathy for him.

"The tragedy of Salieri's life was this: God gave him the desire to be a great composer but not the ability. Salieri had been living under the impression that he was a success. He had royal commissions and the love of his audience and critics. He was upright and religious and he devoted his music to God. All of this came crashing down when he meets Wolfgang Amadeus Mozart.

"When he hears Mozart's music, Salieri recognizes his own inadequacy. He comes face to face with true genius and knows he is incapable of such beauty. This might have been bearable if Mozart were a great man. Instead, he's a silly, immature, whiny over sensitive libertine.

"For me the movie abolishes every notion about justice and fairness. *Amadeus* is about the mystery of genius and the mystery of hate and, following that line, the mystery of God. No matter how much one tries to criticize or explain away Salieri's behavior, you can't get past the feeling that he's been wronged.

"Salieri can no longer make sense of his own life and neither can the audience. The idea that the bestowal of genius or talent is as random and undeserved as the bestowal of, say, Down's Syndrome, is a hard pill to swallow at any age. Salieri chokes on it and the result thrilled and terrified me."

Will Oakley, a tall, gangly grad student from Alabama, had this story to tell about how *Pee-Wee's Greatest Adventure* changed his life: "It was the funniest movie my six-year-old eyes had ever beheld. At a Chinese restaurant afterwards, while my mother and sister ate Mongolian beef, I performed Pee-Wee's greatest scenes.

"That fall I returned to school. I hated it there. I was no good at sports. In Alabama, if you're no good at sports, all you're good for is getting your ass kicked.

"One day the teacher was called out of the room, and the class bully started making his rounds, pounding us athletically challenged kids. When he came to me and was about to sock me one, for some reason I let out Pee Wee's weak, apprehensive high-pitched laugh.

"In that moment everything changed. The bully said, 'Do that again.' I did. The class went into hysterics. When the teacher came in she found me reciting the line from the movie: 'I know you are, but what am I?'

"I got my name on the Frowning Face list that day, but I didn't care. The other students liked me. I started checking out joke books from the library and using my allowance on whoopee cushions and peanut brittle cans filled with spring snakes.

"I stayed up late watching Johnny Carson's monologue and next day did his jokes in class. Humor became my shield, how I made it day to day in the vicious world of the Alabama educational system.

"I was one of only two boys in the school that didn't play football, but I was allowed to live a wedgie-free life. The other boy, a Trekkie, disappeared a month later."

The question I put to these students — what's the movie that influenced you the most? — goes the heart of your creative and emotional impulses. You will probably key in on the genre you should be in. In Will's case, a kind of David vs. Goliath comedy.

The next question to ask yourself: What kind of movie should I be writing?

Some people answer, "Oh, I like all types of movies. I'm not particular." That answer inevitably leads to the writer running through a bunch of story lines, crisscrossing genres, unable to make up his or her mind, and finally meeting that Big Wall: Utter Frustration.

What kinds of movies make you shudder with anticipation? Todd Solenz's weird journeys into family discombobulation? Arnold's action extravaganzas? The Coen brothers studies in how a simple frustration can turn into a bizarre, out of control disaster? The Farrelly Brothers? (What's *with* all these brother teams?) Is it the tone that moves you? The off-beat story lines? The schlubby main character whose desire for a simple sliver, just a sliver of respect, ends with a body coughed out of a wood chipper.

What *is* it about that tingle that says: "I can't *wait* to see this movie!" Familiarity and great expectation joining forces? A signal that this is the seat where, if you had the choice, you'd like to park yourself to watch movies of this kind and no other?

What a tip-off! There's none stronger! That's the genre you should be writing in.

And while you're thinking about that, I'll tell you about an experience I had, which in my creative life could have been the worst thing that ever happened to me, and was for a while. It could have stopped my writing career dead, and almost did.

During my first year or so in the writing business, I had finished a novel and was scouting around for another idea. My William Morris agent and I were sitting in his office in New York one day when he said to me, "I have the next book you're going to write."

"You do?"

"It's about the fur industry," he announced.

"The fur industry?" I said. A bell went off; one of those dull bells that indicates minimal interest. As in making love in front of a fireplace, on a pile of mink coats? That kind of fur story?

"The time is 1600," he says. "We're in Canada, in Thunder Bay. Fur trappers send their pelts down river to St. Louis, where they're bought by traders, who sell them to manufacturers, to rich consumers, who wear these magnificent, elegant warm coats. John Jacob Astor made his fortune in the fur business, along with a thousand other hungry capitalists. The history of America is the history of the fur business, in every aspect. Struggle, opening of the West, glamour, politics, billions of dollars, from dreary Minnesota woods to the great salons in every major city of the world.

"You follow a couple of families over a four-hundred-year period, using the fur business as a metaphor for American commerce linked to family fortunes rising and changing with the times.

"Take these two families, always at war with one another, through the centuries. Take them to St. Louis, gateway to the West. Take them to Russia and the pricey mink pelts, to murder and mayhem engineered by those willing to do anything to embrace this furry goddess."

*Furry Goddess*, I'm thinking.

"To the ultra-glamorous fur salons of Europe and South Africa, the rise of the Communist party, the beginnings of the American mobster. Glamorous on the outside, exploitative and murderous below."

I'm now on the edge of the seat, watching my agent spin this yarn of epic proportions.

"You take us to the grand international salons. You take us through the sweatshops, through the Communist party scandals of the twenties and thirties, through HUAC and Congressional subcommittees. You lead us into the multi-billion-dollar stolen pelt business, to the veldt of South African exotic hides. And through the war against fur, the animal rights groups.

"You've got the whole world to tell your story, but specifically through the multi-billion-per-year fur industry for which thousands of people have given their lives, and from which others have made their fortunes, seen through the eyes of two warring families."

"Okay," I'm saying, my head bobbing up and down.

"And I even have your title," the agent said. "Call it *Mink!*"

Oh my God. I was breathless, flabbergasted at the immensity of it all. But I could see it; a big, rambling epic moving across time, driven by destiny. The history of the world through animal pelts. *Mink!*

So I gathered up my ambition and wits and spent the next four years, off and on, in library stacks, interviewing furriers, charting family ancestries, planning big moments over time, finding anchors or turning points by which to tell the story, jumping ahead sometimes seventy-five years at a clip.

I talked about it to friends. In my mind I made this more than epic. But the truth was, as I realized soon enough, I was failing. I knew it but I didn't stop, or step back, to take a look. I was determined to see it through, no matter what. But deep down, I was panicking.

I had mountains of research; I devoted an entire room in my apartment to this monster. I filed and arranged, refiled and rearranged. I had note cards about note cards. Red, yellow, orange, white.

I built a giant corkboard against one wall to see what I had. What I had was overpowering, and growing out of control. I would sit for hours looking at the movement of my two families, over time and space, intersecting. Fur and melodrama. Fortunes rose, lives fell. I started having migraines; I went into long dark stupors.

I pretended to everyone that I was doing fine, but they knew better. Yet they kept encouraging me because they loved the idea. *They* loved it. *I* loathed it. I wished I had never gotten in, and now I didn't think I would ever get out. My Frankenstein monster was eating his creator.

My first real breakthrough — let's call it break out — came when a friend who saw my dilemma asked me a question I wished I had asked myself. She said, "Hey, Chris, do you even like to read this kind of book?"

The question was like a tsunami crashing over me. She said she had never seen me more dumbfounded. My jaw hung open.

"No," I managed to say, "I hate reading these kinds of books."

"Why is that?"

"I can never keep anything straight. I lose control of the situation. I lose interest. I like stories that take place in short periods of time, all revolving around one central event, with characters in conflict and turmoil, with a ticking clock."

"Then what in the hell are you doing trying to write this book?" she said.

"Committing suicide?" I said.

"Exactly."

What a revelation! I had suspected as much before but buried the thought under those mountains of research, and denial.

What a hard lesson to learn, but that's how I seem to learn all my lessons. I keep making mistakes until they pile up and then one day — KABOOM! — the revelation whacks me up side the head and I finally get it.

I abandoned this dead horse — uh, mink — and got it off my back. Or so I thought. Even today, years later, I sometimes wonder if I had just pulled the truck a little farther over the line.... After which the reality of that situation clobbers me, as it did then. I know I made the best decision.

These days, one of the first things I tell anybody who asks me what they should write, is this, "If it's a novel, tell me where you go when you first enter a bookstore, when you're looking for something to read. Mystery? Woman's fiction? Romance? Sci-Fi? Literary fiction? Where do you go? What draws you to that section? That's the area in which you should be writing your book."

In movies, it's the same thing. You know what grabs you. You know how you feel when that certain movie is out and you *have* to see it.

Thank God *Mink!*'s dilemma made itself known to me. I would still be sailing down the river of no return with those two families. After investing in generation after generation for four hundred years, every seventy-five pages having to kill them off and start again with a whole new bunch of characters, always keeping in mind where each of them had come from and where they were going, I had had it.

I can't remember what I'm supposed to do at three o'clock in the afternoon, or what I did at seven a.m. How in the hell was I supposed to remember every family member from two clans, and what they did — along with their friends and acquaintances and enemies — over four centuries?

Write what you know also means write what you want to know, or what you want to know *more about*. It means genre. It goes back to why you like storytelling in the first place. What *kind* of storytelling? What kind of tone? Or voice? Does the story take place in four hours, four days or over four centuries. What attracts you?

You know the genre. You love it, live for it. It's in you and has been since the beginning. You've had a love affair with it without even knowing it.

That's where you should be. Your instinct lives there. Your passion thrives there. Your anticipation boils over there. You can analyze it. You're confident talking about it. Your subconscious takes baths in it. When you want to write a movie, ask yourself that question. To what genre do I gravitate? What kind of movie really turns me on?

If you're not able to answer this question, you may spend a lifetime writing against the grain, and wondering why you do not love what you do. Your own *Mink!* could smother you!

In fact, you will most likely go through your own *Mink!* fiasco to understand the nature of that beast. Even though experience is the best teacher, I wouldn't wish it on anybody. It's enough that one of us had to go through it. The least I can do, by telling you my sad tale of woe, is to try to steer you away from that pit.

If you're going to fail and learn lessons from it, do it in your own genre, not somebody else's.

I wish I had read something like this, from someone like me, who had been through this, before I took off on that extravagant, time-consuming, migraine-begetting bad acid trip of an experience. But the truth is, I had to go through it in order to recognize it and later to pass it on.

Search in the past for the key to your likes and dislikes. There is no reason for you to go through years of struggle when all you have to do is ask yourself one question: Do I even like to read that stuff? Or in the case of a movie, see that stuff?

It's the Passion, isn't it? You know what the Passion feels like. That singularly elusive, indefinable urge in the pit of your stomach or the center of your head that forces you to pay attention. Not only do I want to write that screenplay, you say, I can write it, and beautifully.

If you don't have the Passion, writing will be just a job, unless of course you develop the Passion along the way. Usually the Passion is born of character, in the emotional threads that stitch together the human condition.

## DRILL

What was it about that movie you saw last weekend that made you take notice? Why'd you go in the first place? What was it about the character or story that drew you in? What was the fever? Get it down. Get it down on the machine, save it. When you're writing your screenplay and you're stuck, you'll come back to it and get unstuck.

## WHAT *ABOUT* THOSE DARK CHILDHOOD MEMORIES?

My earliest dark childhood memory begins with me sitting on the upstairs landing of our home. It's midnight. I'm in my jammies. I'm x years old. I peek down through the slats in the railing and watch my parents and their friends at a party.

I see people drinking and arguing. I see husbands and wives signal to other husbands and wives. I see hands flit across backsides and over shoulders, I see secret looks. And sometimes I see one husband and another wife slip off through separate exits to rendezvous in other parts of the house, then return to the party, fresh and satiated. I didn't know that then.

I listen to very bright, drunken people arguing. The later it gets the more the arguments heat up, driven by intellectual alcoholism and mind-numbing repetition. I hear a lot of repetition down there, loud repetition, as if nobody is listening to anybody, which is probably true. It's a living room brimming with agendas — sexual, predatory, manipulative agendas. I didn't know that then.

I see my mother and father involved in all this. They are the not so young anymore darlings of this community. Successful, smart, a beautiful couple. I notice how through manipulation — intellectual but mainly physical — fueled by alcohol these people seek pleasure in one another.

The things they say are funny and smart and wicked. I sit up here on the second floor, in the shadows, once, twice, three times a week, month after month, year after year, watching. Listening. Obsessed.

It's *Who's Afraid of Virginia Woolf* from a balcony seat. I see double-dealing, deceit, sadness, joy, and heart-wrenching pain. I know these people. They're my parents' friends. I go to school with their children. What I see from my balcony seat are very different people from the responsible parents during the day. Through my young eyes I see this dichotomy and it puzzles me.

Things are not what they seem.

I see my father's best friend slide his hand across my mother's buttocks and my mother lean against him. I see my father slide his hand around the waist of Mrs. So-and-So, and the looks that pass between them. And then they slip out of the room, to a secret place, in the dark. And don't come back for a long time.

My imagination makes me strangely ill. But can I tear my eyes away? No. I want more. I love being this voyeur in the dark at the top of the stairs — with my future forming before from eyes, molded by what I see below.

How dark is this childhood memory? Dark enough.

These nights became the basis for what I do now. Write. The future writer watches, unseen, inspecting his future characters.

By ten years old, I start to write plays, and for the next ten years write dozens, hundreds of them. Snippets of plays about people who use deceit, chicanery, verbal manipulation, and liquor to take from others what will satisfy themselves.

People deceive one another; husbands deceive wives, wives husbands. I am deluged by the absence of trust, a theme that will later saturate my work, and my life.

It's not just the childhood memories themselves that I ask my students to bring into the open, but what the memories *mean*. How they worked their way into their behavior and their thought.

How, I ask them, would you feel if you saw extramarital affairs blossom on a daily basis, watching this nocturnal soap opera unfold? How would you develop a character in adulthood that spent much of his childhood watching this behavior?

Did the young recorder of these events become a later participant in them, slipping from the observer to the observed? Did I climb down from the balcony seat to the field, from the fan to the player?

By asking these questions, you draw closer to yourself: *Why do you do what you do?* And therefore closer to the characters you create: *Why do they do what they do?*

You have to begin somewhere. Why not with yourself? Not your superficial self, the one you paint for others to see, but the one you know, fears and all. You have to be willing to own up to yourself before you're able to peel away the layers of your characters.

Dark childhood memories are a good starting point.

I remember one student who said he used to physically brutalize his brother and sister, and then demand that they make up lies to tell their parents about some strange kids mauling them.

Eventually, my student began mutilating himself. In this way it would seem that (a) he would also appear to be a victim and (b) out of guilt he felt he needed to experience the pain he was inflicting and feel something about it.

By age twelve, he grew out of this behavior. In his early twenties now, he has no contact with his siblings, who want nothing to do with him. They have moved away and will not forgive.

It's a source of great anguish for him. Nightmares haunt him. Drugs and psychiatry have not helped. He has decided to try to write himself to the source of his pain and perhaps in so doing be able to forgive himself.

Dark childhood memories. They themselves can begin a quest suitable for a movie. This student is writing a story about a man who will do anything to get back into the graces of his battered family. His working title: "What comes around…"

Once you extract one fully developed childhood memory, others invariably follow, as if they're all lined up back there in your subconscious waiting to be urged into the light.

A handful of them will make a huge impact. Dorothy Allison, in her remarkable memoir, *Bastard Out of Carolina* (which became a movie directed by Angelica Huston), focuses on one moment in time, the pivotal moment, as it turned out, that established all of her significant behavior later on.

When she was ten years old, her mother had a relationship with an abusive boyfriend. The boyfriend was so abusive, to both the mother and to Dorothy, that Dorothy begged her mother to leave him. Her mother had to make a choice between the boyfriend and her daughter.

She chose the boyfriend because she was afraid she would never find anyone like him again (and everything that implies). Her daughter, on the other hand, had her whole life in front of her and would make her way.

So the child Dorothy was sent off and the mother remained. And this, Dorothy Allison tells us, impacted her life like no other event. Read the book. It's amazing. Then see the movie.

In your screenplay you'll be focusing on the most critical moment of your main character's life — a moment at a juncture of life and death, figuratively and literally.

It can be no other way, or the story is not worth telling. The stakes have to be at their highest. There will be no turning back by your main character, even though she may want to, because as the story progresses that door to the past closes, forcing your character to face the present, and the future.

You will discover what she is made of. Your *character* will discover what she is made of.

Consider *Good Will Hunting*, when Will is forced by circumstances to face his fear centers: his heart, his genius, and his psyche. He tries to run and hide from the confrontations with his girlfriend, the psychologist, and the MIT professor, but there is no place to go. The world keeps intruding. Even his friends eventually tell him he can't stay with them. Will Hunting has to turn and face the harsh light of the world, but first himself, which he does not want to do.

Instead he constructs an emotional wall, hiding his essential yet horrid sense of himself from the world. Will Hunting is so afraid of the world not accepting him that his barriers are impenetrable. So he thinks.

The writers are relentless. They attack Will's fear centers and pull him, screaming and yelling, into the harsh light of day.

The writers close the door to his prison of fears. There is no place for him to go finally but forward. So what is Will Hunting going to do now that he has entered that other cage, of the world at large?

Assailed in the heart, mind and psyche, he is pushed out of his self-imposed isolation. His genius, his love, and his dark childhood memories are yanked from the shadows and cast down before him.

He fights them. He resists. He tries to crawl back to his life in his shanty by the sea. Good luck, Will. South Boston sank into the sea. You're on your own now.

When you look back at your own childhood there are moments, big moments, that slammed you up against the wall of experience. When you came to and climbed to your feet, you were about to become somebody else, or at least felt like someone who had just been through the most extraordinary moment of his life, through the wringer.

Childhood memories boost the critical aspects of story. You give credence to the bomb exploding in your character's life and the ensuing fallout. The bomb illuminates the action your character will take to restore order to his shattered world.

When she was five, Robin C.'s father left home with the next-door neighbor, his best friend's wife. Robin hasn't seen him since. She's twenty now and thinks about him and what he did. She's no longer as angry as she was, or confused. She gets it now, more or less.

Her parents had a rotten marriage. They passed by one another, dozens of times every day, like strangers. They never raised their voices. They didn't need to. They had nothing to say to one another. They'd married the wrong person, both of them. They carried silent resentments that, in Robin's mind, sounded like avalanches. They were always avoiding or turning away from each other, yet always crashing into each other because of the circumstances.

When her father left, Robin went into a deep trance, an excruciatingly painful coma from which she didn't emerge for ten years.

Robin embraces loneliness. She wants to be a writer partially out of her need for solitude. She's agoraphobic but admits that agoraphobia may be an excuse for her need to stay away from people. She trusts no one.

But boy can she write. She writes about couples splitting up and the impact on their kids. Robin says she has written a thousand variations on that theme and will write a thousand more. It's become the lynch-pin of her oeuvre. She's getting better and better, and when she's able to put her characters in more active verbal conflict, she will be there.

Gary N. is from Minnesota, the land of Viking stock. He can relate to *Fargo*; all of the Coen Brothers movies, he says, except *Miller's Crossing*. He is convinced that somewhere in the making of that movie the Coen brothers had been on the verge of splitting up.

Gary is a very funny guy. He was brought up on comic books. Action heroes are his soul mates. He hated *X-Men*, the movie: "Too dull. Wooden characters. The action is predictable. I wanted X-Men as written by the Coen Brothers."

Gary has read all of the Coen Brothers scripts and all the action heroes created by the legendary Stan Lee, from his Incredible Hulk to the pantheon of Marvel Comics marauders. In his writing he wants to humanize, and stylize, action stars.

When I asked Gary how he came to fall in love with these characters in the first place, he said. "Look at me. I'm thin and edgy, very un-Viking like. In my Minnesota town, I was a popular target."

They put small furry animals in his lunch box. The girls ridiculed his skinny hairy body. They broke his glasses. They called him Fairy Gary and other names. Like the kid in those ancient muscle mags who got sand kicked in their faces, Gary dreamed of being an invincible man with one tragic flaw, straight from Stan Lee's cast of characters.

Gary spent most of his childhood alone, buried in Stan Lee's heroes. From them he created his own, adapted the heroes of his youth into the heroes of his imagination.

From his parents, two other non-Viking types who had to fight their way out of an abyss or two, he learned humor as a defensive weapon. Oddball humor. They were Jews among Presbyterian warriors. They *had* to develop wit.

From early on, Gary, pen in one hand and pencil in another, wrote and sketched his way into adulthood. His themes fed David and Goliath modern melodramas; thoroughly unpredictable, riotously funny, and loaded with suspense.

Until he turns things around, Gary's David will get the shit beat out of him by Goliath. It's classic storytelling. The more interesting scenario, until he turns things around, is that a complex David will always get the shit beat out of him by a complex Goliath.

Gary has seen a movie written and directed by Cameron Crowe, *Almost Famous*, two dozen times. Crowe wrote *Almost Famous* out of his experiences as a sixteen-year-old journalist for *Rolling Stone*. Cameron Crowe says he made a significant transformation doing that picture, one of his life's turning points. Big change resulted, along with hard-earned badges of courage, and the loss of innocence.

It matters that you want to put your main character through the wringer. It matters who this character is, this poor slob you're going to send through hell. Where does he come from? What baggage is he hauling with him, that he deserves this transformational journey?

One process is this:

**1.** Write down your darkest childhood memory. Take a look at it. It probably has a beginning, middle, and end. It means something to you; otherwise it wouldn't be your darkest childhood memory. What does it mean? How do you feel when you think about it? Write down the story as you remember it.

**2.** Imagine how this memory might have shaped your later behavior. If you lost your grandfather you might have developed serious abandonment issues, for instance. Trust is a big one. You don't entirely believe people who say they will never leave you, or even that they'll come through on a promise. You may feel that nothing is permanent, like your grandfather, who was suddenly taken away from you. Your kid's mind might have processed this as your grandfather deciding he didn't want to bed with you anymore and took off. That could cause one hell of a problem in a human life and in the life of a character.

From these memories, a human being starts to emerge. He is about to enter a world he has never seen before, and one he is ill prepared to face.

By endowing your character with vulnerability and fear, you establish someone ready for change, and not a pasteboard cut-out character about which the reader doesn't care.

What's the worse thing you can ever hear about your character: "I didn't care about him, so the story didn't matter." See *Troy*. The film-makers made a mistake. In the main characters, they gave us a couple of duds.

Your process begins by tracking back through time and finding the building blocks to construct a human being we can relate to, care about, root for, fear for.

## DRILL

**Take a moment. Think back. That thing that happened to you long ago, the thing that made you feel guilty or shameful or gave you an outstanding sense of well being, or that sent you hurdling into despair. What was that thing? Write it down. See it. Turn it into a scene. Who was there? What happened? How did it make you feel? How does it make you feel now? Can you give this feeling to one of your characters?**

## WHEN DID YOU FIRST START TO WRITE, AND WHY?

This is a bonus question. I have always loved the concept of bonus questions. Like little surprises.

As a kid, my parents read to me from Dickens. They did this because, they later told me, they could not bear to spend time reading to me from "Goo Goo Goes to The Garage" or "What Peter Felt When He Saw a Dead Flower." They read Dickens because they liked to read

Dickens. He told well-written, riveting tales, with driven characters and dramatic set pieces, with many of them about kids.

I spent most of my young life longing for a Dickensian childhood. What does that tell you?

I wrote bread and butter notes, little thank you notes to the neighbors after my mother would take me to lunch at their homes.

A couple of lines would have sufficed, but I wrote essays on how lovely the food was, how much I enjoyed the décor, why I thought their dog was an ideal pet, why I thought their children were first rate. And on and on. Everyone thought they were so charming, so funny. I had an audience who wanted more; always a good sign.

The next big writing moment came at fifteen. I had been scribbling love letters to a girl, big mushy purple-prose testaments about my deep-seated love for her. Reading these things after many years, I believe I was in love with my prose as much as I was in love with her.

One day I picked up the phone in the living room and heard the mother of the girl to whom I had written the love letters reading the latest to my mother, who was on the extension in the kitchen.

I was of two minds. I felt betrayed by the girl's mother reading my heartfelt yearnings for her daughter — to *my* mother! I also had to admit that I was thrilled Mom and Mrs. Babock seemed to *love* what I wrote. Ecstatic. Hmmm, I remember thinking. As her mother read along, pausing in places, dramatizing moments, my mother laughed out loud, got silent, and said things like, "Just fantastic. Read that one again."

So, at this moment, at age fifteen, I was given the opportunity to watch two trains — one named art, the other named commerce — crashing into each other right before my eyes. On one hand my deeply personal thoughts were being thrown haphazardly into the public. I was also surprised by how much Mom and Mrs. Babcock liked it.

I point to these two early episodes as benchmarks that lighted a path for me. I just wrote. All the time. In high school, influenced by the French absurdist theater, I wrote French absurdist plays. In college, influenced by Sam Shepard, I wrote American, Sam Shepard-like plays.

My uncle told me to read Saul Bellow. I did and saw what language and character could do to a story. I kept reading and writing. I couldn't help myself. And I went to movies.

I never read scripts. Like a lot of people it never occurred to me that there were hundreds, *thousands* of screenwriters in Hollywood who toiled every day trying to make art out of their craft.

My first experience with screenwriting came when Paramount bought my first book, *The Hunter*, for the movies. After two other screenwriters couldn't get the job done, the producer asked me if I thought I could do it. I said absolutely, and went off to find out what a screenplay was.

That was the beginning. I had an advantage early on toward becoming a writer. I was a loner, needing something to keep me busy when I was alone. For me, it was writing and golf. My parents handed me a book and a seven iron and sent me off. The perfect pastime and the perfect sport for a solo kid.

With books and golf, I didn't have to deal with people that much, if at all. I didn't have to be on. When I went out of the house into public I didn't have to be the dancing pony, an awful burden that made me, ultimately, want to stay at home.

## DRILL

This drill may do nothing for you. In fact it may be boring as hell to even begin. Or pretentious. Who cares what made you start writing, the influences? The parents who read to you, the uncle who told you to read Bellow. Who cares?

If you turned out to be a serial killer you might want to know why you made that wrong turn, and where. If not you, prob-ably a lot of other people would want to know.

My great friend and part-time mentor, Gary Provost, one of the finest writing teachers to have roamed this earth, said to me one day after I was grousing about something, "Chris, why don't you make a little chronology of what you think led you to become a writer?"

"Why?" I said.

"If you ever get stuck or stumble over some writer's block, I guarantee you the block will go away and you'll write your way out of whatever crap you're going trough."

"Yeah, how does that work?" I said.

"It's different for everybody."

"You did it?"

"Yup."

"And...? "

"You're going to be surprised."

"Like how?"

"Chris."

"What?"

"Shut up."

Notes to yourself. Little scenarios from which short pieces, stories, scenarios, or letters spring. What made you want to express yourself on paper? What drives you to tell and retell, in stories, the history of your life — as if you're trying to solve some mystery or heal some wound that's dogged you for as long as you can remember?

This exercise is a link to the origins of your creativity, your need to write, back to those precious moments a long time ago when that little kid in you one day picked up a pen or pencil and, with one word after another finding its way to the page, this story started to appear. A moment, an indelible mark on your world, an act of creation. Call it whatever you want.

It took a lot more time than I thought. Months. And just when I thought I was done, I wasn't.

Gary was right. You're going to be surprised.

# THE THREE HORSEMEN OF THE SCREENPLAY:
## SITUATION, CONCEPT, STORY

## SITUATION

John Le Carré once defined the difference between a situation and a story as this: a situation is a cat sitting on a blanket. A story is a cat sitting on a *dog's* blanket. By adding conflict, a story can begin to be told.

*Nothing moves forward in any screenplay except through CONFLICT.*

Hamlet going home for the weekend to see his mother and step-father is a situation. Hamlet going home and discovering that his mother and stepfather had been having an affair long before his father's death, and that they conspired to kill his father, in fact *did* kill him — that's a story.

By putting your character in emotional and physical hell, the story becomes your character doing whatever she can to resolve the big problem she faces, thus showing what she's made out of: *character.*

In the Coen Brothers' *The Man Who Wasn't There*, the *situation* is Billy Bob Thornton's barber finding out that his wife is having an affair with her boss, adding to the barber's already pathetic life. The *story* kicks into gear when the barber, seeing an opportunity, anonymously blackmails the boss (as payment for having an affair with his wife), thus sending everybody spiraling out of control.

Almost all Coen Brothers' movies begin with a small urge or need in the main character that spirals out of control, destroying everything in its path. In *Fargo*, it's William H. Macy's character, Jerry, who just wants to be his own man and step out from under his father-in-law's long shadow. And boy, does that start something that ends up in a wood chipper, among other things. In *Raising Arizona* it's the simple desire for a baby to make the happy couple feel complete. But why wait, they figure, let's borrow one.

At the beginning of each story, the main character should always be unsettled, *really* screwed up. He's got a problem that's about to become a disaster like nothing he's ever seen.

Furthermore, you try to put him in the place where he wants to be the least. Automatic conflict. You're always trying to make your main character uncomfortable, annoyed, pissed off and frustrated beyond belief.

He gets into one "why me" situation after another, until he can barely breathe.

It's this bad *and* he's got a long way to go, from whatever bad situation we find him in, to a much worse situation, so bad in fact that he believes there is no way he'll ever get out of this mess. And then, at the end of Act II, you throw him over the falls.

And only then can he start seriously thinking about crawling his way back, solving the big problem of the story and the emotional dragon he's been carrying around inside forever, the source of his true agony.

To help him along the way you throw in a ticking clock with time running out and some treacherous villain who's only desire is to bury this pest.

Now you've got the beginning of a decent character.

But along the way you still have to keep asking yourself the question: How can I make it worse for him? How can I *really* screw up my main character's already screwed up life?

As the writer you've got to be nasty to your main character.

Here are some situations and stories I thought worked.

*Blood Diamond.* **Situation:** Two unlikely guys, a South African mercenary, Archer (Leonardo DiCaprio) and a Mende fisherman, Solomon (Djimon Hounsou) join forces. **Story:** They recover a rare pink diamond and, with an American journalist (Jennifer Connelly), go on a journey through rebel country to save Solomon's family and give Archer a second chance.

*Candy.* **Situation**: A heroin-addicted poet (Heath Ledger) falls in love with an art student (Abby Cornish). **Story:** To grow closer to him, Cornish takes up heroin, which leads to oblivion, self-destruction, and despair. Cheery little piece of heaven.

*Perfume.* **Situation:** A European perfumer, born with no sense of smell, develops an extraordinary nose. **Story:** When he starts on a quest to discover the perfect scent, his life takes a dark, murderous turn.

Notice in all of these that life is going along on its own even (or uneven) keel, at which point the writer drops a bomb into it, then waits for the fallout. This is storytelling.

## DRILL

Make a list of movies you've recently seen. Strip away story and concept. Take out the conflict. See the Situation for what it is. Then restore the conflict. This is how Situation becomes Story. *See what's there.* These are building blocks. How to get the cat to sit on the dog's blanket, knowing the dog's going to show up in about ten seconds.

## MOVIE CONCEPT

For our purposes, a Concept is a general movie notion or idea that seems to have enough appeal to attract talent, a director or producer, along with audience. A high concept is an idea ripped from today's headlines or the result of baking two disparate, seemingly unrelated ideas into one big original box office pie.

You've heard it before. Eighty percent of all screenplays are bought on concept. When a script comes in it matters how well it's written, but it's the concept that sells it. The producers can always hire another writer to clean it up.

Studios buy a book or a magazine article or somebody's life story because they believe it can sell a lot of tickets. The studio hires an established writer to make movie sense of it and hopes that it reaches the screen through the laborious development process.

*Cold Mountain*, a very well-written book, spent a lot of time in development and had attached to it many big actors, all of whom fell away. The concept was not that strong — after the Civil War, a soldier walks across North Carolina to reach home. The studio could not get a strong script. It wasn't until many drafts later and a significant change of cast that the movie came together. The concept stayed alive because the producers continued to believe in it and the book had won so many awards.

There are two messages here. *Cold Mountain* does not have a high concept, an idea that a studio or producer can grasp in one sentence.

*Cold Mountain* is about a lot of things, but on the surface it's about the soldier returning home. It's a period piece. It's beautifully written. When a studio buys a book it buys the story, not the writer's voice. The writer's voice does not travel well to the screen. Witness *Bonfire of the Vanities* and other book-to-movie disasters.

The second message: If the story is strong enough, or hot enough, or if a bankable star agrees to do it, it stands the best chance of getting made. "There's no accounting for good or bad taste" and "Nobody knows anything" are two of the most often repeated lines in Hollywood.

So, what does a "concept" look like?

The short version:

*Speed*: *Diehard* on a Bus. *Star Wars*: *Wagon Train* in the sky. *The Car* (a car that eats people): *Jaws* on wheels.

*Shallow Hal*, the concept: What if a guy spent his life seeing only the inner beauty of women, never the outer blemishes — in this case, extra weight? The problem: He's the only one who does see the inner beauty. Everyone else, seeing the weight, stays superficial and ignorant.

The object of affection in *Shallow Hal* is a Rubenesque Gwynyth Paltrow, the point here being that beauty is skin deep and therefore you almost never get to the good stuff beneath — to a world where inner beauty is the only beauty that matters. A big reversal on the norm. Good concept. Makes you think. We can all relate.

For his good idea, along with his story, characters and execution, the writer, in this, his first screenplay, made $1.6 million, and launched a career.

What got the ball rolling? Concept. Situation becomes story becomes concept. The screenwriter formulated the story from the concept. He pitched both the concept and the story to the studio.

Good writing sells the writer. Concept sells the movie.

From the moment you start to conceive of your idea start thinking about the one line — the LOG LINE — that will sell your movie.

A *lot* of people need to buy your concept before it can proceed: agents, producers, studio mavens, directors, actors. *You* need to buy it. If you're fuzzy about what your script is about, how do you think everybody else will feel?

You've got this idea. Somebody asks: "What's it about?" Your answer: "Well, there are these two guys, a CEO and his Number One. The CEO is great and powerful but he's got a problem. He's got a girl-friend or wife he's crazy about. His Number One wants to take the CEO down, so he fans the fire. He whispers to the CEO that his wife is fooling around with another guy in the company. The CEO's jealousy drives him mad. Everything crumbles around him. As he falls the Number One to rises up to take his place of power."

Not bad. Good general idea. Wordy. How about *Othello* meets *Bad Lieutenant*?

Strong concept + audience attraction = box office action.

What does *Othello* meets *Bad Lieutenant* have going for it? And what does it NOT have going for it?

**1.** *Do we get it?* What's not to get? A tenth-grader can get it. A giant among men is taken down by his own fatal flaw: insecurity. Specifically, jealousy.

**2.** *Strong enough to attract a big star?* A modern-day Othello? Denzel Washington? Jamie Fox? The original *Othello* has a strong but down-beat ending. Hollywood might try to dress it up by having the main character turn things around.

On one level, this is a workplace movie about a disgruntled employee and his need for revenge. Iago is passed over for promotion. He sus-pects that Othello might have had an affair with his own wife. He plots revenge on his boss, and carries it out by exploiting his boss's fatal flaw.

It's a plum role, a star turn. A three-star turn: Othello, Iago, and Desdemona. A modern-day Othello, in a corporate environment? Sex with an interracial couple: Desdemona, the white woman, and Othello, the black titan. And Iago, the white lieutenant, who himself may even lust after Desdemona, or have hidden loathing for blacks in general (for a reason we discover later in the story), and Othello in particular.

Iago believes he deserves to be on top and has been waiting for the right time to make his move. Iago chooses this moment to whisper in Othello's cuckolded ear — Desdemona is screwing around. With whom? The guy who got Iago's job, whom Othello chose over him. How perfect can revenge be?

You the writer (or in this case, Shakespeare the writer) have chosen the most critical moment in all three lives to tell the story. The stakes will never be higher. People will die, fortunes will change.

**3.** *Sequel possibilities?* Maybe in the end Iago escapes and runs off somewhere, but he'll be back — if the movie turns good box office numbers.

**4.** *Emotional and dramatic hot buttons?* Lust, power struggles, betrayals, a fallen hero who rises out of his own ashes to slay his former friend and comrade, now betrayer. What else do you need?

Shakespeare knew what he was doing. I'm getting so lathered up with this, I ought to go out and write it myself. This concept has legs.

Many less appealing concepts, often tired and cliché ridden, still manage to crawl out of the lame barrel. Here's one: The Old Pro Called Back to Do One Last Job.

Hollywood is forever putting new spins on this because there are old pro actors out there who can still draw, especially if they are teamed with a younger actor with rising or even established star power. As an extremely conservative business (conserving one's own job), studios rely on so-called "safe" concepts, which themselves often backfire and lose money. Redford and Pitt in *Spy Game*. Hackman and Co. in *Heist*. Kevin Costner and Ashton Kutchner in *The Guardian*. De Niro in anything.

This doesn't mean you shouldn't write for this genre. If you're convinced you've got a new twist and love this kind of movie, write it. But know going in that ten thousand people just like you, along with A-list scribes, are building the same derivative house.

## DRILL

Call it The Tweak Factor. If you're searching for something original, try taking your idea and melding it with another idea by constructing a bridge between them. If they don't work together, try another one. There's something in your original idea that's on solid ground. It may only need another element to turn it into a strong concept. Take your time. Remember: Impatience kills.

## STORY

You discover stories in the strangest places.

I discovered this one in my school mailbox: "Dear Mr. Christopher Keane, I attended your script writing workshop last Wed. when there were ten extra kids that showed up. I'm gonna show up again tomorrow. Hopefully someone dropped the course, or you might be willing to let in one extra kid (that would be me). I NEED this class. If you don't let me in I'll go crazy. *PLEASE*. If you do, you won't be sorry. I promise. Thank you." (signed) Andrea Portnoy.

Andrea said she would "go crazy" is she didn't get into my class. Here's what I did: I let her in. And then, in my imagination, over the next several weeks, out of a situation I concocted a story.

In my **Story**, based on a **Situation**, I turn Andrea into a mentally disturbed stalker-student. In this **Concept**, I am a teacher, married with a kid, and Andrea is a younger, crazier version of Glenn Close in *Fatal Attraction*.

Eventually the teacher, who fears being punished for bad behavior — by getting too close to Andrea's craziness — tries to pull away. But can he?

He senses this woman's power and he *still* lets her into class. What's that all about? Testing fear? Maybe he wants to get close to the flame but not get burned? He wants to test his resolve? He has an inflated sense of his ability to say no? Maybe he wants to get laid? Oh boy. What does this say about his relationship with his wife and kid, or about himself?

What about the student? She has her own issues with authority figures. There is something about the teacher that ignites dark and dangerous images from her past. And somehow — through transference, who knows? — she wants to punish the teacher. But not just any teacher. One who reminds her of something bad that happened to her long ago. We will later learn that this is not the first time that Andrea has played out this scenario.

As is, this is too close to *Fatal Attraction,* so do we throw in a little *Something Wild* into the mix?

Notice that Andrea and the teacher are now drifting away from the real Andrea and the real me. Andrea's wires get crossed (they've been crossed for a while) and she becomes dangerously aggressive. She wants revenge but wants it sweet. But she's smart and canny and manipulative and bright and good looking, and she has spent twenty years of her life going after and getting what she wants, all of it driven by fear and a hunger for retribution.

This isn't supposed to turn the teacher into a victim, except if he wants to play the victim. That's another trail we can follow if we wish.

The teacher is about to become her next target. But the audience doesn't know any of this yet because one of your obligations as a writer is to *never give the audience any information until the audience needs to know it.*

Keep the reader in suspense. Let the story unfold naturally. Andrea's past is back-story, which should be revealed in drips and drabs throughout the story to create suspense, shock, and tension.

The **Situation** is that Andrea writes a note, a funny note, an innocent-seeming note. The note might have a sort of sinister twist to it, but not if the teacher doesn't see it that way.

The teacher, in any case, thinks it's charming, aggressive, and he likes women who are aggressive. His mother is aggressive; the woman he married is aggressive.

Now you start building toward tension points, searching for the major dramatic beats of the **Story**.

Your main objective is to keep the readers interested: interested, fascinated, on the edge of their seats, wanting more — as long as it's upsetting the readers' expectations. They may be expecting another *Fatal Attraction.* Surprise them. Don't ever dump information on the reader; *dramatize* it.

Bad Example:

```
              TEACHER
     Andrea, how'd you find out I'm
     a big collector of goldfish? I
     started collecting my fish when,
     as a child, I had no friends.

              ANDREA
     Oh, gee, Mr. Moon, I love fish. I
     was a lonely kid, too, and I'm
     also a collector.
```

I'm nodding out writing this. You must be comatose by now. Let's try again:

                    ANDREA
Hey, Teach, I hear you collect fish.
Could I see them?

                    TEACH
I have some in my apartment.

                    ANDREA
Big?

                    TEACH
Huh?

                    ANDREA
How big is your equipment?

                    TEACH
Equipment?

                    ANDREA
        (smiling)
How big are you, teach?

                    TEACH
Big? I mean, I collect fish.
I'm not SeaWorld.

                    ANDREA
What about your wife?

                    TEACH
What about her? She's knows about my fish.

                    ANDREA
I'll bet she does. Do you invite other students
up to see your big fish? I would love to swim
with your big fish. How about today?

                    TEACH
Today?

                    ANDREA
Now.

                    TEACH
You wanna see my fish, now?

> ANDREA
> Have you got a big, eager fish or
> a shy fish that needs coaxing?

> TEACH
> Ahhhh...

> ANDREA
> I live right near your apartment.
> And I adore big fish.

> TEACH
> You know where I live?

It ain't Shakespeare, but at least it's got energy, some meat on its bones. Who knows if Andrea will like swimming in these metaphorical waters with Teach's big fish. Will he be, at night's end, as they say, *swimming with the fishes*?

What have we got here? Sexual innuendo, anticipation. A married guy. Danger. We are working this concept and story. Is this perhaps more of a very black comedy? Does this distance it from *Fatal Attraction*?

You have created potential. You have started to build Drama, and the Anticipation of More Drama.

Flat writing is dead writing. The reader tunes out.

Back to the **Concept:** What happens when a young twisted student exacts revenge on her teacher for reasons that neither one of them understands — until it is too late? Sound promising?

This concept can also be used as the temporary **Log Line,** a one- or two-line titillating pitch or hook that gets the agent, producer, or studio exec excited. The log line is also for the sales department.

This log line, after it's developed and spun into fine gold, will become the pitch your agents feed to the rest of the industry, selling it up the movie food chain until it reaches a big studio cheese who can say yes.

Your intention with this log line is to get the food chain salivating. Other movies will come to their minds. Stalker movies. Movies about secret intentions. Glenn Close/Michael Douglas in *Fatal Attraction*. Diane Lane and Richard Gere in *Unfaithful*. *Play Misty for Me*, Clint Eastwood's first directorial effort. Michael Douglas and Gwyneth Paltrow in *A Perfect Murder*. Or the Michael Creighton/Demi Moore/Michael Douglas sex-in-the-marketplace feature, *Disclosure*. Harrison Ford and Michelle Pfeiffer in *What Lies Beneath*. Movies that made money and got strong notices.

Now you're starting to get savvy. You focus on the simplicity of story: The stalker and her target. This is the axis, or spine, around which the story will spin. Don't spin off it. *Stay on the axis.* Camp on the spine. Most scripts fail when the writer wanders or spins off in another direction, forgetting the core of the story.

Three-quarters of the way through the story, you know that the teacher will have to turn the tables and go from the stalked to the stalker. His life is nearly ruined and he's got to somehow resolve The Problem. He can't run, he can't hide. His only alternative, he believes, is to turn and face the enemy.

At this point, though, it doesn't look as if he will ever be able to get out of this jam. What can he do? He will have to start thinking, in significant ways, just like her.

Like any good sociopath, the stalker (Andrea) has separated the target from the rest of the world, leaving him alone out there, so that she can have control over him, manipulate him in the web she's created.

Let's back up for a second. A key element here is that there's something missing from the teacher's life, some **Internal Demon** that has been stalking him forever, which has allowed this to happen in the first place. This is the main character's **fatal flaw** (the incapacity to commit? an itch that can't be scratched?), which he has to face up to if he's going to move on.

Without this fatal flaw, none of this would have happened in the first place. Remember: without Othello's fatal flaw, jealousy, Iago's nudge, "Hey, Othello, I saw Desdemona downtown making out with your Captain," would mean little. If Othello says, "Oh, she does that.

Means nothing," that's the end of the story of Othello. Jealousy drives Othello, Iago knows, and this in turn drives the story. Your main characters' fatal flaws drive the story. Therefore, if logic serves, they need their fatal or tragic flaws.

# DRILL

> **Close your eyes. Think. What fatal flaw drives *your* main character?**
>
> **Make a list of five movies that grabbed you. What drove each of the main characters? One of the seven deadly sins? What was his or her fatal flaw?**

In this story, a fatal flaw dogs our Teacher, always has. He's got to face up to it. Insecurity? Fear? Your character eventually has got to face the terror, head on, which will be the hardest thing he has ever had to do — to identify it, to admit it, to face it. What's he afraid of? Why can't he resist allowing the young woman into his class when he knows she's trouble. Why would he want to risk putting his family in jeopardy?

Fatal flaws often become comforts and therefore hard to shake. Even though flaws make our lives miserable, even though they blot out what goodness we may possess, they become security blankets to us. "I'm comfortable in my awful behavior," he is saying. This is the teacher's problem, has been forever, and now this problem can have the most terrifying consequences ever.

The familiar is never as terrifying as the unknown, and so we embrace it, thinking the flaws are not as bad as they could be. Wrong. They are our worst nightmares, under the guise of comfort. Great fodder for characters to deal with.

We stay in a relationship or marriage because it's familiar, because at least we're secure in our grief. They become hedges against the unknown. But we wonder why we're not getting on with life, or getting joy *from* life, why we're always in a rut, why we seek others to fill the gaps left by the ones we're with.

Your main character probably has a suicidal attachment to his fatal flaw. In this story, the teacher does. The student does. The story is about the one last chance the teacher has to break the chains, to face this THING and get rid of it once and for all. Or, failing that, to live with it forever. *Because there will never be another chance like this.*

Back to Henry James' comment: your story must take place at the most critical moment of your main character's life. Otherwise, the story is not worth telling.

In *Fight Club,* the Ed Norton character has for a long time been dogged by the ordinary life he leads, so what does he do? He creates Brad Pitt to give him some excitement — the Mr. Hyde to his Dr. Jekyll.

And look where Hyde leads him, and see how hard it is for Jekyll, once he brings out Hyde, to get rid of him.

In almost all stories your main character needs to change the shitty life he's leading, but can't because he's locked into and comfortable with the prison his life has become.

So you, the writer, bring in a stranger to shake things up. This stranger represents the personification of all your main character's fears, often under the guise of his hopes, wishes, and dreams.

What can this stranger be? A person, a disease, an accident, a disaster. It will take a big disaster to dislodge your character from his or her routine life. To break the chains.

Your character thinks the disaster is the worst thing possible. But it's not. It's the cure, the antidote to the fatal flaw. Screenwriting is, in large part, the act of turning the worst possible situation into the best possible situation.

Let's go back to *Fight Club.* Brad Pitt looks like the best thing that could ever happen to Edward Norton. As the story progresses, Brad

Pitt starts taking over — literally everything — until Edward Norton's life becomes totally unmanageable.

Edward Norton now must act by trying to get rid of this monster Brad Pitt. He battles this creature he has created and defeats him. And his life improves. But what a journey!

What does it takes to make a good story? For one, putting the character at the most dangerous, wild, terrifying moment of his or her life, and seeing what happens. Have some fun with it!

What will your character do when the stranger comes to town? Force your character to face his demons and to eventually escape from his strangulated existence. There's your story.

For two-thirds of the story, you throw everything you can at your character, at which point your character says ENOUGH! and begins to fight back. In Act III, Edward Norton goes after Brad Pitt, who represents, literally, all of Edward Norton's worst intentions, and ultimately, if Norton gives in to it, his downfall.

In our story, this is the moment in our Teacher's life when that internal demon will rear its ugly head again — that demon-based flaw.

Let's say that failure to commit to anything is the Teacher's fatal flaw — life, partner, profession. He's mired in lethargy, seized by the paralysis of inertia — until out of a need to save his own life he feels compelled to destroy the student before she destroys him.

How about a twist, which you've set up early on? He's fallen in love with the student. Yes, she's a monster, yes, she's tried to kill him by this point. The Teacher thinks this may not be love but obsession. He wonders if he destroys her, will he also be destroying himself. By this time we know he's a goner when he starts rationalizing the end of his sanity, or his life.

The teacher realizes that to save his life he will have to confront and slay his *own* dragon/demon in order to stop the evil student. He has to kill off a part of himself that has perhaps given him comfort all his adult life. Is he willing to do this? Not a simple thing. He has to give up his flaw *and* recognize her flaw so that he can wage war in it.

Never be too easy on your main character. He has to earn the change you put him through. I'd be glad I'm writing this and not living it.

In Act III, the character takes on huge, startling adversaries. Many fights to the death. The student to the Teacher is Brad Pitt to Edward Norton. Edward Norton courted Brad Pitt's evil intentions, just as the Teacher courted the student's desire for revenge. Until it was almost too late.

As the reader, and later the viewer, I should not be able to tear my eyes away from the battle. I *need* to find out what happens. And so I turn the pages, breathlessly.

Even with all this tension and conflict you've created, as the writer you must always up the stakes. Borrow from your past, from research, from any source you can, and from the characters as you know them, to jeopardize your protagonist and raise the stakes even higher still.

Your characters begin to take shape. They possess motives (murky), and pasts (sketchy). In this case, the Teacher is insecure about his relationship with his wife, not because his wife has given him any reason to be. He's insecure to begin with, from way back, let's say from a debilitating relationship with his parents. Maybe, maybe not. At least it's a start. Something to begin with.

He's never worked out these issues (the inner demon), but he's about to. Does he learn some hard-won lessons? He had better.

See how a simple note from a student who wanted to get into my class has progressed to this? So far, we have merely scratched the surface. A simple situation has turned into this.

When working on your screenplay, ask yourself these questions: What situation began it? What's the concept? The idea or notion behind the story? What gives the story focus?

In Hollywood, they ask *what* it's about, not *who* it's about. The concept gets you in the door, the story will find you a seat, the characters will keep you in the room.

Stories are the meat on the bones of the concept. Stories take great effort. They're like relationships. They don't come fully realized. You have to develop them, grow with them, participate in them, create, manipulate, seduce and love them, all in the service of forming a dynamic, satisfying, passion-and-drama-filled relationship.

What about that moment when a great idea strikes you, or when a concept is suddenly fully formed? When you've hit upon something and can run with it, all the way to picture? You've never seen this concept on screen before. Nobody has. You *know* that it's unique. It's got chops, as they say in the business.

Time passes. You begin to wonder why you keep this idea or concept close to you for so long, why you haven't started developing it more thoroughly. Days go by, weeks, months, without adding to or subtracting from it. Why is that? You want to savor the brilliance of it in its pure initial state?

Most likely it's because you have the sneaking suspicion that this concept or situation, or idea, has many miles to go before it reaches home. Too many miles.

You refer to this brilliant idea as a story. But it's not a story. It's barely a concept. Maybe it's no more than a situation.

At some point you can't stand to let this thing fester any longer. It's time to take the jewel out of its box. Get on your computer, or get out your pad, and start to write. Start with the big dramatic beats, the highs and lows, the turning points. In other words, you start with broad strokes leading to structure.

Almost immediately you run into trouble, in the sense of problems. Problems you hadn't seen before.

This brilliant idea is unraveling before your eyes. Context creeps in, and behind context, content lurks, or doesn't. Maybe there's no real content.

The thing — and that's what it's becoming, no longer the brilliant story but the THING — has become a festering, out of control sore. It's in your brain and it's giving you a migraine.

You want to drive it out but your brain tells you that it's not yet time. You've had this THING in your cerebral womb for some time now. It *must* be good. All it needs is a little oxygen, to breathe.

Like any potentially brilliant child, it's got growing pains. Appendages, limbs, body parts — call them what you will — are sprouting up all over the place. The core idea is changing, transforming before your widening, shocked eyes.

Remember the old days — just weeks, or months, ago — when you were so happy with it? When you dreamed of this love child becoming your grand gesture to the world, an emblem of your width, breadth and depth?

This Incredible Story that would make it to the silver screen, with your name up there attached to it. Your creation.

But look what it's become — a virus, a *thing*. I get this virus every time I begin a project. It's as if I'm caught in a bipolar swing, traveling at supersonic speed from absolute ecstasy to utter despair. Call it creative post-partum depression.

Everybody gets it. *There is no perfection*, the voices keep reminding me, *it's all progress towards something*. Nothing ever comes out fully or perfectly formed, no matter how strongly we will it to. This is a metaphorical child, buddy. At this point it hasn't got enough flesh and bones to last the hour.

Take it easy! Step back, look at it, see what you've got. Go back to the beginning. It's still there, this brilliant idea. It's taken on new components, but the essence is there.

What's the rush!?

How do you think I felt about *Mink!* The book that ate its author? I let that concept, or idea, get way out of control. I dressed it up so quickly and so lavishly that it never had a chance to return to its essential self. I frantically built and built until I had constructed an architecturally untidy heap.

How do you stem the tide? How do you steer this original idea, concept or situation away from the hell it's heading toward and into a solid story? What tools do you need to make that happen?

## DRILL

This story idea of yours: where did it come from? Think back. How'd you come up with it? With all the story fodder you hear every day, why did this one stick? There's something there for you. What is it? Write down the progression or germination of the idea.

Just type for now; you'll edit later. Let it pour out of you. Something in there is worthwhile. Go find it. If you do it'll probably act like tumbleweed, picking up all sorts of stuff along the trail. And little by little you'll be watching a full-fledged story coming to life.

# WORKSHOP 5

# WHAT ARE THOSE STORIES?

As far as I can tell, stories are not found, they're discovered, revealed through observation and hard work. Often they spring out of the closet, needing to be dusted off and studied before they're ready to be written.

A situation, concept, or character begins the process, followed by the plot, the character's motivation, and the dramatic build. All have to be formed, molded, and structured before you can even call it a story.

*Good Will Hunting* started out as a thriller about a reluctant genius embroiled in the high-tech world. The only scene left from the original is where Ben Affleck's character, posing as Matt Damon's character, applies for a job at a high tech company.

The Miramax producers who read the first draft saw something they liked — the screwed-up genius character. They didn't like that the story was heading into big-budget, high-tech thriller country.

Director Rob Reiner read it and told the guys to tone it down, avoid high-tech country but keep the location, Cambridge and Boston's Southie neighborhood.

Forget about trying to compete with the big studio writers and their thrillers, Reiner told them. It's not that kind of picture. It's a neighborhood movie, about a reluctant genius tormented by his fears.

Miramax sent it to other heavy hitters, like William Goldman, who also saw a more personal story with big implications that audiences could relate to. Damon and Affleck went back to work and wrote another draft.

Now Goldman and other writers had a script they could polish, with the genius aspect intact and high tech stripped away, making it the personal movie it was destined to be.

Goldman and the others emphasized university versus the working class, and a main character with a superconductor brain who lives in blue-collar land, straddling two worlds — comfortable with one, slipping into another. The new writers were also conscious of the theater-going public's demographics (18-26) and decided that driving the story into the high-tech world would be missing a grand opportunity to put the Damon character at risk in a school atmosphere, which the audience had all experienced. They also kept it classy, at Harvard and MIT, where even geniuses have big problems.

Goldman and other uncredited writers built on the foundation established by Damon and Affleck. The rest is history. The reason Damon and Affleck received credit: The Writers Guild of America assigns credit to the original writers if at least half the story that made it to the screen belongs to them, or if no challenge was mounted by subsequent writers. To the best of my knowledge, nobody challenged them. I was told, but don't know for sure, that the deal made with the A-list writers precluded them from challenging credits and going before an arbitration board.

That's one way to break in. Don't let Matt Damon and Ben Affleck being already established actors put you off. I can't tell you the number of famous stars who have tried to write screenplays or pitch ideas, and only out of deference were not hustled, like regular folks, out of studio offices.

In your own stories, find the central flawed character and drive him or her into the heart of the story, as these guys did. Affleck and Damon were young scribes with an idea. They were no further along than anyone else. Just because they had Hollywood access doesn't mean they were guaranteed of anything. They had to fight hard to get their script cast.

In other words, don't let their celebrity prevent you from going after your own story. If they didn't have a knock-out idea at the center of their high-tech thriller, they never would have been invited into the room. In fact, you probably already know how producers and directors feel about actors with ideas for movies. Enough said.

In your stories, build through conflict. Conflict. Conflict. Conflict. Nothing should ever move through a story without being driven by conflict. What do they call scenes without conflict? That's right: flat, flabby, dull, and boring. Have enough of those in your script and you might as well take up lawn bowling.

When I talk about conflict I'm talking about physical and emotional conflict. I'm talking about conflict implied through dramatic irony in which the reader knows more than the character. The reader immediately gets nervous about what's going on in a particular scene, knowing that when the main character gets up and walks out through the restaurant door, there's someone lying in wait for him. The tension and conflict is that we don't want him to get up and go.

Every ten pages your main character gets thrown for a loop, called by some a WHAMMO! — just when the main character looks as if he or she is going to get the prize, WHAMMO!, something or somebody races in and snatches it away from them.

In other words, as the writer you lead the character (and the audience) up to a point where everything looks certain and you throw a bomb into it.

Your character, injured and dizzy, now has to find another route to the prize. These are called **reversals**, as in reversals of fortune. Build your story through a series of reversals that make life hard to nearly impossible for your character and demand that she dig deep to find an alternate route.

In this chapter we're going after story:

• How to recognize one.

• Compression of time, space, and language.

• The art of adaptation.

• If you haven't lived it, where do you find it?

• Indie love.

• Taking smart chances.

## HOW TO RECOGNIZE A STORY

If only it were that easy. Then again, it *is* that easy — if you're tuned to the right station. How do you get tuned and stay tuned?

Like the photographer who carries her camera everywhere, you have to be actively on the lookout. The late Gary Provost scoured newspapers and magazines. Some writers go to old movies that did well and try to find an angle to update them. They try to figure out why the movie did well, they read reviews and the script, they watch the movie and break it down. Then they ask themselves how they would take certain elements of the story and reconfigure them to take place in a present day setting.

Others go to obscure periodicals, or to books like *The 100 Greatest Crimes in History*.

Look around you. Do you see people in crisis, even among your closest friends or people you know? Surely you've been witness to tragedy and how victims have either fallen before it or shown great courage against it. Or even the dissolution of a family; the pain and anguish of trying to disengage from someone with whom you've had a long-term marriage or relationship.

A story I like to tell happened to a writer back in the 1970s. She was living with her family in Lake Forest, Illinois, outside of Chicago. She was a writer, then and now, always on the lookout for a good story

She had had some success but no breakout book. Yet. She could craft excellent sentences and delineate character with the best of them, but she didn't have a strong enough vessel — a story — to feed all this talent into.

For quite a long time she had been living in a lovely neighborhood with her family. During one stretch she noticed that something was going on with the neighbors.

Across the lawn and over the low fence that separated her yard from the neighbors, she watched the daily disintegration of a loving, smart, and passionately involved family.

The reason for this disintegration was that the older son, 17, died in a boating accident, tearing the family apart. The writer saw the toll this tragic death took on the family. The mother, heavily into denial, went catatonic. The victim's younger brother, who was with him in the boat when it capsized, blamed himself for his older brother's (his hero's) death. The father, a professional man, tried to keep the family together, failing at every turn.

This was the real-life story that writer Judith Guest would turn into an international bestseller and Oscar-winning movie, *Ordinary People*.

Judith Guest did not have to go to space or to another city or even down the street to find her story. There it was, unfolding before her eyes. She was familiar with it, she knew the people, she was canny and compassionate enough to see what emotional devastation can do.

She witnessed a single awful event, at the center of a family, which nearly destroyed its members. She watched the concentric circles of pain caused by the death of the hero-son sweep through the family and drive them to the brink of madness, with one in particular, the mother, falling over the edge.

She saw how a once strong, resilient woman lost her mind. She watched how the father, a man who might have faltered when his son died, instead came to the fore and pulled what he could together. She saw a loving brother who himself teetered on the brink of insanity, and fought his way back.

The key to this story lay in the family's reaction to the tragedy. Who would make it, who wouldn't? Shocking and surprising the readers and upsetting their expectations at every turn as each family member reacted, in his and her own unique unexpected way, to the tragedy.

People around the world who face tragedy in their own lives (who hasn't?) related to *Ordinary People*. Judith Guest told a simple story with characters hurled by circumstance into the most devastating time of their lives, violently tearing to shreds the fabric of their family life.

Through her writer's filter, Judith Guest changed some elements. She altered characters, she moved events around, all in the service of the story and the people who inhabited it.

Look around your own family, into your own neighborhood, and you'll find — like the photographer who carries her camera (or Judith Guest) — stories to tell.

In almost all good stories written for the screen (and more often than not in books), ten to twelve minutes in a bomb explodes. The characters spend the rest of the story trying to restore order to their shattered world. This is how stories are built. Take any (good) movie. You'll see these elements: Simple story, complex characters. Rather than the other way around.

One of my best students, Rachel Grissom, a slender, energetic blonde from the South who now lives in Hollywood, doesn't have to look very far to find potential stories.

Part of Rachel's family lives in New Orleans, where her script, about cemetery thieves, takes place.

Here's Rachel's take on finding stories: "Finding stories is actually very easy for me, and a very unconscious thing. I always write about things that interest me.

"How did I get the idea for my script? I had a friend in New Orleans, and found the city fascinating. I have family all over Mississippi, so I grew up with the culture. And I have always found the way a community buried its dead intriguing, its manner towards them (wakes versus funerals, Judeo-Christian beliefs versus reincarnation, etc.) fascinating as well.

"So when I saw an article in the newspaper about a ring of cemetery thieves in New Orleans who had been busted, but only after they had stolen and unloaded over a million dollars worth of stuff, it was an easy jump.

"I see stories everywhere. They usually have to do with what people do to survive. Example: What kind of people, what kind of lives, do you see in the background of your daily existences? What is it like, for instance, to drive a subway? What is it like to work the coatroom of a Boston club?

"I'm currently working on a story about a woman who is a professional eulogist. Whenever someone in my family dies, they make me give the eulogy, because few people in my family have a college education (which I do) and none have public speaking experience (which I have). Therefore, up to the podium I go. Sometimes it is difficult to give a eulogy for someone who was a bad person. That can't be uncommon. What do families do if they don't have someone to give that speech?

"A story is born. I think this is easy for me, partly because of my improv experience. Often, to get people comfortable with speaking off-the-cuff, if you will, teachers will make you only tell stories that are true, so you don't have to work at making it up as you go along. Doing that, you quickly learn that *everyone* has a story. Everyone.

"Each and every story is wonderful, complex, sad and funny. Every single one. Everyone is afraid of something. Everyone has lost something.

"I can look around at my family, easy. I have a cousin who was dropped on his head, causing brain damage, who now works for SeaWorld. My grandmother was offered a basketball scholarship to the University of Missouri but had to give it up because girls in her family did not leave home before marriage.

"She married a drunk gambler, had three kids, worked her way through college and taught in inner-city Memphis during integration.

"One of my brothers slept with my other brother's fiancée. My father could've been a golf pro, until his back was damaged by polio. My stepfather raced stock cars and motor cross. My other grandmother was reborn (for the better) when her husband of fifty years died.

"When my best friend's father's wife was paralyzed in a car accident, he left her for a prostitute he met doing drugs in Singapore. Another friend of mine has a disease where her collagen is disintegrating (it's worse than hemophilia). A bump would kill her.

"I'm thinking about writing a collection of linked stories, all about the way the men on the maternal side of my family have died. Almost every single one of them has died an early, unnatural death. Burning to death. Shot in the back. Falling off a ladder. Suicide. Drunk driving. A friend of mine insists that I warn any man I date.

"Another friend once asked me for advice on how to get started with a story. She had lots of beginnings, lots of characters, but couldn't finish it. She couldn't think of how to move forward.

"I told her, 'Take the character you know the best, the one you've fleshed out the most. Then figure out what the most important thing in the world to them is. Then take it from them, never to be returned, and see what they do.'"

Rachel is now in Los Angeles working as a screenwriter, bringing her world of the South into the culture of Hollywood.

## COMPRESSION OF TIME, SPACE AND LANGUAGE

A writer's journey to the heart of a story is filled with obstacles, detours and reversals. Distilling the story's essence to get the most potent effect requires an understanding of one of screenwriting's flagship concepts: **compression**.

One definition of a movie is a rapid acceleration of events happening over a short period of time. A chief component of that definition is compression. Squeezing things together so that there's no flab hanging from the story.

The three elements of compression: time, space, and language.

## COMPRESSION OF TIME

When you think about your story, one of the things that will come up is length of time. If your story takes place over a six-month period, ask yourself if it's possible for it to take place over a week or even a weekend.

Take *Three Days of the Condor*, staring Robert Redford and Faye Dunaway. The book upon which the movie was based is called *Six Days of the Condor*. For Hollywood, six days were three too many.

Some movies demand five years or more (*Lawrence of Arabia; A Beautiful Mind*), in which case the writers used compression in other areas.

The key is to eliminate dead time. If, for instance, a character must go through a pregnancy, a weekend won't cut it. The problem might be what to do with those nine months waiting for the pregnancy to unfold, in which case you ask yourself: can my character already be pregnant for, say, eight months? Maybe the story is not the pregnancy in its entirety, but the events leading up to the birth.

## COMPRESSION OF SPACE

A rule of thumb: never separate your characters for long periods of time, no matter what Nora Ephron may tell you. In Ephron's *Sleepless in Seattle* the characters meet only at the end. It's a tribute to writer Jeff Arch and Ephron's talent that they were able to sustain the tension for as long as they did.

They say that the best way for turmoil, drama, conflict and tension to prevail is to throw the characters into a closet with and lock the door.

One of the best uses of compression of space is in one of the most popular movies ever made, *The Graduate*. In this movie the writers have a situation in which they want to put the main character through a series of life-altering events. They want to make him squirm and sweat bullets so that he *earns* the rewards from changes he goes through. This will be no walk in the park for Ben Braddock (Dustin Hoffman).

So what do the writers do? The first thing is to put the character in a place he does not want to be, where he will be in constant conflict.

They came up with the only place guaranteed to make him miserable — at home, with his parents, who give him sports cars instead of love and treat him like a stranger. Pressure from the get-go.

In your stories you have to put your character where he is most uncomfortable. In that way he needs relief, and in order to get the relief he needs to act.

You never want your character comfortable. Or if he is comfortable, make sure it isn't for more than a second or two before the shit hits the fan.

Next the writers say, okay, what life-altering experience can we give to Ben that he has not had before? How about — sex? Okay, what shall we do? Bring in an old flame from school, or maybe somebody he used to have a crush on? Too easy.

They look around and their eyes fix on next door, right across the hedge, to the neighbor. Who's living there? It's Mrs. Robinson, an older, wiser woman who smokes like a chimney and drinks like a fish.

Perfect! Older woman, young man. Ben falls into her clutches, right in plain sight of his parents (if they happened to glance across the hedge), who also know and disapprove of Mrs. Robinson.

So off Ben stumbles, to have this eye-opening sexual experience with Mrs. Robinson, who can't believe her good luck. Nice fresh, young meat, next door, marching into her clutches. Ben gets an education.

What exquisite pressure. Right next door to his dreaded parents, and he's with a woman old enough to be his mother. Ben gets laid for the first time.

Compression of space under these conditions is pressing the characters together in a confined space, in this case, as next-door neighbors. If these two houses were separated by even an empty lot the sense of claustrophobia would have been lost.

The story doesn't have to veer off somewhere in search of a woman. She's right there, and ready. Lesson: look around before you go traipsing off in search of adventure that may be under your character's nose.

Now that he's in this awful place with his awful parents, the writers are thinking, and no longer a virgin, having given it away to the hawk-like, booze-swilling Robinson — what else has Ben never experienced? Ah. Love.

The writers start searching for an object of his love. They go through the same drill: What about somebody from college? What about a girl he knew from high school, still in town, maybe across town, or even in the neighborhood?

Wait a minute, they cry in a sudden burst of inspiration: Doesn't Mrs. Robinson have a daughter? Perfect!

And so Ben, while boinking Mrs. Robinson, or, more appropriately, getting boinked by her, falls in love with her daughter, and *she* falls in love with *him*. Next door neighbors, upstairs/downstairs. Compression.

And all of it right next door, and in just a short period of time. Ben goes through a life-altering experience and in the end heads off with the girl towards an uncertain, but possibly more promising future. *The Panic Room*, *Phone Booth*, etc., all used the compression of space to their great advantage.

## COMPRESSION OF LANGUAGE

This is Strunk and White territory. I am not one of those who believe that screenwriting has no author's voice. There's some ridiculous press out there that says that because screenwriting is a bastard art that other people will eventually turn the script into digital or celluloid, the writing by definition is without much originality. These critics have not read many screenplays.

The voice or style of the writer may not be in evidence as much as in novels, but read some screenplays. Read screenplays by screenwriters and not necessarily directors with laptops. Not that directors can't write, but it's not usually their primary concern. They want to *make* a movie, not write a movie. Screenwriters want to write movies.

I mentioned earlier that some studio people insist that 80% of all screenplays options or purchases are due to the concept, not the writing. Fair enough. That's true in publishing, too. You can write up a storm of a story but if it's not going to entice an audience, it's not going to be bought.

I once read a 40-page short story about a guy watching and cogitating over a rock he found by a river bed. It was beautiful, profound; it transported me, as all good storytelling should, from one place to another. Would it have made a movie? No. A book? No. A short story in a book with other such well-written evocative stories? Probably.

How many times have I heard agents and producers say, "Boy, can so-and-so write. All she needs is the right idea." Sometimes if a script is well-written an agent will take on a writer and send it as a writing sample to producers or studios with open writing assignments.

Even if you have an idea but the writing stinks, readers at agencies and production companies will toss your script by page ten. Nobody wants to slog through a badly written script.

## MAJOR PROBLEMS TO WATCH OUT FOR

**1.** *Big blocky paragraphs chock full of* Architectural Digest *descriptive passages of rooms and lawns.*

**Bad:** Raffi passes by a 150-year-old weatherbeaten house with gables and a widow's walk. A tire hangs by a rope from a tree branch. The lawn has needed mowing for months. Chipped paint flakes lie on the ground from where they have fallen from the house. Stringy curtains hang inside the house. The veranda is lopsided.

**Better:** Raffi passes by a dilapidated Victorian mansion.

In screenplays always search for the essence of things.

**2.** *Dialogue that sounds as if it's come out of a law book, or a crashing bore who can't shut up, or someone who uses "Really?" or "Totally!" every other sentence.*

**Bad:**
Raffi: I absolutely adore that outfit you're wearing you purchased yesterday afternoon at Bonwits on 5th and 57th. Did you go there with your husband of five years and his kids from a previous marriage?

The Key West Woman: Oh thank you, Raffi, for saying that you admire my outfit from Bonwits, and yes, my darling much older husband

Reggie and his two college-aged children came down from Columbia and Sarah Lawrence in that luxurious Cadillac Reggie ordered just last week when we were visiting Count Olaf in Norway.

I've seen much worse.

**3.** *Characters who incessantly explain the plot to each other.*

**Bad:**
Raffi: Did you get the feeling that Samuel, who, by the way, spent 13 years in prison for pistol whipping his Aunt Jane, could have stolen the paintings, which I think he's hiding in his brother-in-law's basement?

The Key West Woman: I think we should follow the both of them while at the same time bringing Detective Blue in on this, though did you know that Detective Blue four years ago had been questioned in conjunction with those stolen Rauchenbergs?

Raffi: Before we get into that why don't we go back to your place and have sex before your husband gets home from target practice?

The Key West Woman: By the way, did you wear protection last time, Raffi? I meant to tell you that I forgot.

Raffi: Having a baby might complicate the investigation and create pressure on us to marry, which in both cases would constitute bigamy, but I'd chance it. How about you?

The Key West Woman: That would drive my terminally ill sister to suicide. Then we'd never know what she did with the stolen paintings. Oops. I sure let the cat out of the bag on that one.

Had enough? I have.

**4.** *Herds of characters galloping across the first ten pages.*

The reader will have enough to do in simply familiarizing herself with the set-up without having to confront a hoard of newbies. The old British spy movies used to brutalize their audiences with this device. I am convinced the whole point was to throw in as many characters as they could so that the audience could spend the rest of the movie trying to sort out who they were.

## THINGS TO DO TO PREVENT THESE PROBLEMS

**1.** *Build Active Sentences.* The ball was not hit by the boy. The boy hit the ball. Use basic active sentence construction. We tend to forget this. A movie is about someone in *active* pursuit of something: a way to get into it or a way to get out of it. The language should reflect that. If you offer us dollops of passive sentence construction you'll interrupt the reading experience, sabotage your characters and lose story momentum.

**2.** *Kill All Adverbs.* Adverbs are lazy, showy accessories that prevent the writer from utilizing the power of the verb. How many sports announcers, those great saboteurs of the power of the verb, make good writers? None? Right answer. Those "l-y" weasel words ruin more good scripts. They're like vermin. Use a simple noun, a strong active, visual verb, and move on.

**3.** *Avoid Long Paragraphs.* If you must write a long descriptive paragraph, write it out and then *edit, edit, edit,* breaking it down into smaller paragraphs. Read it aloud. Does it sound too phony or overwritten or purple? This also goes for characters. When they speak let them go, edit later. In that coal mine of babble there is a diamond hiding. If they talk too much, put a sock in their mouths and condense.

Don't write to fill space. Don't worry about how long, or short, the script is supposed to be. Keep in mind what each scene itself is about. Don't get the characters jabbering about what we can already see, or have already seen. You don't need a Greek chorus to explain action. Compress and distill.

See *Monster's Ball* for compression of language and absence of dialogue. We are inundated by TV, in which people never shut up, even on clever shows like *Grey's Anatomy* and *Desperate Housewives.* On TV, silence is anathema. If we hear silence we think the set is broken.

**4.** *Kill Excessive Description.* Do you NEED all that description? The essence of the place or object or character will do. Ask yourself this: if you were looking at a room or a vista you're about to describe, what are the one or two things that would grab your attention first? There's your answer. Get them down and move on.

Are the character's ears huge? Is her face pasty white below a shock of dreadlocked red hair? Is the house a faded blue, a small stucco box on a gravel lawn, with orange sprinkler stains running up the walls? Essence.

**5.** *Watch out for clichés.* If you've heard it before, and still use it, you're being either lazy or plagiaristic.

### *Do you really think, Uncle Arno, that your life would make a great movie?* The Art of Adaptation

Someone once said that the true art of adaptation — adapting a true life story, or a book or play, into a movie — is *not* being true to the original.

So many students get screwed up trying to remain faithful to every aspect of the story, especially true stories. Let's face it, almost every story has elements of truth.

Case in Point: *A Beautiful Mind.* Based on the life and times of John Nash, game and chaos theory mathematician, Nobel laureate, MIT professor and schizophrenic, *A Beautiful Mind*, in perfect three-act structure, charts Nash's life: the build, the destruction and the rebuild.

In Akiva Goldsman's script, under Ron Howard's direction, Nash becomes a modern tragic hero who survives through his own will power and the love of a woman, who sticks by his side throughout.

The truth, according to Sylvia Nasar's biography on Nash, is this: Nash was mean-spirited, a master of the cruel put-down. Before he married Alicia Larde, he had married another woman with whom he had a child, abandoning them both to poverty. He had many intense sexual relationships with men and was fired from the Rand Corporation for soliciting sex in a Santa Monica men's room. Alicia

Larde did not stay with him. When his illness became intolerable, she divorced him, remarrying him in 2001. The filmmakers left all this out because they felt these truths would tarnish the image of Nash they wanted to portray.

Was this ethical moviemaking? Moral? Was it smart filmmaking? Or were Ron Howard and Akiva Goldsman and the studio worried that including these facts would diminish box office potential?

Might these excluded facts have made a better movie, with a far more complex character?

The point here is that they did leave out these items. They slanted the stories to their own purposes. You can do that. You can keep or get rid of anything you want, in the service of a better story. You are not writing biography. You are making movie essence. Even biographers leave critical stuff out.

Remember T. S. Eliot's words: "All history is a contrived corridor." Everybody becomes an editor to suit a point of view.

This behavior by the filmmakers reminds me of the whitewash job Mike Nichols did on Meryl Streep's character in *Silkwood*. The writers, and later Nichols, backed away from the booze-guzzling, promiscuous Karen Silkwood because they felt that her behavior would diminish the force of her protests. What we got was a character (played magnificently by Streep) whose behavior was skewed. It was that very wildness that brought her to protest against the evil. What a missed opportunity. Yes, it was up for and won Oscars, but instead of being a good movie, it could have been a great one.

I hate it when smart guys like Mike Nichols and Ron Howard back away from good controversy, in the name of *possible* loss of box office receipts. But Hollywood is first and foremost a business.

The point? Take what's available and use your art and craft to remain faithful to the essence of the story. Trim the fat. Add drama and strong visuals. Bring to high heat. And hope you succeed.

## IF I HAVEN'T LIVED IT. WHERE DO I FIND IT? – TRACKING THE STORY BEAST

Let's say your life is boring beyond belief and the idea of finding material for a story is as remote and distant as an old love interest. Let's say you're sitting around feeling sorry for yourself, wracking your brain for something to write about, when suddenly you wonder why you're so angry! Why *are* you angry? You're angry because your former love interest blew you off, and you want satisfaction, call it revenge! You like to take revenge on people who fuck with you, don't you? He or she got away with that shit! Who did she think she was! Who did she think you were, to be treated like that!

The truth is that the love interest is gone, but not the thought or the feelings associated with that awful betrayal. As a writer in need of a story, this might be one. You're pissed. There's conflict. This may be the only time drudging up old memories like that can be profitable. There could be revenge, getting the girl back. Maybe some treachery, double-dealing, even death.

So, how would you do it? How would you get back at the love interest that screwed you over, and that evil bastard who her away in the first place? Man, you want to get some satisfaction. You have suffered enough, right? Damn right you have. Make them pay, make them suffer. Write about them, show the world what low rent creeps they really are.

A thriller writer I know and I were both in love with the same woman. She chose me. The thriller writer was pissed and in his next book I became the evil brother, the *beyond* EVIL brother, who paid for his sins (my sins) with his life. There he/I was, looked just like me, and the thriller writer, I am told, had a blast slicing and dicing me up into little insignificant pieces of Chris.

Maybe what you want is revenge with a twist, even getting the love interest back again maybe, making him or her realize what a stupid move it was to leave you in the first place, and then once you have her back, you dump her.

Start thinking, start writing. Start remembering. Drudging that shit up. Wallow in it. Get MAD!

Stories can find a good start with emotional pain, or feelings of retribution born of longing.

That's what my Emerson College student, Duncan Birmingham, did with his story that became a screenplay and opened Hollywood doors. He started thinking about a young guy who lost his father and took his father's place with his mother — in all ways but one.

Duncan, tall, lanky, with a bemused straight-arrow way about him (hiding a wicked wit), wrote the script, *Mama's Boy*, in class. After getting his MFA he moved to Hollywood and in short order, with the script as his calling card, got an agent, a manager, and an attorney and created a stir. In October 2002, after five months working on a script with producers, Universal hired Duncan, age 26, to write a big-budget baseball comedy. His career was kicked-started into high gear. He made a big chunk of dough up front; if the movie is made he stands to make in the high six figures.

Here's Duncan talking about *Mama's Boy*, a small indie dark comedy that paved his way to a career as a Hollywood screenwriter: "*Mama's Boy* is the story of Ed, a serious-minded young man who is over-protective of his beautiful but flighty mother. When his womanizing Shakespeare teacher begins a public romance with his mother, Ed sees this as a personal attack and declares a war on him that quickly snowballs out of control.

"For me, the sparking idea was the relationship between an eccentric young man who acts more like an adult than his young, party-girl single mother. I really liked the idea of this strange family dynamic and thought a long time before I figured out what the actual plot would be.

"As a fiction writer, some ideas for screenplays come from stories I've written. Newspaper and magazine articles often spark ideas — the problem is those same articles often spark similar ideas to other writers or even Hollywood producers too.

"Overall, for me everything spirals from the main character. Thinking up someone who would be interesting to watch for two hours inherently gets the ball rolling for your story. Once you establish a strong character, then you ask yourself what would really turn this character's life upside down.

"In Ed's case, he is a very lonely kid always jealous of his mother's shady suitors. When he finally does make a friend (his teacher), he then experiences the double-bombshell of having his friend betray him to get to his mother. All this when he's fighting the uphill battle of starting at a new school."

Ed longed to be something. Important? A protector of his mother's virtue? What would a young guy like Ed do to carve out a place in his mother's heart? You start with a feeling, a need, and begin to play it out, spin the yarn.

Duncan just recently sold a comedy, *Swingles*, to Paramount.

## DON'T BACK AWAY JUST BECAUSE IT'S NOT MAINSTREAM — INDIE LOVE

A big question in the mind of every screenwriter is whether to take his or her screenplay mainstream or independent. High budget or low budget? High concept or low concept?

Mainstream means major studio. I hear "It's not big enough to be a studio picture" all the time. This means that the agent or producer does not feel that the studio machine will be willing to pony up big bucks or big promotion for a movie so small, or too low-concept, to attract a big audience. In other words: Sorry, not enough potential profit. Won't attract a major star. Next.

I say to new screenwriters: Come up with a good story and write your heart out. If it's a well-written, strong story you'll get noticed by agents and producers, who will guide your career. An A-list star in the stable of one of these agents, or with whom one of these producers loves to work, will get the script from the agent or manager.

Do you want to write about incest (*Happiness*), or about a narcoleptic, transsexual who longs to get rid of eight inches (20 centimeters) of equipment that separates her from being the glamorous woman she dreams to be (*20 Centimeters*), or murder without morals in one of my favorites *(Portrait of Henry: Serial Killer)?* The studios will touch some taboo subjects, but with a feather. If, however, an A-list (or even B-list) actor comes aboard, your worries are over.

How long did it take them to make a real life movie with gay main characters (*Brokeback Mountain*)? Low dollar return doesn't encourage big production companies or studios to go out on a limb. Not those limbs.

If you have a story about a cross-dressing, hypochondriac, Oedipal-driven homicidal maniac with a pet piranha, the indie route might be for you. You never know if it's precisely the character Johnny Depp has been dying to play forever.

The catch here, of course, is that you have to write a great script. With a hypochondriac, Oedipal-driven cross-dressing homicidal maniac as your main character, you had *better* write a great script.

But there is a dilemma. You've created an excellent cross-dressing, homicidal maniac character. However, you should know how tough it is to break into the business. An agent or manager wants to see a future in a client, one in which money is present. But you don't want to write ordinary drivel. What do you do?

You're caught in the crossfire between art and commerce, or between what producers think audiences want and what the audiences genuinely want — which sometimes is the same thing.

When William Goldman said that the only given in Hollywood is that nobody knows anything, he wasn't kidding.

When I teach I rarely try to talk anybody out of a story they want to tell. Something drives the writer towards certain subject matter. To deny that urge, especially at the beginning stages, usually sends the writer, already frustrated, chasing after derivative trains, and ending up with formulaic crap we've all seen before.

So what do you do? Find out what the driving force is. What are you tapping into here? Take a look at some of last year's Sundance entries' log lines and concepts:

***The Quiet:*** A deaf mute woman goes to live with her godparents and their daughter where she discovers just how silently crazy a family can be. Popular cheerleader Nina Deer's world is turned upside down when her parents adopt a recently orphaned deaf girl, Dot. Things are not what they seem. Dot's arrival puts a crack in Nina's idyllic social life and her family's dark secrets become exposed.

***Quinceanera:*** Magdalena's 15th birthday approaches. Her simple life goes haywire when she finds out she's pregnant. Kicked out of her house, she finds a new family with her great-granduncle and gay cousin who aren't the salvation she thought they were, and now she has to grow up in a hurry.

***Little Miss Sunshine:*** A family determined to get their young daughter into the finals of a beauty pageant take a cross-country trip in their busted VW bus.

***Half Nelson:*** Dan Dunne battles both his own fears of not reaching his teenage students and his accelerating drug addiction. An idealistic inner-city junior high school teacher with a drug habit hooks up with Drey, one of her troubled students. Through her newly acquired drug habit, she gets closer to him. Will this undo them or give them the courage to move forward in their lives?

***Factotum:*** Hank Chinaski, the fictional alter-ego of *Factotum* author Charles Bukowski, wanders around Los Angeles trying to live off jobs that don't interfere with his writing. The same old temptations — women, drinking and gambling — try mightily to tear him away from this course.

***Mutual Appreciation:*** Alan, a musician, leaves a bad local band for New York. He tries to stay focused while fending off an attraction to his good friend's girlfriend, searching for the perfect drummer, practicing his own self-promotion, and falling in love with a radio DJ to whom he can't express his feelings.

What these movies have in common is damaged youthful desperation, the need for drugs, alcohol, and sex to fuel relationships, and the fear/realization of being truly alienated to those closest to them. Take Heath Ledger. He played a heroin addict in *Candy* (2006). He played the role of Dan, a poet with an addiction for heroin and for Candy, a girl who falls in love with him and his addiction. A powerful movie about a raw subject, written well enough to attract an A-list actor.

# WORKSHOP 6

# You're Writing in What Genre?

A romantic comedy/Western/action thriller with fish-out-of-water, psychological, women-in-jeopardy, period-piece elements, supported by sci-fi/horror/fantasy links with supernatural overtones?

Sure, send it over. My address? The moon.

In some of my film and book projects, I have committed a cardinal sin. I floated over borders and crisscrossed genres, making it impossible for sales departments in studios and publishing houses to sell the projects.

In a screenplay on which I worked for a year, about a couple of airplane repo men who mistakenly kidnap a beautiful young woman from a very powerful father who will do anything to get her back, I met a wall.

The kicker is that the woman is an extraordinary android and the plane jockeys, who have had huge relationship problems with women to begin with, unwittingly fall in love with her.

The fliers will do anything to protect her, while her powerful father/creator will do anything to get her back. And the chase was on.

What did we have here? A buddy movie trying to cross-fertilize with a futuristic sci-fi thriller, and a love story. This was the pitch and perception. When the agents and managers sent it around town, it was turned down everywhere. *Skyjax* never got off the ground.

More heartbreak in the city of heartbreaks. No one budged. It was an $80 million movie that nobody wanted to take a chance on. I learned a lesson — actually a couple of them.

One was that you don't write an $80 million movie that crosses genres because nobody in his right financial mind is going to risk that much dough on a hybrid that a studio sales department can't figure out how to sell. This was one that didn't make it.

Then there was one that did make it. In 1997, a nonfiction book I wrote, *The Huntress,* was published, a true story about a mother-daughter bounty hunting team in Los Angeles. Dottie and her daughter, Brandi Thorson, lost their husband/father, Ralph Thorson, legendary bounty hunter, when one of the cons he put in prison got out and planted a bomb in his car, killing him. After his death, Dottie and Brandi discovered that Ralph had sold the house and had accumulated debt to the tune of $150,000. What were the women going to do?

They knew one thing very well, the family bounty hunting business. They grew up in it. And so they became partners. USA Network shot a movie-of-the-week/pilot and shot 34 hour-long episodes. I wrote for the series, was a co-producer, made some money.

Why one and not the other? For one thing, in *The Huntress* there was no mistaking what the story was, who the characters were, and what genre it fit into. The studio could sell it.

It had two women in jeopardy against a male-dominated world. The "women as bounty hunters" theme was different and plausible. They went after bail jumpers who ran big companies and others who ate rats under bridges, very bad guys. They chased bail-jumping women who killed, old men, young women. In other words, they went after their prey everywhere.

The studio could *see* the story. They could sell it. And viewers watched it. It fit into a genre–action with a subgenre: women in jeopardy.

The movie business, like most businesses, is category driven. Sales departments sell categories and rarely will venture outside of that tightly controlled atmosphere. Even though studios or networks may love everything about a series, they will turn it down because they don't know — or don't have time to figure out — how to pitch it to the public.

This practice, or lack of it, is, to fiscal-minded people, bottom-line, iron-clad wisdom. To the creative instinct, it stifles.

I'm of two minds about this. One mind says, yes, if you cross genres your script will be tougher to sell. But if you love what you are writing, my other mind says, don't stifle yourself.

My practical side tells me to use my creative juices to saturate a genre with new and more wonderful characters, details, reversals, etc. My creative mind keeps moving toward the genre borderlines, trying to stretch as much as possible without getting cramped.

My advice is to understand the categories or genres and then, if you must, stretch their borders.

Everything about your story may work, except how to sell it — which is the kiss of death. If you confuse the sales staff, you lose.

# CATEGORIES

## 1. THRILLERS

The very mention of "thriller" makes me sit up and pay attention. Thriller means suspense, not just action. It points to that most fabulous of all writing devices — dramatic irony — in which the audience knows more than the main character. "Don't go through that door!" we cry silently. "Don't get in that car!"

Look at all the subgenres attached to the thriller: romantic-thriller, comedy-thriller, action-thriller, suspense-thriller (a redundancy if I ever heard one), psychological-thriller, political-thriller. I've heard X-thriller and noir thriller. You name it, it's a thriller of some kind.

A thriller usually has one main character who stumbles in where he or she doesn't belong and screws up some major operation already in progress, usually run by the bad guy. This main character should be a major pain in the ass to the villain who spends the whole movie trying to get rid of this pest.

Wouldn't you, if you had a plan you'd worked on for months, even years, and now some jamoke strolls in — the main character — and starts botching the works?

Somebody once said, and I agree, that we should have more sympathy for the villains. These poor souls spend time, effort, and money planning this big deal (usually illegal and often lethal, but it's a living), and then one afternoon the pest (stranger/hero) comes to town and starts ruining everything. So what if what the villain is doing this illegal thing? THAT'S NOT THE POINT.

Anyway, that's the thriller: Your main character bumbles in and spends the next two hours of movie time isolated and in danger, trying to reestablish order from the chaos he has unwittingly created.

Take *Blue Velvet*, a noir thriller, the David Lynch sicko extravaganza that made more of an impact on me than any film I have ever seen. The kid/hero comes home to see his ailing father. One afternoon, in the middle of a vacant lot, he stumbles upon a severed ear, and the story kicks into gear.

The ear leads him to the discovery of love and sex and demented townie creeps, led by Dennis Hopper, who are running the town from the shadows behind the town's red rose-blue velvet exterior.

The hero/pest keeps finding clues, which lead to the downfall of the bad guys and an awakening by the pest in his journey from innocence to experience. It took my breath away.

David Lynch, an NYU art major, brought his visual world to the picture. I've seen *Blue Velvet* at least fifteen times. It changed forever my perception of what was possible in writing movies.

Lynch roars on. *Mulholland Drive*, which TV turned down as too odd, went on to star Naomi Watts and won Best Picture and Best Director of 2001 by both the NYC and L.A. Film Critics respectively.

As a tyro scribe, you should stick to the tenets of the genre. Add dollops from other genres, but don't let them overtake the solid foundation of the genre you're working in. And read produced scripts in the genre you've decided to tackle.

The last point here is to keep in mind that A-list actors are very conscious of genre. They don't want their reputations getting hung up in a hybrid that may look good on paper but confuses mightily after it's made. Remember when you're writing for an A-list actor, he or she may never get the script. The agents and managers will cut it off at the pass as something too genre-conflicted and therefore a poor career move for their client who, God forbid, may take a drop in salary or, if the movie tanks, may *have* to take a drop in salary.

**Musts for Thrillers**
• Isolate and put in nail-biting jeopardy your main character.
• Concentrate on suspense and tension over action.
• Make us identify with the main character's fears, needs, and the depth of each.
• Give us a villain more driven and often smarter than the main character, and more dramatically terrifying — until at the end when the hero usually digs deep and, by discovering the villain's Achilles Heel, prevails.

## 2. ACTION ADVENTURE

Fifty-five percent of all pictures fall into the Action-Adventure category. The reason for this is just what the term "action-adventure" (including comics adaptations) implies: Lots of high-tech elements, blood and adventure, and more visual than talky, which means foreign markets won't have to worry about language nuance. Any dialogue is so simplistic that foreign audiences get it quickly. Action-adventure aims at the testosterone-driven teen market.

The hero can be an action-hero or a main character who sheds his identity to become the fantasy creature who does the bad guys in. Jean Claude Van Damme, Arnold, Wesley Snipes, George Clooney's Batman; that crowd.

A main element of this genre: *reversals of fortune*. The hero hops in a high-tech truck to chase after the villain, BUT: The truck has a ticking bomb under it the hero doesn't know about.

The hero is just about to rescue the girl, WHEN: the girl turns into the villain, and then morphs into a beautiful woman who looks just like the hero's dead girlfriend come back to life.

The hero realizes what is going on and is about to nab the villain, WHEN: the bomb explodes, sending the truck and the hero into a ditch. A dog comes up and guides the hero out, BUT: the dog bites the hero, filling his body with a virus. And so on until the hero figures out a way to get well and return to battle with the villain.

Action pictures have simple plots and simple characters, with one main objective that usually screws up the main character, who now has to take an alternative route to fulfill his objective. Psychological insight muddies these shallow waters. Clever, ironic dialogue confuses the issues. Keep it simple.

Examples in this genre: the Vin Diesel movies, the James Bond movies, some of the Arnold movies, the old Stallone movies. You know what I mean. Simple, often stupid, stuff.

In Stallone's movies, for instance, when it's time for the love interest to appear, she does, as let's say a breathtakingly gorgeous Laotian national. He meets her in the jungle or on a ledge overlooking the raging river she's just saved him from. Their passion for one another makes the banana trees blush. They make love, the two of them, their sweat-glistened backs stealing all focus, and when they're spent a shot is fired, the woman falls off the ledge, just barely out of Stallone's reach, and perishes in the river below.

Now it's Stallone's eyes that glisten with tears over the death of what's-her-name. What a waste. But like any soldier who knows his aphorisms, the one that comes to mind is this: He who travels farthest travels alone. Now our hero has another reason to single-handedly wipe out the Laotian army by tomorrow afternoon.

### Musts for Action Pictures
• Concentrate on action and adventure over suspense.
• In the main characters, what you see is what you get.
• Use many reversals of fortune for the main characters in his or her quest.

### 3. ROMANTIC COMEDY

When you write to attract an A-list romantic comedy star, you probably think of Jennifer Aniston, Julia Roberts, Sarah Jessica Parker, Jennifer Lopez, Cameron Diaz, or Sandra Bullock.

In romantic comedies, girl gets guy, girl loses guy, another girl gets guy, original girl fights for guy and gets him back. These date movies and "chick flicks" draw big audiences.

The key here is to find a territory that hasn't been exploited to death and then provide enough twists and turns to make the story itself and the outcome unpredictable — at least until the last moment, at which point the man and woman overcome ludicrous odds to show, once again, that love does win in the end.

Former *Boston Globe* film critic Michael Blowen and I wrote a romantic comedy, "Best of Boston," about a couple, both reporters, working for a *Globe*-like paper. They love each other but take each other for granted. She's a dogged crime reporter. He's the gossip columnist who once was a dogged crime reporter until he screwed up.

One day, the local magazine names her Boston's Best Journalist, and names him Boston's Worst. The story is what happens to their relationship as a result.

Not a bad concept. A production company optioned it. There was a lot of gab about the potential. Our problem was that we didn't make it tough enough on the main characters. They were too jokey and glib. None of that fierce sense of loss and betrayal showed up in them, to make the audience respond as they should have. If we had gone for the turmoil of *The Wedding Planner* or *My Best Friend's Wedding*, we might have fared better.

But we were too easy on them. In our version, the moment in their lives was not critical enough. The stakes were not high enough. Though the concept was strong, "Best of Boston" did not generate enough studio interest in the *plight of the characters.*

If you're going to work in this highly competitive genre, not only do you need a high concept but vivid, dynamic characters the A-list talent want to play and audiences want to *root for*, characters in an emotional life-or-death, high-stakes game.

What are your all-time favorite romantic comedies? The Katherine Hepburn-Spencer Tracy or Hepburn-Cary Grant, or *Pretty Woman, Shakespeare in Love, An American President, Legally Blonde, When Harry Met Sally, Sweet Home Alabama*? What did you respond to in these pictures?

**Musts for Romantic Comedies**
• A fierce battle of the sexes.
• Two main characters at the most critical moments of their emotional lives.
• A barrage of unspeakable, often zany horrors they have to overcome in order to reach each other.
• Strong, compelling characters we can identify with, in situations we can relate to.

## 4. STRAIGHT COMEDIES

I would give anything to be able to write a movie like *Big*. I would give not much to write an *American Pie* franchise flick (though I would like to have the box office numbers). Straight comedies rely on timing, with foundations in tragedy, rising out of a dire situation, from which the humor emerges.

In these movies, if you strip away the jokes you will find a pathetic, vulnerable human being in the midst of the worst crisis he or she has ever faced.

One of the tenets of great comedy is not to play for or write jokes. The characters have to play it straight; no mugging, please. Humor rises out of situation.

I have read scripts in which the writers tried to be too funny or clever, replete with old jokes, Marx Brothers routines, anything to get a laugh. I once saw a rendition of Neil Simon's *The Odd Couple*, in which every actor mugged, winked at the audience, you name it. It received not one laugh; not one, through the entire performance. *The Odd Couple*! Can you imagine how hard the cast had to work, *and how bad they had to be,* to pull off that miracle!

They say that comedy is the most difficult to write. The Coen Brothers come close to perfection in *Brother, Where Art Thou?*, *Raising Arizona*, and *Fargo*.

The subgenres are dark comedy, farce, slapstick, and others.

Remember how Billy Wilder worked comedic wonders with *Some Like It Hot*? *Tootsie* depended on a strong, driven, main character in jeopardy, one who is willing to do *anything,* including changing his gender, to get a job acting. *Best in Show*, an event comedy wrapped around a dog show, is one of the funniest movies of all time. Why? Against the characters' passions and obsessions to win, they play it straight.

*Wedding Crashers* was funny, even though the actors came close to the line many times but pulled back before crossing the line into farce. I was so glad to see Will Ferrell in *Stranger than Fiction* because, in my humble opinion, he had begun to chew the scenery so much and so often that he was single-handedly ruining entire motion pictures. That over-the-top scene chewing was not acting but emoting in a single overwrought key. In *Stranger than Fiction*, he showed restraint and was good at it.

Then there's the strange case of Nicholas Cage, possibly the finest comedic actor working in films today, if he still has his touch. I remember his brilliant star turns in *Raising Arizona, Red Rock West*, and *Fast Times at Ridgemont High*. Probably the worst thing that could have happened to American audiences was his Oscar-winning performance in *Leaving Las Vegas*. It convinced him somehow that he was a male ingenue/leading man. Nick Cage is not a male ingenue/leading man. He's a goofy-looking guy with perfect comedic timing. But for some reason he didn't want to do comedies anymore and started taking roles for which he was unsuited, like *Con Air*.

In *City of Angels*, he played an angel. If I were the Meg Ryan character in that picture and had to convince the world that this goofball with the Bronx accent was going to save my day, I would have laughed until I died. Ludicrous is the nicest thing I can say about that experience.

When you think about his performance in *Leaving Las Vegas* you could say that as a self-pitying, pathetic alcoholic bumbler, he played the saddest of clowns who had fallen so far he would never be able to make it back. As sad drunken clown, he was magnificent.

My point here is that when you write a part with Nicholas Cage, or any A-list actor in mind, you should always write to strength.

At the same time, make sure that the first thing you think about is the story or the character, not the actor. Your passion for the story should always trump who you would like to play it. Get the story rolling, have the main character growing before your eyes, and then let your mind slip through the A-list, watching carefully for the actor who would best suit you.

Remember what the actor's true strength is and choose accordingly. By the time you're done with the outline, that A-list actor will feel entrenched.

I would always write for a star. You have a persona, you have a face, you have physically a fully developed human being before you at all times.

I'm convinced that a major reason preventing screenwriters from being able to capture a character as fully as need be is that no face or body has ever been developed sufficiently.

The writer has used a ghost, an amalgam of this and that. Agents and managers always ask their clients who they see in the role. Who you choose to play the most important role in your screenplay says a lot about you and your choices and more importantly your character. You've cast him or her. Think about that. You've been willing and able to go that far in a short period of time.

**Musts for Straight Comedies**
• Put the characters into utterly hopeless, tragic situations.
• Pull their obsessions from them, put them on display, and exaggerate them.
• Make sure the characters do not mug or play for comedy but treat their dilemmas as if they were Hamlet. What may seem slightly absurd to us is deadly serious to them.


## 5. HORROR

I can't tell you the number of times during the past couple of years that producers have ask me if I had a horror movie in the works.

Horror flicks scare the hell out of me. I watched *Alien* through my fingers. In theaters I've listened to more horror films than I've watched. I remember seeing *Night of the Living Dead* with a clicker in my hand, every couple of seconds cutting back to the ball game.

For days afterwards, the *Scream* flicks made me sick. You might wonder why I keep watching these things that scare me to death.

Aside from my own dark needs, the horror movies I've seen have been well made. In *The Shining*, for instance, Kubrick decided to eliminate all shadows, formerly a mainstay of this genre. Then he gave us an incomprehensibly evil villain who for his own demented reasons wants to kill innocent, unsuspecting people.

The writers accomplish this through shock and surprise and hiding the creature until the last possible moment. We didn't see how crazy the Nicholson character in *The Shining* was until his wife did. We heard the shark in *Jaws* long before we saw it. We felt the Alien's presence long before it showed up.

The horror story creature runs on the fuel of human fears. Usually the evil has been dormant, living a relatively quiet existence until somebody shows up and disturbs it. The shark and the alien were getting along quite well, until humans tramped all over their territories.

Good horror writers know how to manipulate the readers' emotions visually. If you write in the horror genre, make your villain fiercely original, while at the same time so familiar in the villain's emotional logic that we can identify with it and are horrified at how close we live to that line.

**Musts for Horror**
1. The villain is a monster-like human or human-like monster. If your home comes under attack from the neighbors, might you become a monster-like human? Take time to look at the story from the monster's point of view.
2. The farther the main characters go into the hell the greater the escalating, unspeakable horrors they meet.
3. In his fiction, Stephen King assails our own greatest childhood fears. So should you — perhaps your own greatest childhood fears.

## 6. STRAIGHT DRAMA

Straight dramas fall into a large category called everything else. There are period pieces like *Marie Antoinette* and *The Good Shepherd*, crime dramas like *Departed* and action romances like *Indiana Jones IV.*

The tenets of this broad genre fall into the same batch as in other genres, except here the idiosyncrasies of the subgenres dictate much of the pictures' tones.

*Fargo* can be called a crime drama, a character piece, even a horror flick, and finally a straight drama, when none of the other categories fit.

One could make a case for straight drama being spun off into all of the above categories. But the more specific the needs of the genre, the better off you'll be to follow them closely.

Studios need to know how to sell the movie, what to sell it as. In many cases, as mentioned above, the studios pass on cross-fertilized or hybrid pictures because they cannot define the genre. Or after the movie is shot it's somehow become something else.

"It was nothing like the trailer" is a familiar lament.

The key to mastering the genre you're writing in is to rent at least five movies in the category. Even more importantly, read five scripts of movies in the genre. Seeing is not enough. Reading is essential. You have to see how the pros do it on the page. Without this, you will remain hopelessly inadequate.

Here are three websites that offer downloaded scripts or can steer you to sites that have them. Once you find what genre you want to write in, you can find scripts that match the genre and read them.

• *http://sfy.ru/* publishes award-winning shooting scripts in their professional format.

• Movie Script Database (*www.iscriptdb.com*) is a search directory for scripts online. Some scripts are free downloads, others require a fee. Most of these scripts are properly formatted and the draft is identified.

• *http://www.script-o-rama.com*. This is the oldest and one of the most reliable of the script websites.

# THE FOURTH HORSEMAN:
## PLOT

What is plot? A tourist meets a poor Scandinavian rug salesman up near the fjords. He feels sorry for the salesman and insists on buying all his rugs. The next morning he returns to find that the salesman has died of frostbite. But did he? Was the tourist so insensitive as to not realize that if he bought *all* of the rugs he would have nothing to keep him warm?

**Plot** is a story's particular *action*, from the Greek *praxis*. Plot equals the actions of a story. With no story there is no plot, only a series of random actions.

If story is a series of events or situations strung together, plot puts the "how come?" or "why?" into the series of events, their cause and effect. Cause and effect examines the characters' patterns of behavior.

**Story**: Once there was a ring forged long ago in the depths of hell. This ring, over time, found its way into the hands of a young man, and forever changed his life and those around him.

**Plot**: Once there was a ring forged long ago in the depths of hell.

This ring, over time, found its way into the hands of a young man, whose destiny it was to try to return it to the depths of hell in order to destroy the ring and save mankind.

**Structure**: Act I: Boy meets ring. Act II: Boy goes to hell on a mission to return ring. Act III: In hell, boy destroys ring.

The **Story** of *Lord of The Rings* gives us the overall concept and situation: a chain of events about an ancient ring, a kid, and what happens to them both along the way.

**Plot** brings the character's motivation and drive into play. The kid has to face great odds to get the ring back, *to save Middle Earth and mankind*. The motivational *why* creates a pattern of thought and action on the part of the characters. **Story** is comprised of tidbits of action and event. **Plot** inserts a beating heart, filled with need and want, into the story.

When Jim Thompson said there are a total of 32 stories ever told but only one plot — things are not what they seem — he could have been referring to J. R. R. Tolkien's story. The kid has no idea what's going to happen, and neither do we.

If he had, he would have run off screaming for his mother. As is, this innocent kid has been chosen, in Tolkien's story, to save Middle Earth.

```
                    MANKIND
          Hey, kid, got a minute?

                    KID
          Sure, what up?

Mankind holds up a pretty RING:

                    KID (CON'T)
          Hey, nice…

                    MANKIND
          Yeah, well, how'd you like to
          make ten bucks?
```

                    KID
Sure.

                    MANKIND
I'm a little busy right now, so
could you drop this ring off for me?
It's just over that rise. Take
you no time at all.

                    KID
No prob.

                    MANKIND
The sooner the better. And, kid…

                    KID
Yeah?

                    MANKIND
I been told that of all the
kids living in these parts,
you're the go-to guy for this
kind of thing. Am I wrong?

                    KID
No, no. I'll do it.

Mankind gives him a look…

                    KID (CON'T)
No, no. Believe me, I'll get it done.
                    MANKIND
No matter what?

                    KID
No matter what.

So off the Kid goes on his "no matter what" mission, with his best
friend and a couple of other tag-along buddies looking for something
fun to do.

Along the way they meet some very bad people who also have an
interest in this ring.

The farther they go, the stranger things get, and the more *things are not even close to what they seem.*

Even though the Kid wonders what in hell he's gotten himself into, he's more determined than ever to get the job done.

Welcome to plot.

If **Story** is a chronicle of events, **Plot** is a chronicle of events *pushed from behind by cause and effect* — the *why* of storytelling. Why the characters do what they do.

Plot = story + motivation.

I don't think that any writer ever starts out to write anything but a character-driven plot. Many end up as pieces of action-junk because the writer has no idea who his main character is, or what he wants. Even if the writer knows what he wants, he can't figure out how he can get it. "I'm stuck," the writer shouts, and promptly brings in a PLOT DEVICE: another ugly helicopter with its ugly pilot to try to mow the hero over.

Story is a misshapen though often exciting conglomeration of idea, concept, and notion. It's got some half-formed characters, some half-assed ideas floating around that give it some energy. So the writer snaps to this ***Story Idea.***

Climb inside this story room and see what you've got. One thing you notice is the *type* of story you have. You remember these labels or categories you've learned from childhood: ***Types of Stories.*** Add characters and motivation and you have: ***Types of Plots.***

You ask yourself: is this about a Quest? Revenge? Coming of Age? David and Goliath? What type of plot *is* this?

As you build on it, you discover that it's fitting more and more into one of these categories. So off you go to look up with these categories are.

This is all about motivation. Is your plot character driven or plot driven, or both? Is this Claude van Damme you're talking about, or Lawrence of Arabia? Is this Ben Braddock in *The Graduate*, an *Election*-type story, or the adventures of Shrek?

If you get stuck, grab your character by the neck, hold her up and shake violently until the character tells you what she wants in this plot. Revenge? Retribution? The Holy Grail. What!?

Once you get that information, you ask: What would you do and be willing to give up to reach this objective?

One of the big problems with most scripts is that all the characters sound as if they come from one set of sensibilities (they do — the writer's), rather than from a smart, canny, thinking source that makes it look as if the characters act on their own and are not manipulated by the writer who unwittingly plays God.

# PLOT CATEGORIES

From Aristotle on, writers have been trying to categorize plots.

When you're creating and building and writing, and finally pitching to the agents, producers or studios, it helps to know where your movie sits.

Like most businesses, moviemaking is category driven.

### 1. SAVE THE WORLD? NO PROBLEM — THE QUEST PLOT.

In his excellent book, *20 Master Plots*, Ronald Tobias says, "Before plot there was story. Plot is story that has a pattern of action and reaction."

A strong character with flaws goes after something that will save the world, himself, his mother, somebody. The plot involves a series of episodes, each one more dangerous than the last, with heightened stakes, derring-do, loads of reversals. We should be on the edge of our seats.

**Hits**: The *Indiana Jones* series, *Star Wars*, *Lord of the Rings*, *Harry Potter* series. *The Matrix* series.

**Flops**: *Aeron Flux, King Kong, End of Days, War of the Worlds*.

The key to the Quest category is the quest itself. Your character goes after something or someone and will not give up until she gets it.

If you're writing a Quest plot, put a sign above your computer that says something like: "This is a story about so-and-so *who will do anything* to get such-and-such." Set your character in motion and, through a series of increasingly more life-threatening episodes, your character hopefully learns something while also saving the day.

It should be a simple story. The objective is always right in front of the character, but out of reach. Just when she's about to lay her hands on it, it slips away. Frustration and anger creep in, then a great desire to say, "Screw it. I'm not going another foot!" But by this time, she's too invested and there is no turning back.

Your job as a writer is to come up with all sorts of external (visual) hurdles and internal (emotional) demons to prevent the main character from reaching her goal — thus making her work harder than she has ever worked before, which builds character.

In movies, character is as character does. Characters' wants and needs drive strong, savvy, compelling plots. Weak plots rely on external action to keep them going. These writers know so little about their characters, or care so little about them, that they seek objects to drive the plots forward.

T. E. Lawrence in the Robert Bolt-written *Lawrence of Arabia* drives the plot by his obsession to be an Anglo king of the desert and to right what is wrong. In *Munich* it's the obsessive drive by five men ordered to eliminate those Black September members who killed the 11 Israeli athletes.

Fundamentally, you've got to have a goal for the character to chase after. Without a goal, you have no story or plot.

Though most quest movies are big-budget pictures like *Gladiator* and *Spartacus* and those mentioned above, some independent pictures share many of the same tenets, on a smaller scale.

**Musts for Quest Plots**
• The main character, perhaps a modern-day Don Quixote, is on a search for real meaning in a cynical world.
• The character changes significantly as a result of the quest.
• The character starts after something he wants and instead ends up with something he needs.

### 2. GO AHEAD, HONEY, I'LL GIVE YOU A TEN-MINUTE HEAD START — THE HIDE & SEEK PLOT

Guys chasing each other. Women chased by guys. James Bond chasing the bad guys in *Casino Royale*.

What I like to call "hide and seek" movies are typically episodic, big-budget, multi-location pictures fueled by low-tech characterization and lots of pyrotechnics. These movies usually waste big name talent by hauling music video directors in to soup up the story with hot visuals and name bands. These flicks, like *The Cell* and *Vanilla Sky*, target 18- to 24-year-old males.

On the smaller scale, you could write your own *Memento*, about a guy chasing after his own memory, if it *is* his own memory. He can't remember anything and so has written his recent past on his skin in order to try to discover what is real or not. It's brilliantly written as a puzzle that makes the audience work. It's tightly focused on the central character and his quirky, fanatical need to find the truth. It was shot on a low budget and won all sorts of awards.

The key to Hide & Seek is its constant movement and suspense. Take *The Panic Room* with Jodi Foster. Mother and son move into a large city apartment. One of the rooms is a secret place, which the son makes his own room. Bad guys break in. Mother and son hide in the Panic Room. The entire story revolves around Jodi Foster and her son — the Innocents — trying to outwit the Uglies, who will do anything to get at them and the dark secret.

Vulnerable characters. Tight budget. Enclosed area. Pressure, tension and suspense. Mother and child, innocents in a box, versus a half dozen black op-alpha males. Uglies trying to pry the box open. Innocents become experienced as they elude the Uglies, then turn on them.

In your Hide & Seek plot, how large is your field of play? An apartment? A city? A world filled with expensive locations? The TV series *Alias* travels the world. Each location is ID'd by music and a murky set, or a high-angled cityscape shot over rooftops of, let's say, Cairo.

Think compression. Compression of time and place and language are essential elements (see Workshop Five). The main characters are squeezed into tiny spaces with a clock ticking. Will the bad guys figure out how to get inside the panic room? Will the air give out before they do?

In Hide & Seek flicks, you want BIG SUSPENSE and TENSION, not just action. Simply put, action is two riders on horseback chasing down another rider. Tension is the audience knowing that the rider being chased has a cobra crawling out of the saddlebag, up over the horn, toward his neck.

In other words, play up **Dramatic Irony,** which means that the audience knows just a little bit more than the hero. In this case, that cobra. You want the audience to cringe, to want to rush up into the scene and shout: "*Watch out for the cobra*!" Tension and dramatic irony are key elements in this category.

Put your main characters in a vice, or lock them in a metaphorical closet (or a real one), and never let them out. If they do manage to get out, *let them do it by their own wits,* not your contrivances. Never bring in that Greek invention, the *deus ex machina*, the god out of the machine, who suddenly appears and saves the day. In today's movies, there are no cavalries to bail your characters out.

When you're trying to figure out how your characters will get out of each jam, don't try so hard. Ask your characters. They have the answers, believe me. The readers don't care how *you* will get your characters out, but how your characters will get themselves out.

Remember, in this kind of movie, the chase is the thing. We're not in westerns anymore where John Wayne chased down the bad guys. These days, the hero, or heroine, is the one being chased. For better or worse, John Wayne is dead and gone. Today's hero, or heroine, is in constant, nail-biting jeopardy. In *The Matrix,* for instance, the machines chase the freethinkers who broke from the Matrix. You'll notice that some movies combine one or more plots. For instance, *The Matrix* can also be characterized as a Quest Plot.

These Hide & Seek plots have subgenres — rescue, kidnap, etc. — all having to do with a simple straightforward plot: somebody chasing somebody else toward some bad end.

Your challenge is to make it original. Save the kid. Save the girl. Save the world. A race against time.

These plots all have Ticking Clocks. If you don't save the kid by midnight the ducks will be let through the trap door and peck his flesh to death.

A Ticking Clock frames the time line. It puts pressure and tension on your characters to get the job done. Keeping your eye on The Ticking Clock also helps to create what movies ought to be — tension-filled stories.

One of my favorite ticking clock movies happens to be the movie that changed forever my way of looking at the movies — *Blue Velvet.* Here the main character finds himself in the clutches of a corrupt town and its sadistic leader, played by Dennis Hopper. The hero sheds his innocence as he goes. Will he be able to solve the crime and stem the tide of corruption *before it's too late*? Will he be able to keep from becoming the next victim? Will he be able to save the dark woman (Isabella Rossellini) who took his virginity, or the girl next door (Laura Dern), who stole his heart? I was on the edge of my seat, transfixed, scared to death, knowing what was waiting for him, and knowing also that he would never turn back.

Put a ticking clock into your story and watch the stakes rise.

### Musts for Hide & Seek Movies
• All the characters revolve around one central event.
• The story unfolds in a series of rapidly accelerating events over a short period of time.
• The stakes are higher than they have ever been.
• Everything culminates in a riveting, slam bang climax.
• Tell your characters: "You're on the clock!" Put pressure on them to get the job done. No characters should be hanging around the plot. If they are, write them out.

### 3. You Done Me Wrong, You Evil Bastard, and I'll Track You Till My Dying Day — The Revenge Plot

Many moons ago, Charles Bronson starred in a movie about a guy whose wife was killed. Nobody had time to go after the killer, so Bronson's character decided to take matters into his own hands. *Death Wish* was so popular that it spurred three remakes.

Revenge is a popular motivation. The hero often lives a regular life. We get to know him and his friend or wife or dog. Some wretch comes in and knocks off the friend, wife or dog, and the movie kicks into gear.

The hero, or heroine, goes to the cops, who aren't much help. Against everybody's advice, the hero, who knows next to nothing about tracking a killer, starts tracking the killer.

Along the way he battles the cops, his own ineptitude, and finally the killer himself. Straightforward stuff. Once again, we have a simple story, nothing too complicated. As it should be.

If you want to write a compelling revenge plot, complicate the characters, put them in a venue we haven't seen before. Maybe the crime is off beat. Maybe the killer isn't who the hero thinks he or she is. Take *Reservoir Dogs*, a low budget indie about a handful of gangsters who screw up a jewelry store job.

They rendezvous at a small house. In this confined place suspicions mount, accusations are made and the men, all wanting revenge for unsubstantiated despair, start killing each other off, thinking there's a cop/snitch among them.

Space and time compress. The story is told in non-chronological order. The pressure mounts. The men, and the audience, feel as if they're in a cell. They can't breathe.

In many of these movies, the hero's moral justification keeps him going, and keeps us riveted to the screen. We want him to succeed. But it looks as if this hero, world-weary or off-kilter as he is, won't be able to fry an egg, much less catch a murderer.

The hero meets an army of reversals. Just when he thinks he's about to catch the culprit, bad stuff happens to him, throwing him off at every turn. Reversals are big items in revenge plots, which is another version of a chase movie, only in this case the good guy is the pursuer, not the pursued.

For instance, the plot to *In the Bedroom* is about a father avenging the murder of his son. *Hamlet* is about a son avenging the murder of his father.

The plot is the engine, driving the story forward. Remember that note above your computer: "This is a story about so-and-so *who is willing do anything* to get such and such?" When you get fuzzy about what you're supposed to be writing, stare at that note. It will get you back on track. This simple sentence illuminates the spine of your movie: everything revolves around the spine. If you find yourself sailing off somewhere, away from the plot, tack back and get on course. Otherwise, you'll be carried away on a bed of seductive trade winds, never to be seen again. Why? Because, out of confusion, avoidance and terror of being lost, *you will never finish the script!*

The reason I'm laying out these categories is to try to keep you in line with the kind of story you're telling. It's so easy to get swept away. God knows I've done it.

In the end, it's the most awful feeling, being lost at sea, with no way home.

### Musts for the Revenge Plot
• The Hero is usually an ordinary person who suffers a grave injustice, for which he seeks revenge.
• But first he tries and fails to get official help.
• The better revenge plots show action *and* examine the motives for the revenge.
• The plot may be a Revenge Suspense (*Hamlet*), in which we know the villain's identity OR a Revenge Mystery, in which we don't (*Patriot Games*).
• However the hero punishes the villain, the punishment should never exceed the crime. *The War of The Roses* was one of the most intense revenge plots of all times, as Michael Douglas and Kathleen Turner, a married couple about to get divorced, went after each other. A lot of people hated that movie because it reminded them of how their divorce went, or how bad it was about to become.

## 4. KICK SAND IN *MY* FACE, WILL YA — THE DAVID VERSUS GOLIATH PLOT

One of the most successful genres in movies, the David versus Goliath Plot gives the A-list actor a huge advantage. If he or she can find the right role — one that is meaty and will enhance his or her career — it means, in this genre, the audience leaves the theater with a good impression of the A-list actor. Win win. Good script. Story of David overcoming Goliath leaves audience with favorable impression of actor.

It's little guy versus big guy. Take *The Insider*, the Russell Crowe movie about the tobacco company whistle blower. He has to fight his company, the industry itself, his own conscience, the breakup of his family, and TV network news phonies. He's exhausted. It looks impossible, out of the question, for him to go through this, with all this at stake.

We think the guy is nuts, but his determination and need to right a wrong make us root for him against these insurmountable odds.

The key here is that it appears as if little David is no match for Goliath, but during the course of the story we find out that he is, and so does he. He just hasn't realized it yet. He has reserves he hasn't tapped. That slingshot of his, if used properly, wields loads of power.

Sometimes the enemy is not human. A disease, like alcoholism, becomes the Goliath. In *Leaving Las Vegas* Nicolas Cage's character goes to Vegas to die from booze. But there he finds new hope, in a woman, but even she proves no match for the insidious nature of the disease.

Do yourself a favor and rent *Requiem for a Dream*. Ellen Burstyn won an Oscar for best actress. Jennifer Connolly did a star turn that radically changed her career. The director Darren Aronofsky (*The Fountain*), became, overnight, one of the top directors in Hollywood.

Here also is a movie with a non-human (but human-made) villain: drugs. Street drugs, pharmaceutical and prescription, and how they, also insidiously, turned the characters into their own worst monsters.

In the Old Hollywood, in the standard texts on screenwriting, the Goliaths were almost all human, or superhuman. In the New Hollywood, they are more sinister, more subtle, more devastating. They are human-created villains (like drugs) that become the characters' Frankensteins.

Watch and read *Requiem, Blood Diamond*, and *The Good Shepherd*, and you will not see old standard stuff. As a screenwriter you cannot afford to play the old games, or seem dated. The rules have changed.

One thing for certain is that A-list actors' representatives are always looking to put their clients in sharp contemporary stories build on solid foundations, like David versus Goliath.

If you are not willing to scout new territories you will get left behind. Look around. Read science journals. Read abnormal psychology books. Look at the behavior of your own family or friends in times of severe stress.

What comes out of them? What's the Goliath? Why did that woman down the street beat her son with a curtain rod, while he just stood there and took it? Because he would take anything she delivered, just so long as she paid attention to him. That's the kind of stuff that makes the readers of screenplays pay attention.

The Screenwriter's Mantra*: Explore the human condition at great risk, in the modern day.* In a sense, almost all stories are a form of David versus Goliath. In war, it is the hill (Goliath) that has to be taken. In *Good Will Hunting*, a young man's locked-down psyche (Goliath) has to be opened for him to find his way.

In my workshops people sometimes complain that I'm a hard teacher because I don't agree with what other teachers have said about their work. "My other teachers said I was great," they whine.

And my answer: "You have lots of potential but your subject matter is too derivative. You're stuck twenty years ago, or ten years ago. That stuff's been done. You're worrying too much about formula and not enough about what you see in the world around you — why people do this or that, even in your own neighborhood."

The old Goliaths are fuzzy dead men. They haven't got a shot against these new, often non-human, Goliaths.

Remember Duncan Birmingham and Rachel Grissom, former students now working in Hollywood? Duncan's spec script was about a 16-year-old kid who literally climbs into his dead father's shoes and becomes him in his relationship with his mother (in all ways but sexually, and that might be next). Rachel's heroine hooks up with a weird and fascinating gang of three cemetery thieves who lure her into their dark world.

Original stuff. If you're not original, and you decide to follow conventional means, you will fail. If your capacity to work creatively is there, take chances. Use standard means of laying out the screenplay but get down inside and find the rare juice of creativity that you possess and free it.

After you get the necessary lowdown from screenwriting books, put them aside. Don't read all the retread junk they lay on you. Much of it is old, standard and lazy.

Read new scripts, some old scripts. Language changes. Ideas move forward and take on new colors. If anyone tells you, as someone recently told me, to not read anything made after 2000, tell him to take a walk.

Some screenwriting gurus travel throughout the land, espousing the early movies as models for the modern sensibility. How about breaking down *American Beauty* instead? Something relevant to today. It's not to say that *Chinatown* and that ilk are clunky; they're not. They have reached the venerable level and should always be read. I'm talking about losing the hackneyed retreads and trying to connect yourself, and then the A-list, and ultimately the audience with the modern sensibility.

The old villains, the ancient Goliaths of movies past, wear frayed, ordinary armor and see-though masks. They are not sophisticated or complex enough for today's modern hero. Not when we have characters like the ones played by Phillip Seymour Hoffman in *Capote*, where he was both the David and the Goliath. Or in *Fight Club*, where

Edward Norton played the David (himself) and the Goliath (himself as Brad Pitt), or Charlize Theron, who played both in *Monster*.

Write roles like these, and the A-list will come calling.

Goliaths drive movies towards disaster. The more fascinating, deeply rooted and dangerous the modern villain is, the better off your script will be. Make your Goliath the best, most daring, potentially devastating creature you can.

Who's the Goliath in *American Beauty*? Kevin Spacey's inner modern man at war with society and himself? Yes. The world at large? Yes. The family he is tied to but can't let go of? Yes. Is this the story of a modern man who is not buying the bullshit family ideal story/pabulum fed to us from the Conservative Right — keep your family together, protect family values, even if they kill you — and decides to do something about it? Yes.

This ain't Jimmy Stewart's neighborhood in *It's a Wonderful Life*. In *American Beauty's* neighborhood they brutalize each other, they come apart at the seams, a father lusts after his daughter's friend, a wife screws her competitor. The next-door neighbor is gay *and* homophobic, beats his son and, in the end, murders the hero. Now *this*, ladies and gentlemen, is a modern American neighborhood. Face it. Love it. It's what goes on behind the modern façade that matters these days.

Jimmy Stewart probably thought about screwing the next door neighbor's daughter and maybe he even did. But that was then, when things like that were not put up there for all to see, and this is now.

In fact, Kevin Spacey came to realize what Jimmy Stewart did — that family is important, loving your wife and family matters above all else, yada, yada, yada. And then he gets killed. If that's not the modern sensibility at work....

What I'm also talking about here is man against self, the most severe villain of all. John Nash, Russell Crowe's character in *A Beautiful*

*Mind,* battles imaginary enemies created by his own fear, by his schizophrenic twin self.

Ed Norton in *Fight Club* battles Brad Pitt, Norton's creation, his other self brought out from behind his own human wall. The main character in *Memento* fights for control of his own memory. Man against self. In *In the Bedroom,* the couple fights their own grief that comes from loss.

Our Goliaths are the fears we possess within and how we manifest them into the villains without. It's your job to take these internal demon-monsters and to create from them visible and visual monsters we can see up there on the screen, in whatever form they take.

**Musts in David versus Goliath Movies**
• Goliath must far outmatch David in his or her power.
• The David character uses wits to overcome the power of Goliath and there is never a secure moment for him.
• The plot builds in a series of plans made, plans enacted and plans thwarted, until reaching the climax where David, in a last-ditch effort through his cunning, prevails.

Epics fall into this category. The little man against the big bad villain. *Gladiator* worked. *Hercules vs. the Moloch* did not.

## 5. I Mean It, Ignorance Was a Much Easier Gig — The Coming of Age Plot

Change is at the center of this category — young change. This is the favorite category of young writers because they haven't lived to be old, so don't know what it means or how it feels. Most Coming of Age scripts I've read lack conflict and drama. This is because the writers haven't been willing or able to take chances with their stories or characters, or to stack the deck against the young hero.

Let's take a look at *Tadpole,* an indie that came out in 2002. Like *Rushmore, The Graduate,* and *Spanking the Monkey, Tadpole* is a coming-of-age tour de force. Fifteen-year-old Oscar Grubman, son of a wealthy Manhattan family, arrives home from prep school. Oscar is in torment; he's madly in love with his stepmother (Sigourney Weaver). Oscar quotes Voltaire and is determined to make love to her. Instead he gets seduced by her pal, Diane (Bebe Neuwirth), and hit on by all their friends. He learns a big lesson in the end.

Learning big lessons, and small, is a capstone for coming-of-age flicks.

When most people in the industry hear "coming of age," they roll their eyes and head for the hills. With the exception of the titles above, coming-of-age scripts run through the pipeline have been pretty awful.

But...

### Musts for Coming-of-Age Movies

• Your character ought to be sliding, screaming or erupting into adulthood.
• Establish your character so that we know him well enough. When the bomb explodes we want to see a big change before and after.
• How does your character handle this bomb — tries to run, confronts it, etc.? It will say a lot about him.
• How do little moments become, for him or her, big moments? How does he or she handle each one in this process of maturation?
• What emotional or psychological price must your character face in the transfer from innocence to experience?
• Make sure he or she *learns* small important lessons about growing up; don't rush the transition. You've got 100 minutes of screen time to tell the story.

*Harold and Maude* was brilliant. *Zapped!* was not.

# IN THE FINAL ANALYSIS

In my classes, I rarely try to steer a student away from an original concept. We play around a lot with plot and characters, looking for the best way to tell the story — always keeping in mind that there is something about that concept, that *urge*, which the writer continually needs to feed.

That is what I try to get them to respond to. Sometimes it's impossible to get to right away, but eventually, as the story unfolds, the writer understands the urge to stay with and pursue that original gust of creative wind that carried the story in the first place. This comes out the writer's *need* to tell the story.

Some stories arise out of the need for the main character to choose at the end. Maybe a woman feels she must choose between two men. It may be that the writer herself feels that she would need to make this choice. As the creator she has to understand why she possesses this need, and why she would give it to her main character, or perhaps why the character might choose neither of the men. She would instead tell the guys to take a hike and choose herself, to be alone for now. In other words, the choice should be the character's, not the writer's.

In some cases, when the writer can't decide what to do and throws up her hands, and decides to go on to another story, she will invariably come back to the same concept, but from a slightly different angle. It's funny that way, and telling, and it happens all the time.

As a writer, recognize your need to tell a particular story, and then allow the character to live it. Ironically, the character may show you the way out of a dilemma you've been facing for a long time.

As I mentioned earlier, I always seem to write the David versus Goliath plot. The main character is a victim of his own weaknesses who in order to overcome the odds must reach way down and pull out a handful of slingshots to slay the dragons of his fears.

I try, in all my work, to slay my own insecurities, over and over, in different forms. I respond to my gut fears and try to write my way out of them. It's a lifetime preoccupation that's become an occupation. A lifetime obsession turned into a profession.

In my attempt to overcome these odds, my character moves from innocence to experience.

## DRILL

Each week in my classes I ask the students to read at least one, usually two, scripts of produced movies that have something to do, whether in theme, genre or plot, with the script they're writing.

I ask them to turn in at least one sheet on each script, listing all the things they didn't know about how to put a screenplay on a page.

By jotting these down as you read along, and typing them out afterwards, you'll get an education that money can't buy.

# The Fifth Horseman:
## Structure

A few weeks after the Spielberg war movie, *Saving Private Ryan*, came out, *Newsweek* invited a few top-notch screenwriters for a symposium, among them Robert Rodat, who wrote the picture, Tom Stoppard (*Shakespeare in Love*), and Don Roos (*The Opposite of Sex*). In the symposium, Rodat railed against three-act structure as the bane of young screenwriters' existence:

*Newsweek*'s question: *In film school screenwriters are taught formulas. Screenplays have to have three acts: 30 pages, 60 pages, 30 pages.*

Rodat: "It's hideous! And they get you when you're *so* young and *so* malleable that you believe this stuff. It's been a real challenge to for me to take that stuff and try to blast it out of my brain. Otherwise, you're going to end up with real formulaic films."

Hmm. Can you imagine that? Ironically, I can't think of a major well-received film that follows a more rigid three-act structure than *Saving Private Ryan*. Could this be a case of do as the screenwriter does, not as he says?

So, should you write your screenplay in the three-act structure or not? "If it was good enough for Aristotle," a student once said to me, "it's good enough for me." Fair enough. Can you write a screenplay not in the three-act structure? Yes. Can you write a screenplay without structure? Yes. Will they turn out any good? Possibly. But probably not. Then why take the chance? *My Dinner with Andre* may have a three-act structure but I'll be damned if I'm going to try to find it. Lots of foreign films try to stay away from three-acts partially in defiance of what they call the American Paradigm. Like any other regimen — or in this case, paradigm — first you should know the rules before you can break them. Rodat and other nay-sayers can call how they structure anything they like. The truth is that they use the principles of three-act structure in their work.

Every writer I know, or have read, who works in Hollywood, writes with a beginning, middle, end, which is three-act structure. Studios and producers think in three-act; their notes address three-act paradigms. Storytelling of almost any kind, from the simple tale told by a boy about his day at school, to newscasters trying to tease their audiences to tune in more, to board rooms where concepts are pitched in three-act structures.

I have seen diagrams of river beds, ski trails, fence posts. They all say the same thing: beginning, middle, end.

Ah, structure. You need to know a few things up front.

People mix up plot and structure. Structure is the bones, the architecture, the plans on how to hold plot up. Plot has no bones, no skeleton. It's an organic process.

Plot is the sweet or sour-smelling people that drive through and around a story, to make it a living force. Structure is the Lego network of shapes and forms that hold up your story. Structure is static, plot is kinesthetic. Structure is the Fifth Horseman of the screenplay.

Structure without story and plot is like that half-finished building, just standing there, waiting for the builder to either get out of bankruptcy, or for another builder to come along.

## STRUCTURAL MUSTS

• Make the first ten pages so startlingly dramatic that only someone who gets hit by a truck mid-read will be prevented from going on.

• Read the first ten pages of twenty scripts from the same genre in which you're writing. See how those writers did it. Study how they introduce characters, story, tone, place, etc. Take notes.

• After you write your own startlingly dramatic ten pages, promise yourself that none of the pages that follow will fall below their excellence.

• In every script there's what's known as **The Bomb**, or **Inciting Incident**. You'll find the explosion at around page ten.

The Bomb starts the story. This is a Bomb that blows up in the main character's face, throwing the main character and most of the other characters into utter chaos. The rest of the story is about your main character trying to pull his or her life back together, and not doing a very good job of it.

• Sprinkle powerful REVERSALS throughout, usually every ten pages or so, to keep the story exciting. For instance, John Nash in *A Beautiful Mind* meets a secret government agent who hires him to decode Communist infiltration through magazines and newspapers.

In reality, as we later discover, this is the moment that Nash's paranoid schizophrenia kicks in big time. The agent is a figment of his wild mind, and so is a lot else about his life, including, as he (and we) find out, his roommate.

• Set up the story like this: in the first ten pages we see life as it's lived by the characters. When the Bomb hits, that life is forever changed.

The Bomb could be schizophrenia kicking in, or a car accident, a murder, a plague, or a young genius janitor being discovered solving an impossible equation on an MIT blackboard. The Bomb stops one life and starts another, and begins the movie. *Whatever problem erupts at the Bomb will have to be resolved by the end of the movie.*

Draw a line from the Bomb to your climax. This is the SPINE of your movie. Nothing should waver from that spine. Hamlet learns from the Ghost that Claudius and Gertrude killed his father. For the rest of the story everything Hamlet does has to do with proving if what the Ghost said was true. Period.

If you wander from the spine, you'll lose the story thread, give up, and the story never gets told. This is the chief reason why, without structure, you fail.

| ACT I | ACT II | ACT III |
|---|---|---|
| Problem/set up | characters in conflict | problem resolved |
| page 10-15 bomb explodes, establishing problem | leading to: | climax where problem is resolved |

# ACT I

### THE SET-UP AND OVERVIEW.

The first ten minutes of any movie establishes the world as your main character knows it. It may be a world at war, or in a meadow (but there had better be something interesting going on in the meadow).

Almost always the main character faces something that has something to do with the big PROBLEM he will face later on. One of my favorite romantic movies, *Splash!*, shows two things about the Tom Hanks' character. As a child he gets saved by a mermaid and he has no idea what a male/female relationship is all about, his big problem.

At around pages 10-14, the Bomb explodes, hurling your character out of whatever comfort she has in that world. The character finds herself in a new hell where nothing will ever be the same and the past cannot be recaptured. Confusion, uncertainly and fear grab her. She reaches out only to find nothing but more misery or danger. She desperately searches for some way out of the chaos and, finding little, has to start reaching down inside herself for some answers. Villains and other obstacles rise up and inner demons stalk her. She goes to a trusted friend or mentor for help but doesn't like the answers she gets. But she has to do something.

The friend or mentor suggested a journey of some kind to find the answer or escape from the problem, or both. The reluctant heroine approaches the end of Act I terrified. Adventure calls, along with the unknown, danger, fearful consequences.

Throughout the rest of Act I and into Act II the character tries to restore order to her shattered universe. At one point, at the end of Act I another bomb hits — the first Big Turning Point that gives her a notion of what's she's really up against.

She faces more danger but at least she is now prepared (sort of, she thinks) for it. This only means that she has prepared for only a small part of what she will encounter. The hand of hell will beat down on her with greater ferocity.

She fights her way through Act II, the confrontation act, in which she battles the villains who want to prevent her from solving the problem and internal demons who have always acted against her own best interests.

She reluctantly has to face these demons (triggered into being at childhood usually) and is having an awful time of it. But what else is she going to do? The doors to the past have closed and at present she can't stand still without being devoured by enemies.

She has to keep moving towards something — a solution — that she can only vaguely see, or understand.

She tries to restore order, and fails. And fails again. This is not about restoration but discovery. This is a journey. She is *forced through circumstance* to go on. As the main character she is the one most challenged, who will make the biggest change by the end.

She is on the mission: to resolve the problem in any way she can. With good luck and her own canniness she will try to slay or shed her demons and beat back the adversaries, and prevail. But this is, after all, the most critical moment of her life. She will not have it easy. In fact, one of the tenets of screenwriting is that you shall *never make it too easy on your main character.*

Fear motivates the character, and drives her on. Fear of failure. Fear of what failing may bring. She will pick her way through hell and hopefully find wisdom, self and otherwise, along the way.

She will screw up, fall back, get whacked by major reversals, but through hit and miss, trial and error she will, let's hope, gain understanding and clear away the debris of her life.

In this wake-up call of a story we will root for her. She becomes a heroine to us. We want more than anything, considering what we see her go through, for her to succeed.     By the end of Act II and beginning of Act III she is more conflicted than ever, but sees a dim light way out on the emotional and physical horizon. A mirage? Who knows? But she wants out of this misery, and will do anything to fight or think her way to freedom.

Out of this need, and from what she has learned along the way, she sees that dim light as a solution. She stands alone at the edge of the swamp, standing between her and the jungle thicket, and wonders if she has the stamina or juice to go on.

She would turn and run if it were not for two things: one is that she can't turn and run because there is nowhere to go back to. Two, she knows in her heart that if there is a solution it's up ahead, through the nest of vipers living in the swamp of her dark past beside the city of the undead.

She buckles up, gets the lay of the land, makes a plan based on what she knows so far, and moves ahead.

In Act III, the Resolution Act, she fights her greatest battle. If she thought she had already been through hell, the last leg of this journey will make the earlier stuff pale by comparison.

She knows the problem will not go away by itself. She commits herself to go through this last door, and does.

The rest of Act III is the working out of the decision to move forward she made at the beginning of Act III. She fights the chieftains of her own inner demons and the mightiest of her adversaries.

In Act III the main character *acts* by vigorously pursuing the objective that will make or break her — the problem's resolution. At the climax she'll meet her greatest challenge, face to face.

In the Climax, the biggest scene in the movie, everything gets tied up. She wins or loses, or partially wins, leaving a modicum of hope.

Make sure the climax is the pay-off to what began back at The Bomb.

Your job is the make the journey fascinating, original, exciting — through your fascinating, original and exciting main characters. Not an easy thing, as many of you already know. But possible, if you have the tools. And the story. A story that is not clichéd or derivative. Something original.

I'm getting ahead of myself. Let's go back a step to Act II.

# ACT II

## THE CONFRONTATION

General wisdom says that most movies collapse in Act II. As the longest act (half the movie, between fifty to sixty minutes long), Act II is the stretch where the main character meets all sorts of obstacles from the visual and visible world of people, places and things, and from the internal world where she faces and overcomes her own demons.

Act II is where the writer and her character often wander off together into the desert and get lost. They perish and the script dies, and another fifty-page story gets buried in the drawer.

Why does this happen? The writer doesn't bother to get to know her character well enough, stuck in the mire of character ignorance. She didn't do enough prep work on the story. She forgot to refer to her character bios. She doesn't have a clue as to her character's fears or wants. She was impatient to get started on the story, thinking she would work it all out in the actual writing. She forgot to do a mini-treatment or a scene breakdown (see Workshop Nine).

She forgot to explore the chief mental and physical problems the main characters had before coming into this story — the backstory — their insecurities, fears, phobias, bad attitudes, you name it. She ignored her characters' personal saboteurs.

I like to use *In the Bedroom* as an example. Almost everybody loved this movie, everybody except me and a few other crank souls.

The movie's about a middle-aged couple (played by Sissy Spacek and Tom Wilkenson) who have a college student son who's dating an older woman (Marisa Tomei), with two kids and an estranged husband, the scion of a local powerful family.

One day the estranged husband, in a jealous rage, murders the college kid, and the rest of the story focuses on his parents trying to pull their own lives back together by grieving and then avenging their son's death.

When I read the story idea I could not wait to see this movie. It had all the elements of great storytelling:

• Small, elegant Maine coastal town, Camden

• Younger man/older woman affair torn apart by murder

• Class struggle. Middle-class family versus town big-wigs

• A couple forced to face the death of their son, and each other, against great odds, on a small, personal scale

•A low-budget movie that attracted top acting talent

So, with all this wonderful material, what could go wrong?

After I saw the movie I went home and wrote a review. I often do this when a movie affects me. I vent. I toss out ideas that often makes me sound like a sour, irritated ass.

Call it mental masturbation. Here it is:

In the Bedroom *is like a film school effort, with a tension-absent Act II and self-conscious directing.*

*While Act I starts with an original world, Act II is glum and tedious. How many ways can two characters show grief — dozens, in this rendition. The actors work overtime to bring the material to life, but they can't overcome the weight and quicksand storytelling. As the lights came up, I heard a woman behind in me in the theater say, "Insufferable." That about sums it up. The characters were not delineated enough, even for fine actors to capture.*

*With less self-conscious directing — with its lingering shots and "meaningful" pauses — the movie could have been the jewel some critics have called it.*

*I feel that some of these critics wrote more about what they would have liked to see than what was in front of them. Or maybe they felt that* In the Bedroom *was one of the best in a batch of generally mediocre movies that year..*

*In Act II, the pacing plodded, stumbling along on spindly legs. The director held his shots for so long he must have been brought up on Eastern European cinema. Where was the editor on this? Or better yet: why did they (whoever* they *is) allow this director, and editor, to take this self-indulgent route?*

*Once the son is murdered, even the dialogue takes on a halting, artsy fartsy "meaningful" first-year film school feel to it. The pace slows to inertia, as if grief is supposed to stultify the world and so let's stultify everthing else, too.*

*After a well-paced Act I, the filmmakers had nowhere to go, the movie went to sleep for sixty minutes, and then picked up again when the father decides to take revenge and kill his son's murderer.*

And so on.

The point is that *In the Bedroom* has lots of good things going for it — the concept, the twists, the actors, the *potential*. Let's go back to the origins, the script and story.

After the murder, the story had nowhere to go but inside the parents' grief. Of course they were devastated by their son's murder, who wouldn't be? But did we have to spend sixty screen minutes watching people pine over a lost one, in such deadening repetition?

Penny Marshall had the same problem in *The Awakening*, in which a troubled Robert De Niro spent Act I in craziness, Act II in recovery, and Act III in craziness again. In Act, II Marshall and her filmmakers had nowhere to go. They found nothing to build upon the tension of Act I.

What did the filmmakers do? They bloated, or floated, the story with other characters and events that didn't matter. In *Awakening* we were forced to watch other mentally challenged people make it through the day — all the while waiting for the chaos of Act III to give the story energy again.

So it is with *In the Bedroom*, in Act III, when the father takes revenge.

# DRILL

**In Act II, aren't characters supposed to be reacting, in constantly escalating turmoil, to the Bomb of Act I? The movie shouldn't go flat, should it?**

**• In your script do you feed on the Bomb in Act I and take the main character(s) on a horrendous, escalating journey through hell and self discovery?**

**• In Act II, do you bombard your main character with external visual and visible villains, environments, hurdles?**

**• At the same time, do you bombard your main character with demons from the past that have become obvious, debilitating behavior patterns in the present?**

Maybe the *In the Bedroom* writer-director saw Act II as a way to explore grief. Great, but hold the moping. We are bombed and we retreat, we fall back, we head for cover to recuperate. Only when the coast looks clear do we come out again.

Not in movies. Movies are not real life. They are acts of compression — real life compressed into a few terrifying, damning, exalted, wild and wonderful moments, filled with sound and fury, signifying everything.

Movie characters should not be allowed to retreat for more than a few moments, and screenwriters shouldn't encourage their characters to go into their bedrooms and whine for half the movie before challenging them to move ahead.

Your job as writer is to force the characters out of their retreats and into the heat of frenetic life. The characters will resist. Who wouldn't want to go back to bed and pull the covers over their heads?

But that's not allowed in movies. Your job as screenwriter, especially in Act II, is to:

— *Force* your characters out of their comfort.

— *Close* all escape routes.

— *Identify* and then attack their fear centers so that they won't be able to sit still for one moment.

— *Make sure* the villains know where they are, forcing your heroes out, if the heroes can't bring themselves to do it.

— *Create* an unrelenting vice pressing against the characters. Once the characters are out in the open again, *don't let up*. These characters are abruptly forced to change habits, outlook, list of priorities — in preparation for radical change, on this the most critical moment of their lives.

— *Compress* time, space and language in an all-out effort to force the characters to face the brutalities of the outside world and the terrifying demons of their inner selves.

Act II is all about confrontation. It's about breaking behavioral chains that your character has dragged along behind her all her life, and is now compelled to break — at this most critical moment in her life.

The question: What is the single most powerful force dragging your main character down? It's a behavior pattern. You need to know it because in the course of the story your character will have to face it and start to shed it before tacking the greater problem.

Don't be afraid to put your character through the wringer. That's your job. Act II is the place to do it, with physical and emotional violence. Rain down on your character torment, doubt, and living on the edge of madness. And never let up on her. If you do, the story turns soggy. Never give her a break.

In *In the Bedroom,* the writer/director had already set up characters who could have been more vitally affected by the death. Instead of relentlessly inspecting in numbing detail Sissy Spacek's grief (a tour de force performance), why not concentrate on others in that cast that I want to know about? How might they have been truly affected, inspected, etc.?

# DRILL

- Read screenplays in the genre you're writing in.

- Watch for and pay attention to Act Breaks.

- Divide the script into three acts.

- In each act make a list of the central actions.

You'll see how the three acts break down. This exercise will take time, but when you're through you will know better than ever how the pros do it and why the pros almost always have an A-list actor in mind. I can't stress enough how valuable this exercise is.

We have not been brought up reading screenplays. We don't know the form unless we study it. And we certainly won't be able to write strong screenplays without knowing the form.

Do yourself a favor and buy or download five of your favorite screenplays, read them and break them down into acts. They will become templates for all future scripts you write.

# ACT III

## How To End the Damn Thing

The word is that European filmmakers don't know how to end a movie so they just stop somewhere and allow the audience members to trail off, using their imaginations.

American filmmakers don't know how to end movies either, so they have three, four, sometimes six endings, mini-endings, that jerk and bump along asking the audience member to take whichever one it prefers, until the movie sputters to a stop.

I prefer movies to end as satisfactorily as they can, considering what the main character has gone through. After all, it's the main character's movie, isn't it? We've followed this person through endless highs and lows for two hours, more or less. We've linked our fortune to his or her own. We want to see the ending as the most satisfactory one, given what we've learned.

If Hamlet had lived, let's say, would he have gone back to England to finish his degree? Satisfactory? Given to some filmmakers who refuse to allow any main character to die at the end, it might be.

In *Casablanca*, Rick and Ilsa get together in the end.

The Kevin Spacey character in *American Beauty* lives in the end.

The point is that you should test all legitimate endings, write Act III out in one sitting in three to ten pages, beat by beat, in outline or text, and pay attention to how you feel about each, and record it. If you do this, whittling down one ending after another, you will arrive at the ending that is most satisfactory.

# WORKSHOP

# 9

# THE DREADED MINI-TREATMENT
## & THE TEDIOUS SCENE BREAKDOWN

The mini-treatment, the most difficult pages you will ever write, takes up just four pages, but encapsulates the entire story you will write in the screenplay. It's almost as onerous as the Terrifying Scene Breakdown which you'll learn about later in this section. If there were ever evil twins from Hades, here they are.

To get to the mini-treatment, you should follow a simple regime. The first thing to do when you start to formulate the movie idea is to write down anything that comes into your head that looks as if it belongs to your idea. Shotgun the idea. Let it rip. Soon your mental editor will come on the scene and start to dismiss certain extraneous ideas as soon as they come up (though some of them you'll retain for later when you write the actual script).

By the time you've shotgunned a number of pages, you will start to whittle down and condense, whittle and condense, until you can fit the major plot and story elements into a workable six or seven pages.

At this point you go through it again, eliminating anything that is not absolutely necessary to the plot or story. By the time you finish this process you will have that double-spaced, 12-point Courier font, four-page mini-treatment.

Basically the mini-treatment is as it states: a four-page summary of the highlights of the story, broken down into acts. Page one includes the action of Act I; pages two and three carry the action of Act II; and page four carries the action of Act III to the climax.

The mini-treatment is the first step in a process that will eventually culminate in the writing of the script itself. This is the first layer of the story foundation. If you're able to complete this step you'll save time and effort and substantially reduce the possibility of giving up on it. People give up on scripts because they think screenwriting is diving into the screenplay and having at it.

Wrong. This step and the ones that follow is the guts of the writing process, from which everything else flows. In the Writers Guild of America (WGA), a screenwriter has twelve weeks to complete the first draft. Twelve weeks. They'd spend ten weeks on the gut work and two on the actual writing. The actual writing is the easy part.

This is not for spec work, of course, but it's an example of how quickly the pros have to get out the work.

I assign my students the mini-treatment, in this form, so that they can focus on the main story points. Without a rigid, four-page, double-spaced at 12-point Courier font, they would tend to run the story out to seven or more pages, put it in single space format and make it 8 or 10 point. The reason they give: not enough space to tell the whole story.

That's the point. You don't want the whole story. You want to focus only the major elements and turning points so that they can *see* the story unfold. It's all about spotlighting the story and not about how many details you can cram into a half-dozen pages.

I warn them that if I get anything other than four pages of double-spaced 12-point Courier prose I will turn it back to them unread. During my teaching life, I have been met by a number of shocked and disappointed faces belonging to students who didn't believe me.

Write it as if you're telling a story to a five-year-old with a short attention span. Use generalities to keep the flow and specifics to nail the big turning points.

You'll notice that the styles in each are slightly different. Pick the one you're most comfortable with. Like scripts themselves, styles also vary slightly.

## Untitled Mini-Treatment
## by Katherine Follett

Katherine Follet, quiet and determined, is a grad student from Vermont.

```
Act 1
Upstate New York in the present day. Four
friends await news from NYU film school
concerning their ambitions to be stars in
the movie industry. Rachel, a smart, funny
college-age girl, bides her time working
in a bookstore. Her closest friend, Riley,
unassuming but razor-minded, runs his own
shady internet business. Kind, reliable Mike
is hoping to escape a life of apprenticeship
for his father's electrician's practice. They
spend their afternoons at the shabby diner
where Dale, classically tall, dark, and
handsome, waits tables for minimum wage. They
meet there one afternoon, letters from NYU in
hand. When they open them, they each find a
rejection. Their egos are crushed; the working-
class surroundings of the tacky diner seem
to spell their fate. But back at Rachel's
apartment is an old screenplay she and Riley
have co-written; it's a caper film about a
bank robbery. Convinced that they're bound for
```

stardom, they decide to film their movie on their own terms. Problem: they have no money for sets, actors, costumes, etc., only a super-8 camera, some sound recording equipment, and a couple lights.

**Plot Point 1:** While mulling over how to film a blockbuster on a shoestring, Rachel jokingly says, "Hey, why don't we just rob the bank, and film it that way?" The foursome exchange looks; they've been dissecting this screenplay for years — it seems air-tight. It just might work.

## Act II

The bank in the next town over is unglamorous, but it has money. Super-8 in hand, they begin scoping out the place. Dale opens an account and shamelessly flirts with the dippy blonde teller. Mike waits in the lobby, studying the security cameras. Rachel observes the parking garage, orchestrating their getaway. Nights, they meet at their diner to lay out plans, thought out mostly by Rachel and Riley. Guns or no guns? Dale and Mike don't want this to get too real, but as co-directors, Riley and Rachel win out. Dale ineptly learns how to aim and shoot a gun.

The plans are set, a timed rehearsal run gone through. On Tuesday morning, Dale, Mike, and Riley walk into the bank. Mike sets up lights and Dale, all charm, explains the situation while Riley films. They're going to be filming a bank robbery for a "school project," and they need to "borrow" the bank, so act scared, duck when I point the gun at you, give us the money in this conveniently large duffel bag. Mike, masked, shoves an enormous wrench through the front doors, cuts the power to the security cameras.

Meanwhile in the parking garage, Rachel hops into an unmarked white van they have seen parked there every weekday, unlocked. Reading from a manual, she hot-wires the van.

In the bank, they shoot. The tellers are far too nonchalant; Dale did his job too well. Riley yells at them. The blonde teller can't help smiling at Dale, even when Riley insists he point the rifle in her face. Each time they must re-shoot, Riley cleverly insists that they leave the money in the bag and add new cash. But as they continue to pile money in their bag, the bank staff starts to get antsy. Something's up. The manager demands to see some proof that they're doing this for "a project." Meanwhile, Rachel carefully drives the van to a pre-determined spot, a handicapped parking space on the second deck. She hangs a stolen handicapped card on the rearview mirror.

Dale and the manager argue, while Mike and Riley become very nervous. Finally, Riley insists that this bank robbery is going to go down how a bank robbery should — he forces Dale to point the gun at the manager, insists that everybody get down or they'll be killed. When the manager questions the legitimacy of the gun, Riley insists that Dale fire it — it is, in fact, real and loaded. They insist that the bank staff get on the ground, not to touch the alarm. They finish the job with almost everyone involved (Dale, Mike, the manager, the teller) quite shaken. Riley, by contrast, seems jazzed by his sense of power. On their way out, Riley tosses Dale the camera. Mike arrives at the parking spot first, hops in the back. Riley follows next. Sirens. The cops see Dale and chase after him, but with Dale's athleticism and small-town cop ineptitude, he manages to lose them on the first floor of the parking garage, all while filming the chase, until he lands safely in the van. Slowly and casually, Rachel drives out of the parking garage. They return to the apartment, jubilant.

**Plot Point 2:** Later that night, while the foursome parties, the cops knock at Riley's door. It may be just the noise, but they're spooked, and Riley insists that they run.

**Act III:** In the van. Arguments ensue about whose fault it was that the cops came, the alarm was pulled. Riley is furious at Dale, Rachel at all three of them. She is driving north, towards Canada. By dawn, they're at a laughable border crossing, one old man in a brick shack. Despite coy Rachel, he insists on seeing the back of the van. When he does, Riley, gun in hand, forces him inside, filming while he ties him up. It's clear that Riley is over the line, but finally Rachel concedes, and they drive on. They see lights, imagine sirens. In the back Riley taunts the guard, aiming the rifle at him. Mike gets up front and insists Rachel pull over. In a cornfield, there's a showdown. Riley wants to keep running, this is the best scene yet, and take Dale with him. Trying to win back Dale, Rachel reveals her feelings for him. Riley is furious; they had been a team, he thought. Mad with jealousy, he takes Dale and the guard off in the van. Rachel and Mike walk back to the road, and Mike reveals that he had been accepted into NYU. Realizing what their crimes have cost them, Rachel tips off the police on Riley's possible whereabouts. In the police car, finding the van, Mike and Rachel are horrified to discover that Riley has insisted on filming the guard's death scene by Dale's hand. Riley is arrested; the film will prove that Dale, now an emotional mess, was coerced. As Riley is taken to jail, Rachel insists that Mike take the film they have made and create a masterpiece at film school.

## Strengths and Weaknesses

**Act I** (Page 1) sets the story nicely. We meet the four main characters and their variety of personalities. They all have hopes of getting into NYU film school. Hopes are dashed. At the Bomb depression sets in. Then: they discover an old screenplay about a bank heist. Act I ends with Rachel suggesting actually robbing the bank while shooting the movie. Solid set-up act. We get to know the characters and their mood swings as they deal with disaster and hope. A small indie feature, not expensive, movie within movie.

The problem is that here Plot Point 1, which happens at page 25, should be the Bomb, happening on pages 12-15. The Bomb starts the movie: They decide to stage a phony bank heist. They argue. Some like it, some don't. Sides are taken.

Plot Point 1, in which the characters typically have made the decision to go, enters an entirely new world where the real challenges begin, in this case, the bank. They enter the bank. They've stepped across the line from intention to actuality, from thinking to doing. They are committed. They can't go back. They can try, but forget about it.

**Act II** (Pages 2 & 3) puts the confrontation into play. They stake the bank out. Dale and Mike, the conservative ones, argue with the more liberal "co-directors" Riley and Rachel. They hit the bank, a clever rendition of movie/robbery/chaos/humor, and by the end of Act II they escape. But later that night a cop comes to the door and they freak, making their escape once again.

There's potential for all sorts of trouble and reversals of fortune. Anything could go wrong both inside and outside the bank, and does. This all depends on the execution but at this point the story remains strong. The escape can be dramatic, and even the knock on the door and flight set up well.

This is where character starts to shine. One character pitted against another. This is an ensemble cast. Ensembles are hard to get made for many reasons. One of which is getting five actors of equal stature to want to share the lead. Schedules are such that the chances for getting them all at the same time are almost non-existent. Budget-wise, you can afford one star, not five, or you can afford five B- or C- list actors. No horse.

You want a horse. You want a bankable A-list or high B-list actor to generate financing.

It's hard enough following the fortunes or writing the lives of one lead actor, much less five. Out of every movie a leader emerges. As the writer, you need to figure out which one that is and write that character to be the lead. And then present it to an A-list actor whose presence will generate interest from other, slightly less prominent actors.

Back to the story.

Thus far the pieces of the puzzle fit well. I don't see any fat on the body, no dangling subplots to carry the story off somewhere. The locations are simple, the budget moderate. I want to find out what happens to the characters, who are showing pressure from the heist itself. The action and tension are changing them in interesting ways. We have an ego loose cannon case in Riley.

Everything will depend on the details and execution, but so far so good.

In Act III, the characters are trapped in a moving vehicle, arguing, blaming, tense. Good. Tension rises. Crisis looms. Their intention is to get away clean, but will they?

Now they split up and the movie takes a dip. With Riley, Dale, and the guard going off in the van, and Mike and Rachel walking down the road, with Mike's admission that in actuality he had been accepted to NYU, the stakes flag. Then they discover that the guard died. Rachel calls the cops, and so on. To me the ending is not as satisfying as it could be.

The climax should have more oomph! That Michael takes the film to NYU is not the climax but a little ironic twist at the end.

When you split the characters up, a movie automatically spreads out and loses steam. The end needs work to make what comes earlier achieve its optimum effect.

Katherine did a very good job, though. She carried me through the tough set-up and the very difficult Act II confrontations, only needing work on the resolution.

You've noticed that a mini-treatment contains no dialogue, only narrative. It should sweep along from one point to another as if carried by a big wind.

The mini-treatment establishes the foundation for your story, which will change as you write the screenplay. I write at least a half dozen of these mini-treatments along the way. I need to; otherwise I'll lose focus.

As the story changes, even during the writing, I need to refocus on what I have. The mini-treatment is the way to do it.

## Scene Breakdown

After the mini-treatment comes the scene breakdown, which is a scene-by-scene delineation of the story. By using the location and the central action of each scene (the reason why the scene exists in the first place), you can see the story from yet another perspective. If the mini-treatment is an overall rendition of the story, the scene breakdown nails it down point by point.

We've all written scenes cluttered with off-focus material. This exercise makes you concentrate. Each scene is about one central thing. Each scene has a beginning, middle and end, like a mini-screenplay. Focus and structure are the keys. Each character in the scene has a personal agenda that flies in the face of the others' agendas — creating conflict, the juice that drives story forward.

The initial idea has become the mini-treatment, which is a general overview of the story in four pages, as if you had to explain the plot to a five-year-old with a short attention span.

Now we're getting more particular. In this, the scene breakdown view, we see the story from a closer angle, by way of a detailed account of the entire script.

Take a look at what Katherine did with this:

**Scene Breakdown**
**Act 1**
1. Bookstore where Rachel works: Riley films Rachel's intro.
2. Outside Mike's Dad's electrician's shop: Riley films Mike's intro.
3. Daisy's Diner: Riley films Dale, the foursome discusses NYU; their hopes for stardom become apparent.
4. Rachel's Apt.: They watch their awful student films.
5. Rachel's Front Porch: She finds a letter from NYU in her mailbox — rushes to…
6. Daisy's Diner: the foursome collect and open their rejection letters. They are devastated.
7. On the Job with Mike; Rachel films Mike's bleak future
8. Daisy's Diner: Rachel secretly films Dale sucking up to fat, stupid customers.
9. Riley's cavernous bedroom: Rachel films Riley working; they decide they can't live this way. The contents of Riley's room hint at a darker side.
10. Rachel's Apt: They collect equipment and try to adapt their screenplay; each person has about 12 roles.
11. Bleak Early Spring, Railroad Tracks in Industrial Park: They scope out locations, potential "banks." Looks grim.
12. Daisy's Diner: Decide it's impossible. Rachel jokingly suggests they rob the bank.

**ACT II**
1. Next Town Over: the foursome scope out the bank, notice the parking garage next door.
2. Inside Circle Bank: Dale opens account, flirts with cashier. Mike scopes security system. Cross cutting to
3. Parking Garage: Rachel and Riley rolling thru the run down parking garage, formulating getaway.

4. Rachel's Apt.: Specs laid out — who gets masks? Do we need guns? Mike agrees to steal Dad's hunting rifle and teach Dale to shoot.

5. Residential Street: Rachel sees handicapped tag in car, gets idea, steals the tag.

6. Sand Pit Behind Town: Dale incompetently learns to shoot, Riley watching, fascinated by firepower.

7. Circle Bank. Practice-run/scope-out. Riley, Mike, and Dale subtly choreograph their robbery. Cross-cut to

8. Parking Garage Rachel drives around, checking the getaway plan.

9. Circle Bank, Next Morning. The day of the robbery: lugging equipment, Riley, Dale, and Mike enter and assure bank tellers/customers it's "only a movie." Cross cutting with

10. Parking Garage Rachel driving through garage, excessively nervous.

11. Circle Bank: First take. Dale flirts and teller giggles. All other employees circle around and ogle the shot.

12. Parking Garage Rachel ditches her car, is able to open the van. She is the only one conscious of the severity of their actions.

13. C.B. Other tellers want turns being the one "held up." Mike has dismantled both the camera and the alarm system while the filming provides a diversion.

14. P.G. Rachel unloads the van, hot wires it from a manual

15. C.B. Riley gets nervous, yells at the employees. The cash starts to pile up, and the manager becomes testy.

16. P.G. All set, Rachel begins to sweat. Where are they?

17. C.B. Manager demands to see credentials, Riley starts to lose it. He insists it start to look like a real robbery. People are scared, a shot is fired. Mike's turn to take off to…

18. P.G. Mike makes it to the spot, into the van. Informs Rachel of the breakdown of their plan.

19. C.B. Bank robbery ensues. Riley exits, followed by Dale. They make it to…
20. P.G. Riley makes it to the van, while Dale runs in afterward, terrified. Sirens. They force themselves to be calm while pulling out of the garage.
21. Rachel's Apartment Celebratory Party. Bought tons of shit. A late knock on the door turns Riley paranoid, sets them running.

**ACT III**
1. The Van, Near-Dawn Friendship Breakdown. Argue over who is to blame for bungled robbery, how they are going to get out of it. Riley wants to run, Rachel wants to stop and plan.
2. Somewhere in Farm Country. They pull over, and Riley takes the gun and threatens to take Dale (the star) to finish the movie by any means necessary.
3. Corn Field: Trying to pull Dale to her side, Rachel reveals her feelings for him. Furiously jealous, Riley takes Dale, the cash and runs off.
4. Corn Field: Rachel and Mike chase after. Mike reveals he got into NYU.
5. Corn Field: Standoff: Riley's madness enables Rachel and Mike to seize the gun, camera, and cash. Leaving Riley there, they get into…
6. The Van. Swing back to town to drop Mike off, with the tapes, to head off to NYU. Rachel and Dale head towards Canada.
7. Train Station. Mike films himself getting on the train.

Now we can see the characters begin to emerge. In Act I, Riley is darker (even his cavernous bedroom suggests it) and the frustration at having been rejected at NYU is more poignant. The environment in which they live takes on character. Mike's bleak future with his father comes up. "Bleak early spring" sets a mood. We get a better sense of smart, driven young people with some hope in a murky place, only to have the hope dashed. Until the suggestion to rob the bank arises.

In Act II we get the sense of new hope, with the plan. The cross-cutting sequences among the characters and between inside the bank and those outside give us the sense of space, danger and anticipation. A key here is the juxtaposition of their bleak world and their young hopes, and that the only way out of this world is by taking the biggest chance ever. The stakes are high.

They pull it off and celebrate, after which the cops knock and they are on the run again, in more trouble than ever. They might now have to pay for their crime. The mood swings and changing fortunes make this compelling. Katherine is building a story through her characters.

In Act III, the friendships break down, there's a gun, and a cornfield standoff. A man dies. Mike will carry the banner for them all. Rachel and Dale head for the border to an uncertain future. Bittersweet ending brings complexity to the story.

Here's another example of the mini-treatment and scene breakdown by one of my other students. As a genre piece, *Hell, Inc.* is a dark comedy. The same rules apply.

## "Hell, Inc." Mini-Treatment
## by Mike Demers

Mike Demer's last script was about a shrink who holds his sessions while driving a cab through Manhattan. Mike is tall and thin and works like a dog, and he's funny. His bio: "I was the youngest of three brothers, meaning those two connected and then there was me. I was ignored a lot growing up. But I had things to say, stories to tell, and after spending a half-dozen years in the 'real world,' I applied to grad school, and found my way at Emerson College. Writing screenplays. It's hard as hell, inventing worlds, but it's rewarding like nothing else."

> Mini-Treatment: *For a good time, go to Hell...*
> *Exit 6 off the Mass Turnpike*
>
> **Act 1:** Nobody's heard of Hellick, Massachusetts.
> With Lenox next door, a plush green example
> of wealth and pride, Hellick is the opposite,

riddled with potholes, dead brown grass, and dilapidation. Lenox has wanted to buy Hellick for years, to store their trash there and make it the muddy doormat to lovely Lenox, which naturally offends Hellick. But with bankruptcy looming, and the likelihood of losing Hellick to the state, which will sell it to Lenox, the selectmen scramble to turn things around. While Buck Barnum lobbies to sell the town to a celebrity, like Chevy Chase or Kim Basinger, the selectmen call Granger Todd after they see him on the cover of an old *Ad Week* magazine.

Meet Granger Todd, a brilliant ad man whose inability to keep "it" in his pants destroyed his career. He can't buy a job until he's asked to change Hellick's image from the decaying zero that it is to a wealthy tourist destination. His pay is a storefront downtown and if he succeeds in Hellick, his property value skyrockets, and he's back on top. Hoping to score a couple bucks, and a couple babes, Granger heads for Hellick.

Shacking up in the guesthouse of the virtuous chairman of selectman and high school principal Dawnie Collins, the comedy begins. The men love him and the women "love" him and at the town meeting, Granger dazzles, proposes dropping the "ick" from Hellick because a town called Hell commands attention.

**Plot Point 1:** Despite the virtuous Dawnie's resistance, they drop the "ick" and the transformation from Hellick to Hell begins, a deal with the devil that proves to be ruinous as well as rousing.

**Act II:** Reverend Baker, a quiet family man resigned to empty pews and a church in decay, just wants to save somebody, anybody, and is convinced by Granger that if he jazzes up his sermons and renames his church, the pews will fill, and the church will get the paint job it's desperate for. Told he'll save more souls in a populous Hell than a dilapidated Hellick, the reverend agrees to become a public access TV evangelist at the First Church of Hell, which irks his wife, who wears the pants in the family. PJ McKay, the town cop who once promised his wife a baby "the day Hell freezes over," and whose job is to chase out the riffraff from Lenox, is persuaded to be nicer, make Hell a friendly place so visitors come back and spend money. Lola, a high school senior/Martin Scorcese wannabe who needs an original film short to get into film school, gets her chance at something original, and damning, when Hellick becomes Hell. Clyde Lyman, another selectman and owner of the hard-up Hellick Watering Hole, is engaged to Dawnie Collins but when he gets a whiff of money, Dawnie becomes second fiddle. Clyde renames his bar "Hell Hole" to attract business, and becomes driven by greed, to Dawnie's dismay. As tension mounts between them, Granger moves in. Meanwhile...

Merchants get into it, replacing old awnings with new ones reading *Hell of a Diner*, *Drugs from Hell* (pharmacy), etc. The school symbol changes from the Hellick Ducks to the Hell Devil Ducks, which are ducks with horns and pitchforks. Tourists begin appearing and Hellick's profitable transformation to Hell parallels Granger's own return to success. But when Dawnie tires of Granger's lechery and goes to kick him out, he tells her his wife and child are dead, appealing to her sympathy. It works. He gets to stay.

Granger creates publicity stunts to put Hell on the map.

Stunt #1: In the search for a famous fugitive, Granger instructs Clyde Lyman, owner of the Hell Hole bar, to claim to have seen him, promising media attention for the town and a full cash register to boot. It works. Media and police converge on Hell, seeking quotes and information, and Clyde's bar is packed. Hell makes the local news.

Residents are overjoyed but Dawnie expresses the usual concerns at the next meeting, wanting a virtuous town, but Clyde, her fiancé, says Hell will make them rich! Dawnie is disgusted with Clyde, love on the rocks, and she soon leaves Clyde for Granger. But just as Granger's reeling her in, psyched to be finally getting the girl, his wife and child show up. They're not dead, as he'd said. Dawnie's pissed, blows him off. But the show goes on.

Stunt #2: When winter arrives, and the town freezes over, Granger has Lady McKay, once promised a baby by PJ "the day Hell freezes over," take him to court. It's all a sham, and the judge rules PJ must have the baby or do jail time. It makes national news and a Jay Leno monologue. Hell, Massachusetts makes the *New York Times*.

Lola sends out her video, and Hell is exposed as a sham, a publicity stunt, and tourists begin arriving in droves to have a burger in Hell, to buy tee-shirts reading: "I've been to Hell and back," to send postcards from Hell to family and friends. Hell has become the Vegas of Western Massachusetts, famous, rich, and saved from Lenox. But where there is Hell, there is evil. The reverend's children, once meek and giving, are now fighting over the Gameboy. Clyde is stealing from the town treasury. Debauchery is widespread.

At a "Taste of Hell," an extravaganza with costumes, bonfires, and tourists, everything erupts. JP is a celebrity cop, and the reverend is defrocked by the diocese for escorting sin into God's house.

**Plot Point 2**: As Granger tries convincing Dawnie that advertising is harmless, still trying to get her in the sack, his own son catches fire.

**Act III**: He tries rescuing his boy, but tourists block him, cheering the burning boy on, snapping photos. They've seen Hell on *Hard Copy*. They think it's a show, a stunt. The reverend finally appears and saves the boy's life. He finally saves somebody, which is all he ever wanted. Granger, in tears, tries confessing his advertising sins to the media, but they're more concerned with the priest that just saved a burning boy in Hell. Granger gets knocked unconscious by a snowball. When he wakes, he learns that Hell has burned down. The town is ashes, broke again, and doomed. All seems lost.

For Sale signs pop up everywhere as residents sell their Hell property to relocate to obscurity. To hell with Hell. Hell votes 2-1 to put the "ick" back, though the reverend moves his family to Lenox. Clyde, caught stealing from the town, is impeached, and Granger quits advertising, opening a candy store full-time instead. But the town is broke, foreclosed on by the state, about to be sold to Lenox, until:

Famous celebrity director brothers show up and buy the town for a cool couple million, pleasing Buck to no end, who wanted a celebrity from day one. They're going to make a movie about Hell going to Hell, calling it, "Drop the ick." The town is saved from bankruptcy. Lola is on set for the shoot, working as a production assistant, her path toward directing having begun. Dawnie, Granger, and Granger's boy are there, too, as they film a dripping brush painting over the 'ick.'

## Strengths and Weaknesses

Handled properly, probably as a satire, this could be a fun movie. It takes aim at small town mores, community anger and envy, and desperation. A former star ad man on the skids, with a sex addiction, coming to bail this town out is a riot. The story is strong, but execution is all.

In Act I, we have a strong set-up, a dying town on the verge of bankruptcy. The town next door, Lenox, wants to annex this dump, but the people of Hellick will fight back. The stakes are high: survival. Enter the formerly successful Granger Todd, who we know is a rake and slightly crooked, and his sex addiction. On his last legs, with one final gasp, Granger is the human embodiment of the town. He will take the job, mainly for the bucks and Dawnie, to whom he takes a liking. So far, so good.

A lot of characters parade by us in Act 1. I worry when this happens because usually it means that the central characters lose their thrust and identities amidst a thundering herd. But Mike seems to have this under control.

In Act II the merchants smell dough and go for the makeover. Meanwhile, Dawnie leaves her ugly, capitalist boyfriend for Granger, whose wife and child suddenly show up. The writer knows how to play comedy by using a series of quick reversals that put the reader in the position of knowing just a little bit more than the characters do. This dramatic irony works wonders on a story like this. Granger works his magic with publicity stunts, along with the "when Hell freezes over" promise. Hell itself becomes a self-fulfilling prophesy.

I am not wild about the coincidental nature of the fire that destroys the town and the snowball that knocks Granger out, although these events do pull everything together in Act III so that the town can come back from its ashes, and bankruptcy. These events also allow Granger to get the girl and have his boy.

The mini-treatment provides an overall view of the story and the scene breakdown particularizes that view. In the breakdown you'll notice that the writer has added and subtracted elements to make a better story. So if you see items in the mini-treatment that are absent in the breakdown, or vice versa, you'll know what happened. The breakdown is essentially a way for the writer to find, on a scene by scene basis, a logic and pacing to the story.

**Scene Breakdown (in this one you'll notice the absence of numbers beside each scene — another, less accepted way to do this. Numbering allows us to go directly to the scene in question)**

**Act 1:** Various images of Hellick decay: swamps, sign for water ban, and town meeting *tonight*!

3 selectmen (Dawnie, Clyde, and Buck) phone Granger Todd, best advertising guy in the biz, to offer job of jazzing up town's image, to attract tourists. He readily accepts.

Granger, in crappy NY apartment, hangs up phone, resumes shameless womanizing.

At town meeting, selectmen explain Hellick is bankrupt, but Granger Todd, a NYC image expert, is coming to save them!

Residents talk hopefully about Granger, Granger, Granger Todd.

On school bus, selectmen pick up slovenly Granger, have second thoughts, but he's smooth and wins them over perfectly. Granger instantly has eyes for Dawnie, Clyde's girl.

Bus passes Hellick sign, Inc. 1705, pop. 665.

Granger tours Hellick with selectmen, gets the scoop.

School bus drops off Clyde Lyman at his bar, then Dawnie at her high school, after she offers her guesthouse. Dawnie's shocked when Granger kisses her.

Granger's dropped off at guesthouse.

Dawnie tells Clyde that Granger kissed her, gets angry when he doesn't believe her. Lola, a high school senior, says she needs an original film short to get into film school.

Granger locks up guesthouse, starts walking.

Granger harassed by town cop, PJ McKay, then wins him over.

PJ tells Granger his wife wants a baby, and that he'll have one when hell freezes over. Ha ha ha.

Granger visits his storefront, hooks up with random girl #1.

Reverend Baker tells his wife about Granger, says town meeting is tonight.

**Plot Point 1:** At town meeting, Granger's smooth, wins residents over perfectly, persuades them to drop the 'ick' despite Dawnie's reservations, wanting to be virtuous for the children.

Dripping brush paints over the "ick," rewrites pop. as 666.

Dawnie, on phone with Clyde discussing Granger's immorality, sees random woman #2 leave guesthouse, says she's kicking him out.

Granger tells Dawnie his wife and son died, gains Dawnie's sympathy.

Granger tells PJ about Taste of Hell, the extravaganza that'll save the town from bankruptcy.

Various shots of new awnings being hung, school bus and cruisers being repainted, etc. Town's taking on decidedly red hue and residents have skip in step.

Granger comes up with plan to save the church, which is being closed by the diocese for low attendance. Reverend says he'll try the first idea, but must ask his wife about renaming church.

Wife says no damn way.

New "First Church of Hell" sign being hung anyway, the reverend shaking head, in big trouble with wife.

Granger hanging sign of his new candy store, Sweet as Hell, as PJ pulls up.

Dawnie begins to have feelings for Granger, but fights them.

At Clyde's bar, Granger talks Clyde into first stunt (publicity stunt #1).

Police and media converge on town to interview Clyde Lyman who claims to have spotted the famous fugitive, the Animal Cannibal. Hell makes the news.

Lark! Police find actual fugitive by swamp!

Residents celebrate. Various shots of growing debauchery: drunks, littering, fights.

Clyde and Dawnie fight. Love on the rocks. She wants Granger.

First sermon at First Church of Hell is a huge hit, moneymaker.

News gets hold of damning video footage, Hell is humiliated, Granger's plan in jeopardy.

Granger spins the bad publicity into good publicity.

Knock on Granger's door. Dawnie? Nope. It's his wife (Ivy) and son (Evan, age 8), *alive*. Ivy says she's fed up with motherhood.

Dawnie sees Granger's wife and son, is hurt, lied to by Granger who said they were dead.

Town meeting, Granger says Taste of Hell

is seven days away, has devil costumes for residents.

Granger apologizes to Dawnie, says he loves her. Dawnie says Clyde's a crook, but Granger's a liar, no better. Ouch.

Various shots of town preparing for Taste of Hell. It's Halloween meets Vegas: costumes, games, rides, bonfire supplies.

Weatherman says freezing temps overnight, an early winter. Granger asks PJ if he's ready for his stunt.

At McKay house, Granger sends PJ off in one car, accompanies Lady McKay in another.

Granger and Lady arrive at town courthouse. Media frenzy awaits, in the center of which is PJ.

Reverend's wife says the town's become the devil's playground as kids fight over Gameboy.

Dawnie visits Ivy and Evan, Granger's wife and son.

Ivy says Granger's an advertising liar, a chameleon, whose sperm made son retarded (kid has weird fascination with fires and firemen). Dawnie's flabbergasted at this woman.

Judge rules in favor of Lady; PJ has to have the baby. Outside, reporter says history has changed. Hell's frozen over. Anything can happen now.

Dawnie says Granger's not saving the town, he's destroying it. The devil! To think that she trusted him! Granger's hurt.

The reverend, in a devil costume, winds up a dazzling sermon for parishioners who throw money at him, entertained, but not saved. The reverend looks tortured.

Man approaches the reverend, pulls down his stretchy devil neck, yanks out white collar. Defrocked by the diocese for escorting sin into God's house.

The reverend wanders outside to: Bonfire, costumes, games, media, a marching band of devils playing the devil's music. It's Taste of Hell, a smash hit. And it's snowing.

PJ, now a celebrity cop with horns, signs autographs while Clyde Lyman prods women into bar with pitchfork.

Granger, dressed as shepherd, tries to convince Dawnie advertising is harmless.

**Plot Point 2:** Screaming erupts. Granger's boy, Evan, is on fire.

Granger tries to reach him but tourists have surrounded the boy, taking pictures. They think it's a show. Granger flips out, tries to save him, but the music is too loud. Finally, the reverend appears, saves the boy's life.

Granger's in tears, tries to confess ad campaign to media, but media won't give shepherd the time cuz a priest, dressed as a devil, just saved a burning boy in Hell.

Snowball cracks Granger in head. Knocked out cold.

Granger wakes in hospital, learns Hell burnt down, and media blames the candy store owner who ran around throwing snowballs saying, "I made them drop the ick!" It caused a riot.

Town meeting is in the school auditorium, until they find money to rebuild town hall. Selectmen approve adding the "ick" and impeach Clyde Lyman, crook.

Granger tells the reverend his boy is okay, minimal burns cuz he wore fireman's flame-retardants. The reverend says he's moving to Lenox, the spiritual capital of western Mass.

Famous director brothers offer to buy the town for two million dollars, so they can make a movie about Hell going to Hell called, "Drop the ick". Now they can rebuild Hellick.

Granger says he's quitting advertising and going into candy full-time.

Outside, for sale signs everywhere sticking through thick snow that blankets street. Mass exodus from town.

Close up on "Hellick" town sign, population 566. Pull back to reveal production company, and famous director brothers filming a dripping brush painting over the "ick", crossing out 566 and rewriting 666.

## DRILL: STRENGTHS & WEAKNESSES

It's your turn. In a few sentences what do you feel the strengths and weaknesses of this scene breakdown are? Are there fundamental problems with the story or structure? Be hard on it. Don't mince words. The very toughness with which you go after this should reflect the toughness and thoroughness you would use on your own.

Here's another example from my student, Rob Arnold, whose genre is drama and story is on the dark cerebral landscape of a *Sling Blade*.

## Manifest Destiny Mini-Treatment
## by Rob Arnold

Rob is mild mannered, a poet, with a fierce sense of place and dedication. Here's what he says about himself: "I grew up in the Midwest with five sisters and a brother. Out of that turmoil emerged a strong sense of the world around me and a sensitivity to its stories. I was educated in writing at the University of Washington in Seattle and at Emerson College in Boston."

### Mini-Treatment

"In a Midwestern wasteland, a young man's newfound daughter forces him to reconcile a criminal past."

### Act I

JIMMY HICKS, 23, comes from a nothing background in central Nebraska. His father is an alcoholic trucker prone to fits of violence. His mother died when he was fifteen. Jimmy has been in jail on and off since he was seventeen and is now doing time for attempted armed robbery and drug offenses. He hates his father, who beat him regularly, and resents his brother who took responsibility for him when their mother died. At the prison, Jimmy works on a road crew, cleaning litter and roadkill off the highways. He is up for parole soon. Jimmy's older brother, DAVID HICKS, 28, a recovering alcoholic, writes obituaries for a local newspaper and attends church and tries to lead a decent life with his wife, away from his family's history of failure. One day David visits with news: their estranged father, BILL, is dying of cancer. Jimmy receives the news with self-interest: perhaps it will help in his parole hearing in a month. He asks David to attend the hearing because it looks better if family is present. David leaves without promising anything. When Jimmy's parole hearing date arrives, David doesn't show.

Jimmy makes parole, and travels to his hometown to stay with David but receives a cold welcome, especially from David's wife, PAM. He gets a job at a local slaughterhouse to convince David he's changed. At a tavern after work, he runs into TAD, an old friend and bad influence. Tad tells Jimmy he saw Jimmy's old girlfriend, ANGIE, 22, with a child.

Plot Point I: Jimmy looks Angie up and finds her a gaunt waste. She reveals that she spent Jimmy's abortion money on drugs. Jimmy is furious, but suddenly her jealous boyfriend pulls up and Angie panics, making Jimmy leave out the back door. Outside, Jimmy sees a six-year-old girl playing alone. She sees him and waves. He runs off.

**Act II**
Jimmy is convinced that the girl he saw is his daughter but Tad tries to make him forget about it. They go on a drinking binge and get in a fight with some guys at the bar. They run away and decide to visit Jimmy's brother to harass him. David is asleep when they arrive and is not pleased to see them. He knows Tad is a bad influence on Jimmy. He yells at Jimmy for his irresponsibility and tries to make Tad leave so he and Jimmy can talk. Instead, Jimmy leaves with Tad. David yells after him to remember they have a sick father. Jimmy shrugs and gets in the car.

The next day at work, Jimmy talks to a co-worker about family. The co-worker talks about his children and how he wants them to have a better life than he's had. Jimmy nods.

Tad is waiting for Jimmy after work. At Tad's house, Tad and a friend share some crank. Tad and his friend plan to build a meth lab but need money for supplies. They offer Jimmy some crank. Jimmy declines but Tad insists. Stalling, Jimmy borrows Tad's car to go to the store and get some beer. Instead, he drives to Angie's house and parks outside. He hears raised voices and sees Angie and her boyfriend arguing in the window. The boyfriend hits Angie and she falls to the floor. He continues yelling. In another window, the little girl is looking out at Jimmy in the car. They make eye contact and Jimmy drives off.

Back at Tad's house, they pressure him once more to join the team. Unnerved by his experience, he agrees. They decide to rob a liquor store, using Jimmy's meat-packing smocks as disguises, and Tad's BB guns as decoy weapons. The next night, they do the last of Tad's crank and drive to the liquor store. As they're psyching up for the robbery, a police car pulls up. An off-duty police officer, KIM, 28, goes in. On her way out, she sees Tad and recognizes him as David's younger brother and comes over to talk. She asks how parole is going, wishes them luck and leaves. Spooked, they decide to hit a convenience store by the highway instead.

At the convenience store, they rush in, weapons drawn. The clerk ducks beneath the counter and comes back up with a shotgun. He fires at them several times, injuring Tad. They barely escape. In a parking lot, Jimmy assesses Tad's wounds and decides he'll need medical attention, dropping him off at the hospital and taking his car. Tad is not happy. The next day, Jimmy goes to David and tells him what happened. David wants him to get help. Jimmy agrees but he wants to see his daughter again. In the morning, David awakes to find Jimmy gone.

Nobody seems home at Angie's house so Jimmy breaks in. As he's looking at some photographs, he realizes he's being watched. The little girl

has come out from a back bedroom. He sees she
has bruises on her arm and ask if she wants
to leave. She nods and they go. In the car, he
tries to talk to her but she doesn't talk back.
He explains he's her daddy, but she doesn't
respond. He realizes she'll need clothes.

Plot Point II: Jimmy returns to get clothes,
but Angie and her boyfriend, BEN, return.
They're arguing and Ben is getting violent.
Jimmy grabs the girl and hides in a closet.
Angie opens the closet door and sees Jimmy.
The boyfriend is furious and pushes Angie out
of the way. Jimmy tries to run but is caught.
The boyfriend draws a gun and beats Jimmy with
it. They scuffle. Somehow Jimmy manages to get
the gun and shoots the boyfriend several times,
killing him.

**Act III**
Angie, in shock from the events, hits Jimmy.
Jimmy, also in shock, pushes her away and grabs
the girl. Angie tries to call the police but
he rips the phone out of the wall and throws
it out a window. He runs to the car and drives
off.

On the road, Jimmy tries to talk to the
child. She remains silent. He begins to think
something is wrong with her. Jimmy calls David
from a payphone on the road. The girl still
hasn't spoken. David's wife tells Jimmy that
their father has been hospitalized and that
David is with him. Jimmy gets directions.

Jimmy and his daughter find David outside
Bill's room. Jimmy confesses the shooting
and cries on David's shoulder. His daughter
wanders off into Bill's room. Realizing she's
missing, Jimmy looks for her. David takes the
opportunity to call the police. Jimmy finds
his daughter on Bill's lap, and explodes in
anger, physically intimidating the weakened
man and blaming him for all his problems

```
and difficulties. He tells Bill to stay away
from his daughter. Bill apologizes but Jimmy
is relentless, wishing him a painful death.
David enters and calms Jimmy. He has news: the
police are after Jimmy but David gave them
misinformation, buying some time. Jimmy grabs
his daughter and they rush down the hospital
corridors.
    At his car, Jimmy thanks David and says
farewell. David wishes him a good life. Then,
Jimmy and his daughter drive away, into the
West.
```

## Strengths & Weaknesses

In Act I, Jimmy Hicks, the protagonist, is in jail for armed robbery and drugs, and has a history of violent fits. He has an alcoholic brother and a violent alcoholic father, who is dying of cancer, and a dead mother. The Nebraska landscape is as desolate as his life. Jimmy has nowhere to go except up, we think. We also know that Jimmy can also be violent and will take advantage of any situation — including his father's cancer — to get him out on parole, which works. At home he finds coldness, an old pal, a former girlfriend with two kids and her angry boyfriend. In order to keep our interest, we have to hope that Jimmy has a sense of humor or at least a cynical take on the world.

In Act II, Jimmy in convinced that the six-year-old girl he saw while escaping from his ex-girlfriend's house is his own daughter. It's been six years (during which he's been away in jail) and the girl even looks like him. Now he's got a mission and reason to live.

Jimmy's alcoholic brother David wants Jimmy to stay away from his friend Tad, a bad influence. Jimmy defies him. At Tad's, where a meth lab is about to be built, they decided to knock off a store for dough. Jimmy also goes over to see the girl he thinks is his daughter and finds bruises on her arms. They meet a female cop. They rob the store. There's no end to the pressure and action. The key here is to make Jimmy sympathetic, which the writer does. He's a victim of his father's violence and drinking. He wants to save his daughter. And everyone around him the writer has made out to be worse than Jimmy. It's almost as if Jimmy is the only one we *can* like. The writer wants the audience (in this case, the reader) to pray for Jimmy's recovery. But let's face it: this could be a hard guy to like, and a tough story to get involved in. It's so damned desolate. But so, on the surface, was *Sling Blade*.

At the end of Act II, Jimmy kills the boyfriend. Now he's really in deep shit. There is no way out, it seems, and this is just where you want your character at the end of Act II, in a place from which it seems he will never escape. Because in Act III you will send him on the most harrowing journey he will ever face, with no guarantees.

In Act III, Jimmy is on the run. He senses something wrong with his daughter, as a result of the beatings and bruises and probably fetal alcohol syndrome. He kidnaps the girl and goes to his brother's, where he finds out that Dad is on his last legs. At the hospital we have the family showdown. Father, two sons, source of all pain. When Jimmy sees his daughter with his father he flips out, taking her away, as if the mere thought of his father will infect her, as it did Jimmy.

Family still prevails, though, when brother David waylays the cops, allowing Jimmy and his daughter to get in the car and head west, to perhaps a better life together.

Once again, the proof will come out in the execution, but Rob Arnold's story resonates. I care for what happens to Jimmy and his daughter, and even though he commits murder and robs a store, he battled his way through and earns then love of his daughter and the promise of a better life.

Do you think so, too?

**Scene Breakdown — Manifest Destiny**

**Act I**

1: A prison road crew cleans litter along a highway. JIMMY HICKS, 23, is among them.

2: Jimmy in his cell at night. It's decorated only with a photo of his mother. He reads a bad western novel.

3: Jimmy talks with a parole review board. Jimmy is approved for a parole hearing.

4: The road crew cleans along the highway during an autumn rainstorm.

5: Sunday. In the prison, a minister speaks with prisoners about redemption. A guard enters: Jimmy has a visitor.

6: In the visitation room, Jimmy's brother, DAVID, 28, tells him their father is dying. Jimmy, unsympathetic, hopes it'll help his parole case. He asks David to attend the hearing.

7: Jimmy's parole hearing. His parole is granted. David never shows.

8: Jimmy rides the bus into town. He calls David.

9: David takes Jimmy home. David's wife, Pam, is not happy. Jimmy says he'll work at the slaughterhouse to make money.

10: At a slaughterhouse on the outskirts of town, Jimmy speaks with the foreman and is given a job killing horses.

11: Jimmy comes home to hear Pam and David arguing about him. Angered, he goes to his room.

12: At the slaughterhouse, Jimmy is shown how to kill a horse.

13: At a tavern, Jimmy runs into TAD, 23, an old friend and bad influence. Tad tells him about his ex-girlfriend, ANGIE, 22.

14: Jimmy visits Angie and insists they talk. She reveals she spent his abortion money on drugs. A truck pulls up. Angie panics and makes Jimmy leave out the back door.

15: Out back, Jimmy sees a six-year-old girl playing alone in the dirt. She sees him and waves. He pauses, then runs off.

**Act II**

16: Jimmy finds Tad at the tavern. Tad makes Jimmy drink off his concern. They get in a fight with some guys and leave.

17: Tad and Jimmy drive around looking for trouble.

18: On a highway overpass, Tad and Jimmy drink and throw their bottles to the concrete below. They decide to visit David.

19: David is asleep when they arrive and explodes in anger. Jimmy laughs at him. David reminds Jimmy they have a dying father. Jimmy shrugs and leaves.

20: In the bedroom, David's wife asks about Jimmy. David tells her that their father used to beat Jimmy.

21: The next day at the slaughterhouse, ERNIE, 30s, and Jimmy talk about family. Ernie is saving money for his kids.

22: Tad is waiting for Jimmy after work. Tad explains he can score some good crank to make money.

23: Jimmy meets with a drug counselor. Tad picks him up afterward.

24: Tad and Jimmy visit GREG, Tad's connection. Greg needs money to start a meth lab. Jimmy stalls, going to get beer.

25: Instead, he drives to Angie's and sees her boyfriend strike her. In another window, the girl makes eye contact with him.

26: At the liquor store, Jimmy buys some beer and drives back to Greg's.

27: At Greg's, Jimmy is pressured to try a sample of crank. They agree to rob a liquor store for the cash, using BB guns.

28: Outside the store, they do more meth. A police car drives up. The officer recognizes Jimmy and talks to them. Spooked, they decide to rob a convenience store, instead.

29: They rush into the store, BB guns drawn. The clerk gets a shotgun and shoots several times. Tad is hurt. They flee.

30: In a parking lot, they inspect Tad's wounds. He took some shot in the side and arm and needs medical attention.

31: Jimmy drives Tad to a hospital and leaves him on the curb. Tad is not happy: Jimmy has taken Tad's car.

32: At David's house, Jimmy confesses and claims he wants to go straight and not back to jail. David says he'll help.

33: In the morning, David wakes to find Jimmy gone. A police car arrives, looking for Jimmy.

34: Outside Angie's house, Jimmy makes sure nobody is home and then breaks in through a back window.

35: Inside, he looks at some photographs. The girl comes out of her room, bruises on her arms. He takes her.

36: At a park, he asks her name. She doesn't reply. They play together on the playground. Jimmy shows real tenderness.

37: At a diner, Jimmy tries to talk with her. She is quiet and unresponsive but smiles a bit when he offers ice cream.

38: Jimmy and the girl go shopping for food. She still won't talk; it's clear something is wrong with her.

39: They sleep that night in the car by the highway. Jimmy realizes she'll need some clothes.

40: In the morning, they drive back to Angie's house. Nobody seems home. David tries the door: it's open.

41: In the kitchen, he finds a grade report: her name is Emily. The report shows that she needs special education.

42: In the girl's room, David roots around for clothes, throwing some in a bag.

43: As they're about to leave, he hears a car door and voices approach the front door. He panics and hides in a closet.

44: From in the closet, he hears Angie and her boyfriend, BEN, argue about Emily's whereabouts. Ben is getting violent.

45: Angie opens the closet door and finds Jimmy and Emily. She screams. Ben draws a gun and beats Jimmy with it. They wrestle. Jimmy grabs the gun and kills Ben.

## Act III

46: Jimmy finds Emily hiding in a corner, scared. Angie hits Jimmy and tries to call the police. Jimmy breaks the phone.

47: Jimmy puts Emily in the car and stops. He has forgotten the clothes.

48: Inside, Angie is screaming. Jimmy grabs the bag of clothes, wiping blood off it.

49: David finds Emily terrified and hiding in the back seat when he returns. He tries to calm her but hears sirens.

50: Jimmy drives fast down the road, trying to coax Emily from out of her hiding place. She doesn't respond.

51: Jimmy calls David from a payphone. David's wife tells him that David is at the hospital, visiting their father, BILL.

52: In a gas station bathroom, Jimmy washes his face. His eye is swollen shut, and his lip is cut open.

53: Jimmy buys an ice cream treat from the gas station. He offers it to Emily. She takes it.

54: Jimmy and Emily drive in silence to the hospital.

55: At the front desk, they get directions to his father's room. The nurse wonders if Jimmy needs some patching up.

56: They find David in the hallway. David is concerned about Jimmy. Emily wanders into their father's room.

57: Jimmy tells David what happened and starts to cry. David grimly holds him.

58: Jimmy enters the room and finds Emily in Bill's lap. He becomes furious and fights with his father, slapping him.

59: Out in the hallway, David phones the police.

60: In the room, Bill apologizes but Jimmy is relentless, blaming Bill for all his problems. David enters and calms Jimmy, saying he called the police to buy time to escape.

61: Jimmy, Emily, and David rush through the hallways of the hospital.

62: David wishes Jimmy a good life.

63: Jimmy and Emily drive west.

Once again, the scene breakdown particularizes the generality of the mini-treatment. In this case, Jimmy's journey is the focus and we follow him through jail, parole, home, discovering his daughter, drugs, armed robbery, homicide, family woes, and finally hope.

The scene breakdown gives the writer a chance to focus on the beats of a story, how the story unfolds through character and turning points.

Once you complete the scene breakdown and feel that you have the story in hand, begin to write. Start with the opening scene and build through the structure. Remember the Bomb that appears around page 12, then Plot Point I, on page 25-30, that takes the character in a completely new direction (either emotionally or physically or both). Act II will find you and your character in the vast desert of conflict in which he or she battles external villains, environment, etc. and internal demons. At the beginning of Act III (three-quarters of the way through the script) the character finds him or herself in position to make a final assault on the villains and the demons — as Jimmy does here against his father, his brother (who in the end turns out to be his ally) and against his own fears. In the end, he deserves another chance.

It's the most frightening journey, this last leg, because once into it, there is literally no turning back. The character is usually alone and running scared. The committee in the character's head is screaming at him. He keeps losing focus and getting it back. Up ahead he sees the climax, the biggest battle of the story. Is he prepared? Can he face this, and win? This is, let's face it, do or die.

Never forget that this is the most critical moment of your character's life. Life as he or she knows will change forever; it already has. This kind of crunch moment is why we go to movies and can sit back watching events unfold that we, thank God, don't have to face in our own lives. Yet we can identify, we can root for, we can weep and scream out.

Structure is the bowl into which you pour your story and plot. The mini-treatment and scene breakdown are the intermediary steps between the concept or idea and the actual writing of the script. They are the bridges to give you form and substance and a path to follow.

Now you're ready to take the final plunge yourself.

# WORKSHOP

# 10

# HOW TO BREAK INTO HOLLYWOOD

Y ou need a crowbar, otherwise known as a Great Script.

Breaking into Hollywood as a writer means having a knockout script as your calling card. This masterpiece should have "talent" written all over it, money-making talent. As you gaze west cross America, with the masterpiece tucked into your laptop case, you know you've taken the screenplay as far as you can. You've rewritten it at least half a dozen times, you've given it to anyone who's agreed to read it and offer take-no-prisoners analysis. You've pored over the notes they've given you, taken what you truly believed to be good ones, and made the changes. You've spent months crafting it and now you're ready to take it to the marketplace.

One of my favorite stories concerns writer/director Colin Higgins, who made a number of big pictures. While Colin was at UCLA Film School, he worked part-time as Robert Evans' pool boy. While cleaning the pool one day, Colin asked Evans if he would read a script he was going to submit for his thesis project. Evans said, sure kid, and tossed it into a pile.

A few days later Evans picked it up and started to read. When he finished reading *Harold and Maude*, he knew he had found a masterpiece. A movie was made, a career started, and one of the great independent pictures of all times went off into the world.

Let's say you have finished, rewritten and polished your own masterpiece to a point where you are satisfied, what do you do now?

## THE POSSIBILITIES

• move to L.A.

• don't move to L.A.

• make the movie yourself

**1.** Move to L.A. and get a real job. Do it! What's the problem? You're young. You want to write movies for a living, or get into the film business in some capacity. How many movie jobs are in Sadsack, Tennessee? How many producers or agents have you run into in downtown Sadsack?

Take the plunge. Drive that rickety old piece of junk out there and find a place to live. Get a shit job at Bobo's Eatery in the Valley. You hate it, but you have this script, this masterpiece, and it keeps you going when you're down.

In your non-Bobo's Eatery hours you hound everyone for names and contacts and generally make a sweet pest of yourself. And you keep working. You don't get discouraged, which is easy to do in this movie town.

You meet tons of people doing what you're doing: trying to get their script read. And with persistence you will get it read. I know someone who sent an agent a dozen white roses every day for two weeks, begging her to read his script. Finally she did. She didn't like it, but she read it. It's called access. Gaining access.

You might even land a job as a production assistant at a production company, placing you closer to the flame. You might get hired in the mailroom at CAA or William Morris or Warner Brothers, at Paramount or at an independent production company.

Your only aim is to get your masterpiece read by somebody significant who can get it to somebody *more* significant, pushing your script up Hollywood's tree. If the masterpiece is good, it will get attention. *You* will get attention. Everybody wants good material, and they don't care from whom.

Once you get close to the flame you start to talk about the script, maybe casually spark an industry person's interest. Maybe they ask you what it's about. This is what you've been waiting for: to pitch your idea. If they like it, they'll hopefully ask for the script. Are you ready to pitch your heart out? You had better be.

## WHAT EXACTLY IS A PITCH?

A pitch is a brief, compelling, verbal rendition of your movie. You want to pitch agents, producers, studio heads, anybody who can move the script forward. You practice your pitch on strangers at cocktail parties, mirrors, in the shower. All the time. Try it out on your friends. You need to be ready with the pitch because who knows?

Start with a short pithy attention-getter, a Log Line, which is a dramatic one or two-sentence rendition of the movie. Example: What would you do if a very rich man offered you $1 million to spend a night with you wife? *Indecent Proposal*. How about *Departed*: In Boston, two undercover agents on opposite sides of the law, one in the Massachusetts State Police and the other in the Irish mafia, spread violence and bloodshed searching out each other's identity.

In pitching to producers, agents, etc. you have, at most, five minutes. Some of the great story pitchers give Oscar-caliber performances. They get down on their knees or fly around the room, playing all the parts. If you're not a thespian or drama queen make sure the pitch is straightforward, original and dramatic. It should unfold logically and stun the audience with its visual and storytelling brilliance.

After delivering the log line, begin the story in a casual but visual way, with the opening scene and the main character. Draw us into the world. "It's a hot humid night in Phoenix. Gisele, 22, a breathtakingly beautiful Italian diamond merchant, stumbles her way out of a bar. She's a little drunk, and a lot unhappy. She wants to go home tonight and climb into bed, alone. But that's not going to happen...."

Move rapidly through the rest of the story, introducing the other central characters as they appear. You hit the big moments — the Bomb, the turning point at the end of ACT 1, the turning point at the end of ACT II, *but no climax*. Never give them that — unless they ask.

And then stop talking.

If the person you're pitching is asleep, get up and tiptoe out of the room. If the person starts asking questions, you've got interest.

If you need a jump start in developing the log line, check the newspaper listings for movies showing on TV that night, or *TV Guide*, or websites like *Scriptsales/Done Deal*. These are industry-grade log lines to movies *that the money people are buying*. The cost is $39 a year.

There are other pitching venues: organized pitch fests where studio execs, directors and producers listen to your pitch and comment on it, suggesting changes. If they like the pitch, they'll tell you to finish the script and even send it to them. Instant contact.

Santa Fe *www.scsfe.com/general/testimonials.aspx*

Nashville Screenwriters *www.nashscreen.com/*

Austin Film Festival *www.austinfilmfestival.com/*

American Screenwriters Association *www.goasa.com/*

All the film festivals hold contests. At the Screenwriters EXPO, in L.A. every Fall, people pitch hundreds of movie ideas.

If you live in L.A., you will have access; it's where the business is and where the people who run the business live. It is as simple and clear as that. Everybody struggles in the business, even the top dogs, *and they all live in L.A.* They moved to L.A. because that's where the action is.

But the action is not for everyone. It may not be for you, but you'll never know unless you take a shot at it. From Kansas City you can *say* you don't like the action, but you won't know unless you live in it. I say go, take the chance. You're not going out there cold; you've got your best friend with you — the masterpiece.

There is no substitute for living close to the flame. You meet the people who will hire you because they live there. If you don't live there it's like trying to get a job as a whaler while living in Memphis.

It's been my experience that the judges in these contests, most often well-known agents, managers and production house executives, look for star–driven vehicles: A-list properties. These judges know that a strong A-list script generates more interest than, say, an ensemble or theme-driven script. In fact, these agents often have in their stable or in their agency an A-list actor who might be interested.

**2.** Okay, so you can't move to L.A., just yet. You've got family, a job, and other responsibilities. You may be better off, for the time being. You may be buying time to work on your masterpiece, sculpting the script into the fine piece of art that it deserves to be. You may not be like the others — the Impatient Ones — who wrote their screenplays in a hurry and left in a hurry.

You're more cautious, more deliberate. You plan. You're not into spontaneous combustion, but logic. Call it good sense.

From your home far away from L.A. you can seek out, via phone, mail, and internet, agents and managers and production companies, writing and calling them. You can build a log line and hone your mini-treatment. You can develop your pitch. You don't want to pitch anyone, however, until you have a completed script. What if someone says, I like what you've told me, send it to me. And you say, well, it's not quite ready?

The agent or producer on the other end is hot to see your work, and you don't have it to show? There goes your chance. Almost as bad as sending your sort of okay masterpiece before it's time. There's no better way to kill interest than with a bad script or a great pitch and no script to back it up.

When you finish your screenplay, you can send it to screenwriting competitions. On search engines like Google, Yahoo or Ask.com, call up "Screenplay Contests", where producers and agents look for new talent — new talent that wins or comes close to winning.

If you need help, you can send your work to script doctors who charge anywhere from $200 to $3,000 to $65,000 for a page-one-to-production extravaganza.

I personally feel that with basic research, you can find someone qualified, who provides a good service — reading and evaluating your script.

There are various types of services:

1. The standard script analysis shop where eager young screenwriters turn out pro forma script analysis. They use solid formulas and offer reliable, if not personal or original, takes on the work.

2. Cheapy one-offs for $100 or less, for which you get the real formula: an already prepared analysis in which they plug the name of your script and characters into the blank spaces.

3. Name analysts who pass your script off to hired help who are never identified as such.

4. I (and a few others) provide a service (see *Keanewords.com*) in which I write up an eight to twelve-page analysis of the most severe problems in the script. It's personal, I have fun writing it, it's sometimes off-beat and original in its treatment of the problems, and I pull no punches.

Some people say NEVER PAY ANYTHING TO ANYONE! They seem to have control issues that you shouldn't have to get involved in. Legitimate agents don't charge a fee. I've used online services for a fresh set of eyes. And invariably I've come away with some good advice. Isn't that what I was looking for? The best method is having someone in the industry, or close to it, read with your best interests in mind, and give you excellent feedback.

You can give the script to your friends and family. I would avoid your mother, for instance, who loves, or hates, everything you do. Does your sister the fashion designer know how to read scripts and give cogent criticism? If you're giving it to her, let's hope so.

To reach agents, the best method is through contacts. Some say it is the only method because agents do not have time to read query letters. Do you know someone in the industry? A friend, relative, someone you meet at a party or conference or seminar, a production assistant, a recent film school grad who knows her way around a script. Get them to read your script. If they like it they will pass it on.

I agree that agents don't have time but I also know people who have sent query letters to agents who have read them and asked for the scripts, and the writers got representation.

This method is about writing a one-page cover letter, explaining to the agent or manager that you've written a script: a romantic comedy or a psychological thriller about such and such (this is where you insert your powerful log line), followed by a two or three-line brilliant pitch about the rest of the movie, without the ending.

If you have some expertise in the subject matter of the screenplay — you worked for the very same CIA your main character works for in the story — include it. Or include anything that might get the agent's attention: awards, special expertise, or skills. Agents read scripts for two reasons: they like the idea, or they think some other agent might like the idea and beat them to it.

Go to *http://www.hcdonline.com/* (requires a fee) for the most comprehensive lists of agents, managers, production companies, etc., or to various websites that list theatrical agents. Send them the letter only (not the script), along with a stamped, self-addressed postcard, with two little boxes marked: "send the script" or "don't send the script." This works under the same principle as creditors who send bills with everything done for you: just add money. In other words, make it easy for them to either accept or reject your idea.

To ingratiate yourself, in the letter you might mention that you saw a movie you loved written by one of their clients. Next time you see a movie you love, write down the name of the writer, call the Writers Guild of America, West or East, and ask for "Representation." When the person comes on ask who represents the writer. They'll tell you. You can go to *www.wga.org* for many industry resources, including registering your script.

Production companies normally will not read scripts unless you sign a release form indemnifying them from stealing your idea. Production companies have many projects in development. Your script may have elements they are already using in another project. Worry not. If something unsavory happens you will have recourse, with proof, later on. The big odds are they will steal nothing from you or anyone else. It's not worth it.

Screenwriting is an ongoing process and buying scripts can be costly. If you want to view screenplays online, go to any of the search engines and type in "screenplays." Any number of sites will pop up.

**3.** Make your own movie. You've heard the stories about maxing out credit cards, begging relatives, borrowing from anybody, defraying all costs. Will you beg, borrow, or steal to make your own movie?

Why would anybody want to? Lots of reasons. There is nothing like the on-the-job training of making your own picture, from script to shooting to post-production to editing, to marketing — always with the idea that you might strike it rich. What a rush!

What a headache. It may be one of the most emotionally draining, spirit-destroying, ego-gratifying, neurosis-inducing exercises of all time.

Valerie Weiss was on the last leg of getting a Harvard PhD in biochemistry while at the same time writing, shooting, and directing her first feature, *Dance by Design*. I met Valerie when she asked me to speak at the Harvard Film & Drama Program, of which she was the head.

Here's the story:

The Making of *Dance by Design*

by Valerie Weiss, PhD
Filmmaker in Residence
Dudley Film and Drama Program
Harvard University

I always wanted to make movies. Growing up, the closest, most accessible thing to it was theater. I honed my acting and directing skills by doing plays. Then everything changed. Digital video technology became a consumer's medium and, like a painter or a poet, a filmmaker could afford to practice her craft.

I was in my third year of graduate school at Harvard University working towards my PhD in biochemistry. I had been studied theater and biology in parallel since high school. I had been directing plays Boston and at Harvard University's graduate student center, Dudley House (*http://go.to/dudleyfilm*).

Since Harvard does not have a graduate program in film, our students earn their doctorates in a wide range of disciplines including math, archaeology, Spanish literature, computer science, history and biology.

Half our participants are scientists. We invite filmmaking professionals to teach workshops on areas such as screenwriting, directing, editing and producing: Debra

Winger, Michael Corrente, Jim Toback, Hal Hartley, and Chris Keane.

We decided to write and produce our own collaborative feature film, starting in September, 2001, completing it by the following May. A feature film in nine months, written, produced, edited. No problem.

Our highest priority was that it be a fun film. Growing up in the eighties, I was influenced by dance films like *Footloose*, *Flashdance* and *Fame*. That must explain why I always hear a soundtrack in my head and live to go dancing. We decided that the feature would be an eighties dance movie.

I had learned about treatments from Chris Keane's lecture. I was impressed with the way that he organized ideas and provided guidance for avoiding pitfalls of the first screenplay. I watched all of the movies he recommended.

I had always been involved in the performances of the actors in films; it was difficult to switch gears and observe story structure. (I had a similar experience editing when I began to cut the film.) I began to understand the level that the story worked on and to separate the screenplay from the production.

We needed to work quickly but we all were full-time students. I recruited a team for the project: PhD candidates from the divinity school, computer science, architecture, Romance languages; Spanish literature, English, graphic design; an MD/PhD student. It was an international crew from Spain, Mexico, Holland, Puerto Rico and the United States.

We agreed on the basic story. We identified plot points. Plot Point 1 would be when Angela's best friend Andre's night club got closed down. Angela needed a final project for her thesis in order to graduate; she offers to design him a new dance club.

This rekindled her passion for architecture which sets up the conflict: to pursue dance or design. We focused on character development. What they did in the story, who they were. We used Chris's section on "Some Character Considerations" to guide us.

Angela was not different from any of us, which is why we were drawn to the story. She succeeded in a traditional academic way, but her heart was yearning for something creative. Thus our collective epiphany.

We found the theme: a real-life story about how one decides whether or not to go for one's dreams, and the effects of the decision. This was the most important moment in the whole project — the moment when *Dance by Design* became our movie. We had moved past the model that had inspired us and began to put our real beliefs and impressions into the film.

Then came homework. I assigned people sections of the screenplay. By the next meeting we had a first draft — very rough.

This method almost backfired. We were close to a final draft. I went away for Thanksgiving. While I was gone, the architecture student put some final touches on the script and check for authenticity. When I returned, we met to read the draft. It was a mess! He had expanded all of the dialogue and inserted foreign phrases everywhere to capture the pretentious culture of the design school. He gave Angela and Gigi a lesbian relationship. We were outraged, even though some of the language changes did add flair.

In December we cast the film with local professionals. We found a lead who could act and dance. We found a director of photography. Because the writing team had bonded so well, each of them took a role.

We began shooting February 3, 2001, on weekends, and wrapped April 1. While we kept to our schedule we did not complete the editing by May. As we learned, post-production is the longest phase.

We asked Chris Keane for feedback. "If it's not on the page, it's not on the screen" is 100% true and so is the corollary: "If it shouldn't be on the screen, it shouldn't be on the page."

We got feedback from professional editors and directors. Our most common mistake was writing scenes that were too long. We learned to dip in and out of a scene without needing to start at the beginning each time. You want to start right at the action.

Luckily, rewriting dialogue is possible in editing, but there would have been be so much time and money saved on the set and in the cutting room if the story were pared down to its essence on paper.

We had the premier in Boston, after which we sent it to festivals, now awaiting word. I am eager to begin writing my next film using the lessons that I learned from this one. My advice is that when you are developing your craft as a writer or filmmaker, keep working on it. Take Chris's advice for applying structure and force yourself to put in the time every day.

Even when your project does not have the shape that you want, you need to keep working on it

```
until it does. It is easy to give up a project
that is frustrating, for a promise of a new
one, but you will make the same mistakes on
that second project. Don't move on until you
have learned all you can from the first.

Good luck!

Val
```

# THE REJECTION PITFALL

One of the things you will encounter is rejection, from everyone. Writers get rejected almost as often as actors, about whom I've heard get rejected on the average of thirty-four times before they get a callback.

People in Hollywood don't like to say no. Instead they say "It's not right for us," or "We're not making this kind of picture right now," or "Thanks, but we have something similar in development." What they're saying is no. The writer doesn't get solid feedback. Call it silent rejection.

Michael Schiffer (*Colors, Crimson Tide*) tells the story about early in his career when he needed a job. He had pitched an idea to a woman studio executive who loved the idea. In fact, she was on the verge of making an offer.

The phone rang, she took the call in the other room and came back a few moments later. She was not nearly as receptive, however; in fact, she did an about face, thanked Michael for his time, and passed on the idea.

Michael called his agent, saying he thought for sure he had it. The studio executive as much as said she would buy it for development. What happened?

His agent said that he knew why it happened. That phone call she had gotten was from her boss, who fired her. "You were pitching to a person who no longer worked for the studio."

Rejection is a way of life. Don't take it personally; it's not about you but about so many other things that the best thing for you to do is nod and move on.

# TITLES

While we're at it, a title can be a real turn off. It can sour the pitch. If a title is boring, tasteless, derivative or forgettable, call it untitled. It's a reflection of your general ability to write.

Would you see a movie called *Always* or *Forever* or *Next Door, A Black Veil for Lisa,* or *Drifting Souls?*

Don't let anyone tell you otherwise: Titles mean a *lot*! If you can snag a great one right away, go for it. If not, get as close as you can.

Don't drive yourself crazy trying to find it. It will show up, like the beginning of a great relationship, when you're least expecting it. It might come out of something a character says, or from that thesaurus you've been scouring for days, or you might reshape it from an already existing title.

I found the title for one of my books, *Dirty Words,* in a conversation with my niece at dinner one night, at an Outback restaurant in Orlando. The story was about plagiarism and she said, "You mean, dirty words. There's your title." Just like that.

How about *Bad Day at Black Rock?* Says it all, doesn't it? How bad can a bad day at a place called Black Rock be? Exactly. How unforgettable is *The Good, the Bad, and the Ugly? American Beauty. American Psycho. Little Feet. Apocalypto. Snakes on a Plane.*

Will the title fit on a movie marquee? Or does it have so many words that they will trail down the building and onto the sidewalk?

*Pearl Harbor.* I knew a woman once whose name was Pearl Harbor. A father's cruel joke? An homage to war? She was quite happy about it — proud, in fact — because nobody ever forgot her.

Here's how *New York Times* critic A. O. Scott began his review: "The Japanese sneak attack on Pearl Harbor that brought the United States into World War II has inspired a splendid movie, full of vivid performances and unforgettable scenes, a movie that uses the coming of war as a backdrop for individual stories of love, ambition, heroism and betrayal. The name of that movie is 'From Here to Eternity'."

How about *Snakes on a Plane*? The title bangs you over the head. It sure does. But it says compression. It says terror. It strikes fear into anyone who's flown. Fear of flying ranks just below fear of snakes. *Pythons in Your Toilet. Piranhas in the Pool.*

A boring movie title means, to me at least, that the creators put about as much imagination into it as they did into the rest of the movie. *Enormous Changes*, a 1983 flick about New York City women, starring Ellen Barkin and Kevin Bacon, was written by the inimitable John Sayles. It could be the worst title ever. "Hey, Bob, have you seen *Enormous Changes*?"

A title should titillate*: Whatever Happened to Baby Jane?* It should perhaps create mystery: *The Haunting.* It should allude to something about the picture itself, with irony or a double or triple entendre: *Dead Wringer.* Or how about a title that overstates what it is*: Atom Man vs. Superman*, or *Triumph for the Son of Hercules.* Pass the sledge hammer.

A title should suggest some kind of action and intrigue. It should startle. *Fight Club.* In the dark city, in an underground fight club, a deviant soap salesman entices an overeager insurance adjuster to rule the world. *Dirty Pretty Things.* Hard to say but says a lot. *Black Snake Moan.* What? *Babel.* Babble?

In *Psycho*, we get exactly that in the person of the Anthony Perkins' character. Hitchcock loved one word titles. *Vertigo, Frenzy, Notorious, Spellbound.* They fit on the marquee, the grab you, and notice how each one conjures up a feeling or sense of emotional or psychological danger.

A good title titillates, it points you in a direction, and guides you toward the center of the movie.

## DRILL

**What are some of your favorite titles, and why? What was it about those titles that grabbed you? Write down the title and a paragraph or two on what struck you about each one. This exercise might open up a path into creating better titles for your own work.**

## LAST WRITES

Before you do anything, get that masterpiece written, edited, and pored over until there is not one more thing you can do. The script has become a living thing, deep within you now, deeper than any creative effort you have ever made. It is now part of you. And now you have to let it go, send it of into the world for others to embrace and rip apart and reject and maybe option or buy, and then to give to complete strangers to change and rip apart and do unspeakable things to.

Meanwhile, you, the fickle lover, are onto a new passion, a new script, a new lover. The muse has introduced you to a new toy — a fresh idea. And something strange happens.

That old passion gets put into perspective, that wonderful place where art can rest in the world outside of yourself, while you have already entered a new world with your new work.

I get out the note cards, call up Final Draft on the Mac and start plugging in ideas. I write and rewrite myself into another world, with new, barely formed creatures roaming around. I'm as lost as they are but we'll find one another and start relationships and, who knows, we might find another way to chart the story of our lives. There are no vacations in this racket, only exits and entrances.

# WORKSHOP

# 11

# ADAPTING ANY IDEA INTO A SCREENPLAY

I n this case I chose a best-selling novel, *Christmas Babies*, that I wrote (with Dr. William Black) and which Pocket Books published. I've included here the stages I went through in adapting the book to screen. The process is time-consuming and straightforward. My purpose is to find the story before I try to write the screenplay.

The process starts with a short synopsis and then treatment. I then figure out where I went wrong and make a list of the problems I found. Then I write a revised treatment.

This is the foundation for the screenplay.

Anyone foolish enough to start off with the screenplay itself will find trouble down the road.

### *Christmas Babies*
### A Work in Progress

A few years back I wrote my one and only medical thriller, *Christmas Babies*, which I adapted for film. Writing the novel was an experiment, to see if I could understand and execute one of the more popular genres in publishing.

I read the top men and women. My favorite: Tess Gerritsen. I read her books and others to see how they did it. A thriller with a medical theme. To everyone's surprise (except the publisher's), it sold a lot of copies.

Usually doctors write these books, so I went out and found a doctor, Dr. William D. Black, a fascinating guy who knew a lot about genetic engineering of children. Among other interesting things I learned about Bill, during delivery he uses hypnosis rather than anesthesia on his patients because he does not want the anesthesia to have an adverse effect on the birth.

He was also an unwitting participant at the center of a scandal called "Switched at Birth" by the media, about a diabolical scheme by a physician in Bill's hospital who as a favor to a friend replaced her own ill baby with a healthy one.

When I wrote the synopsis, treatment and first draft I did not give enough focus to the two main characters, who needed it to drive the story forward.

In fact, that script failed because of it, as I realize now. I had no stars in mind. No stars were waiting in place. I've since learned that the top professional screenwriters almost always have a top star in mind, whether they're under assignment or not. Why? It helps them focus.

In my first draft I allowed the story itself to dictate the direction and focus. The story has power but the characters got lost in the shuffle of other equally strong characters. And this was *not* an ensemble cast.

I made the classical mistake of following the story — an adapted story from a book in this case — instead of shaving away the less important elements that would have opened up the main characters and their interpersonal plights.

Let's say that the writers of *Titanic* decided to spend seventy percent of the story on the ship with other passengers and every once in a while ambled back to the love triangle. Hello disaster of another sort.

In *Christmas Babies*, the novel, the characters had a lot to lose and a lot to win. The stakes soared. But a writer cannot afford to give to everyone what everyone might need. It's the writer's responsibility to find the main characters and make sure that they run the show.

After the first run-through, in this case the synopsis and treatment (I have not included the script here for purposes of length), I was fortunate enough to get good advice about what was wrong.

First you'll see the original synopsis and treatment. Below that you'll see a second pass I recently wrote.

**Christmas Babies**
Based on the novel *Christmas Babies*,
by Christopher Keane & William D. Black, M.D.


**Synopsis**

In this spine-tingling thriller we are taken inside DNA, Inc., where men of power and twisted scientific ambition join in a terrifying scheme — and the miracle of childbirth is turned into a chilling nightmare.

DR. JOSH HELLER can't explain the alarming rise in difficult labors among his patients at Tampa Memorial Hospital. Many of these women — young, low risk, in perfect health — are dying in the delivery room.

And then there are the babies, tiny infants distinguished by wisps of red hair and luminescent green eyes.

PAT HELLER, Josh's wife and a seasoned medical reporter, begins to unravel the enigma. She uncovers a dangerous alliance between a Florida senator and a psychopathic doctor. They share a deadly secret: a genetic experiment utopian in premise and horrifying in practice.

DR. BRADLEY BURNS of DNA, Inc. thinks he has the answer to the health crisis and longer life: bringing babies into the world, disease free.

Through genetic splicing, Burns and his genetic engineers can remove a fetus's capacity for disease without the mothers ever knowing about it — in their gynecologist's office.

A genetic miracle? The ultimate solution to skyrocketing health problems? An answer to man's quest for immortality?

Or a medical nightmare? A genetic disaster of monumental proportions?

Burns wants to be able to recognize these children. He has spliced into their genetic makeup the exact colors of his own red hair and green eyes.

Then things start going wrong. Complications arise: chromosome abnormalities; deformed fetuses; death. Some make it through to birth, as living time bombs. Some of these "miracles" probably live in your own hometown, possibly in your neighborhood, are perhaps the children of your closest friends, even your own children.

They all carry a tiny, unstable virus Dr. Bradley Burns used to transport the genetically altered cells.

Next time you see a pregnant woman, or woman with red hair and green eyes, you might wonder, what exactly was her gynecologist doing down there?

**Christmas Babies**

**Treatment**

In Washington, D.C., U.S. SENATOR CURTIS MANHEIM gives a rousing speech on health care reform. This is his ticket to the White House. Reporters shoot questions at him. He is controversial, and this is his most radical proposal ever.

His health care plan will make or break him. He calls for billions to be invested in private sector high-tech genetic research firms, leaving them virtually unchecked by government watchdogs. This will lead to a world without disease, genetically removed at birth.

In ten days Manheim will go before both houses of Congress to unveil the details of this master plan. He promises a disease-free society in the not too distant future and he knows how to do it.

Manheim is driven; he believes in this cause, and he wants to become chief executive.

In Florida, the marriage of Dr. John Heller, a Tampa ob-gyn, and his wife PAT, a medical reporter for the Tampa *Tribune*, is on the rocks. Caught in the middle is their twelve-year-old daughter, ARIANA.

And that's not the half of it.

Many of Josh Heller's pregnant patients miscarry. Others give birth to misshapen and horribly deformed children. Others give birth to children who look nothing like their parents. Still others' medical records have been mysteriously altered.

A computer saleswoman, SAMANTHA BARROWS (red hair and luminescent green eyes), arrives at

Josh's office. Ms. Barrows shows interest in Josh beyond selling computers.

Meanwhile, Josh's wife Pat is disturbed by U.S. Senator Curt Manheim's (D-Fla.) health appropriations bill — to inhibit government control over experimental genetics research firms. She believes this could lead to a license to kill in the name of science and medicine.

His plea, which he says will lead to virtually the end of health insurance we know it, has the voters' ear.

Pat, who when she married dropped out of medical school, knows this territory. She is against high-tech genetic firms going unchecked in their research. History is filled with mad scientists and their human guinea pigs.

She starts to investigate. Her interview with Manheim turns nasty, bringing the ire of her editor (an old Manheim friend) down on her. She is told to back off or take a vacation for a few weeks.

Meanwhile Dr. Josh Heller's patients experience more startling side effects. Josh and his new research associate, DR. RIDLEY ELLIS, are stumped. Dr. Ellis, a recent arrival to Josh's office, came bearing a $100,000 research grant to study under Josh.

Josh pays an unscheduled visit to his office and finds Pat. He wonders what she's doing here. After hemming and hawing she admits that she is pregnant and has been seeing Ridley Ellis for treatment. She and Josh were having so much relationship trouble she didn't want him to know.

He takes a look and discovers, with a fetal

scanner, extraordinarily rapid growth areas of Pat's fetus. He can't explain them, but since the baby seems healthy he decides to closely monitor her.

Pat continues to pursue Sen. Manheim, discovering that he has poured millions of his own and government money into private sector research, in particular into an umbrella company whose holdings are difficult to trace. She flies to Washington to find out.

Sam Barrows, computer saleswoman, arrives at Josh's home. She has an appointment with him set up by his medical partner, Dr. Ellis, to replace both partners' office with home systems.

Daughter Ariana, who is charmed by Sam Barrows' warmness and wit, takes to her. Ariana is not so charmed by the way Sam flirts with her father.

Josh Heller receives a call from his best friend from medical school, DR. TED TOZIAN, who's in the midst of a crisis and needs help. "You, too?" says Josh, who agrees with meet with him in Miami.

Sam Barrows explains why they need a new system. The old one is outdated, incapable of properly marking, storing, and sending data.

In Washington, D.C., Pat Heller placates Sen. Manheim. She gets him to promise a trip to DNA, Inc., the genetics firm into which he's been dumping money. For Sen. Manheim, the media empire that owns the TV station Pat works for is strong and a good place for him to state his position.

In Miami Josh meets his friend, Dr. Ted Tozian, ob-gyn, whose patients, Josh is astonished to discover, suffer similar miscarriages and give birth to children with the same birth defects, especially in behavioral areas.

In Washington Pat wakes up next morning in her hotel room. Manheim arrives and they take a ride to Virginia and DNA, Inc.

Back in Tampa, Dr. Josh Heller is worried. There's been no word from Pat. His office is in shambles. His patients are baffled. His partner, Ridley Ellis, works round the clock.

Josh gets an e-mail from Pat, who wants him to meet her in Washington. She has discovered something about Manheim and a company called DNA, Inc, in Falls Church, Virginia.

Ariana tells him that Sam Burrows had come by. Ariana found her in his office. Josh explains about the new computer system. Ariana adds: "And speaking on the phone to Dr. Ellis about some problems with the babies."

"What did you hear exactly?" Ariana says enough for Josh to be concerned. Sam calls Josh, asking him to meet her at her home on Tulip Key. She has something important to discuss with him.

On the way to Samantha's place, John stops by Ridley Ellis's where he discovers newly pregnant women's records and dates of procedures he did not know Ridley had performed.

In other reports Josh Heller sees the name Dr. Bradley Burns, DNA, Inc., the genetics firm that originally had sent Ridley Ellis and the $100,000 grant to work in Josh's office.

Confused and angry, Josh arrives at Sam's and confronts her with this information. Attempting to seduce him in order to later kill him, Samantha accidentally drowns in the pool.

Josh knows that Pat, somewhere in Washington D.C., is in danger.

Unfortunately he can no longer go to the police with his information. They will soon be looking for him in connection with Sam Barrow's death. And there is little time. He must get to Pat.

In Falls Church, Pat arrives at Dr. Bradley Burns' DNA Inc. genetics lab and immediately becomes his prisoner. She learns how Burns has been creating his Perfect Ones, the disease-free babies.

It's quite simple, he explains. He has sent doctors (like Josh's grant partner, Jim Ellis) armed with $100,000 to train with established ob-gyns throughout the country. These doctors remove fetal tissue from newly pregnant women, which they send to DNA labs where the cell properties are established.

Through genetic splicing, disease capacities are removed or spliced out while other characteristics — size, weight, genetic safeguards against disease itself — are spliced on. The altered cell tissue is returned to the ob-gyn's office, where the temporary doctors reinsert it in the pregnant woman without her knowledge.

The cell tissue, by way of a retro virus that speeds cell growth, expands and in effect dominates the fetal growth, its properties taking command. The child, disease free, arrives on time.

The problem is the retro virus, which has not been thoroughly stabilized. Thus the deformed babies.

Burns explains that sometimes his virus goes awry and shows Pat the terrible evidence of it — horribly deformed babies. She reels from the sight.

The implications are staggering. In the wrong hands, in this case Brad Burns and Sen. Manheim's, ob-gyn offices have been surreptitiously turned into experimental labs, working out the kinks at the grass roots level.

Burns says to Pat that his medical breakthrough — a disease-free world — is the greatest gift one could ever give to his fellow man. What's your objection?

That it's in your hands, she replies, and Manheim's.

How many of these disease-free children exist? she asks. Hundreds, thousands, Brad Burns replies, soon to be tens of thousands. Burns says that by telling her these things she must realize that she'll never be allowed to leave.

Josh Heller arrives at DNA, Inc., prepared for anything. He decides that the only way to get inside this fortress is to announce who he is. He does so and is brought to Bradley Burns.

By using Dr. Burns' own virus against him, Josh and Pat Heller manage to escape. Bradley Burns dies a miserable death in the process.

On the Senate floor that afternoon, Sen. Curt Manheim delivers an impassioned speech, televised throughout the nation. In it he calls for a disease-free world and goes on about the steps he will take to bring this about. It's impressive.

Down on the senate floor Manheim sees two people — a woman and a man carrying something in his arms — walking down the aisle towards him. He thinks he recognizes them but the glare from the lights is too strong.

The man, Dr. Josh Heller, carrying the object, speaks out. His words condemn Manheim, who calls for the sergeant of arms to throw the

man out. The sergeant starts down. Some of the
senators stop him and the woman, Pat Heller.
They want to hear more.

As the couple draws closer, Manheim sees what
the man is carrying — one of the deformed ex-
perimental children from DNA, Inc. Manheim draws
away in horror, knowing that this is the end.

In Tampa, Pat and Josh and daughter Amy are a
family again.

In an obscure but extravagantly equipped
genetics laboratory in Michigan near the
Canadian border, Dr. Ridley Ellis and his
colleagues secretly carry on the work of Dr.
Bradley Burns and DNA, Inc.

The following December 20, a beautiful baby
is born to Dr. and Mrs. Josh Heller. An eight-
pound, five-ounce boy with thick auburn hair
and bright green eyes.

**The Major Problems**

1. This is supposed to be a thriller. What happened to the thrills? The
characters too often stand around explaining the plot to each other.
I've got to get them moving and in more physical danger.

2. One the major hurdles is the broken relationship between Pat
and Josh Heller. You wouldn't know it by this story. They are rarely
together, which cuts out the emotional impact of a broken marriage.
In fact, their relationship is so weak that that it would hardly matter if
the marriage were on the rocks. That has to be fixed.

3. The villains. They're like lemmings, there are so many of them.
Burns, Manheim, Dr. Ellis. The good thing is that the villains are all
in cahoots with each other, under one central control. One big cheese
needs to run the show.

4. The beginning doesn't have enough snap. A speech? By a U.S.
Senator? Please.

## The Revised Treatment

The revised treatment will give you an idea of the difference between allowing the story to run away with the movie (version #1) and characters created for A-list talent to play the key parts (version #2).

In this case I had Hugh Jackman and Jennifer Connolly playing the lead roles.

You'll notice what happens when I focused on putting A-list stars' faces on the characters. Even though I had no contract, no commitment, no real contacts with the actors, I revised with them in mind.

I have written for stars attached to projects. Some of them dropped out; others remained. The point is that by keeping in mind an A-list star, whether you have one or not, will enable you to keep your main characters where they belong. You give the movie to them. You make them the leads and that's what they do — they lead the pack and occupy the story's center, on screen the vast majority of the time.

Without the full script you won't get various nuances, but you'll see a few structural differences that put the emphasis n the right place.

### Christmas Babies

### Revised Treatment

At Tampa General, a baby is born to a young couple. When they first see it they scream to high heaven.

JOSH HELLER (37), the family ob-gyn, hears the screams and comes running. He finds the couple staring at their baby — a red-haired, green-eyed eerie-looking thing that looks nothing like either of them.

At home, Josh tells PATRICIA HELLER (33), his wife and a reporter for Channel 4 News, about the baby. Another one? she says.

Their daughter ARIANA (14), listens to them argue about what's to be done. Josh wants to keep the wraps on his suspicion until he knows more. Patricia wants to go public, with the idea of ferreting out more info.

They each have a point. This marriage has lost its chance for compromise, symptomatic of a lot of problems in the marriage.

In Washington, D.C., U.S. SENATOR CURTIS MANHEIM (53) gives a rousing speech on health care reform. This is his ticket to the White House. Reporters shoot questions at him. He is controversial, and this is his most radical proposal ever.

His health care plan calls for billions to be invested in private sector high-tech genetic research firms, leaving them virtually unchecked by government watchdogs. This will lead to a world without disease, genetically removed at birth.

(What he doesn't say is that the plan is already rolling forward. He expects to get some badly needed funding and even some limited Congressional approval. He will then truck out the miraculous results just in time for the election.)

In ten days Manheim will go before both houses of Congress to unveil the details of this master plan. He promises a disease-free society in the not too distant future and he knows how to do it.

Manheim is driven. He believes in this cause, and he wants to become chief executive.

In Tampa Josh speaks with his recently hired junior partner (who brought with him a $150,000 research grant to the practice), DR. RIDLEY

ELLIS (30) about recent problems. Pregnant patients miscarry. Others give birth to misshapen and horribly deformed children. Still others' medical records have been mysteriously altered or are missing.

Ridley Ellis has the answer to the medical records problem. A new software saleswoman, SAMANTHA BARROWS (27; red hair and luminescent green eyes), walks in. Sam Barrows shows interest in Josh beyond selling software.

Meanwhile, at Channel 4, Pat Heller is disturbed by Senator Manheim's health appro-priations bill — to inhibit government control over experimental genetics research firms. She believes this could lead to a license to kill in the name of science and medicine.

His plea, which he says will lead to virtually the end of health insurance we know it, has the voters' ear.

Patricia Heller, who when she married dropped out of medical school, knows the medical business and, despite her husband's protests, wants answers. She is against high-tech genetic firms going unchecked in their research, and airs a story about it. History is filled with mad scientists and their human guinea pigs.

She starts to investigate. Her interview with Manheim turns nasty, bringing the ire of her producer (an old Manheim friend) down on her. She is told to back off.

Josh pays an unscheduled visit to his office and finds Pat. He wonders what she's doing here. After hemming and hawing she admits that she is pregnant and has been seeing Ridley Ellis for treatment. She and Josh were having so much relationship trouble she didn't want him to know.

He discovers, with a fetal scanner, extraordinarily rapid growth areas in Pat's fetus. He can't explain them, but since the baby seems healthy he will closely monitor her.

A moment of caring and joy turns sour. She's frustrated by her boss and Josh, and Manheim, telling her to leave things alone. Josh argues that Manheim's plan could, down the line, become *the* major health breakthrough of the millennium. Government watchdogs stifle research — look at the stem cell issue. She counters with the science-run-amok position of dangerous, insufficiently tested drugs flooding the market. Look at Fen-fen, the Pfizer and Merck disasters.

He says, with perfect health, we won't need health insurance or pharmaceutical multinationals ripping us off. "Or even doctors!" she shouts. "Like all members of Congress, Manheim has his short-term pork-loaded agenda that will make him rich *and* president, with a lot of multinational drugs companies eventually running *everything*."

And so it goes. Patricia storms out. Standing in another doorway is daughter Ariana, who has witnessed this, tears flooding her eyes.

Pat continues to pursue Sen. Manheim, discovering that he has poured millions of his own and government money into private sector research, in particular into an umbrella company whose holdings are difficult to trace. She takes a few days off from work and flies to Washington.

Sam Barrows, computer saleswoman, arrives at Josh's home. She has an appointment with him set up by his medical partner, Dr. Ellis, to replace both partners' office with home systems.

Daughter Ariana, who is charmed by Sam Barrows'

warmness and wit, takes to her. Ariana is not so charmed by the way Sam flirts with her father.

In Washington, D.C., Pat Heller placates Sen. Manheim, who promises a trip to DNA, Inc., into which he's been dumping money.

Back in Tampa, Dr. Josh Heller is worried. There's been no word from Pat. His office is in shambles. His patients are baffled. His partner, Ridley Ellis, works round the clock. Josh decides to go to D.C. to find Patricia.

Ariana tells him that Sam Burrows had come by. Ariana found her in his office. Josh explains about the new computer system. Ariana adds: "And speaking on the phone to Dr. Ellis about some problems with the odd babies."

"What did you hear exactly?" Ariana says enough for Josh to be concerned. Sam calls Josh, asking him to meet her at her home on Tulip Key. She has something important to discuss with him.

On the way to Samantha's place, John stops by Ridley Ellis's where he discovers newly pregnant women's records and dates of procedures he did not know Ridley had performed.

In some of these reports Josh Heller sees the name Dr. Bradley Burns DNA, Inc., Falls Church, Virginia, the genetics firm that originally had sent Ridley Ellis and the $150,000 grant to work in Josh's office

Confused and angry, Josh arrives at Sam's and confronts her with this information. Attempting to seduce him in order to later kill him, Samantha accidentally drowns in the pool.

Josh knows that Pat, probably at DNA, Inc. is in danger.

Unfortunately he can't go to the police with his information, not now.

*Here's where some thrillers will have high-speed chases through Virginia farm country. Not a bad idea. But to make chases interesting you ought to have the main character — in this case, Josh — not suddenly become a racecar driver, Xtreme kick-boxing champ and acclaimed equestrian. He is a doctor. He may get trapped in a thoroughbred barn. He will know how to administer drugs to thoroughbreds, who are known to be high strung and unpredictable.*

*It's not hard to find good places in the story where both Pat and Josh, who are already trying to fix the marriage whether they know it or not, use the tools of their professions and emotional need to reach one another to prevail. And to saddle up, and try again.*

*This emotional need to repair their marriage is the real juice flowing through the story — this is the main subplot. Subplots carry the emotion. The plot — which is the action — is stopping Manheim, Burns and company before they're able to launch their master plan — which will be hard, if not impossible, to stop once it gets going.*

In Falls Church, Pat arrives at Dr. Bradley Burns' DNA Inc. genetics lab and immediately becomes his prisoner. She learns how Burns has been creating his Perfect Ones, the disease-free babies.

It's quite simple, he explains. He has sent doctors (like Josh's grant partner, Ridley Ellis) armed with $150,000 to train with established ob-gyns throughout the country. These doctors remove fetal tissue from newly pregnant women that they send to DNA, Inc. labs where the cell properties are established.

Through genetic splicing, disease capacities are removed or spliced out while other characteristics — size, weight, genetic safeguards against disease itself — are spliced

in. The altered cell tissue is returned to the
ob-gyn's office, where the temporary doctors
reinsert it in the pregnant woman without her
knowledge.

The cell tissue, by way of a retro virus that
speeds cell growth, expands and in effect
dominates the fetal growth, its properties
taking command. The child, disease free,
arrives on time.

The problem is the retro virus that has not
been thoroughly stabilized. Thus the deformed
babies.

Burns explains that sometimes his virus goes
awry and shows Pat living examples of horribly
deformed babies. She reels from the sight.

The implications are staggering. In the
wrong hands, in this case Brad Burns and
Sen. Manheim's, ob-gyn offices have been
surreptitiously turned into experimental labs,
working out the kinks at the grass roots level.

Burns says to Pat that his medical breakthrough
— a disease-free world — is the greatest gift
one could ever bestow upon his fellow man.
What's your objection?

That it's in your hands, she says, and
Manheim's. Playing God isn't that attractive
either —and what else beyond this altruistic
gesture — pretty soon you'll altering everything
in the name of what's fashionable, like green
eyes and red hair.

How many of these disease-free children exist?
she asks. Hundreds, thousands, Burns replies,
soon to be tens of thousands. Burns says that
by telling her these things she must realize
that she'll never be allowed to leave.

Josh Heller arrives at DNA, Inc., prepared for anything. He decides that the only way to get inside this fortress is to announce his presence. He does so and is brought to Bradley Burns.

After a lot of bodies falling and the horrific genetic "mistakes" they witness, by using Dr. Brad Burns' own defective virus against him, Josh and Patricia Heller manage to escape. Bradley Burns dies a horrific death of his own.

On the Senate floor that afternoon, Sen. Curt Manheim delivers an impassioned speech, televised throughout the nation. In it he calls for a disease-free world and goes on about the steps he will take to bring this about. It's impressive.

Down on the Senate floor Manheim sees two people — a woman and a man carrying something in his arms — walking down the aisle towards him. He thinks he recognizes them but the glare from the lights is too strong.

The man, Dr. Josh Heller, carrying the object, speaks out. His words condemn Manheim, who calls for the sergeant of arms to throw the man out. The sergeant starts down. Some of the senators stop him and the woman, Patricia Heller. They want to hear more.

As the couple draws closer, Manheim sees what the man is carrying — one of the deformed experimental children from DNA, Inc. Manheim draws away in horror, knowing that this is the end.

In Tampa, Pat and Josh and daughter Ariana are a family again.

In an obscure but extravagantly equipped genetics laboratory in Michigan near the

Canadian border, Dr. Ridley Ellis and his colleagues secretly carry on the work of Dr. Bradley Burns and DNA, Inc.

The following December 20, a beautiful baby is born to Dr. and Mrs. Josh Heller. An eight-pound, five-ounce boy with thick auburn hair and bright green eyes.

# EPILOGUE

I'm just going to have to keep working on it. I have some ideas, some of which are not that great, some of which are not that bad. It's the nature of the beast. You work and work and get to a point where you think you might have something, and then you work some more.

It beats going to an office and working for someone else, at least it does for me. But the wolf is at the door and I can't afford to sit around and wait for the muse to ride down in her Lexus or on her aluminum broom with the answer.

I have to ask the two or three characters who knows what to do, who haven't I done enough for. Maybe because I don't know them well enough yet to get a satisfactory answer — or even to ask a satisfactory question.

My main characters are my best collaborators. They're my muse. The answers lie in them. They're my horses. When I get them up and running at a full gallop, the rest of the herd will follow.

# About the Author

Christopher Keane has written fourteen fiction and nonfiction books, several of which have been adapted for film and television including *The Hunter* (a Paramount feature), *The Huntress* (a USA TV series), and *The Crossing* (WB). He has taught screenwriting at Harvard, Emerson College, and New York University, and has spoken on screenwriting at the Smithsonian Institution, the National Press Club, Maui Writers, and L.A. Screenwriting Expo. He recently completed a feature, *Lost Light* and a TV series pilot, *The Nob Hill Social Club*.

Website: *www.keanewords.com*
Email: *keanewords@aol.com*

# THE WRITER'S JOURNEY
## 3RD EDITION

## MYTHIC STRUCTURE FOR WRITERS

### CHRISTOPHER VOGLER

## BEST SELLER
### OVER 170,000 COPIES SOLD!

See why this book has become an international best seller and a true classic. *The Writer's Journey* explores the powerful relationship between mythology and storytelling in a clear, concise style that's made it required reading for movie executives, screenwriters, playwrights, scholars, and fans of pop culture all over the world.

Both fiction and nonfiction writers will discover a set of useful myth-inspired storytelling paradigms (i.e., "The Hero's Journey") and step-by-step guidelines to plot and character development. Based on the work of Joseph Campbell, *The Writer's Journey* is a must for all writers interested in further developing their craft.

The updated and revised third edition provides new insights and observations from Vogler's ongoing work on mythology's influence on stories, movies, and man himself.

*"This book is like having the smartest person in the story meeting come home with you and whisper what to do in your ear as you write a screenplay. Insight for insight, step for step, Chris Vogler takes us through the process of connecting theme to story and making a script come alive."*
> – Lynda Obst, Producer, *Sleepless in Seattle, How to Lose a Guy in 10 Days*;
> Author, *Hello, He Lied*

*"This is a book about the stories we write, and perhaps more importantly, the stories we live. It is the most influential work I have yet encountered on the art, nature, and the very purpose of storytelling."*
> – Bruce Joel Rubin, Screenwriter, *Stuart Little 2, Deep Impact,*
> *Ghost, Jacob's Ladder*

CHRISTOPHER VOGLER is a veteran story consultant for major Hollywood film companies and a respected teacher of filmmakers and writers around the globe. He has influenced the stories of movies from *The Lion King* to *Fight Club* to *The Thin Red Line* and most recently wrote the first installment of *Ravenskull*, a Japanese-style manga or graphic novel. He is the executive producer of the feature film *P.S. Your Cat is Dead* and writer of the animated feature *Jester Till*.

**$26.95 · 300 PAGES · ORDER NUMBER 76RLS · ISBN: 193290736x**

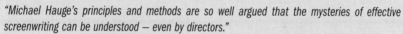

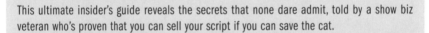

# SAVE THE CAT! GOES TO THE MOVIES
## THE SCREENWRITER'S GUIDE TO EVERY STORY EVER TOLD

### BLAKE SNYDER

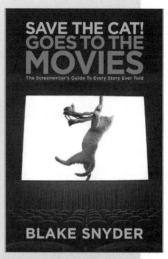

In the long-awaited sequel to his surprise bestseller, *Save the Cat!*, author and screenwriter Blake Snyder returns to form in a fast-paced follow-up that proves why his is the most talked-about approach to screenwriting in years. In the perfect companion piece to his first book, Snyder delivers even more insider's information gleaned from a 20-year track record as "one of Hollywood's most successful spec screenwriters," giving you the clues to write *your* movie.

Designed for screenwriters, novelists, and movie fans, this book gives readers the key breakdowns of the 50 most instructional movies from the past 30 years. From *M\*A\*S\*H* to *Crash*, from *Alien* to *Saw*, from *10* to *Eternal Sunshine of the Spotless Mind*, Snyder reveals how screenwriters who came before you tackled the same challenges you are facing with the film you want to write – or the one you are currently working on.

Writing a "rom-com"? Check out the "Buddy Love" chapter for a "beat for beat" dissection of *When Harry Met Sally*... plus references to 10 other great romantic comedies that will make your story sing.

Want to execute a great mystery? Go to the "Whydunit" section and learn about the "dark turn" that's essential to the heroes of *All the President's Men*, *Blade Runner*, *Fargo* and hip noir *Brick* – and see why ALL good stories, whether a Hollywood blockbuster or a Sundance award winner, follow the same rules of structure outlined in Snyder's breakthrough method.

If you want to sell your script and create a movie that pleases most audiences most of the time, the odds increase if you reference Snyder's checklists and see what makes 50 films tick. After all, both executives and audiences respond to the same elements good writers seek to master. They want to know the type of story they signed on for, and whether it's structured in a way that satisfies everyone. It's what they're looking for. And now, it's what you can deliver.

BLAKE SNYDER, besides selling million-dollar scripts to both Disney and Spielberg, is still "one of Hollywood's most successful spec screenwriters," having made another spec sale in 2006. An in-demand scriptcoach and seminar and workshop leader, Snyder provides information for writers through his website, *www.blakesnyder.com*.

**$22.95 · 270 PAGES · ORDER NUMBER 75RLS · ISBN: 1932907351**

# THE HOLLYWOOD STANDARD

### THE COMPLETE AND AUTHORITATIVE GUIDE
### TO SCRIPT FORMAT AND STYLE

### CHRISTOPHER RILEY

## *BEST SELLER*

Finally, there's a script format guide that is accurate, complete, and easy to use, written by Hollywood's foremost authority on industry standard script formats. Riley's guide is filled with clear, concise, complete instructions and hundreds of examples to take the guesswork out of a multitude of formatting questions that perplex screenwriters, waste their time, and steal their confidence. You'll learn how to get into and out of a POV shot, how to set up a telephone intercut, what to capitalize and why, how to control pacing with format, and more.

"The Hollywood Standard *is not only indispensable, it's practical, readable, and fun to use.*"
— Dean Batali, Writer-Producer, *That '70s Show;* Writer, *Buffy the Vampire Slayer*

"*Buy this book before you write another word! It's required reading for any screenwriter who wants to be taken seriously by Hollywood.*"
— Elizabeth Stephen, President, Mandalay Television Pictures;
Executive Vice President Motion Picture Production, Mandalay Pictures

"*Riley has succeeded in an extremely difficult task: He has produced a guide to screenplay formatting which is both entertaining to read and exceptionally thorough. Riley's clear style, authoritative voice, and well-written examples make this book far more enjoyable than any formatting guide has a right to be. This is the best guide to script formatting ever, and it is an indispensable tool for every writer working in Hollywood.*"
— Wout Thielemans, *Screentalk* Magazine

"*It doesn't matter how great your screenplay is if it looks all wrong.* The Hollywood Standard *is probably the most critical book any screenwriter who is serious about being taken seriously can own. For any writer who truly understands the power of making a good first impression, this comprehensive guide to format and style is priceless.*"
— Marie Jones, *www.absolutewrite.com*

CHRISTOPHER RILEY, based in Los Angeles, developed Warner Brothers Studios script software and serves as the ultimate arbiter of script format for the entertainment industry.

**$18.95 · 208 PAGES · ORDER # 31RLS · ISBN: 9781932907018**

THE 100 MOST POWERFUL FILM CONVENTIONS EVERY FILMMAKER MUST KNOW JENNIFER VAN SIJLL

# CINEMATIC STORYTELLING

### THE 100 MOST POWERFUL FILM CONVENTIONS EVERY FILMMAKER MUST KNOW

### JENNIFER VAN SIJLL

## BEST SELLER

How do directors use screen direction to suggest conflict? How do screenwriters exploit film space to show change? How does editing style determine emotional response?

Many first-time writers and directors do not ask these questions. They forego the huge creative resource of the film medium, defaulting to dialog to tell their screen story. Yet most movies are carried by sound and picture. The industry's most successful writers and directors have mastered the cinematic conventions specific to the medium. They have harnessed non-dialog techniques to create some of the most cinematic moments in movie history.

This book is intended to help writers and directors more fully exploit the medium's inherent storytelling devices. It contains 100 non-dialog techniques that have been used by the industry's top writers and directors. From *Metropolis* and *Citizen Kane* to *Dead Man* and *Kill Bill*, the book illustrates — through 500 frame grabs and 75 script excerpts — how the inherent storytelling devices specific to film were exploited.

You will learn:
- How non-dialog film techniques can advance story.
- How master screenwriters exploit cinematic conventions to create powerful scenarios.

"Cinematic Storytelling *scores a direct hit in terms of concise information and perfectly chosen visuals, and it also searches out... and finds... an emotional core that many books of this nature either miss or are afraid of.*"
— Kirsten Sheridan, Director, *Disco Pigs*; Co-writer, *In America*

"*Here is a uniquely fresh, accessible, and truly original contribution to the field. Jennifer van Sijll takes her readers in a wholly new direction, integrating aspects of screenwriting with all the film crafts in a way I've never before seen. It is essential reading not only for screenwriters but also for filmmakers of every stripe.*"
— Prof. Richard Walter, UCLA Screenwriting Chairman

JENNIFER VAN SIJLL has taught film production, film history, and screenwriting. She is currently on the faculty at San Francisco State's Department of Cinema.

**$24.95 · 230 PAGES · ORDER # 35RLS · ISBN: 193290705X**

# STEALING FIRE FROM THE GODS
## A DYNAMIC NEW STORY MODEL FOR WRITERS AND FILMMAKERS

### JAMES BONNET

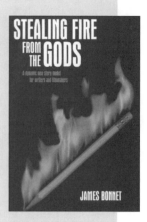

In the tradition of Carl Jung, Joseph Campbell, and Christopher Vogler, James Bonnet explores the connection between mythic story-telling and personal growth. *Stealing Fire From the Gods* investigates the elements that make traditional tales so enduring, and shows how modern writers can use those same elements to make their own stories more powerful, memorable, and emotionally resonant.

*"For anyone interested in structuring feelings and thought into words and story, Bonnet provides the reader with insight and an overview of the creative process. I recommend it highly."*
— Elliott Gould, Actor, Academy Award Nominee

JAMES BONNET, founder of Astoria Filmwrights, is a successful screen and television writer who has been elected twice to the Board of Directors of the Writers Guild.

**$26.95 | 235 PAGES | ORDER # 38RLS | ISBN: 0-941188-65-5**

# WRITING THE SECOND ACT
## BUILDING CONFLICT AND TENSION IN YOUR FILM SCRIPT

### MICHAEL HALPERIN

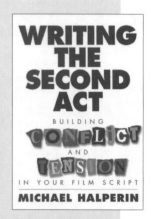

Every screenplay needs an attention-grabbing beginning and a satisfying ending, but the second act is the meat of your story, where your characters grow, change, and overcome the obstacles that will bring them to the resolution at the end of the story. Consequently, it's also the hardest act to write, and where most screenplays tend to lose momentum and focus. This book will help writers through that crucial 60-page stretch. Structural elements and plot devices are discussed in detail, as well as how to keep the action moving and the characters evolving while the audience stays wrapped up in your story.

*"A must-have tool for beginning writers and a valuable reminder for professionals."*
— Lynn Roth, Writer-Producer, A Will of Their Own

MICHAEL HALPERIN is also the author of *Writing the Killer Treatment*.

**$19.95 | 161 PAGES | ORDER # 49RLS | ISBN: 0-941188-29-9**

# MICHAEL WIESE PRODUCTIONS

Since 1981, Michael Wiese Productions has been dedicated to providing both novice and seasoned filmmakers with vital information on all aspects of filmmaking. We have published nearly 100 books, used in over 600 film schools and countless universities, and by hundreds of thousands of filmmakers worldwide.

Our authors are successful industry professionals who spend innumerable hours writing about the hard stuff: budgeting, financing, directing, marketing, and distribution. They believe that if they share their knowledge and experience with others, more high quality films will be produced.

And that has been our mission, now complemented through our new web-based resources. We invite all readers to visit www.mwp.com to receive free tipsheets and sample chapters, participate in forum discussions, obtain product discounts — and even get the opportunity to receive free books, project consulting, and other services offered by our company.

Our goal is, quite simply, to help you reach your goals. That's why we give our readers the most complete portal for filmmaking knowledge available — in the most convenient manner.

We truly hope that our books and web-based resources will empower you to create enduring films that will last for generations to come.

Let us hear from you at anytime.

Sincerely,
## Michael Wiese
Publisher, Filmmaker

www.mwp.com

# FILM & VIDEO BOOKS

**Archetypes for Writers:** *Using the Power of Your Subconscious*
Jennifer Van Bergen / $22.95

**Art of Film Funding, The:** *Alternate Financing Concepts*
Carole lee Dean / $26.95

**Cinematic Storytelling:** *The 100 Most Powerful Film Conventions Every Filmmaker Must Know* / Jennifer Van Sijll / $24.95

**Complete Independent Movie Marketing Handbook, The:** *Promote, Distribute & Sell Your Film or Video* / Mark Steven Bosko / $39.95

**Creating Characters:** *Let Them Whisper Their Secrets*
Marisa D'Vari / $26.95

**Crime Writer's Reference Guide, The:** *1001 Tips for Writing the Perfect Crime*
Martin Roth / $20.95

**Cut by Cut:** *Editing Your Film or Video*
Gael Chandler / $35.95

**Digital Filmmaking 101, 2nd Edition:** *An Essential Guide to Producing Low-Budget Movies* / Dale Newton and John Gaspard / $26.95

**Directing Actors:** *Creating Memorable Performances for Film and Television*
Judith Weston / $26.95

**Directing Feature Films:** *The Creative Collaboration Between Directors, Writers, and Actors* / Mark Travis / $26.95

**Elephant Bucks:** *An Insider's Guide to Writing for TV Sitcoms*
Sheldon Bull / $24.95

**Eye is Quicker, The:** *Film Editing; Making a Good Film Better*
Richard D. Pepperman / $27.95

**Fast, Cheap & Under Control:** *Lessons Learned from the Greatest Low-Budget Movies of All Time* / John Gaspard / $26.95

**Fast, Cheap & Written That Way:** *Top Screenwriters on Writing for Low-Budget Movies* / John Gaspard / $26.95

**Film & Video Budgets, 4th Updated Edition**
Deke Simon and Michael Wiese / $26.95

**Film Directing: Cinematic Motion, 2nd Edition**
Steven D. Katz / $27.95

**Film Directing: Shot by Shot,** *Visualizing from Concept to Screen*
Steven D. Katz / $27.95

**Film Director's Intuition, The:** *Script Analysis and Rehearsal Techniques*
Judith Weston / $26.95

**Film Production Management 101:** *The Ultimate Guide for Film and Television Production Management and Coordination* / Deborah S. Patz / $39.95

**Filmmaking for Teens:** *Pulling Off Your Shorts*
Troy Lanier and Clay Nichols / $18.95

**First Time Director:** *How to Make Your Breakthrough Movie*
Gil Bettman / $27.95

**From Word to Image:** *Storyboarding and the Filmmaking Process*
Marcie Begleiter / $26.95

**Hollywood Standard, The:** *The Complete and Authoritative Guide to Script Format and Style* / Christopher Riley / $18.95

**Independent Film Distribution:** *How to Make a Successful End Run Around the Big Guys* / Phil Hall / $26.95

**Independent Film and Videomakers Guide – 2nd Edition, The:** *Expanded and Updated* / Michael Wiese / $29.95

**Inner Drives:** *How to Write and Create Characters Using the Eight Classic Centers of Motivation* / Pamela Jaye Smith / $26.95

**I'll Be in My Trailer!:** *The Creative Wars Between Directors & Actors*
John Badham and Craig Modderno / $26.95

**Moral Premise, The:** *Harnessing Virtue & Vice for Box Office Success*
Stanley D. Williams, Ph.D. / $24.95

**Myth and the Movies:** *Discovering the Mythic Structure of 50 Unforgettable Films* / Stuart Voytilla / $26.95

**On the Edge of a Dream:** *Magic and Madness in Bali*
Michael Wiese / $16.95

**Perfect Pitch, The:** *How to Sell Yourself and Your Movie Idea to Hollywood*
Ken Rotcop / $16.95

**Power of Film, The**
Howard Suber / $27.95

**Psychology for Screenwriters:** *Building Conflict in your Script*
William Indick, Ph.D. / $26.95

**Save the Cat!:** *The Last Book on Screenwriting You'll Ever Need*
Blake Snyder / $19.95

**Save the Cat! Goes to the Movies:** *The Screenwriter's Guide to Every Story Ever Told* / Blake Snyder / $24.95

**Screenwriting 101:** *The Essential Craft of Feature Film Writing*
Neill D. Hicks / $16.95

**Screenwriting for Teens:** *The 100 Principles of Screenwriting Every Budding Writer Must Know* / Christina Hamlett / $18.95

**Script-Selling Game, The:** *A Hollywood Insider's Look at Getting Your Script Sold and Produced* / Kathie Fong Yoneda / $16.95

**Selling Your Story in 60 Seconds:** *The Guaranteed Way to get Your Screenplay or Novel Read* / Michael Hauge / $12.95

**Setting Up Your Scenes:** *The Inner Workings of Great Films*
Richard D. Pepperman / $24.95

**Setting Up Your Shots:** *Great Camera Moves Every Filmmaker Should Know*
Jeremy Vineyard / $19.95

**Shaking the Money Tree, 2nd Edition:** *The Art of Getting Grants and Donations for Film and Video Projects* / Morrie Warshawski / $26.95

**Sound Design:** *The Expressive Power of Music, Voice, and Sound Effects in Cinema* / David Sonnenschein / $19.95

**Special Effects:** *How to Create a Hollywood Film Look on a Home Studio Budget* / Michael Slone / $31.95

**Stealing Fire From the Gods, 2nd Edition:** *The Complete Guide to Story for Writers & Filmmakers* / James Bonnet / $26.95

**Ultimate Filmmaker's Guide to Short Films, The:** *Making It Big in Shorts*
Kim Adelman / $16.95

**Way of Story, The:** *The Craft & Soul of Writing*
Catherine Anne Jones / $22.95

**Working Director, The:** *How to Arrive, Thrive & Survive in the Director's Chair*
Charles Wilkinson / $22.95

**Writer's Journey, – 3rd Edition, The:** *Mythic Structure for Writers*
Christopher Vogler / $26.95

**Writing the Action Adventure:** *The Moment of Truth*
Neill D. Hicks / $14.95

**Writing the Comedy Film:** *Make 'Em Laugh*
Stuart Voytilla and Scott Petri / $14.95

**Writing the Killer Treatment:** *Selling Your Story Without a Script*
Michael Halperin / $14.95

**Writing the Second Act:** *Building Conflict and Tension in Your Film Script*
Michael Halperin / $19.95

**Writing the Thriller Film:** *The Terror Within*
Neill D. Hicks / $14.95

**Writing the TV Drama Series – 2nd Edition:** *How to Succeed as a Professional Writer in TV* / Pamela Douglas / $26.95

## DVD & VIDEOS

**Field of Fish:** *VHS Video*
Directed by Steve Tanner and Michael Wiese, Written by Annamaria Murphy / $9.95

**Hardware Wars:** *DVD* / Written and Directed by Ernie Fosselius / $14.95

**Sacred Sites of the Dalai Lamas– DVD, The:** *A Pilgrimage to Oracle Lake*
A Documentary by Michael Wiese / $24.95